Dedicated to

Ann Marie Medeiros

With much love and heartfelt gratitude

Where would Joanne and I be without your loving heart?

In Loving Memory of My Sweet Jackie
9/18/73 – 2/18/90
Forever in My Heart – Always on My Mind
Mom

Readers' Comments – The Same Smile

"As an 'outsider,' someone who has not been affected by adoption and does not have a relationship with someone who has, it was eye-opening to get a perspective from those who have lived their lives surrounded with the issue. If I loved this book and could relate to the characters so well, it must be a good book – it's not as if I had a specific interest otherwise... It was very personal and touching. Instead of reading about Susan, I felt like I was living her life with her through all the ups and downs... The 'dual voices' throughout the chapters add another dimension to the story. It's great to read about how they were both feeling simultaneously. Joanne's honesty and bluntness was refreshing... It brought out more emotions than most... It is a well-told, interesting account. I especially think it would be a good book for a person affected by adoption to read because it turned out happily ever after – it would provide some hope for them." *Jacqueline Doucette (Textbook Editor)*

"What a tremendous work Susan and Joanne have put together! I could sense from the very beginning the heartfelt nature of this book. No doubt they have both searched deep inside their own beings to bring together this story of the true and undying love between mother and child. They should be very proud of the heart and soul that they have so eloquently depicted through their story... My understanding of the birth mother's vision about the reunion has been broadened. And hearing another adoptee's concerns and opinions helped to qualify my own." *Jennifer Turner (Reunited adoptee)*

"I have been immersed in Susan's life all day today. I closed my office door, put my DND on and devoured her book. I was right there with her...as I marveled at all she has come through, not bitter and closed down, but open, honest and loving." *Shelley Sequin, ICADC (Reunited Birthmother)*

"The book, overall, was excellent. I couldn't put it down. I started it the day I received it and didn't stop reading until I was done... I laughed, I cried, I cried some more. Susan did a great job giving clear explanations of places and people. Her descriptions of the unwed mother's home she stayed in, her clothing and the people she came in contact with were very visual. Her descriptions of her daughter's illness and death brought me to sobbing they seemed so real. Joanne's descriptions of her feelings about her birth mother were unashamed and real. I applaud her honesty." *Jennifer Baldino*

"The 'Same Smile' is an excellent and articulate recount of what kind of treatment young women received at the hands of those associated with adoption in the '60's. There are moments in this book (especially the birth and relinquishment) where you could have substituted my name for Susan's. A loving tribute to her daughters." *Suzanne Henry (Reunited Birthmother)*

To my good friend Anne, Follow your heart

The Same Smile

The Triumph of a Mother's Love After Losing Two Daughters

Susan Mello Souza
with
Joanne Medeiros Harrington

Fulfill your Dream
Love & Hugs
Susan
12/12/02

GATEWAY PRESS, INC.
Baltimore, MD   2002

Front cover photo credits:
Top Left: David Oliveira
Middle: Susan Souza
Bottom Center: Tom Pacheco Studio

Please direct all correspondence and book orders to:
Susan Souza
mama_mazenga@thesamesmile.com

Library of Congress Control Number 2002113450
ISBN 0-9725100-0-1

Published for the author by
Gateway Press, Inc.
1001 N. Calvert Street
Baltimore, MD 21202-3897

Printed in the United States of America

Acknowledgements

With Much Love, Thanks, and Appreciation

Kristine and Beth, my lifelines - I love and cherish you both beyond measure. Without your unselfish love, patience and understanding, I would be just another heartbroken mother living a day-to-day existence. Your unfailing support during the most difficult days of my life - losing Jackie and searching for Joanne - means everything to me.

Joanne, my precious first-born - Your smile melted away the pain of remembering. Your spirit fueled my resolve. Your love filled my heart.

My angel, Jackie - Has time stood still? For it seems only yesterday you were my little girl in pigtails. Then again, it seems a lifetime since I held you in my arms and told you how much I loved you. You are always with me.

Jay, you loved and rescued me when I thought no one else could. Thank you for enriching my life and the lives of my little girls. Only to go one step further by accepting what I had done as a teenager, and then readily loving the daughter I had so foolishly given away. I will always love you.

Mom, my first best friend - You cried through every draft of my story; repeatedly saying, "It's perfect, don't change a word." Thanks for believing in me, but mostly for loving me even when I was a "bad girl."

For my father, who sadly passed away during the writing of this book - I did good Daddy, just like you said I would. The magic really happened. I miss you terribly.

Madeline Jean - Your words of faith and inspiration written inside the cover of my "how to" book helped to get me through the difficult chapters. I can't say how many times I opened it just to read your encouraging words. I'd be lost without your love and loyalty.

Carol Schaefer - How did I get so lucky to find you at such an important time in my life? Thank you for sharing your extraordinary talents with me.

Rachel Jupin - Without you, I'd still be laboring over my initial draft. The things I couldn't remember, you taught me. When I couldn't learn, you persisted. Through your teachings, I rediscovered my love of words and writing. What simply started out as the telling of my story, turned into a welcomed learning experience.

To all my Sunflower and Firstmom sisters - Without your support, encouragement and unconditional love, I never would have made it this far.

The Same Smile

A smile

A simple thing

Something we inherit

Something we take for granted

Something that shows the world our personality

Something that validates who we are and from

where we came

A smile

Prologue

Shadowy, bare branches loom ominously over the familiar streets. Christmas lights decorating our neighbors' houses seem frighteningly wrong. During the one-hour drive home, waves of intense pain grip my chest and back, pain that is always a prelude to my mysterious and ever-worsening bouts of pneumonia. I pray I will make it to our house and not become ill again. And, with every ounce of my being, I pray that my daughter will survive the night. My world is crashing down around me for a second time.

My husband, Jay, is staying with her. Jackie is too scared to let him leave, but our two other daughters need one of us, and I must go to them. Such a delicate balancing act between all their needs. Although it's against hospital rules, Jay is allowed to sleep in ICU with Jackie, since it is Christmas Eve. To think, in the early days of our relationship, I had a hard time letting Jay into my daughters' lives, because I was so overly protective.

It's heart wrenching to tear myself away from her. I'm terrified I will never see her again and, for the first time in twenty-one years, I feel the same way I did when I kissed my first daughter goodbye, when she was just eight days old.

Despite the pain, I stop by our parish church and manage to slip the daily novena Jackie and I write each evening to St. Jude, the patron saint of lost causes, through the slits in the church doors. Most nights I sleep at the hospital, so I usually bring our novena down to the hospital chapel and place it on a table that serves as the altar.

The house is dark and silent when I let myself in, and I am suddenly frightened of my big, empty new home, this home that was to hold all of our dreams and happy memories as a family. During the nine long months it took to build, I supervised the entire project, keeping our camping trailer on the site as an office. From time to time, the whole family stayed the night to keep an eye on things and prepare the house for the next day's construction, sweeping sawdust off floors and keeping the area ship shape for the carpenters. Even with my intense schedule, working part-time and taking care of the girls, that was the first time in ages I was not plagued with my recurring pneumonia. And, amazingly, it was one of the few times when my mind was not preoccupied with thoughts of my first daughter, whom I had named Madlyn.

This is our first Christmas in our new home. As I gaze at the unlit Christmas tree, shiny presents so lovingly wrapped by my girls beneath it,

1

everything seems unreal, eerie. This can't be Christmas. Jay can't be holding vigil with my dying daughter. Our very first Christmas together ten years ago, Jackie was six and Kristine was nearly four. The girls and I had spent the better part of two days setting up and decorating our tree, making it perfect because Jay was coming for dinner. Just when we had finished setting the table and dressing up for his visit, we heard his car door slam. We found him peering in through our front window, admiring our handiwork. Jackie had run to the door to let him in, and we stood around our beautifully decorated tree awaiting his much desired approval. He took his time admiring our handmade ornaments, and then pulled at one of the branches.

"This tree's fake!" he exclaimed, appalled.

Right then, he wanted to dismantle our fake tree and rush out to buy a real one. Protesting all our hard work and Kristine's allergies, I was able to win our little tree a reprieve. The next year, Jay suggested we donate the tree to our church. Before I had a chance to remind him of Kristine's allergies, Jay had the girls dressed in hats and coats, and out on the porch, on their way to buy a new tree. No sooner had the door shut, when I heard squeals of laughter coming from the street. A tree was already hanging from the trunk of Jay's green, 1975 Plymouth Volare. Grinning from ear to ear, he had the girls convinced that Santa must have put it there, while he was in the house. And, as Jay had predicted from the start, none of our Christmas trees have ever made Kristine's allergies flare up.

My cold, dark house is now filled with sadness and impending loss. This just can't be Christmas. Where are my girls? I need to see Kristine and Beth! A note on the kitchen counter says they are with my parents at my cousin Madeline's. Mom senses my panic over the phone, and promises to bring them home right away.

As I await their return, I pace and pray. "Oh, God, please help our Jackie. I promise never to ask for anything else. Haven't I already paid my dues for being a bad girl getting pregnant and a bad mother giving my baby away? Please, why can't You forgive me? Why do You have to take it out on Jackie, making her pay for my sins? I want You to take me instead."

Helplessly watching Jackie suffer and slowly wither away before my eyes, knowing death is about to take her away, is horrifyingly similar to when I watched my first child grow within me, knowing all the while she was going to be taken away.

When the girls arrive home, I hold them close, not wanting to let them go. I find, as we go through the motions of lighting the tree and creating some semblance of Christmas Eve, that I have a hard time speaking to my parents. So many conflicting emotions are flaring up inside of me that I just want to be left alone with my girls. As I say good night and thank them for taking care of the girls, I can't keep from thinking that if it weren't for their decision, Jackie wouldn't be my second child lost.

Chapter One

It is February, 1968. "Oh, just stop worrying and get dressed," I scold myself, as I put on my favorite outfit - a pink and green plaid kilt with matching green sweater worn over my white Peter Pan collared blouse, thinking they'll make me look more mature for the doctor's appointment this afternoon. I'm on the verge of throwing up and can't get my tights up because my hands are shaking so badly.

On my way out the door for school, Mom offers breakfast. I can't imagine being able to keep anything down, and I'm surprised Mom doesn't notice. "No thanks," I tell her, as I grab my lunch money and leave.

When I get to school, Mark, my boyfriend of nearly two years, is absent and no one answers when I call his house, which is odd. I usually know where he is. The day drags and, when the dismissal bell finally rings and he isn't outside waiting for me, I really begin to worry. He said he would go to the doctor's with me, and he's never before disappointed me. If I thought he was going to stand me up, I would have asked my best friend, Paula, to come with me.

The doctor's office is just around the corner from New Bedford High, so I leave Mom's car parked at school and walk over. Opening the door, I peek into the waiting room and suddenly it hits me. What if a neighbor or, God forbid, one of my aunts is sitting in here? Jesus, help me! I implore. Why didn't I think of this? How will I ever explain myself?

The office is filled with pregnant women - all strangers, thank goodness. To me they look so old. I feel I stick out like a sore thumb.

My sick, churning stomach is empty and I feel faint. I reach for the Three Musketeers bar I carry in my purse, to ease my increasing bouts of nausea.

Figuring we'll be married soon, I give Mark's last name to the receptionist, who hands me a clipboard with a medical history form to fill out. I barely summon the presence of mind to figure out the bogus date of birth I'm about to give. Okay, if I want to pass for eighteen, I would have had to been born in '49, right?

Somehow, I manage to fill in all the blanks and return the form to the receptionist. In an effort to calm myself, I sit back, close my eyes and reminisce back to the first time Mark and I met. It was the summer of '66.

Busy preparing supper and trying to put Paula and me off, Mom had protested that we were only fifteen and the dance we were pleading with her to let us attend was way out in the next town of Dartmouth. "Will you even know anyone?" she reasoned. "I don't think either Daddy or Paula's father would approve of your going."

"Of course, we'll know lots of kids there," I reassured her. "Plus, Daddy's on duty and Mr. Roderigues will never know," I said, not caring at that point that Paula's dad was even stricter than mine, which was pretty bad, considering my dad was a New Bedford City cop. When that didn't work, I shamelessly begged, "Please Mom, we really, really want to go. Please bring us?"

After dinner Mom gave in and dropped us off at Dartmouth's Old Town Hall. The place was dank and gloomy inside and gave us the creeps. Just as Mom had predicted, we didn't know anyone there.

"Paula, let's get outta here," I said, searching for the mad money in my shoe, to call for an early ride home.

"No, not yet. Those two cute guys in the Barracuda jackets keep staring at us," she insisted, turning her face away so they wouldn't think we were talking about them.

"Okay, but if they ask us to dance, I want the tall one."

"No way," she said through clenched teeth, her lips not even moving, so as not to betray herself, "It's my turn, I get the big one!"

"Oh, all right! The short one's cuter anyway," I whispered under my breath, while readjusting the dime in my shoe.

The tall one headed straight toward me, and I smiled my prettiest smile to win him over. When he stood before me, he cocked his head in the short guy's direction, and said, "My friend wants to dance with you."

Disappointed that he didn't want me and, not particularly interested in dancing with the other guy, I said, "Well, if your friend wants to dance with me, he's gonna have to ask me himself."

In an instant, the short one, who barely reached my tall five feet, eight inches, stepped forward, gave me a remember-forever smile and asked, "Wanna dance?"

His smile immediately melted my hard-ass-no-short-guys-allowed heart. The cute little creases at the corners of his mouth complimented his perfect white teeth. Plus, he was wearing my favorite shoes - penny loafers.

Be still my heart! I was hardly able to utter that one tiny syllable, "Yes."

As we finished our "cha-cha" he asked me where I was going to school.

"I'll be starting at New Bedford High in September," I was so happy to tell him. After badgering my father all summer, he finally let me transfer from the Catholic high school, Bishop Stang.

"Hey, me too. I'll be a junior," he said, with a teasing smile and asked me to dance again, only this time, to a slow song, *When A Man Loves A Woman,* by Percy Sledge. He held me just right - close, but not too close. Oh, how I wanted that dance to last forever.

Just as I'm remembering the delicious scent of his English Leather aftershave, the sound of the nurse's booming voice calling my name jolts me back to reality. Her voice seems to reverberate throughout the whole waiting room, and I'm certain all eyes are on me. She asks me to follow her.

In a small anteroom, she asks the date of my last period and a few other personal questions, weighs me, takes my blood pressure and draws a vial of blood. Next, she places me in an examining room and asks me to remove all of my clothes and put a "johnny" on, with the opening down the front, promising the doctor will be in soon.

"All of my clothes?" I protest, panicking at the thought of getting totally naked. "Doesn't he only need to check my bottom half?" This is crazy; I still go to the pediatrician, for crying out loud!

Without replying, she smiles and closes the door.

How the hell will I ever get through the rest of this exam, if I can't even be naked? I do as instructed and sit, waiting on the edge of the examining table, warily eyeing the two gigantic, hook-like metal gadgets attached. I can't help concocting a frightening scenario of how they are used. I'm not liking this. Nope, not one bit. And, what's with the temperature? It's freezing. Never mind this johnny, I need a blanket!

Just as I begin to think I'll never thaw out, the doctor walks in. He's an older gentleman and gracious enough not to question me about the why or the wherefore. After the ordeal of the examination, he simply gives me the facts. "You are, indeed, pregnant and your expected due date is September 26. You appear to be in good health and should have no problems. If you have any questions during the next four weeks give my office a call. My nurse will give you all the information you'll be needing."

He then smiles, nods and walks out. His nurse hands over the necessary pamphlets, reminding me to return in four weeks and asks if I have any questions.

On the inside, I'm screaming, "Questions? Of course, I have questions. I have a million questions. I know nothing about being pregnant. I know even less about delivering a baby. When will I start to show? When will I feel better? How much is this going to hurt?"

"No, I have no questions," I answer meekly.

I don't want to go home and I don't want to find Mark, either. I'll deal with him later. I need to be alone to think, and I have to think fast. Right now I have two big problems - Mom and Dad. Oh, no, now they're gonna know I "did it." They're gonna know that Mark and I have been having sex. What can I tell them so they won't think I'm a tramp? I know, I'll say that we only did it once. Yeah, that's it. We only did it once.

Driving around aimlessly, I envision telling them - Daddy will be pacing the house, smoking Lucky Strike after Lucky Strike and, when finally nothing else can pacify him, polishing and loading his gun. All the while, Mom will be silent and sobbing. How do I tell them their only daughter, the light of their life, is pregnant? I don't show yet, so unless Mom figures it out the moment she sets eyes on me, there's plenty of time for Mark and I to make a plan. In any event, I'm as prepared as any teenage girl can be to deal with what we've done. After all, I love Mark and Mark loves me. We'll be married, have our baby and live happily ever after. So what if we have to quit school? So what if we have no money? We'll live on love and the help of our parents. Who am I kidding? My father is going to kill me! Kill me right where I stand. Shit, I'm in big trouble!

The next day, when Mark picks me up for school, I want to know why he wasn't in class or anywhere else to be found the day before. He gives me some lame excuse about helping a friend move. I accept his explanation, because I have bigger problems right now than his skipping school.

"Do you remember that I went to the doctor's yesterday?"

"Oh, wow, that's right. How'dya make out?" he asks.

"The rabbit died," I say, attempting a joke.

"Is that good or bad news?"

"Well, it isn't good," I say.

"Now, what?" he asks.

"We'll get married," I declare, playfully humming the wedding march.

"Shit!" is all he says.

"Don't worry, we have plenty of time to figure this out," I assure him, as he stops for cigarettes and coffee before heading off for school.

On my way out of my room five days later, Mom is sitting in the parlor, lying in wait. "Come sit on my lap," she says, while patting her knees. Although this isn't uncommon - we always spend special time together - the expression on her face says it all. She puts her arms around me, looks straight into my eyes, and asks, "Susan, are you pregnant?" Just like that. "Are you pregnant?" There are no hysterics, no anger, just sadness in her voice.

Of course, I deny it and try to look offended.

"When was your last period?" she asks, still appearing calm.

Now, I'm forced to tell her a bold face lie. "I just finished."

7

"Susan, I checked your sanitary napkin, it wasn't soiled," she explains quietly. Too quietly.

That's it. I'm cornered. Tears pour down my face and everything I have been harboring comes gushing out. It's almost a relief to tell her the whole story. As she holds me, we both cry.

"Please, don't tell Daddy," I plead.

"Honey, he already knows. We discussed my suspicions last night."

"Is Daddy mad?"

"No, just disappointed."

"Mommy, I'm so upset with myself. I hoped that Mark and I would have everything figured out before telling you and Daddy."

My biggest fear in life has always been disappointing my father, and now I've done it in such a huge way. He's always looked at me with such pride. I remember the night of my eighth grade prom, he was standing in his police uniform watching me through the glass doors at the CYO, beaming, with a grin as wide as can be. How will I ever make this up to him? Can I ever be "Daddy's little girl" again?

Considering the mess I've caused myself and my family, there's been no yelling. My parents have remained pretty cool, because they, like me, have grown to love Mark. He's respectful of them and abides by my father's rules. He's never late to pick me up and always has me home on time. When Mark got his license, Daddy even modified his dating rule and allowed me to "car date" while I was still fifteen.

Mark even treats my annoying kid brothers like real people. He often brings his guitar to my house and, with more patience than I'll ever have, teaches Tom and Russ some chords. Last Easter, as Mark played *Here Comes Peter Cottontail*, he and the boys danced around the parlor, singing and acting crazy. Tommy and Russell, to the beat of the music, started banging themselves on the head with their bags of jellybeans. Before we knew it, the bags burst and there were jellybeans everywhere. Dad, Mark and I were practically rolling on the floor laughing at the surprised looks on their goofy little faces, as the jellybeans went flying. Even Mom, who had to clean up the candy from under the table and all the chairs, was smiling.

Mark is everything I ever dreamed a boyfriend should be. He has a way of making me feel not only beautiful with his many compliments, but special, too, because there's nothing he won't do for me. Kind and considerate, he takes me wherever I want to go, from window-shopping in downtown Boston to just sitting in his VW Bug at the beach, listening to music and looking out over the water, watching the "submarine races" - that's what my mother calls parking and making out. He's not only my boyfriend, he's my best friend, and I'm madly in love.

When he picks me up for our usual Sunday afternoon date, I'm so excited that I can hardly wait until the car door is shut. "My parent's have agreed to let us get married! Daddy says that we can live with them as long as you get a job to help support us and the baby."

"Where am I gonna get a job that pays enough for that?" Mark asks, as if it's impossible.

"I don't know. You'll find something. Hey, how about out fishing with your Dad?"

"Not a chance. I'd hate it out there," he's quick to admit. "Sue, we've got to talk. Let's go down to the beach."

Though cold, the day is sunny. The beach seems eerie with its deserted jetties and empty lifeguard stands. The windows and doors of the bathing house are boarded up for the winter and the frigid water appears dark and menacing. Even with all this, the beach, one of the constants in my life, feels safe and familiar. Until Mark begins to speak.

The tone of his voice tells it all. My heart is pounding hard and my insides begin to knot. "Sue, I don't want to get married," he says, with no ifs, ands, or buts. "Do you?"

"Yes, I'm having your baby. Of course, I want to get married."

"Don't you think we're too young?"

Relax. He's just nervous. After we talk, he'll calm down and realize it's the only thing to do.

"Susan, I'm not living with your father," he says. "Yeah, he's an okay guy and all, but I don't want to live with him. He's a cop for Christ's sake."

"What does that have to do with anything?"

"Nothin', I guess. I just can't see myself married."

We talk, we cry and we hold each other for what seems like forever trying to figure out what to do, or should I say, what Mark wants to do. We're getting nowhere fast and haven't resolved a thing. The sun is sinking, just like my hopes, and it's getting cold, so I ask to be brought home. As I get out of the car, he kisses me and says he'll be back in the morning to pick me up for school. I manage a faint smile.

Yep, he loves me. He's gonna marry me. All he needs is time.

The following weekend, Mom invites Mark and his mother to our house to discuss our situation. All week, Mark has still insisted that he doesn't want to get married. Although I'm certain he'll come around, so I don't bother to mention this itty-bitty fact of his resistance to my parents.

Once they arrive, before anything is said, done or decided, Mark and I are sent to my room to talk about what we want to do. I find this humorous, because it's the first time he's ever been allowed in my bedroom. They must figure, what the hell, she's already pregnant!

My bedroom! Oh, how I love my room with its pink Priscilla curtains and matching bedspread, covered with all my favorite stuffed animals. Mark is trying his best to buy some time by commenting on the many ticket stubs pinned to my bulletin board from every movie we have ever seen.

"Have we really been to this many movies?" He's amazed. He then checks out my tiny closet, jam-packed with clothes. As he stands at my bureau combing his hair, he notices the many photos of the two of us I have tucked into the frame of my mirror. "Can I have one of these pictures?" he asks, while admiring himself in the reflection.

It's strange to see him walking about in my pink bedroom. When he finally sits on the edge of the bed next to me, we just look at one another helplessly. This decision is huge.

As usual, I speak first, "Mark, please tell me you've changed your mind."

Eyes downcast, he takes my hand in his and says nothing.

"Why won't you marry me? Don't you love me, anymore?"

Still no reply.

"Talk to me!" I nearly shout.

"I want to, but I can't. I do love you, Susan, I can't, I just can't do it."

He won't bring himself to look me in the eye, all the while holding my hands and softly touching my fingertips. When, at last, he does look at me, he gently wipes the tears from my face. Oddly enough, the feel of his hands is calming. He has smooth, long fingers with perfectly shaped nails. He writes music and plays the guitar effortlessly with these hands, has even written a love song for me, played it on his guitar with these same beautiful hands that are now rejecting me, rejecting our love.

I'm disillusioned and confused. We've talked about marriage so many times over the past year, I've had no reason to even doubt that he would marry me, when I found out I was pregnant. True, our wedding plans were for the future. Still, I can't believe he means it. Oh, my God, maybe he does.

Now, I'm desperate. I have to convince him. "This isn't just about you and me, Mark. There's a baby, our baby involved now, and this child is going to need both of us."

Again, no reaction. I'm talking to a wall. I want to shake him and scream, "I can't do this alone, Mark. I need you to be here for me." But, I don't scream.

His demeanor says it all; there will be no talking him into it. He's adamant. He loves me, but he doesn't want to get married. Never before has there been anything he wouldn't do for me. I'm crushed and in shock.

When we return to the living room, his mother is open and sincere. "Ed, we all know you can insist that Mark marry Susan," she says to my father. "Personally, I only see heartache and hard times ahead for them. Mark is my baby and I've spoiled him. He's neither mature nor responsible enough to take care of himself, never mind Susan and a baby."

She stops talking for a moment. She must be waiting for a response from my parents. However, they say nothing. I can see that Daddy is fuming and Mom, well I think Mom is in a state of shock, too. So, she turns to me. "Susan, you know there is no one else I would rather see Mark marry than you. But, I'm convinced he'll disappoint you by not being the husband you expect, then hurt you by wanting out of the marriage."

As I listen through my fog of disbelief, the only thing that helps me cope with the grim reality of her words is that I know how much she loves me. She has always showered me, the daughter she never had, with love and kindness and, as a result, we have a genuine friendship. She prepares my favorite meals when I visit and has spent hours at her sewing machine making me pretty outfits.

Before Mark leaves, he hugs me. Just the look on his face tells me he doesn't want me anymore. I'm pregnant, therefore, undesirable. I won't be climbing any sand dunes or body surfing in the waves with him this summer. No drive-in movies, drinking lemonade and eating fried clams. No more starry-eyed evenings sitting at West Beach watching the sunset. When he kisses me goodbye, I know this is the end of our fairy tale romance. Only thing is, in this story no one lives happily ever after.

Once they're gone, I'm inconsolable. The thought of being pregnant and unmarried is frightening, unimaginable. How can he leave me to deal with this alone?

In the past couple of days, I've had time to calm down. I can now see that Mark's mother has been the only one thinking rationally. This situation is far too emotional for either my parents or me to see clearly. Everything she said about Mark is true, even the number of days he's absent from school is growing. He's been out more than he's been in and, when I'd call him during lunch break, I could always tell he was still in bed. His explanation was always the same, "I'm tired, but I'll be there to pick you up after school."

How can his mother allow him to stay home so often? Doesn't she realize how far behind he's getting in his studies? He'll never graduate at this rate. And why is he so damned tired all the time? We never go out on school nights, so he should be in bed early enough. Unless, of course, he goes out after we talk on the phone. Where would he go? What would he do?

He hardly ever showed up at the job my grandfather gave him, a part-time office job in the textile mill he runs. "Gee, Grandpa," I'd have to explain. "He said he was going to work when he brought me home after school." Grandpa made it quite clear he was irritated and, even though he was my boyfriend, he let Mark go.

What could I say to explain? I had no idea where Mark went once he dropped me off. Mark's behavior was irresponsible and disrespectful, but none of this seemed to bother him. He didn't need the job; his mother gives him whatever he wants. As much as it kills me, I have to admit his mother is right. Mark is far too spoiled and could never commit seriously to me or our baby. Why hadn't I seen this before? Why is Mark behaving differently all of a sudden? Was it all my imagination that he was so great before? Is there another girl? A new group of friends?

My options are bleak. A cousin, who's a physician, knows of an abortion clinic in upstate New York and, though he doesn't recommend it, offers to accompany me. He warns it's a risky procedure, both physically and emotionally. However, "getting rid" of my precious unborn baby just because I don't have a husband is not an option I could ever take.

When I mention the possibility of having and keeping my baby without the benefit of marriage, it poses a number of problems. First, if I keep my baby, I can't return to school and my father wants me to graduate. Second, Daddy says he can't afford another mouth to feed. Third, I can't expect Mom to quit her job to help care for my baby because they need her income. So, my only other choice is to go along with my parents' wishes to give my baby up for adoption.

Mom and I meet with Father Anderson, our parish priest, who also happens to be head of St. Mary's Orphanage. I tell him what I've been told, I'm not prepared to take care of the child I'm carrying and have agreed to place my baby for adoption. I wonder how a priest can understand my feelings? How can I trust my own?

Sensing my reluctance, Father attempts to comfort me. "Susan, you have made a wise decision. Any one of a hundred childless couples are ready to love and care for your child, as if it were their very own."

I'm scheduled to enter St. Mary's Home for Unwed Mothers on July 8.

We must now come up with a "story" of where I will be spending my summer. It's decided that I have taken a job as a counselor at a summer camp in New Hampshire. It's a far stretch considering I hate bugs and I've never been to camp before in my life.

12

Chapter Two

Despite the fact that Mark and I have broken up, my parents insist I tell him I've suffered a miscarriage. This way he won't bother me, or reconsider marriage. Fat chance of that happening. I hear he already has a new girlfriend. Plus, he hasn't called or been around since the night he and his mother came to my house two weeks ago. The word is out he's quit school. Still, my mom believes he'll be back. "Just wait and see," she says.

From the windows of the second floor art room, I spot him parked outside of school. My heart drops, along with my stomach. I've missed him so much and seeing him only makes me miss him more. A huge piece of me hopes he's waiting for me, but something is telling me otherwise. This could be a good time to talk with him, and I run to my locker, get my jacket and hurry toward the exit. Even though a swarm of kids is ahead of me on the stairwell, I can still see him through the glass in the doors. Just as I reach the exit, I see a girl with long blonde hair walking toward him. He smiles when he sees her and my heart breaks at the thought of him loving and touching another girl. When she turns to get into the car, I see that I know her. She's in my homeroom. Now, I'll have to look at her face every day. Could life get any worse?

Once home, I know I have to call him. Not just yet though, I'll wait a bit. By the time I finish my homework, I'm a nervous wreck and can't put this off any longer. Shaking, I dial Mark's number. He's probably not home, anyway. It's ringing. How am I going to say this? He answers. Do I just blurt it out? "Mark, its Susan," I say softly, not wanting my brothers to overhear. "I had a miscarriage. There's no more baby."

Although he says nothing, I can hear him breathing heavily.

"You don't have to worry anymore. There's no more baby," I repeat. Then, without another word spoken, I hang up.

I've been sleeping for hours, and the ringing of the telephone awakens me. Mom always worries when the phone rings in the middle of the night, especially if Dad is on duty. I get up to listen. When I look into the kitchen to see if everything is okay, Mom hands me the receiver. "It's Daddy. He wants to talk with you."

Oh, brother, this can't be good. Taking the phone, I'm petrified of what I'm about to hear.

"Guess who's in jail?"

"I don't know. Who?"

"Mark. He's here, downtown at headquarters, arrested for being present where drugs were found."

In shock, I can't take in anything else my father is saying. Mom wants to hear every detail. I can't remember anything except that Mark is behind bars. I feel helpless, and hell will most certainly freeze over before Daddy does anything to help.

Mom is her usual sympathetic self and tries to calm me. "Honey, everything happens for a reason. You're better off without him."

How can I be better off without him? I'm carrying his baby! I wish so much that I could say that out loud. I'm about to burst, keeping all these feelings bottled up inside. Her words are only irritating me so I crawl back into bed before I say something I'll regret later. While lying here, I struggle to figure out how I missed seeing all this about him during our relationship. His oversleeping, his skipping school, his inability to keep the job Grandpa gave him, his not wanting to marry me. How could I be so blind? Sure, lots of guys sniff glue and some even smoke pot. But, Mark? He went out of his way to protect me from that scene. When did it start? Last week? Last month? Last year? His mother must know, and that's why she is keeping us from marrying. If only she had been the one to tell me, and not Daddy. Maybe then it wouldn't hurt so much.

The Mark I know is such a good and kindhearted person. Maybe he loves me enough not to marry me.

I hear through the high school grapevine that Mark has left town. Rumor has it that he and Robert, the tall one, are driving cross-country to visit Mark's brother in California. It's just not fair. Here I am, left alone hiding my pregnancy from the world, while he's out having an adventure. The only good part about it is I don't have to see him with that girl anymore.

As May turns into June, I'm beginning to fill out, and the end of the school year can't come fast enough. I look silly and feel conspicuous wearing these new, fuller clothes Mom's making for me. One of the outfits is a new style called a tent dress. Made from a colorful flowered fabric, it has an empire waist, short sleeves and two patch pockets in the front. Even though they're very pretty and fashionable, between my weight gain and the "tent" dresses, the rumors are flying.

School's been out a week and I've been stuck in the house the whole time. Needing some sun and fresh air, I walk over to Clegg Field to sit with Mom and watch my brother, Tommy, play baseball. As I approach her in the bleachers, a look of panic comes across her face, which makes no sense until she leans over, her brow furrowed, and whispers, "Susan, what are you doing here? You need to go home before anyone sees you."

"I came to watch Tommy play," I say, fighting back tears. "I only wanted to get out of the house for a while." My pale yellow shorts and white baggy sleeveless shell look presentable to me.

From the sadness in Mom's eyes, as I turn to walk away, I can see that sending me home hurts her just as much as it hurts me. She's only protecting me from the vicious neighborhood gossips. Already, one of the ladies, who lives on our street and works for Catholic Charities, has blabbed the "confidential" news of my pregnancy to the neighbors. Mom filed a complaint with the agency, but nothing has come of it so far.

I realize my pregnancy is difficult on everyone, and having to serve this sentence of "hiding out" until it's time to go away is torture. I don't belong at home any longer and that hurts. Home is supposed to be safe, the one place where you can be yourself, not where you have to hide, the walls closing in on you.

Pulling up the shiny white blinds on my open bedroom windows, I see it's going to be another hot summer day. How I wish I was going to the beach or shopping downtown with my friends. Anything other than what I'm about to do - move into St. Mary's Home for Unwed Mothers for the next ten weeks to give birth to, and surrender, my precious unborn child. Dad packed the car late last night, so the neighbors won't see my suitcases when we leave this morning. It's sad having to say good-bye to my little brothers. I already miss them. They have no idea where I'm really going. They believe what they've been told. I'm on my way to summer camp. I wonder if they'll ever learn the truth?

I hate that this place has the same name and order of nuns as my grammar school. After all the trouble I went through to convince Daddy to let me transfer to public school! Tired of ill-tempered nuns and their senseless rules, I was also sick of wearing that dreary maroon and gray plaid uniform, with a skirt so long it had to be rolled at the waist three times to keep the hem from meeting the edge of my athletic socks. I wanted to wear real clothes, like the newest fad, the mini skirt. The idea of being able to talk in the halls at the public school thrilled me. Only silence is allowed at Stang. Luckily, the tuition payments were difficult for my parents to meet, so I used that in my plea for freedom. Being sent to this St. Mary's seems like the ultimate punishment. My days will be spent with the very scary women I so desperately campaigned to escape.

It's hotter than hell and this ride to Boston seems endless. My father is exceptionally quiet, while Mom can't seem to stop talking. I don't remember it taking this long when we visited back in April. No one will want to visit me. I'll be stuck way out here, pregnant and alone. How many girls will be there with me? Hope I have a decent roommate. God, what if she's a slob, or worse, snores?

St. Mary's sits at the top of a hill and my father parks our 1965 white, two door Chevy Impala, with its silvery blue interior, on the incline. At such a steep angle, it's awkward getting my now round body out of the back seat. "Mom, you gotta pull hard to get me out," I joke. It's the first time we've laughed today. While Daddy takes the suitcases from the trunk, Mom caresses my shoulders and we cross the street. By the time we reach the sidewalk, my legs are wobbling in fear, and I can see my nervous heart pounding through my "tent dress." Stopping for a moment, I stand straight, take a deep breath and proceed to climb the stone steps up to the huge wooden doors that beyond hold my future and that of my unborn child. As soon as Daddy catches up, Mom rings the bell.

We are greeted by a young, smiling nun. Introducing ourselves, we tell her we have an eleven o'clock appointment with Sister Mary Theresa.

"Welcome to St. Mary's," she says proudly. "Please come in, I'll take you to her office."

All the way down the hall, the hollow, clunking sound of the rosary beads, hanging from her belt, brings me back to the days when I'd be led back to my first grade class, after getting caught talking in the girls' room, my knuckles cracked for something so benign. Then, I'd be sent to stand in the big, dark dressing room, alone. "Next time I catch you talking, Miss Mello, it will be off to the Spanking Machine for you!" Sister would scold, as she towered over my skinny six-year-old body. It was pretty easy to bully a defenseless, gullible little girl into thinking such a contraption truly existed. I was petrified of both Sister and her infamous machine. Worst part, I didn't dare tell on that nasty nun for fear I'd get into trouble at home. The evening of open house I was distraught, certain Sister would tell my parents how badly I'd behaved. Her remarks to my mother, as it turned out, did not include the necessity of using the spanking machine with me. "Mrs. Mello, Susan is a nice girl. However, she is a chatterbox and a busybody and must learn to keep to herself."

None of her idle threats ever worked, because my talking and visiting with my "neighbors" never ceased. At six years old, I had lots to say and even more "help" to offer my classmates. Even though I was well mannered and received good marks, I suffered the wrath of most of the nuns in the following grades, all because of my love of people and conversation. Each had their own personal method of disciplining my "disgraceful" behavior. One dug her thumbnail into my chin whenever she wanted my undivided attention. Another was famous for insulting me about my taller than average height or harassing me with her weekly threat to keep

16

me back. Then there was the hundred-year-old nun, who passed gas, fell asleep at her desk and used my ears as handles. Only Sister Marie, who stayed with our class through both seventh and eighth grades, was different. I somehow managed to tiptoe through her classes with no bumps, bruises or abrasions.

The sound of the young nun's voice brings me back to the present, as she opens the office door. "Sister Theresa will be with you in a moment. Please have a seat and make yourselves comfortable."

I'm anything but comfortable. All eyes seem to be on me in this barren room. Jesus stares down from the cross. Saints, I vaguely recognize, stare out at me from their black wooden frames. Even my parents sit quietly, watching me. I'm about to explode and start to fidget. I don't want to be here. I don't want to be pregnant anymore. I don't want to be nice to this nun.

Sister enters the room like an icy winter wind. My father stands. She's as tall as Daddy and just as broad. Briskly walking toward her desk and with not even a hint of a smile, she sits, then nods and gestures for Daddy to be seated, too. The silence is oppressive.

Sister speaks first. "I trust the traffic wasn't too bad, Mr. Mello. You're right on time," she says, as she glances at her pocket watch then carefully tucks it back into her thick black belt.

"No, the traffic wasn't bad," Dad replies.

"That's good, now let's get down to business," she says, as she shuffles through my paperwork on her desk.

Now that the small talk is out of the way.

"Susan, how do you feel about being here today?"

Startled she is addressing me, I respond, "Just glad to finally be here, Sister." Good grief, how does she think I feel? I'm nervous as hell!

"That's how most of my girls feel, Susan. You will find it to be quite a relief, once you are settled in." Her business-like tone makes me feel like I'm just one more "bad girl" entering her home.

"I'm sure it will be, Sister," I reply. Anything would be better than my days spent hiding at home.

Sister then sets down what seems to be "The Hundred Rules" at St. Mary's, and I can't believe what I'm hearing when she casually informs me I will be assigned a "house" name for the duration of my stay. "Everyone is given a new name here, Susan. Yours will be Stella."

"Sister, I don't want to be called Stella!" I exclaim. Stella! Of all names, she chooses the family joke! Whenever my dad wants to tease me, he calls me Stella. He knows how I hate it, how it makes my skin crawl the way Marlon Brando screams, "S-t-e-l-l-a!" in such a primal, crude way in *A Street Car Named Desire*.

17

My dad doesn't make a move. I'm to handle Sister myself, apparently.

"I know it's difficult for you to understand, right now, but you'll be glad in the long run," she explains. "No one uses her given name here. This way, no one knows anyone's true identity."

"I'm sorry Sister, I will not be called Stella. I'll use my real name." Am I supposed to be ashamed of who I am, as well as having the shame of being pregnant and unmarried? How Sister thinks twenty teenaged girls won't find out everything possible about each other amazes me. Who does she think she's kidding? So, I figure speak up, this isn't school - take a chance. "Sister, I don't care if everyone here knows who I am. Who cares? No one knows me."

Sister's getting impatient and looking to my parents for support. She's getting that icy glare nuns have, when things aren't going their way. "Susan, isn't secrecy the reason you're here?"

Still, Mom and Dad make no move in my defense.

"No, not really Sister. I'm here so my neighbors, teachers and kids at school won't know I'm pregnant. The girls here are no threat to me."

Finally, Sister throws her hands up in desperation. "Very well, have it your way."

I haven't been here thirty minutes and already I'm in trouble. It's going to be a long ten weeks at this rate. Boy, am I glad I've had an entire lifetime of dealing with nuns, or I'd certainly be a dead duck named "Stella."

Sister stands with such abruptness, she pushes her chair right off of the rubber mat. "Mr. & Mrs. Mello, if you have no further questions, it's time to bring Susan up to her room." She then turns to Dad. "Mr. Mello, you must remain in the visitor's lounge," she adds, with no further explanation.

Looking down at my father from the stairway breaks my heart. He looks so sad, small and lost standing there alone, compared to the tough, hard-nosed, burly cop that is the father I've always known. Thinking I've reduced him to this leaves me with such a feeling of guilt and shame. I will do everything in my power to make this up to him when I get home. I WILL make him proud of me again!

Once upstairs, I meet my roommate, "Debbie." Hey, why didn't they offer me a decent name like that?

The room is drab and sparsely furnished with its twin beds, one chest of drawers to be shared, two wooden rockers and drapes that have been hanging long past their time. My creativity shifts into high gear, as I wonder how I can dress up this room. I put my bags on the empty bed, the one nearest the door. Debbie, having arrived last week, already laid claim to the one by the window. "I hope you deliver soon, so that bed can be mine," I say joking.

"The view is only the back of the hospital and every other morning at six, the garbage truck backs in waking me up," Debbie informs me, laughing.

The bed by the window quickly loses its appeal.

From there, Sister shows us the rest of the floor. The place reminds me of the dorms on *Ozzie and Harriet,* where David and Rickie went to college. The bathroom is pretty much the same as the gym at school, with shower and toilet stalls all lined up. Only these are clean and tidy and smelling of disinfectant. The laundry room is equipped with washers and dryers, irons and ironing boards. There's not a "dust bunny" to be found on the polished wooden floors. Pregnant girls are all around, busy doing one thing or another, and, I'm quick to notice, there isn't a thing out of place. Sister runs a tight ship.

I'm anxious for the tour to end so my parents can go home. Seeing these girls talking, laughing and just being pregnant together makes me realize that, once Mom and Dad leave, I'm off the hook. There'll be no more pretending I don't feel anything, physically or emotionally, no more hiding behind my tired, smiling face. At last, my charade will be over. There are no tears as Mom and Dad say goodbye. I sense that their leaving me here has let them off the hook, too. Relief certainly seems to be the emotion of the day, for their carefully laid plan has now been set into motion. As far as they're concerned, the end of my "situation," as it is so absurdly called, is only ten weeks away.

Once I settle in, it's not so bad. Connie, Debbie's real name, is a great roommate. I love hearing about her South Boston escapades, imagining how much fun it must be to live in a big city. My life is pretty boring, compared to hers. A big night out for Mark and me is a double date with Robert and his girlfriend, going bowling or to a movie at one of the downtown theaters. Unless of course, we go dancing. Now that's an entirely different story. Dancing is my absolute favorite thing to do.

As we talk, *Tell It Like It Is,* by Aaron Neville comes on the radio. It's one of Mark and my favorite songs, and I tell her how much he and I loved to go dancing at Lincoln Park Ballroom in Westport. I recount how our slow dancing together always sent shivers up my spine. "When I was in junior high, my friends and I would peek in at the YMCA to watch the high school kids slow dance. They all moved so gracefully, holding each other close, cheek to cheek, like no one else was in the room. My one wish was to learn to dance that way."

"Well, why didn't you just go in and learn?" Connie asks puzzled.

"I wasn't allowed to go to the Y. My father said I was too young and the crowd was too rough," I explain, with eyes rolling and exasperation written all over my face.

Again, she looks puzzled. "Yeah, so 'cause your father said you couldn't go, you didn't?" she says, shaking her head and squishing her face up in disbelief.

"Nope." Why didn't I just do it? Why am I always so afraid of doing the wrong thing? Too late to worry about that now, I guess.

"Anyway," I go on, "you can imagine how excited I was when Mark said he knew how to dance like that. I think it's similar to the Fox Trot." As I grab her by the hand to demonstrate the footwork, our big bellies make my demonstration a bit tricky. "During our first dance, I felt like a klutz, having never had a chance to try before, but I caught on quickly. Before I knew it, we were gliding across the dance floor, past all of the couples just hanging on to one another, hardly moving their feet. Gee, Connie, just thinking about it gives me goose bumps."

As different as Connie and I seem, we're exactly the same - seventeen, pregnant and heartbroken that our boyfriends abandoned us, our families sent us away and society forces homes like St. Mary's to exist. Nonetheless, we do enjoy living together in a place where we can be at peace with our pregnant selves. It was nearly impossible, towards the end, to hold in a seven months pregnant belly, despite being thin, just so my little brothers would never find out. By simply being here, I have blossomed into full motherhood, looking healthy, content and very pregnant. I can relax and enjoy all the incredible feelings I'm experiencing, as an expectant mother, that I had to otherwise ignore while living at home. Comparing belly size and weight gain with the other girls is fun. Just the freedom to ooh! and ahh! over my baby's hiccups, somersaults and kicks is thrilling. Mostly, it's comforting to be able to share my innermost thoughts about my fear of relinquishment and the frightening prospect of moving on.

It seems hotter than usual this summer and one of our many rules states, "No Bermuda shorts." I miss the comfort of shorts. Mostly, I miss having a bathing suit when I sneak up to the roof with the other girls to sunbathe.

Just as I am getting settled on my towel, Sister comes storming through the rooftop door. "Girls, what in heavens name are you doing up here?" she gasps, her hands on her hips.

"Just trying to get some sun, Sister," Connie says, with the biggest grin, as she applies more iodine tinted baby oil to her legs.

"But, you girls are in your underwear!" she shrieks, horrified.

"We don't have bathing suits," I say brashly, rubbing cocoa butter onto my exposed round belly.

"Girls, you'll be seen up here," she says, surveying the other rooftops surrounding us

"Sister, who's going to see us?" I ask, very bold now. "We're on the tallest building around." Hey, maybe she means God will see us. Who knows?

"Put your clothes back on right now, and go downstairs," Sister demands. "I'll deal with you girls later." She turns and, with the veil of her habit twirling about, disappears through the doorway. After dinner, she bans us from the roof for all of eternity.

I'm sure we'll sneak up again, only next time we'll keep our dresses on to be safe.

We're expected to be "properly dressed" at all times, as if someone can ever be properly dressed in an ugly maternity outfit. We're not even allowed to lounge around in our pajamas while watching TV in the evening.

There's a common closet filled with used clothing from all the girls who have come and gone from St. Mary's. When someone comes here to live, and doesn't have what she might need, she can freely take anything she wants. Some things have been hanging in there for years. There are smocked blouses, with puffy sleeves and bows, and long straight skirts with slits up the back, just like what my mom wore when she was pregnant with my brothers in the fifties. I can see why the closet is full. There isn't a chance in hell any of my maternity clothes are going home. Who needs such a painful reminder?

When boredom sets in, we watch game shows and our favorite soap operas, *Another World* and *The Love of Life*. Although I'm not fond of it, *Dark Shadows* is popular among the girls. There's a record player in the TV room, and Sister allows us to play our records softly and dance gingerly, but only during the day. Maybe that's how she thinks we got pregnant - singing and dancing at night! The Moody Blues' big hit is *Tuesday Afternoon*. But it's Steppenwolf's song, *Born To Be Wild*, that we play over and over again.

The kitchenette is at the end of the upstairs hall, next to the one and only pay phone that's in constant use. The refrigerator, filled with a regular supply of milk, juices and fruit, is the place where we store our snack-time goodies. Pilfering by starving pregnant teens is rampant, and I'm careful to label everything that belongs to me. Mom brings Autocrat syrup, so I can make coffee milk to have with my peanut butter crackers, which Mom calls "Nabs." I guess that's short for Nabisco. When I find that my syrup is gone, I go crazy, and being eight months pregnant, hot and crabby doesn't help. "Mom, the girls used up all my syrup!" I whine, as my eyes well up. "I hate it, Mom, I just hate it!"

"Susan, it's okay. I'll bring more tomorrow. It's not a problem, stop crying."

God, I miss my family. We're all so homesick and scared here that it doesn't take much to set one of us off. The counseling available to us is limited, so, at times, it seems we're barely hanging on by the end of our emotional ropes. Despite the lack of counseling, the nuns do take excellent care of us, especially considering they have no clue what we're going through. After all, they do have a huge obligation, not only to our parents but, also, to the couples who are desperately waiting for our babies. And, they seem to take that responsibility seriously. They watch us like hawks, and I'd give anything to know what they're thinking about us. They make us pray and go to Mass, however it seems a little too late for prayer. I already did most of my praying back in February, when I prayed that I wasn't pregnant. Obviously, it hasn't helped me much. Seems God is only listening to everybody else's prayers.

Questions about relinquishment go unanswered. Although it's our option, the nuns and counselors advise us not to see our babies. "Once you deliver, you will put this behind you and go on with your young lives. Seeing your baby will only increase the hurt you might be feeling."

Hurt we might be feeling? Even I know this is going to be the hurt of a lifetime!

It seems they never quite want to admit our lives are about to be shattered. Instead they insinuate that giving up our babies is the answer to our prayers. Sure it's the answer to a prayer - my parent's prayer. It's the best decision for my mom, dad and brothers, for the adoptive parents, the neighbors and society. I'm just not so sure it's the best decision for my baby and me.

I'm usually the only one to speak my mind during the counseling sessions. Most everyone else is quiet and agreeable and, on occasion, some even seem intimidated. There are many times I wish I was more like them and able to keep my opinions to myself. I'm so sick of being told what to do and when to do it that keeping my big mouth shut isn't always possible. I'm sure to tell anyone who will listen, "I'm not leaving the hospital unless I can take care of my baby! This is my child, and as long as I am an inpatient and conscious, I will be the one who cares for her." Why don't they understand that we have already made a connection, formed a bond - the powerful bond between a mother and her child? It doesn't matter that I am only seventeen. I know my baby's movements and the rhythm of her heart, just as she knows mine, and no one is going to take her away from me one single moment before absolutely necessary.

My parents have never allowed me to confide to anyone at Catholic Charities or St. Mary's as to Mark's identity. Or, more importantly, about his drug use, causing me to believe something might be wrong with my child. That's another reason I'm determined to see my baby. I need to be sure she is healthy and adoptable, because if she isn't I'll refuse to sign the papers. The very notion of my child having to live her life in an orphanage, because she might not be perfect, terrifies me.

We have a new counselor this morning, and we're all hoping he has more compassion and a better understanding of our needs than the others. He looks to be about forty, has a kind smile, good teeth and a great haircut. And, tassel loafers. This is promising.

While getting his papers in order he scans the room, checks us out and readies himself to speak. Hesitating, he clears his throat and begins. "More than three-quarters of you ladies will be back here within the next year or two," are the first words out of his mouth.

"Like hell!" I exclaim, practically leaping from my wooden folding chair in the back row. "I will never put myself in this situation again. You have no right to make such an assumption about me. Or, any of us, for that matter." Hopes for finding any helpful counseling seem pretty grim at this point.

Our meals are supplied by the hospital and served in the dining room in the basement. Although well balanced and nutritious, they lack taste. I miss my mother's delicious Portuguese soups, marinated meats and roasted potatoes. Sister Ruth, the short, plump nun who runs the kitchen, keeps her transistor radio on the overhead basement windowsill and tuned to the "Top Forty." She sings with us and lets us dance while we set the tables and clean up. Obviously, we love being in the basement kitchen with her. No one ever complains about "mess duty." She insists we all take turns saying grace and joins us for dinner some nights. Until Sister Ruth, I'd never seen a nun eat. No matter how depressed we might be, she makes us laugh with her silly Catholic jokes. Her favorite is the one we've all heard, about petticoats, curious boys and patent leather shoes.

Tonight, there is nothing Sister Ruth can possibly say to make me feel better. This morning, one of the girl's boyfriends made an unexpected visit, saying he had had a change of heart and now wants to marry her and keep their baby. I am green with envy and want to stamp my feet and scream like a spoiled brat. My reaction isn't at all like me, and, I'm ashamed to say, I find myself hating this girl. This afternoon, when she confided that shortly after she told her grandmother about her pregnancy, her grandmother had a heart attack and died, all I could say was, "Guess your news is what killed her!" I responded, without hesitation or thought.

The girl has been crying ever since, and, as cruel as this may sound, I don't even feel bad. I so desperately want Mark to come and rescue me, too, from the horrible fate that awaits our baby and me. I want him to say it's all a big mistake, put an end to this nightmare and bring us home. I need him to be my Knight in Shining Armor and make all my wishes come true. But none of that will ever happen, because he believes I miscarried our baby. He doesn't even know where I am.

We've been assigned regular jobs, as well as chores, to keep us busy. My designated task is to work in the lab a few hours each morning at St. Margaret's Hospital next door. I enjoy the people and the time I spend away from the home. I'm also responsible for my laundry, keeping my room clean and changing my bed linens. I've done my best to make my side of the room cozy, with throw pillows and my favorite stuffed animals. I placed my radio and vanity set on my bureau and family photos on my mirror. I made a floral seat cushion for my rocking chair and crocheted an afghan for the foot of my bed. Mom brought my fluffy bed pillow from home, and the smell and feel of it beneath my head seems to somehow soothe me. But, no matter how hard I try, it just isn't my pretty pink bedroom, at home.

I miss Paula. She's only been able to visit me once, and we can't have our girly telephone chats because it's long distance. Although I shouldn't complain, I'm one of the lucky ones, having company more often than the rest. When claustrophobia sets in, Mom, her sister, my Aunt Mary, and my cousin, Madeline, make an extra visit and take me out for a ride and something yummy to eat. We sometimes go to the Franklin Park Zoo for a picnic and watch the children play. We also go to the beach, close to the Dorchester Yacht Club, where I change into my forbidden shorts for a few hours. However, going to the beach only makes me miss Mark and reminds me of all the fun we had. The best time was driving to Horseneck Beach in the summertime in his black Volkswagen Beetle, on the back roads with the windows wide open and the radio blasting to the tunes of WPRO, Providence, Rhode Island. I loved his car, with its cute windshield wipers and tiny knobs on the AM radio. The defrosters never worked, and the heater left a lot to be desired. But we didn't care, we went everywhere in that little Bug.

Dad visits whenever his police schedule allows. Although he never judges me, seeing my father always makes me feel guilty. I'm all too aware of how expensive it is for me to be here. He has to work a lot of extra details to pay the bank loan they took out to cover my room and board here. Mostly, I'm embarrassed by my appearance. It's just not the way you're supposed to look for your dad when you're seventeen. Many times, I don't know which emotion stings more, the guilt or the shame.

The big day out is our weekly visit to the clinic, located across the street in a blue tenement house that has been converted into medical offices. Walking over there is the only exercise we get most weeks, and we know from the pamphlets we read that we need to keep active if we're to deliver our babies as easily as we hope. Our solution is to race each other up and down the three flights of stairs when anyone's near or past their due date. This way, not only the girls that are due get their exercise, we all do. Oh, dear Lord, if Sister knew, she'd pitch a fit. As far as she's concerned, running up and down the stairs ranks right up there with sunbathing on the roof.

The nuns are very protective and careful never to let us venture out into the neighborhood, fearing we'll go looking for boys. That thought cracks me up. Hunting down boys is the last thing on our minds. Plus, what type of boys would be interested in us, anyway? So, we figure we're safe, duck out the basement doors and head straight to the pizza parlor for that forbidden slice of Chicago style, pepperoni pizza. What a sight we are, four brave unwed mothers waddling down the street on a pizza mission. We don't care if our ankles swell up from the salt - we need pizza!

The thing we do most in this place is talk about our precious babies. Always speculating about who they'll look like and whether they'll be a boy or a girl. I happen to feel very strongly that I'm having a girl. We love our unborn babies with all of our hearts, and we're scared to death about what's going to happen to us. We sit for hours with one another, once labor begins, all secretly wishing it were us, so we can go home, too. I know labor isn't going to be easy, but I also know that leaving my baby here so I can go home is going to be the absolute worst. So many huge emotions to deal with all by myself. I'm frightened and rarely get through an entire day without crying. Nighttime is the hardest, when I feel so alone, and there's no place else to go.

Chapter Three

It's after lunch on Monday, September 16, and Connie and I are watching soaps. Realization has been building and finally I whisper to her, "I think I'm in labor."

"Are you sure? You're not due for at least another week," she whispers back, more like a stage whisper, she is so surprised. "Hey wait, you're not even due 'til after me."

"My back is killing me, and there's pain with my contractions."

"I'll go and get Sister."

"No! She'll call my parents and convince them I shouldn't see my baby."

Mom and Dad haven't said that I can't see my baby, but, like Sister, they haven't encouraged me, either. On this, I will stand my ground.

Avoiding Sister Theresa at all costs, I lie on my bed and leaf through *Seventeen Magazine,* envying all the thin pretty girls modeling the fall school clothes. As I listen to the radio, my mind is filled with thoughts of Mark and the first time he told me he loved me. It was the evening of my sixteenth birthday, in May of 1967, when he unexpectedly presented me with a beautiful pearl ring and asked me to marry him after graduation. My insides turned to Jell-O when the significance sunk in. Wow, he wants to marry me. He really does love me.

Later that same summer, our relationship turned intimate. I was baby-sitting with my friend, Elaine, watching her nieces play in the yard, when Mark and Robert drove up. Mark's detective work impressed me. I hadn't told him where I had gone. When the time came to put the girls to bed, we told the guys to leave, but, of course, they didn't. Despite knowing better, we invited them in.

Elaine and Robert hopped onto the sofa, leaving Mark and I scrunched in an overstuffed flowered chair. His smell was intoxicating, and we could hardly keep our hands off each other. Once the lights were out, his Izod shirt was off in a flash. My sandals went flying, his Top Siders followed. We were a mass of tangled limbs.

"Where are the bedrooms?" Mark quietly asked, as we slid off the chair and down onto the floor. At that point, my headband popped off my head.

"Upstairs," I said, breathless between kisses, while he expertly undid the buttons of my blouse.

"Let's go!" he said, grabbing my hand to pull me up, forgetting all about my partially exposed top.

"Use the first room on the right," Elaine mumbled, from the depths of the couch.

We had been going out for a year and hadn't "done it," so I figured what's the big deal? I'm safe. Only it was a big deal. We never before had the luxury of a bed, and it was a challenge to control our lust in such comfort. It had been much easier to say "no" in the back of his cramped VW Bug. Somehow, I summoned the willpower to stop.

Spoiled from having been in a bed, we were now in hot pursuit of comfort. It only took a couple of days before we wound up in Mark's bed, when his mother was out of the house.

Mark knew I was scared, and although he tried to hide it, he was, too. We had been leading up to this moment for months and had done our best to be good, but the temptation was now overwhelming. Our lovemaking that afternoon, though awkward, was deliberate, gentle, tender and unhurried, just like our slow dancing. Recalling the passion and excitement of that late summer afternoon, I smile as the flurry of precious memories fills my heart.

I stay out of Sister's sight and don't let on about my labor to anyone other than Connie. On my way to dinner my water breaks, and I can no longer conceal my discomfort. Connie freaks out and runs to get Sister Ruth, who calls Sister Theresa. Sister Theresa walks me over to the hospital, saying very little. My water continues to leak the whole way across the yard.

"I'm sorry to bother you, Sister. Am I interrupting anything important?" I say sarcastically, really hoping against hope for some comforting words.

"No, it's just that I have a lot on my mind tonight."

Didn't she care at all about how I might be feeling, or the welfare of this baby I will be giving her? I had to have more on my mind than she did.

At the hospital, she hands me over to a nurse, tells me I'll be fine and goes back to St. Mary's without so much as a smile, a touch, a hug. And, boy, oh boy, do I need a hug.

I change into one of those dreadful johnnies. After getting me settled in, the nurse informs me she has to shave me.

"You're gonna shave me where?" I ask, sitting bolt upright in bed.

"Stella, we can't have a place for bacteria to grow, now can we?"

Stella! Sister must have admitted me as Stella. What a sneak!

"Please call me Susan," I say. "I use my real name."

"Okay Susan, this won't take long."

After my "trim," she sets up an IV in my arm and walks away mumbling something I couldn't catch. I haven't been left alone in weeks, and I'm horrified by what's happening to me. The woman in the next room starts moaning and crying out in Spanish. Waves of panic wash over me, and I begin to tremble and become nauseous. The nurses are talking out in the hall, and I pray that one of them will come in to help me. "Hail Mary, full of grace, the Lord is with Thee..." Footsteps. Do I hear footsteps coming my way?

It's a student nurse - a small, pretty blonde, with a ponytail braid. "Hi, I'm Karen. I'll stay with you until my shift ends. Let's hope you have your baby by then. If you have any questions I can't answer, I'll get someone who can," she tells me. "So, how are you feeling?"

"I'm gonna throw up," I say, between dry heaves.

She reaches for a curved metal tray and places it beneath my chin. "Here use this."

I vomit and wipe my mouth with the damp washcloth she hands me. I'm shivering and on the verge of tears. "Karen, I'm scared. What's happening to me?"

"Of course, you're scared," she says, while rinsing out the basin and returning it to my bedside table. "Someone will be in soon to examine you, and then we'll know how far along you are and what to expect. Don't be afraid, you're doing fine," she assures me with a smile, and covers me with an extra blanket.

Ah, some warmth - literally and figuratively.

Soon, my neighbor starts in again with her Spanish tirade. Some poor guy named Joe seems to be in big trouble. I pity the poor guy when she gets her hands on him. Listening to her outburst, I'm petrified. "Is it going to be so bad that I'll be screaming like that?" I ask Karen.

"No, no, she's a big cry-baby," Karen says, as she reaches out and, with a kindness and compassion I haven't had displayed towards me in ten weeks, holds my hand.

I feel at ease and safe in her care, and I'm certain she'll do what's best for me in the difficult hours ahead. She's someone who can be trusted, so I tell her of my intentions. "I'm going to see my baby and take care of her while I'm in the hospital," I confide, confirming my resolve.

"So, you're hoping for a girl?"

"It is a girl," I say, nodding my head confidently, willing my wish to come true.

"Good for you," she says. "Your baby is going to need you while she's here."

Finally, someone who understands. I think I love her!

Karen gives me ice chips for my parched lips and rubs my lower back, as my contractions worsen.

An older, very serious nurse comes in and gives me a shot that makes me sleepy and causes my mind to fade in and out of reality. I'm sitting at our old green card table making a puzzle with my brothers. My stuffed animals cover my bedroom floor and they are calling out to me. But I can't reach them to put them back in place. I'm at the beach, crying and running after a little girl wearing only a diaper. A policeman is shining a bright light at me, asking why I'm not in school.

In what seems like slow motion, I attempt to roll over onto my side. Karen helps by gently moving my "bottom" to straighten me out. She fluffs and fixes my pillows, one under my head and the other under my tummy.

More ice chips feel and taste good. If the pain is real, it's excruciating, although it's as if someone else is feeling it. I'm merely the spectator. The pain is in my chest, my back, my bum. I'm sweating now. My legs are achy and restless. The glare from the ceiling light is making me nauseous again. Don't throw up, breathe. Breathe again - harder, deeper, faster.

"Susan," someone calls from far away. "Susan, can you hear me? Susan, listen to me." Its Karen's soft, faraway voice. "It's after eleven o'clock. It's time for me to go home. It's not going to be much longer. Your baby will be here soon," she encourages me, as she wipes my forehead with a cool cloth for the last time. "Stay tough, you're doing great."

All I can manage in my foggy state is a grimace and a weak, barely audible thank you. "No, don't leave!" The shouts are only inside my head. My pleas are silent. "Karen, I need you to stay, to hold my hand, touch my forehead and stroke my hair like Mommy would do if she were here." My lips aren't moving.

Two nurses from the next shift enter, smiling and chatting with each other. One examines me and says something to the other nurse, who quickly leaves. She's mouthing words that don't make sense.

Is my bed moving? Yes, I'm moving through the doorway and out into the corridor. Why do I feel so groggy? She's still talking. Is she talking to me? Where am I going? If only I could understand her words.

Now, I'm in a big, bright, cold room. The coldness helps to make me more aware of my surroundings. It's the delivery room. The frosty temperature is clearing my head. I'm helped onto the cold metal delivery table, covered only by a sheet, and told to sit with my legs dangling over the side. I do as they say, even though I don't understand. "Why am I sitting? This is very uncomfortable," I complain. "Shouldn't I be lying down?"

When I'm in the midst of a long, hard contraction and barely able to breathe, the nurse gently pushes down on my shoulders. "Lean forward and be perfectly still, so the doctor can administer the spinal," she instructs.

Now fully alert, I exclaim, "You've got to be kidding!" as I try to bend over my huge, hard belly. "What are you doing?"

"Weren't you told you'd be given pain medication?"

"Sure, but what are you doing?" I repeat.

29

"Don't move," she insists. While holding my hand, she explains the barbaric procedure.

"He's not really going to stick a needle into my spine, is he?" I ask, but receive no response.

Keeping my head down, I hold my breath and wait for the pain that thankfully never comes.

The nurse then lays me down and lifts my tingling, knee-sock-covered legs into the cold metal stirrups. The younger nurse covers my top half with a warm blanket and coaches me on how to push my baby out. She's kind and patient, and it seems my pain has all but disappeared. There's some pressure "down below," but it's nothing I can't handle.

The obstetrician arrives and introduces himself. He's one of the nice guys from the clinic.

After about a dozen pushes, he asks, "Stella, are you certain you want to see this baby?"

"My name's not Stella!" I grunt, while trying to push. "I'm Susan. And, yes, I'm positive. I've never been more positive of anything in my life," I manage to say, as my contraction subsides.

"Okay, you're the boss! All I need is one more good push."

"If I were 'the boss' I'd be married and bringing my baby home," I say to the young nurse standing beside me, as the tears roll down my face.

Finally, at 12:33 A.M. on Tuesday, September 17, my beautiful daughter is born. Seven pounds, two and one-half ounces. The older nurse allows me a close look at my crying, newborn baby girl before she whisks her away to be cleaned and examined. I want to hold her and comfort her, but I'm too weary to argue should they refuse. Before I'm taken from the delivery room, I explain to the pediatrician that I had been born with a dislocated hip and understand it's genetic, passed on from mother to daughter. He assures me she will be checked.

I need to hear the sound of Mom's voice.

"May I call my mother now?"

"Of course, you can," the young nurse answers.

The moment she's done tending to my needs, she wheels me over to a wall phone out in the hall. It's two o'clock when Mom sleepily answers, "Hello."

"Mom, I can come home now," is all I can manage to say, my eyes brimming with tears.

My mother cries as I talk about my baby girl and what my labor was like. By the end of our conversation, we're both in tears and I'm exhausted. It's a very emotional and bittersweet time. On one hand, I miss my family and

I'm looking forward to going home. On the other hand, I must leave my daughter behind to do so and might never see her again.

Hanging up, I wonder why Sister didn't notify my parents of my labor.

I name my baby girl, Madlyn Jeanne, after two women I admire most, my mother and my cousin, Madeline Jean. My mother is an amazing woman and I hope to pattern my life after her. She has raised us kids through some hard times, always making the best of the little we have. By example, she's taught me a number of valuable lessons, the most important being how to be a good person. Madeline and I have been raised like sisters, always living on the same street and attending the same schools. I placed her picture on my mirror over at St. Mary's, and, when the girls ask who she is, I fib and tell them she's my sister. We truly are sisters, sisters of the heart.

The spelling of my daughter's name is the version my cousin actually prefers. "It's more exotic - very French," she says. I'd like to change my own from Susan Mary to Suzanne Marie. French sounds better to me, too.

Sister Theresa has agreed to let me take care of Madlyn for my eight-day hospital stay, so I can hardly wait to get started. The nurse pauses in my doorway, and I can just see the edge of Madlyn's warming crib beside her in the hallway. "Good morning, Susan. Are you certain you want to do this?" she asks.

"I'm certain." I say without hesitation, sitting up straight, eager to hold and inspect my daughter from head to toe.

Wheeling in the small bassinet, she hands me my precious bundle. "I'll be back when I'm done with the real mothers."

Her words just barely register. I'm not even sure if that's what she really said, as I'm enthralled and enraptured with Madlyn and not paying attention to anything else. Then the words just fly out of my mouth, "I'm a real mother!" Hormones are flying.

"I only meant that I have to teach the other mothers, who are taking their babies home, how to bathe and diaper them," she responds apologetically.

"Oh, please, won't you teach me, too?"

After taking a long moment to consider my unusual request, she agrees, and then leaves us alone with a promise to return. I imagine we young mothers from St. Mary's must be unnerving for these nurses to deal with. We're all so insecure, not to mention, scared to death. How would they know the right thing to say?

As I lay this tiny being on my lap, she appears to be no bigger than a loaf of bread. Undoing her tightly wrapped blanket, out pops chubby little arms and legs. I kiss the dimples on her long fingers and toes. The minute I unsnap and remove her little undershirt, she stretches and opens her eyes -

they're a beautiful greenish-blue. She has a pretty cherub face with lovely, delicate lips and the cutest button nose. Her hair is wispy and soft, a light shade of brown. I gently pass my hand over her silky head and find her soft spot; I can feel her pulse. Knowing I must make every moment count, I push my johnny aside a bit and hold her up against my skin, then cover us over with the sheet. Embracing her, she snuggles closer, as I close my eyes and dream of holding her forever.

It's not long before the nurse returns for my "real mommy" lesson. Watching Madlyn squirm and listening to her squeak while being bathed, fascinates me. Once we're finished, the nurse says, "When you're done feeding her, I'll take her back."

Suddenly, I'm panicky thinking she means for good, not trusting Sister's word. "Sister promised I could care for her for the rest of the week."

"I only meant I'll be taking her back to the nursery, so you can have some lunch. I'll bring her back to you this afternoon."

Her smile is kindly. I can believe her. Thank you, God. Oh, please help me get through this.

I sing to her, as I gently rock her and give her her bottle, all the while taking in as much of her as possible. This way I'll never forget what it's like to cradle her in my arms, how sweet she smells and how soft and velvety her skin feels. Staring endlessly at her precious sweet face and into her eyes, I want to forever memorize all of her. I hold her as close to my heart as possible, so she'll know it's me, her mother. I feel the bond in my heart and in my soul, and I know she feels it, too. I am her real mother.

Each day is better than the last. I'm so comfortable caring for Madlyn and she loves being spoken to and held close. The nurses say I speak to her as if she were a grown up, understanding the things I say. We're in our own little corner of the world. I haven't felt this happy in months and I don't want this week to ever end.

On the fourth day, Estelle, the girl I had hurt with my callous comment, delivers a healthy baby boy and is put in the same room with me. It's torture knowing she'll be bringing her baby home and only makes me resent her more, making it hard for me to be nice. Her boyfriend visits everyday and hearing them plan their future together is so difficult, I think I will die. If only I had the courage to call Mark and tell him about Madlyn, and where he can find us. But Daddy would be angry and disappointed all over again if I went against his wishes.

On Tuesday, September 24, when my eight-day stay comes to an end, they bring Madlyn to me for the last time. My quiet, content little girl is fidgeting and crying. Madlyn senses that I will be leaving her behind. It takes a while to settle her down as I undress her, and give her a "cotton ball" bath.

Holding her ever so close while feeding her, I try not to cry, so as not to upset her anymore than she already is.

My head is throbbing and my heart is aching, as I tell her the concerns of my heart, all the while looking into her eyes that appear so wise, and kissing her all over. "Mommy loves you with all of her heart, and I am only doing this because I love you so much. Everyone says you deserve both a mommy and daddy that will love and take care of you." Then I whisper a promise, so no one else will overhear. "Madlyn, I promise Mommy will find you when you turn twenty-one. And, when I see you then, I will tell you again how much I love you." I apologize to her a thousand times for what I'm about to do; give her away. When the nurse comes in to take my baby girl away, my grief is so great, I don't think my tears will ever stop.

I always knew saying good-bye was going to be painful, I just didn't realize it would be to this devastating degree. Just how do I say goodbye to my very own child, the child I love with all that I am? How can this possibly be in God's plan for me? This has to be a mistake. I'm a good person. God is all-forgiving, isn't He? That's what I've always been taught. So, why am I being punished? This pain is so intense it takes my breath away. I'm about to pass out, but the merciful blackness never overtakes me. I must endure the pain of relinquishment consciously.

Aunt Mary accompanies my mother to bring me home. Mom must need her sister's moral support to carry out the plan that was set in motion so many months ago. Visibly shaken, she can't bring herself to go down to the nursery windows to see her first-born grandchild. "If I see Madlyn, I'll be much too tempted to bring her home," Mom tries to explain.

Sitting on the edge of my hospital bed, my head bowed and my empty arms folded over my flattened belly, I listen to her reasoning and it's not ringing true. How can a mother, as loving and caring as Mom, leave this hospital and not bring Madlyn home? Please God, all she has to say is, "Wrap her up, we're taking her home."

Nothing is said, I'm left to face at least twenty-one years without my baby girl. I don't respond to Mom's explanation because I have no more words. What can I possibly say that hasn't already been said and dismissed months ago? What can I say that won't make me sound selfish and ungrateful? What can I say that will change anything? Bringing Madlyn home isn't part of the plan, and I guess we simply have to follow "the plan."

Aunt Mary walks down to the nursery window to see Madlyn, her sister's and daughter's namesake. As she walks back into the room, I see how deeply seeing her tiny niece has affected her. Although she's crying, she remains silent like me.

Now I know I will never get over losing Madlyn. I'm forever changed. If only I had understood what a huge price tag falling in love would carry. As a result of my teenage mistake, I have been stripped of my dignity, my self-esteem, and my faith and trust in others. Most of all, I've been stripped of my motherhood.

As I gather my belongings and prepare to say good-bye to my friends at St. Mary's, thirteen-year-old Carol is standing outside my room crying. She has been living here since the beginning of her pregnancy, and still has another six weeks to go. Not once has she had a visitor. My heart is filled with sorrow, as I hug Carol good-bye then move on to the other girls. We all promise to keep in touch, even though we know we won't. Then, quickly and quietly, I slip out through the same wooden doors I entered eleven weeks ago, the ones that now close shut on any chance of my being Madlyn's mother.

This deep empty silence, this void is the worst and most startling part. For the first time in my life, I have nothing to say. At long last, I have run out of words. Nor can I cry. I have also run out of tears. I am a disgrace, just like Sister said I was all those years ago, when I was in first grade.

Riding home, back to my old life, I'm keenly aware of how strong I've become and how capable I am now of anything that is expected of me, and I feel troubled knowing this about myself. Just how far will I have to go to carry off the rest of this outrageous sham?

Just ten days after my daughter's birth, and three days before beginning my senior year, I return to St. Mary's Orphanage, where the course of my life was set last March, to sign the final relinquishment papers.

When Aunt Mary arrives to pick us up, I become confused when my mother doesn't make a move to come with us. Her excuse is that she needs to be home for my brothers. Why can't Aunt Mary stay? I need Mom, too. My pleas stay silent. On the way to the car, Aunt Mary tries to explain, "Susan, this is very hard on your mother. Everything will be all right. I'll be there with you."

I want to go racing back into the house and scream, "How do you expect me to deal with all of this when you can't? You're my mother, I need you!"

On our way there, Aunt Mary does her best to be cheerful and talkative. I'm nauseous and can throw up any minute. Not having the heart to tell her to please be quiet, I stare out the window and daydream about my precious baby. Is she home with her new parents? She must be. Sister said the man was a doctor, and he and his wife were waiting for me to leave the hospital so they could take her right home. I guess she will have everything she could ever want, except maybe me. Will she ever wonder about me? I try not to cry so my face won't get blotchy.

St. Mary's Orphanage looks all too much like St. Mary's Home for Unwed Mothers, and the sight of it as we approach is so upsetting. St. Mary's School, St. Mary's Orphanage, St. Mary's Home for Unwed Mothers, when will I be free of St. Mary?

Father greets us at the door and leads us to his office. The papers are neatly placed on his desk. I'm polite, even though I don't feel like talking.

"Susan, it must be great to be back home," he says cheerfully, while opening the window to let in the fresh autumn air.

"Yes, Father."

"Have you started school, yet?" he asks, on his way to his desk.

"No, not yet. Monday."

"It'll be good for you to get back into your normal routine," he says with certainty.

"Yes, Father. I'm sure it will," I respond flatly. My life will never be normal or routine again. Of that I am certain. Let him think what he has to. Can't he see my shattered heart? Does he even care? A deal's a deal with the Catholic Church, I guess.

Father glances through the documents, and then passes one of them over to me. None of it is filled in. No names. No dates. Nothing. Without comment or requesting us to read it over, he simply points to blank lines where we are to sign. The typewritten words on the paper are cold and impersonal. "I, _____, ...being the mother and only parent...of the child, _____, who was born of me _____, at _____, HEREBY PERMANENTLY GIVE UP SAID CHILD, and surrender full custody, possession, care and control of said child, to the Catholic Welfare Bureau..."

"Said Child!" My daughter's name is Madlyn Jeanne. Shouldn't Father first fill in all the blanks? Even I know this form can't be left this way. Or, can it? Is this legal? It must be. I've known Father for most of my life; I suppose I just have to trust him.

After Aunt Mary and I sign the papers, Father quickly escorts us out. I'm amazed at myself, as I observe myself from a very detached place. I just signed my daughter away, without so much as a fight or argument. How do I deal with this shame? My spirit and self-worth are gone, along with my baby.

I don't want to go home but, once again, I have nowhere else to go.

Chapter Four

My first day back in school, everyone is quick to inform me that Mark has re-enrolled. I haven't seen or spoken to him since the end of March, and it makes me antsy to know he's around. I dread the thought of having to see him every day, and it hurts to think I'll never be his girlfriend again.

From what I hear, I'm the topic of much speculation, so it's going to be difficult to ignore the gossip and stares. "Just remember, hold your head high and keep a smile on your face," Mom advised me, as I headed out the door this morning. "Before long, the girls will be talking about someone else."

My new figure is a dramatic change. Built more like a tomboy before my pregnancy, these once small breasts have become fuller. More than adequate to feed the baby I will never hold in my arms again. When my milk came in, Mom ripped up an old sheet to bind my breasts. These hips, that bore my baby girl, now round and curvaceous, serve to accentuate my slim waistline. Without so much as a stretch mark, my stomach is as firm and flat as ever, never to reveal my secret child. Hopefully, to the outside world, everyone will just think that Mother Nature has been busy at work. Needless to say, Mom has sewn another wardrobe for me and the kids are sure to wonder what's going on. Two new wardrobes in one year?

Having already missed the first few weeks of school, it's necessary to have a doctor's note stating the reason for my absence. Our family physician has decided Mononucleosis will be the assigned affliction acquired during my hectic summer away at "camp." I don't believe the kids or even the teachers will fall for the mono bit, because I certainly don't appear to have been ill. I look perfectly fit and healthy; except for the tan I should have from being away at summer camp.

It's all Sister's fault," I whined to Mom. "If only she had let me sit on the roof and sunbathe, I wouldn't be so pale!"

Depressed, heartsick, my spirit broken, I keep smiling. Words from St. Mary's about getting on with my life echo in my head. However, my "rose colored glasses" have been smashed to smithereens, and I'm not particularly fond of myself any longer. Giving up Madlyn has left me feeling worthless and empty. What kind of mother just walks away and leaves her cherished newborn behind? What kind of mother goes on smiling and pretending she didn't just lovingly carry and deliver that child? The answer is simple - the kind of mother who is dying inside.

Trying to fit back into my old life, it's painfully clear I'm not the same girl I was. My thoughts and attitudes have all changed. I'm so fed up with hearing how I should feel, I'm not even sure how I do feel anymore. Having no control over the gossip makes me feel exposed and vulnerable. But what am I supposed to do? Do I tell the world I really am a good person and not to think badly of me just because I got pregnant and had to give my baby away? I'm not sure I even believe that anymore. The cruelty of life and people isn't about to change just because I'm devastated. So, there isn't much choice. I have to pretend to be just like any other normal high school senior, having fun, going to dances and attending football games.

The measure of anger I suppress on a daily basis since coming home is incredible. At least at the home, even their meager counseling provided some outlet for my feelings. I'm angry with myself. I'm angry with Mark. I'm angry at the world, and I'm angry with God. I'm still not quite sure why I'm not angry with my parents, but I'm not. They've been nothing but patient and kind, however that prevents me from discussing my feelings with them so I don't appear ungrateful.

Tuesday morning, Mark is standing outside of his homeroom. I walk past, pretending not to see him. Please God, don't let him be waiting for me. I don't have the strength to face him yet.

"Hey, Sue, wait up," he calls out, as he catches up with me in the corridor. "Where have you been?" He's smiling and checking me out. "Wow, you look great." He winks, then automatically leans over, kisses me on the cheek and reaches out to carry my books, just like he always did.

Am I dreaming? Here we are, walking along like old times, Mark and Sue back together, as though nothing has come between us.

"I've really missed you," he admits. Then, in a hushed and somewhat comical tone, he says, "I didn't dare call your house, cause your father would have killed me."

"No shit!" are the first words out of my mouth. "Now, that's the freakin' understatement of the year."

As much as I'm angry with him, something inside of me knows that, although I hate what he did to Madlyn and me, I will always love him. I lie to him about summer camp and then coming down with mono, and he seems to have no problem believing me. It's killing me to stick with that story. I want so badly to tell him exactly what I've just been through and all because he didn't have the courage to share the responsibility of fathering our child.

He keeps after me until I agree to see him and, as hard as I try, I can't set myself free of him. I still have all the same feelings as before, and then

37

some. He's more handsome than ever and certainly doesn't appear to be using drugs. Plus, he's in school everyday, so I'm insanely optimistic that he has straightened out.

Being with him is the only time I feel anything at all like my old self. His presence almost makes me feel whole again - closer to Madlyn. He fills a part of the void left in my life by giving her up. So, even though my parents have strictly forbidden it, I continue to date him, partly also because I'm confused and insecure, afraid no one else will want me after what I have just done.

Mark asks that I meet him at a party and gives me the street address. It's in a run-down section of the South End and, although it's against my better judgment, I agree to go as long as he meets me outside.

The party is on the second floor of a dilapidated three-tenement house. Its dingy hallways are lit by single bare light bulbs, hanging from cracked and partially fallen ceilings. When the door to the apartment is opened, the hazy darkness from inside and the smell of incense comes wafting out, along with the music of the *Buffalo Springfield*. Only candles provide light and, once my eyes become accustomed to the dark, I can see a circle of unfamiliar people sitting on the floor, smoking from what appears to be a pipe. Mark leads me to one of the bedrooms that are also lit by candles. One guy, dressed only in a pair of unzipped dungarees, is sprawled out on the bed. A couple of girls, one with long, straight, parted-down-the-middle hair, the other in braided pigtails, with a red bandana wrapped around her forehead – Indian style, are sitting together in a chair. When Mark trips over someone lying on the floor, he throws them all out.

As we stand in the semi-darkness, I ask, "What kind of party is this? What's going on here?"

"Susan, this is different than the other parties we go to," he says, as he takes my hands. "Its gonna be fun, I promise. Come on, I want you to meet my new friends. You do want to meet them, don't you?" he asks, as he tries to pull me back into the other room.

"No, I don't want to meet them," I say, standing firm and releasing my hands from his.

"Ok, we'll stay in here, if you don't want to join them."

"Mark, I don't know these people. I don't want to join them, and I don't want to stay in this bedroom, either. Please, let's leave and go somewhere else. This is scaring me."

He wraps his arms around me and kisses my cheek. "Don't worry, as long as you're with me nothing bad will happen."

"What if the cops show up and we all get busted?" I ask, as I pull myself away. Good God, that's all I need. I've already pushed my parents to the limit.

"Susan, I love you. You have to trust me, I'll take care of you," he says persuasively, as he puts his arms around me again.

His words and the smooth, velvety sound of his voice makes me feel like butter in his arms, ready to melt at his very touch. He caresses the back of my neck and head with one hand and gently brushes my cheek with the fingertips of his other hand, then softly kisses my lips, my face, my neck. I still love him so much and want desperately to believe in him. Then, as he carefully lays me down on the bed, I know that he wants to make love. Mesmerized by his sweet kisses, his touch and his words, I'm ready, once again, to surrender to my desires, because he's all I've ever truly wanted. The moment I close my eyes, a precious, sweet vision of Madlyn appears, and it's like having a bucket of cold water tossed at me.

"Yeah sure, just like you took care of me seven months ago," I say crying, as I try to shove him aside. "Get off of me. I'm outta here," I practically shout, as I flee from the house.

As frightened as I am of being on this dark, scary street alone, it's better than being in that horrible place. I hear him calling after me. I can't look back. I'm much too afraid I'll run back to him and into his arms.

My hands are shaking so badly I can hardly unlock the car door. To clear my head, I drive to West Beach, to the same spot where we always would go "parking." Looking out over the water where we sat more times than I can count, sharing thoughts of our days together and making out, sharing our dreams of the future and making out and then, making out some more, I try to sort myself out. I sit long enough to have a good cry, blow my nose a thousand times, get rid of my blotchy face and realize that Mark's never going to change. He's gone too far. He's over the edge. And, as much as it breaks my heart, I know I can never see him again.

Mark makes it easy for me by quitting school a second time, and I find myself lost without him, all over again. I recover enough to date a few guys, always feel uneasy, as if I should be somewhere else, doing something different. Maybe it's the constant yearning to be taking care of Madlyn. I can't concentrate anymore and I lose track of the events and conversations going on around me, always leaving me with the sense of being left out of some big joke. Who knows, maybe I'm the joke. It seems the girls have so much to say, and I just stand there lost for words, always missing the point they're all so desperately trying to make. Their incessant pettiness and drivel seems such a waste of time, and I feel as if I have nothing in common with them anymore.

There are many times when I feel disconnected from my very own family. No one ever expresses any concern for me, so I know they don't understand the depth of the heartache I still feel. My parents certainly seem to have moved on, forgetting all about Madlyn, and I figure I'm supposed to do the same, but it just isn't happening for me.

Just to make matters worse, I'm convinced that guys are only asking me out because of the rumors. I can't help it. I've become guarded and suspicious, always assuming the worst, even though that doesn't appear to be the case. They are all very charming and never try to "get fresh." Dating is just so damn difficult now, as is everything else in my life.

I've been cursed with my Grandpa Goley's curly hair and have always wondered why couldn't I, the only girl in the family, have the beautiful straight blonde hair my kid brother Russell has? It kills me to see all that gorgeous hair wasted on a little boy who always has a "beeza." Straight hair is all the rage. So, I spend a lot of time with my hair either rolled up in huge, beer-can size brush rollers or with it spread out flat on the ironing board. While shampooing my hair last night, I felt tiny pimple-like bumps on my scalp, along the hairline, just above my temples, and checked them out, once I got out of the tub. I wondered what they could be, as I continued setting my hair. I soon forgot about them and went to bed.

Removing the rollers this morning, I notice they are full of hair, especially the ones in the front, and I panic. "Mom, my hair is falling out! Oh, brother, this is all I need - a receding hairline like Daddy's."

Mom comes running into my bedroom in her chenille bathrobe and matching slippers, with the toilet paper still wrapped around her hair. "Oh, my, I'll try to get you an appointment with a dermatologist today," she tells me.

Although I'm a new patient, the doctor agrees to see me. As he examines my scalp, he asks me how long ago I delivered?

My eyes are bugging out and my jaw's hanging open, while Mom's face drains of all color.

"What do you mean - deliver?" Mom asks, gripping her purse.

"A baby," he says nonchalantly. "This is somewhat common after giving birth."

"She didn't have a baby, she's only seventeen," Mom lies, sounding indignant. "I think it's from those darn brush rollers she wears in her hair every night!"

The doctor doesn't even bother to argue the point. "Well then, I guess her rollers are too tight." He then writes me a prescription and shows us the door. Walking to the car, we don't know whether to laugh or cry and can't stop talking about the silly looks on our faces, when the doctor made his accurate diagnosis.

There is a guy I'm interested in, however. His name is Brian. He's easy to talk to, and we've been friends since our sophomore year. It's still football season and he's a starting player, therefore, very popular. So, I'm hesitant about approaching him. He has a girlfriend, and I can't imagine his clique welcoming me with open arms any time soon.

When we finally do get the chance to talk, the gossip doesn't seem to bother him and before long, he breaks up with his girlfriend and asks me out. Thanksgiving and the end of the football season are near, and he invites me to the Cheerleader's Dance. This is the function all of the jocks, cheerleaders and majorettes attend. It's held in the Gold Room, on the top floor of the New Bedford Hotel, and I know I'm gonna feel like a fish out of water, so I tell him I'll think about it.

My cousin, Roberta, is head majorette, and she's trying to convince me to go. "Come on, don't worry about those girls. I'll be there, we'll have fun," she promises.

"Oh, I don't know. I'll feel so out of place, they'll all be gawking at me."

"Oh, stop it! You're paranoid, for Christ's sake. It's been two months already and nobody's even talking about you anymore. It's over, so forget it. You're going and that's it."

It's hard to argue with Roberta, she's a lot tougher than I am. I remember shortly after Mark dumped me last March, she and I were on our way to the school cafeteria when his new blonde girlfriend made a nasty comment, gloating over the fact that he had broken up with me to go out with her. Well, Roberta was off in a flash and grabbed that girl by her purple mohair sweater, pushed her up against the lockers and demanded she apologize for being so rude. The girl was so startled, I thought her eyeballs were going to pop out of her head. Fixing her sweater, she nervously apologized and hurried off down the hall, as fast her skinny legs would carry her.

I was as shocked as she was and cracked up when Roberta simply grinned, picked the mohair out from between her fingers and said, "I'm starving, let's get lunch," as if nothing had just happened. I wanted to give her a great big hug for standing up for me in that way. It touched my heart to think she truly recognized how difficult it was for me at the time to be pregnant, jilted by my boyfriend and still in school.

Mom must understand how leery I am about going to this dance, because she offers to buy me a special holiday dress to wear. The Thursday night before the dance, we go downtown to Cherry & Webb looking for the perfect party dress. "That's it!" I exclaim, as I set my eyes on a double-breasted coat style mini dress, made of a polished winter white fabric, with silvery threads running through it and beautiful rhinestone buttons. Mom puts it on her charge card and then leads me to the shoe department. "I can have new shoes, too?" I can't believe this, a store bought dress and new patent leather pumps. Oh, happy day!

The night of the dance, hardly any of the girls are speaking to me, and I begin to retreat. Then I remember my mother's advice to always hold my head high and, strangely enough, it works. I look fabulous in my glittery dress. Plus, my newly attained figure helps to boost my confidence. Roberta never strays far and before long I'm dancing and having the fun she promised.

In a couple of hours I will be a graduate of the New Bedford High School Class of 1969. Thank God! I actually made it. Brian and I are going steady now. We went to the Senior Banquet and prom together. Going to that Cheerleaders dance was the best thing I could have ever done for myself. It broke the ice with most of the kids, and I've been pretty much accepted since.

Brian has been very good for me. He makes me feel safe and treats me like the lady I pretend to be. I enjoy the time we spend together and I happily find myself growing more and more attracted to him as time goes on. The best part is my parents like him. Although it makes me sad to say, that's one of the main reasons I've continued my relationship with him. Pleasing my parents is essential. It's necessary that I redeem myself in their eyes before I can ever have any respect for myself again. I know it's selfish on my part and unfair to Brian, but they finally seem happy for me. And, it's almost as if I'm on the road to recovery, because I'm beginning to feel somewhat better about myself, too. So, even though what I'm doing isn't right, staying with Brian is what I need to do.

Brian's sister is expecting her first baby just before Madlyn's first birthday, and all the painful memories are flooding back, as if they are happening all over again. I envy her when she talks about her pregnancy and all she's going through. I want to share all the feelings I had experienced, just last year. There's always some comment on the tip of my tongue, about to be revealed. Sometimes I slip and say something incriminating, but no one ever seems to notice. Why do I feel as if some huge scarlet letter is stamped on my forehead for all to know my lurid tale? Those who do know my secret never bring it up or belittle me in any way. I do it to myself. I've become my own worst enemy.

Just days before Madlyn's first birthday, she delivers a healthy baby boy. Not quite knowing what to do with my feelings, I hurry over to see her new son. While watching him sleep, I can't figure out if I'm more heart broken or excited, and I ask if I can pick him up. Holding him close, I breathe in his sweet, soft baby powdery smell. His small velvet head is near my face, just under my chin, and I close my eyes and pretend its Madlyn. Stinging tears are about to spill. My head aches trying to hold them back. The lump in my throat causes my muffled sigh to quiver.

With a big yawn, he stretches, rubs his face and opens his eyes. I take in every bit of him. He's a beautiful baby with eyes very much like Madlyn's.

"May I change him and give him a bottle?" I ask, avoiding eye contact with Brian's mother, who's just come in to check on us. "I know how. I've done lots of babysitting," I stretch the truth a bit, so she'll allow me to do it.

While rocking this tiny bundle, waiting for a burp, I overhear Brian's mother say, "She's quite taken with him isn't she?"

On Madlyn's first birthday, I'm nearly paralyzed with sadness. For months, I've been second-guessing my decision, and I'm fearful she isn't enjoying the life that was chosen for her. I'm tormented with dozens of questions that can't be answered. Will she dig her chubby little fingers into her first birthday cake and smear it all over her face and in her hair? Will she even have a birthday party? Will there be lots of family to celebrate with her? Does she have brothers and sisters?

Does she have curly hair? Of course, she has curly hair; both Mark and I have curly hair. Does she have pigtails? I adore little girls in curly pigtails, with pretty ribbons to match their dresses. Does she have a new dress with all the pretty smocking at the top? Is she walking? And, if she is, does she have Stride Rite shoes? Children need to learn to walk in good shoes. When she grows out of them, will they be bronzed, as mine were?

Most importantly, is her hip okay? Even though they assured me that Madlyn had been checked and her hip was fine, I've always wondered if it was true, or did they just tell me that so I would quietly go away.

By Christmas of 1969, Brian has fallen in love and asks me to marry him. Before even considering his proposal, I have to tell him about Madlyn. He has to know the truth about the type of person I really am. I'm so ashamed, as I dredge up the whole wrenching story for him. I haven't talked about it with anyone, since leaving her behind at the hospital. He listens in complete silence, and it's impossible to imagine what he's thinking of me. Still, I'm strong enough to make one condition to the marriage. "Brian, unless you're willing to accept Madlyn into our family, should she ever come looking for me or when the time comes for me to find her, I can't marry you." It's a lot to lay on him, and I tell him to think about it and call me when he makes a decision. I ask him to please understand how important this is to me.

When the phone rings the next day, I know its Brian. "Susan, what happened, happened. It has nothing to do with me," he says, sounding calm and self-assured.

How lucky can a girl like me get? Maybe, just maybe, I'm not damaged goods after all. Somebody really loves me and wants to marry me. Hopefully, now that we'll be engaged I'll fall in love with Brian. Am I about to find some happiness?

It's Saturday, September 12, 1970. As I mechanically get ready for what's supposed to be the happiest day of my life, I'm nauseous and lightheaded. For months, I've been hoping against hope that, as the days passed and the wedding date neared, my anxiety would turn into enthusiasm. I'm disheartened this morning, when excitement doesn't fill my heart the way everyone said it would. As always, I mask my feelings, having become a master of disguise.

It's nearly ten in the morning and my gown still hasn't been delivered for my eleven o'clock wedding Mass. My parents couldn't afford the dress I spotted in Bride's magazine, so Mom hired a seamstress who made me an exact copy for half the cost. This year, it's fashionable to add pastel colors to a wedding gown, and I've chosen a pale yellow sash at my waistline. The touch of yellow somehow eases my guilt about not being "pure" for my husband. While standing at the dining room windows, watching for my dress to arrive, my mind is filled with doubts and reservations.

Sadly, I don't love Brian as much as I should. Even as fond of him as I am, someday I'll be sorry for going through with this. But for now, I must marry him to save myself, to get over Mark and have a baby I can keep. As soon as we're married and settled in, I'm sure to fall in love. And, if not right away, most certainly once I have his child. All I need is to give myself time and be patient.

The wedding is a great success. Dad and my brothers look so handsome in their tuxedos. Mom is positively glowing in her pretty powder blue suit. She even has flowers in her hair. It's so obvious how happy and proud I have made them today. My cousin, Madeline, my maid of honor, looks beautiful in her peach colored gown with her big white straw hat. All one hundred and fifty guests are enjoying the reception, dancing to the music and having a blast, even me! I can tell how much Brian loves me and I love him so much for that. Maybe marrying him is going to work out after all.

Our apartment isn't ready when we return from our honeymoon, so Brian's mother offers us the use of his old room. Living with her is quite nice. She not only makes me feel comfortable and welcome, she also helps with our laundry, makes dinner and keeps an immaculate house, not wanting me to do much of anything. My friends can't understand why I, as a young bride, can be so content living with my mother-in-law. I can only assume that not being madly in love helps.

I've been sick with a hacking cough, congestion and sharp, knife-like pains in my chest and back. The diagnosis is severe bronchitis, possibly pneumonia. As much as Brian wants to care for me, no one else but my mother will do, and I move back home. Brian, not knowing what else to do, moves into Mom's with me.

My wedding album has arrived, and there's a surprise picture of me looking out the window, with my pink housecoat and fluffy slippers, as I waited for my gown to arrive. The photographer, Mr. Rioux, a dear family friend, must have thought it was a sweet picture and included it. If he only knew all the "unsweet" thoughts running through my head, when he snapped that shot.

By the first of November, Brian and I move into our apartment. Everything is brand new, and I love "playing house" and entertaining our friends on the weekends. I work days at an insurance company and Brian works the night shift as a computer operator, leaving me alone with too much time to think about Madlyn and wondering where she could be. Although, I've always had a strong feeling, call it mother's intuition, that Madlyn was given to a family in Fall River, Massachusetts, just fifteen miles away. Each year since we were kids, my parent's would bring us to the Fall River Knitting Mills for our new winter sweaters. At Christmas time, there was always a beautifully decorated tree displayed, with electric trains circling a miniature winter village. Santa would pass out candy canes and balloons to entertain the kids and allow parents time to shop. Now that I'm married, I plan to continue the family shopping tradition and allow myself time to sit on the benches that surround the tree, to watch the children and search for a little girl that just might be mine.

In the early spring of 1971, a physician's secretary calls the insurance office where I work, regarding a rejected claim for a tonsillectomy, and asks that it be checked. While taking down all the particulars, I notice that the patient, a little girl, has the same birth date as Madlyn and lives in Fall River. Immediately, I worry that this could be her. With tears in my eyes, I take the information over to my Aunt Mary, who also works here, and share my concerns with her that this is my little girl. I ask that she do the adjustment for me. If this is Madlyn, it's much too soon to barge into their lives. I must respect the privacy of her new parents and not be the one to investigate the case.

I've been offered a secretarial position by one of the physicians, an OB/GYN, that I handle claims for. He's impressed with my ability to remedy just about any problem and wants to have someone in his office that knows the ins and outs of insurance. When he offers me a ten-dollar weekly raise, I eagerly accept. His office is located in a new medical building near St. Luke's Hospital. As it happens, the doctor I had seen to confirm my pregnancy with Madlyn now works upstairs, in the very same building. Whenever it's necessary to go up to his office to get a patient's file or a lab report, I'm paranoid that one of his nurses will recognize me. Like anyone would believe that the scared, pregnant teenager I was in 1968 is now this newly hired secretary from downstairs.

I eventually learn the charts of patients not routinely seen are stored in the basement. Wondering if the files from the upstairs offices are down there as well, I venture into the cellar to search. Unlocking the door, I pass my trembling hand over the wall in search of the light switch. The room smells musty like old newspapers, and the walls are lined with dozens of old filing cabinets. I need to find the one that holds my chart, the one with my alleged soon-to-be-married name. As I approach "the" cabinet, my heart is pounding.

Opening the drawer, I find my chart. Reading through it, I'm stunned to see that I had also used Mark's home address and phone number. I have no recollection of having done that, and I'm saddened to think of how delusional I had been in expecting he would marry me. As I continue reading, I'm thankful that I've been working there long enough to decipher and understand all the chicken scratch. Reading every word written in my file, I'm relieved to see the doctor's notes are routinely familiar. There's nothing to indicate he suspected I lied.

After devouring all of the information, I tear the chart into a million pieces, destroying any evidence of my ever having been a "bad girl."

Chapter Five

My baby has dropped into position. My doctor has informed me that I'm sufficiently dilated and indeed ready to deliver, even though it's twelve days before my due date, incredibly the very same due date, September 26, as Madlyn's due date was. Last year, my sister-in-law delivered her second son, my godchild, on September 26. I have to wonder if there isn't some sort of divine significance to that date for me. Or, is it just a cruel cosmic joke?

After waiting five long years, my anxiety level is sky-high and I can't wait another moment to hold this baby in my arms. So, without hesitation, I ask to be induced. Since it's Friday, my doctor advises me to wait until Monday, if I don't go into labor over the weekend.

"That's the seventeenth! I can't have this baby on Monday," I inform him, becoming hysterical. Reminding him that's Madlyn's birthday, he kindly arranges for me to go in on Tuesday the eighteenth. Since I also work for him and know him well, I feel safe being honest with him.

The onset of labor never happens, although I can't imagine why not. If stress induces labor, I'd have given birth twenty times by now. I've made myself a nervous wreck by not only worrying about giving birth on Monday, but also fretting over Madlyn's fifth birthday.

When I arrive at St. Luke's early on the eighteenth, all the beds are full. The nurse assures me a bed will soon be available. In the meantime, I should wait out in the lounge area and relax. Brian is sent to admissions to fill out the paper work. In the lounge, there is a woman in labor. Well, I assume she's in labor, since she's in a johnny. The fact that she's smoking disgusts me.

"First kid?" she asks, with the cigarette dangling out of her mouth.

All during my pregnancy, I've tried to think only happy thoughts. Only problem is, happy thoughts are sometimes hard to come by because the secrets and lies surrounding adoption have nearly consumed my life. Even at Lamaze class, I had to lie and pretend this is my first pregnancy.

I must look nervous, but I'm not about to let her think I haven't done this before. "No, I have a five year old. Her birthday was yesterday. She just started kindergarten," I say, seating myself as far away from her as possible. Wow, that felt so good. I've never before admitted to anyone other than Brian, I had Madlyn and can't believe I said it out loud.

I'm finally induced at ten o'clock and deliver my second beautiful baby girl, Jacqueline, shortly after noon. My labor is short and sweet, truly a labor of love and nothing like I had feared. My experience at St. Margaret's was so clouded by the drugs they had given me that I remember very little about my first labor.

When they bring Jackie to me, I hold her tight and close my eyes, and her sweet smell brings me back to Madlyn. Memories flood in, as I unwrap her and tenderly run my hands over her silkiness, count her fingers and toes, and then gently caress her tiny body. The soft feel of her down-like hair and skin against mine is enchanting. Holding my child, the child I am going to keep forever, is nothing less than miraculous. No one will ever take her away from me. I will never let her go. With tears streaming down my face, I place her on my lap and try to see if there is even the slightest resemblance to Madlyn. Yes, they do have the same blue-green eyes, but Jackie is long and thin with (I hate to say it) a smushed nose, while Madlyn was short and chubby with a button nose.

I had convinced myself that, once this new child was in my arms, I would begin to heal from the loss of Madlyn. Her birth would heal me, heal my marriage and heal my heart. However, as much as I love and cherish Jacqueline, that hasn't happened. None of it. Not even months after Jackie's birth. Jackie is Jackie and Madlyn is Madlyn. Now I have to face their two birthdays back to back every year and I can't help thinking that now I should have two precious daughters.

Being a mother comes so naturally to me, and the infinite joy it brings only causes me to realize that, yes, I could have taken care of Madlyn and been a good mother, with or without a husband. All I would have needed was a little bit of help and the chance to prove myself.

I've begun experiencing mild to severe migraine headaches. My dentist contributes them to TMJ and sends me to an orthodontist. He prescribes eighteen months with braces. They better work!

On February 9, 1976, in the midst of a raging snowstorm, I deliver another little girl. Kristine weighs in at nine pounds, fourteen ounces and measures twenty-one and a half inches long. Again, I find myself searching for and happily finding a likeness to Madlyn. Kris has the same chubby arms and legs, deep creases everywhere. Her round, pink cheeks are accented by her cute button nose. Her perfectly shaped head is topped with soft, wispy hair, exactly the same texture and color as Madlyn's. However, her eyes are a dark navy blue. What a thrill to see my first-born in my third daughter, and I welcome the feeling of comfort it brings to my heart.

I'm delighted to be a stay-at-home mom, and from the outside looking in, I have it made. We have two lovely girls, two nice cars and share ownership of a two-family house with my parents in a desired South End neighborhood. But, my desperate attempt to fall in love with Brian has failed. The harder I try, the more frustrated I become. I worry that I have become frigid, and that there must something wrong with me for not being sexually attracted to my kind and handsome husband. The more anxious I grow over the fate of my marriage, the hurt of losing Mark becomes even harder to bear.

As a result of the ongoing unhappiness in my marriage, I become obsessed with the care and upbringing of my girls. They are my lifelines and, as far as I'm concerned, I have to be the best mother ever. My marriage is failing from the obsession.

I struggle, but manage to stay with Brian for only a couple more years. By the fall of 1978, I can't hide my frustration or stay married any longer. I confess my lack of feelings for him, ask for a divorce and apologize, over and over, for hurting him so. Not wanting to upset the girls before the holidays, nothing is mentioned until Brian is ready to move out after the first of the New Year.

I am curiously unaffected by our break up. Frankly, I'm relieved, having reached a point where I've become displeased with myself because of my ever-growing indifference towards Brian. Now that he's gone, the tension my indifference had caused within me is gone. I set us both free. I'm no longer miserable from such immense guilt for marrying this kind and gentle man. Brian deserves a wife who will return all the love he has to offer, and I'm simply not the one for him. Someday, I'll tell my daughters how risky it is to marry someone you don't love with all your heart. My failed marriage will always serve as a brutal reminder of how foolish I was to try and make up for all I had lost.

Being a divorced, single mother of two is no picnic. Money is tight, and I'm trying to make ends meet by working as a cocktail waitress/coat room girl at Alhambra's, a nightclub a couple of towns away in Westport, Massachusetts. I've met a lot of new people by working there. One guy, Jay, a disc jockey, fascinates me. He's tall and handsome, dresses preppy and wears his eyeglasses on the top of his head. He's friendly and funny, although he can often appear distant and serious. Most of the guys who work here are divorced, have kids and are also trying to make extra cash. So, I assume Jay's in the same situation. Unlike the other guys who work the door or the bar, Jay is stuck in the disc jockey booth. So, we rarely have the chance to talk. Our conversations are usually short and on the run, when I either bring him a drink or when he checks his jacket.

Recently, we've had more opportunities to talk, and I'm certain the chemistry I feel towards him is mutual. He repeatedly asks me to join him for breakfast after work and, as much as I'd like to, I must always decline.

Jackie and Kris are early risers and, getting off work at two in the morning, I need to go straight home. Each time I apologize and ask for a rain check. I know he'll eventually get sick of being turned down.

Tonight is "Beat the Clock" night at Alhambra's, when the price of a beer starts out at twenty-five cents a bottle. Every hour, thereafter, the cost increases by another quarter. It's both impressive and scary to witness hundreds of college kids, beating down the club doors at eight o'clock sharp for their twenty-five cent beers.

Before the crowd swarms in, Jay and I are enjoying a drink together. It's school vacation and the girls are with Brian, so I can finally join him for breakfast after work. I'm excited to tell him and dumbfounded at his response.

"I can't," he replies. "I have to get back to Boston, I have an 8 o'clock exam in the morning."

I'm at a loss for words. This wasn't in the script.

"I'm a pharmacy student. You knew that, didn't you?"

"No, can't say that I did." I'm not sure I want to hear his response to my next question. "How old are you, Jay?"

"Twenty-one."

I'm shocked. He doesn't look at all like a college student and certainly doesn't act like one, especially the ones that come into this place.

Seeing my look of disbelief, he says, "Trust me, I am."

I'm feeling so disappointed that we won't have this time to get to know each other better. "Do you realize how old I am?" I rush to ask. Before he even has a chance to answer, I blurt out, "I'm twenty-eight years old. I have two kids." Without realizing it, I'm yelling and my arms are flying, and everyone is laughing.

"I know how old you are, and I know that you have kids. So what?"

"Jay, why would you want to date me?"

He just shrugs.

"I can't go out with you. You're younger than my kid brother," I say, pacing back and forth in front of the bar, while the doormen, bartenders and waitresses watch me make a fool of myself.

"I think you should give me a chance," Jay says calmly.

"Yeah, give the little guy a chance," the smart-ass bartender says, winking at me.

Oh, brother, now what? "I don't know, Jay. I'm gonna have to think about this."

"Good enough," he says confidently.

Two weeks later, after enduring the cradle robbing jokes from my friends at work, I give in and invite Jay for Sunday dinner. Before getting involved, I want to see how he and the girls react to one another. As the weekend approaches, I'm convinced this relationship is doomed, not only because of the seven-year age gap, but because I'm not sure if I'm ready for someone to come into my life, even if it is only for dinner. Besides, I haven't been on a date since 1969, and I'm scared to death.

By four o'clock on Sunday, I'm certain I can't go through with it and decide to cancel dinner. Jay is spending the weekend in Fall River, so I call his parent's house.

"Hello!" says the woman's voice at the other end of the phone.

Oh, this is ridiculous, his mother answered.

"Yes, hello. May I speak with Jay?" Suddenly, I'm feeling like a pushy teenage girl.

"Who's calling?"

Of course, she had to ask.

"This is Susan."

"Jay...telephone. Some girl named Susan."

"Hello."

"Hi, Jay, it's Susan. Sorry to call on such short notice. I have to cancel for tonight. I never got to the store to get what I need to make dinner." I hate lying, but there's just no other choice.

"No problem, I'll take you and the girls out for dinner."

Yikes, think fast.

"The girls aren't home," I lie again. Damn, why did I tell him that? That wasn't very smart.

"Perfect, I'll be there in an hour. Decide where you want to go," he says, then hangs up.

He just hung up on me. Holy shit! I have a date with a college kid. I don't need this. What I do need, however, is to have my head examined. Where can we go? Nowhere too expensive - he can't have much money. Davy's Locker is just down the street. We can eat and come right back. No, we can't come back here, he thinks the girls aren't home. Good Lord, because I lied I have to hide the kids upstairs at Mom's. Okay, calm down and get ready.

Exactly one hour later, the doorbell rings. I check my face and hair. What for, I don't know. He's seen me many times at my worst, exhausted, after work at two in the morning. I take a deep breath, open the door and give him my best smile. He looks so handsome. He has on tan corduroys, a blue button-down shirt, a navy blue blazer and loafers with no socks. He never wears socks. Glasses on his head - I still don't get that.

"Hi, come on in, I'll get my coat," I try to sound enthusiastic.

"Nice apartment," he comments, as he checks out my place.

"Thanks, we bought it eight years ago."

"Oh, you own it?" he asks.

Yes, I own it. I'm a grown up! "Yes," I say proudly. "Okay, let's go."

After being the gentleman and opening the car door, he grins at me through the front windshield, on his way to the driver's side. I smile back. When he starts up the car, he pulls his glasses down from the top of his head. One mystery solved. He needs them after all to drive.

"Where to?"

"Davy's Locker."

I give him directions, only to find out he already knows where it is.

He rushes to open the door of the restaurant for me and asks the hostess for a table by the windows. Already dark, the night sky is clear and the view of the lighthouse across the sparkling water is magnificent. I'm nervous and hardly touch my meal of broiled scallops. Apparently, he's not the least bit nervous, as he devours everything on his plate and mine. We share a little bit about ourselves and his life sounds busy and exciting compared to mine. He has an apartment in Boston, three part-time jobs, on top of being a full time student. When dinner is over, I begin to concoct a way to quickly and graciously say good night without having to invite him in to my place, when he suggests we take in a movie.

Our ride to the theater is quiet and somewhat strained for some reason. I force some light conversation and choose to see *The Blue Lagoon*. After the movie, things lighten up again. Neither of us liked the movie, and we have more laughs ripping it apart. I'm certain he must be out of money by now, and he'll be bringing me home. Just the popcorn and soda ran him a fortune. Now, he's insisting we go to Alhambra's for a drink, and I'm surprised he wants to go where everyone knows us.

The minute we walk in, the doormen are all too happy to give us a ration of grief, because they know the problem I have with the age thing. Nonetheless, I smile good-naturedly, walk past them directly to the bar and order a drink. Thank God, I'm only one "gin and seven" away from the end of this interminable date.

Jay pays for our drinks, and we go up to the balcony to watch the people dance below. One of the waitresses, who is also off tonight, walks up to us and, looking me straight in the eye, asks Jay to dance. The creep accepts.

What a jerk! He's got a lot of nerve dancing with someone else on our first date. That's what I get for dating a college guy. The only thing surprising me more than his rudeness is how much seeing him dance with her bothers me.

I date Jay several more times, each time telling myself that, as much as I enjoy his company, I'm not going to see him again. The age difference is making me crazy. Finally, I stop seeing him, using the excuse that summer is right around the corner, and I'll be busy with the girls.

I date a few other guys, none I care much about. One is a confirmed bachelor and feels the need to repeat that fact to me as often as possible. Another loves himself more than I love my kids. Then, just to make matters worse, neither of them wants to spend time with Jackie and Kris, and I find myself going out more and more without my girls. It's all happening so fast, I barely recognize what I've been doing. Good thing my brother, Russell, takes the time to straighten me out. His words about the girls needing me and being a better parent are all I need to ground myself and put my priorities back into place.

As summer wears on, I miss spending time with Jay more than I ever imagined. By the fall, I've decided I've had my fill of bad dates and have given up on men. However, I agree to go on what I call a "pity date," to a bar in Newport, Rhode Island with Russell and his girlfriend, Denise. Though I love spending time with them, the band is awful, no one is dancing and I'm bored to tears. Looking for an escape, I notice this guy sitting alone at the bar with glasses on top of his head. It's Jay! When I sit on the barstool next to him, he's as surprised to see me as I'm delighted to see him. We chat for a while, and then he tells me he's about to leave and head for Alhambra's.

"Please take me with you," I beg. I really want to be with him again.

"Aren't you with your brother?"

"He won't care if I leave."

"Sure, let me finish my beer."

"There's just one thing. You'll have to bring me home to New Bedford."

"No problem," he agrees, takes his last swig and we head out the door.

Getting into his car, I see its back seat is filled with textbooks, clothes, shoes, and, of all things, an alarm clock. "What's all of this stuff?"

"Oh, you mean that stuff?" he asks, turning around surveying his mess. "I lived in my car this past summer semester."

This guy never fails to amaze me.

"Yeah, I didn't have money for an apartment."

"Jay, that's dangerous. What if you got mugged or worse, murdered?"

"Guess that never crossed my mind."

"What's this?" I ask, holding up an old, dirty and disgusting ski hat.

"Hey, that's my favorite hat," he says, as he tries to grab it out of my hand.

I take one whiff and throw it out the window. He tries hard to appear insulted that I have no regard for his stinky, knitted hat, but he can't keep a straight face and cracks up.

Whatever was I thinking? I really like this guy. I need to give him a chance. After all, not many guys share my sick sense of humor.

This time the ribbing we get from Alhambra's doormen doesn't bother me. All night long, Jay and I talk and laugh and dance. It's the most fun I've had in years. While dancing to *Turn Off The Lights*, by Teddy Pendergrass, I close my eyes for what seems like an instant and, before I know it, we lose our balance and land smack on the lighted dance floor. We laugh so much we can hardly pick ourselves up.

I haven't felt like this since the sixties. I'm as giddy as a teenager.

Once home, I ask Jay in for that long promised breakfast. He scrambles the eggs, while I take care of the bacon and toast. While joking around cleaning up and finishing our coffee, he stands in the kitchen doorway, much like Mr. Clean, not letting me pass. I try to sneak out under his arm to finish wiping off the table, when he grabs me by my waist and kisses me in a way that makes me take notice. He's not just fooling around. This is serious. He meant to kiss me that way. I'm trembling as chills run up and down my body.

It's after three o'clock in the morning, how can he still smell so incredibly delicious? His strong arms feel so good wrapped around me. The warmth and feel of his body against mine is oh, so tempting. It's been a long, long time since I've felt this tingling right down to my toes. To think, I've been romantically starved since the age of seventeen and I'm just now realizing how much I've missed it! I drop the sponge and forget whatever it is I was about to do. My libido is in overdrive, so are my thoughts. Love and sex and loyalty. I can't say I've ever been able to figure that one out. All three should go hand in hand. Somehow, it hasn't yet worked that way for me. I always seem to be missing one component. But I'm willing to give this a shot. Jay seems worthy of my time and attention, plus he's driving me wild!

We're both surprised when, without a second thought, I invite him to share my bed. I almost feel naughty being the aggressor. It's not a role to which I'm accustomed. My new behavior is turning me on even more so, enabling me to experience a passion in lovemaking like never before.

We see each other nearly every day, and I'm overcome with sensations surprisingly similar to those I called love so many years ago. Emotions I haven't felt in far too many years. Have I finally fallen out of love with Mark? Yes! Jay has not only managed to invade life, but my heart as well. I'm at long last, in love.

The girls are with Brian for Thanksgiving, and the time has come for me to share my secret with Jay. He needs to understand why I sometimes get so sad when I still find myself scanning groups of little girls to see if there is one who looks like me and might be Madlyn. Many times, while pretending to admire their outfits or hairstyles, I feel foolish and pathetic. I try not to cry while telling him, but the wounds are just as fresh and painful as when I first told Brian. Time does not seem to heal this wound. I'm terrified that, even though nothing else about me has made him run, this will. But, Jay takes me into his arms and tells me not to cry. "Susan, if she belongs to you how can I not love her, too?"

Over the next three years, our courtship is rocky. At times, Jay can be cold and indifferent, having little appreciation for the needs of others, including mine. Why he's like this, I'm not quite sure. I guess one never truly knows the environment in which another is brought up, so I make no assumptions. His parent's disparaging remarks and incessant disapproval of me, my daughters and my relationship with their son, cause a lot of tension between us. Ultimately, their objections have only caused Jay and I to grow closer and have helped us to realize that we love and need one another more than we ever thought possible. As many times as we have broken up, we never fail to get back together. We're learning that there is something extraordinary about our connection that not only intrigues us, but has also grabbed us by our hearts and won't let go.

Still, I sometimes wonder if I can trust him to be there for me in my most desperate times.

One night, I awake gasping for air, feeling disoriented and nauseous after dreaming the same nightmare that has haunted me for years. As always, I'm running as fast as I can and still can't catch the child running ahead of me. Nor can I run fast enough to elude the person in pursuit of me. Frantically, I try to call out to the child, but when I open my mouth to shout, no sound comes out. As the man catches up to me, I attempt to shove him aside, but my arms are too weighted down to strike him. I'm crying.

This time, I can't control the feelings the dream brings up, and I'm in the midst of a panic attack. My ever-growing anxiety must be due to this reoccurring dream. As I pass Jackie's room on the way to the bathroom, I call out for her to go upstairs and get my mother. The cold tiles feel good on my face, as I lay on the floor waiting for help.

"She's pale as a ghost." Dad shouts out to Mom. "Get her dressed, I'm taking her to the hospital."

"Jackie, call Jay and tell him to meet Mommy and Grandpa at the hospital," I say, barely able to catch my breathe.

It's well over an hour before I'm examined. By then, my fright has passed. Too embarrassed to admit that this has been happening to me for years, I tell no one about the nightmare. As a result of my silence, no cause is found and no diagnosis is made.

Jay never shows up or even calls, and his lack of concern bothers me. I don't understand how he can know I was sick enough to be brought to the hospital, yet not go to be with me. His excuse when I call him later is he fell back asleep. Wasn't I with my father, so why did I need him?

"You were the one I wanted," I try to explain. "You didn't even call to see if I was okay."

"I knew you'd call."

Frustrated, I hang up, finding it inconceivable that he has no understanding of how to comfort someone he loves. Still, my intuition tells me there's a caring soul hidden deep inside and I'm willing to teach him how to love and enjoy life and be there for the people he loves.

It's midnight and the doorbell is ringing. It's Jay. He's been at his buddy's bachelor party, and he's swaying from side to side, trying to refocus on the doorbell. Why is he crashing here? He knows he can't spend the night when the girls are home.

I open the door and pull him inside. "What are you doing here?" I ask, holding him up. "You didn't drive here in this condition, did you?"

"I love you," he slurs, then kisses me and falls onto the couch.

"I love you, too, but you can't stay here, the girls are home. Jay, Jay, can you hear me?"

He's out cold. It's the middle of the night, and I have this two hundred pound, unconscious man lying on my couch. Hearing that my parents are still up, I call Dad, hoping he'll know what to do with him.

"He's passed out!" Dad says, laughing as he inspects the sleeping heap on my couch. "There's nothing you can do. Let him sleep it off."

"Daddy, I can't. The girls are home."

"Susan, you have no choice. He's in no shape to go anywhere," he says, as he goes back upstairs.

Dad's right, so I throw an afghan over Jay and go to bed.

In the morning, I wake to the sound of cartoons and, when I go in to investigate, I find the girls are both lying on top of Jay, watching TV. He's got one in each arm. Jackie's in her pink fluffy feet pajamas, holding onto her favorite stuffed bunny, Bun, and Kristine's in her yellow blanket sleeper, happily sucking her thumb.

"Mommy, Jay slept over last night. Can he stay again tonight?" Jackie asks.

"How about if you girls pack your overnight cases and sleeping bags and camp out at my house next weekend?" Jay suggests. If he's hung over, he's hiding it.

His being here seems to be nothing less than spectacular for my girls.

"Please, Mommy, can we all stay at Jay's?"

"Sure, it'll be fun. Though I don't want to sleep in a sleeping bag," I whine dramatically.

"No, Mommy, you can sleep with Jay. He's got a big bed," Kristine proudly says, as if she's solved the problem of the century.

It's become quite obvious that the girls don't like it when Jay isn't with us. Not only am I looking to him for love and support, so are my girls. So, in April of 1982, the four of us, Jay, Jackie, Kristine and me, have a meeting and decide we need to get married and become a family. We all agree the Friday night after Thanksgiving will be perfect. The girls and I have great fun picking out dresses and planning the wedding. They choose matching Gunnysack dresses and pretty dried flowers for their bouquets. It will be a smallish affair, with seventy-five of our closest friends and family. Once again, I ask my cousin, Madeline, to be my maid of honor, while Jackie and Kris will serve as my bridesmaids. When the time comes to book our honeymoon, Jay thinks it's best if we first take the girls on a family honeymoon to Disneyworld, just so they don't feel left out.

This time, as I stand before the altar taking my vows, every word of the service holds deep significance; every breath I take has meaning. Jay is trembling and crying, too. I hear sniffles from behind, as Jackie tugs on my gown, asking for the tissues Jay has for us in his tuxedo pocket. Jackie, always the caring big sister, wipes Kristine's nose. I'm overflowing with my love for them, and now Jay is part of us. We are a family.

Now that Kristine is in first grade, it's time for me to find a job. I want something that will allow me the freedom to work only during school hours. Sculptured nails are the big fashion craze, so I convince Jay to finance my beauty school education to obtain a manicuring license.

It's Father's Day, 1983 and the girls have a big day planned for Jay. Last week, they talked me into buying Jay the largest blue recliner we could find. "Blue is for boys," they said. It was delivered yesterday and Jay was all choked up as they escorted him to his big blue "throne," when he got home from work. But that was nothing compared to the gift they will give him today.

Last night, when I tucked the girls into bed, they asked me something very important. "Mommy, we've been thinking," Jackie said pensively. "Do you think Jay will let us call him Dad?" she asked, in her shy, quiet voice.

"Not Daddy, cause Daddy is already Daddy," piped up Kristine. "Just, Dad," she explained, with her big brown eyes sparkling.

"I think that's a wonderful idea," I said, complimenting them. "Jay will feel so special." Then I asked, "You know how much he loves you both, don't you?"

"Yeah, we know," Jackie said proudly, as her smile grew wide.

Well, if I thought Jay was choked up about the chair, it paled in comparison to this request. With tears in his eyes, he eagerly accepts their loving offer, as they all sit in his new blue chair.

Over the years, Brian has slowly distanced himself from the girls. I believe his anger towards me for deceiving him and breaking up our family has only escalated since my marriage to Jay. Consequently, it has gotten in the way of his relationship with our daughters. Although I can appreciate his reasoning, I've asked that he consider spending more time with the girls. I've even gone so far as to mention that I'm afraid he might be losing them to Jay. Brian assures me that will never happen, but it's easy to see that Jay is taking over as the dad in our household.

The following April, while shopping in the north end of New Bedford, I'm stopped by a man asking if I know of a particular address. Not recognizing him, I pay little attention and point him in the right direction.

With a broad smile this stranger says, "Thanks."

I know those teeth - that smile.

"Mark, is that you?" I ask, reaching out to touch his arm. "It's me, Susan."

He's as surprised as I am. It's been fourteen years, since I last saw him. His hair is unkempt, and he's dressed all in black - leather jacket, jeans, and funky shoes. His intoxicating, delicious scent is noticeably missing. He seems taller than I remember.

No English leather? Where's his Barracuda jacket and Weejun loafers? Where's my Mark?

It unnerves me when the pounding in my chest and the nervousness I feel is no longer exhilaration, but panic and disappointment. I feel nothing for this man I loved so much and for so long, and I'm taken aback by just how uncomfortable I feel in his presence. As if a switch has been flipped, my brain shuts down. Although I can see that his lips are moving, I hear nothing. I try to concentrate on his words, and can't. My mind only wants to remember the happy, carefree, teenage days we spent together, a time when we loved each other simply because we loved each other. Hell, when you're sixteen, who needs other reasons to love. I feel I'm in a time warp.

"Sue, are you okay?" he asks, as he takes my hand in both of his.

My face must be a blank, so I place my free hand on his, so we'll both know I'm still here, somewhere. Looking down, I see the same beautiful hands that wrote and played his love song for me so long ago.

"Why don't we get a cup of coffee and talk?" he suggests, gaining my attention at last.

"What? You want coffee?" I ask, as if it's an outrageous request. Did I even hear him right? Okay, be nice. All he wants to do is talk. "Sure, I've got a few minutes," I add, not really sure why I have agreed.

As we head toward the coffee shop, he asks about my life. Although I don't think he deserves to know, I tell him a little and then change the subject.

"Are you married?" I ask.

"No, divorced." He proceeds to explain how he had married his buddy's ex-wife many years ago.

Being neither interested in his buddy or his ex-wife, I interrupt. "Do you have any children?" Why am I feeling this indifference towards him? It doesn't make sense. He's been such a huge part of my emotional life for so many years.

Again, he says, "No," along with another explanation I really don't care to hear.

Oh, no! He's never had any other children. He needs to know he has a daughter. Damn, now I have to admit that I lied. "Mark, there's something I need to tell you," I say, trying to find my voice. After unveiling the entire fabricated story, I tell him about being sent away to St. Mary's and describe our daughter as I remembered she looked. When I feel myself getting way too emotional, I stop and ask to hear his thoughts. He's just staring at me, as though in a fog.

"Mark, are you hearing me?"

No response.

"You have a daughter."

Still nothing. Just a laid-back, it-really-doesn't-matter kind of a shrug.

Why is he behaving like this? Why does he have nothing to say? Déjà vu. It's the same as that day in my bedroom. It's 1968 all over again. I'm hurt by his disregard and turn to walk away.

"I know, I heard you," he finally says, and then reaches out to grab my hand. "Sue, don't go," he says, with his sly handsome smile.

With hopes he is wanting to know more about Madlyn, I turn back to him. An instant tenderness building within me.

"Wanna go for a ride in my van?" he asks, winking and apparently unaffected by my words.

After years of fantasizing about just such a moment, it's hard to believe I have absolutely no desire to go with him. Why, just a few years ago, I would have jumped at this opportunity. Or, would I have? Is it my love for Jay that's keeping me from going with him? Or, am I rejecting him based on his appearance? Imagine - me rejecting him! Could it be I've simply outgrown him? I don't know, I just don't know.

This man is in no way the same guy I fell in love with sixteen years ago. He seems so lost and confused. To think he might still be searching for some of life's happiness, when he could have had it all back in 1968, saddens me. I can't help wondering what difference Madlyn and I would have made in his life.

Now, I can't even bring myself to look at him. Once again, I'm transported back in time to when he left me alone and pregnant, feeling the pain of the extreme price I paid for the things we did. So, with head bowed and tears trickling down my face, I pull my hand free from his. As I walk away, I remind myself that I alone survived, became strong and moved on, making the best of the hand that was dealt to me.

On July 9, 1984, I deliver my fourth baby girl, Bethany Jay. She's long and thin and very delicate, with big, beautiful dark brown eyes, the loveliest rosebud lips and Jay's dimples. She looks so much like Jay that I'd have a difficult time proving she's mine, let alone searching for a likeness to Madlyn. After years of never expecting to have another child, because of my divorce, I consider Beth to be my extra special bonus in life. I'm hoping she keeps me young at heart and on my toes.

By the fall, though, I'm feeling unfulfilled and experiencing an emptiness I haven't felt in years, and I don't quite understand why. I have three happy and healthy "kept" daughters, a husband I truly love and a very good life. Although, lately I've been wondering if all the pain and memories of surrendering Madlyn, that came rushing back after Bethany's birth, is the reason. Why is my need to find Madlyn gnawing at me more than it has in the past? I can't fall apart now. I must remain patient. There's only five more years, before it's time to find my baby.

My migraine headaches have reached a level where I completely shut down. Lying in a darkened room with my eyes closed is the only place I want to be. My teeth and jaw hurt so badly I can't chew. My cheekbones ache.

Nothing takes away the pain, and I just have to wait it out, sometimes for days.

Since my teenage years, I've been prone to cold sores, and it's gotten to a point where they are becoming so frequent and large, my family jokingly refers to me as "Herpes Face." Not funny! Regrettably, I'm also losing my sense of humor. Years ago, my pastor told me that the blisters are brought on by stress, and I should try to avoid stressful situations. Easier said than done. I love participating in all the girls' activities, including lunch duty at school and chaperoning their class outings, but it leaves me little time for myself. On top of all that, there's my part-time job, a house to take care of and a husband who works long hours. Often times, I feel like a single parent who is spread too thin. If all that isn't enough, we're also in search of a piece of property on which to build our dream home.

By February of 1985, I've begun getting severe urinary tract infections. Even after an extremely unpleasant procedure called a cystoscopy, the urologist isn't able to find the source of the infection. "Don't worry, it can't be anything too serious," he says, handing me another prescription, "you don't have a temperature, so let's just wait it out and see."

Each cold I catch becomes flu-like, but never severe enough to stay in bed, where I really want to be. I try all the recommended remedies, but as the days pass, I'm becoming so weak I can barely get out of bed.

In the middle of the night, I am awakened by the most severe chest and back pain, and I'm convinced I'm having a heart attack. Jay doesn't seem worried, so I figure I'm over reacting and wait until morning to call my physician. When I do, he sounds concerned and tells me to come right in. Upon examination, he feels confident that pneumonia has developed and sends me for x-rays and blood work. Sure enough, it's pneumonia and it becomes so serious I'm admitted to the hospital to have the fluid drained from my lung. This procedure, thorocentisis, although not pleasant, does make me feel better. However, because my pneumonia isn't accompanied by a fever, I'm promptly discharged and sent home. For ten weeks Jay, Jackie and Kristine take excellent care of both little Bethany and me.

It's early spring of 1986, and I've been caught up in a vicious cycle for the past year now. The depression I'm experiencing must be due to my feeling lousy all the time. But then, I wonder if I'm feeling lousy because I'm always so damned depressed. The pneumonia returns the first of May and I feel buried alive in despair. "When will it ever end?" I cry to Jay.

By March of 1987, I'm feeling much better. My attitude and health are definitely improving, and I can't help but to wonder if its partly because the time is drawing closer to Madlyn's twenty-first birthday, at last, giving me license to search. Then, late in April, just as spring is getting underway, the pains in my back and chest return. The pneumonia reoccurs for a third time, only this episode is worse than the previous two. Still, with no fever associated with it, my physicians, both here and in Boston, are puzzled and can't figure out what causes it. So, after fourteen weeks of taking more drugs than I care to admit, lab tests too numerous to count and dozens of x-rays, they discharge me from their care and send me home to wait for the pneumonia to run its customary course.

Almost a year has passed, when I realize that the pneumonia that has plagued me for the past three years hasn't returned, despite the fact I've been even more exhausted and stressed from supervising the construction of our new house, in addition to everything else. I must be just too busy to get sick.

We move into our new home the week after Christmas 1988, feeling as though we have the world in the palm of our hands. Life is good. Jay and I had set a goal and accomplished it, just in time to get some much-needed rest before my next huge endeavor - finding my first-born daughter.

Chapter Six

It's Labor Day, 1989. While watching a parade in our neighboring town of Fairhaven, Jackie complains she's not feeling well. We leave for home before the parade is over, and she sleeps on and off for most of the day. She's being treated for bursitis in her shoulder, caused by the excessive hours she spends twirling her flag during marching band practice. Our family physician ordered that her practice time be cut in half and put her on the prescription drug, Naprosin. However, it isn't her shoulder that's bothering her today. She describes it as an overall discomfort.

As I watch Jackie sleep, I can't believe she will be sixteen in a few weeks, and that my first-born will be twenty-one. At long last I can keep the promise I made to Madlyn, as I kissed her on her tiny forehead for the last time, to find her when she turned twenty-one. When Jackie is feeling better, I want to tell her about her sister, and then ask her if she thinks Kristine at fourteen and Bethany at five are old enough to know my secret, too. With her maturity, Jackie will certainly have some sound advice with regard to telling her sisters about Madlyn.

The very thought of telling them is terrifying. It has been a forbidden subject for so many years that I fear I won't be able to get the words past my lips. Having only spoken about Madlyn a few times in my lifetime, I worry how to broach the subject. I'm also afraid that their loving opinion of me will change, once they know what I have done. How will they ever be able to identify with the narrow thinking of the sixties, when children were to be seen and not heard?

After dinner, Jackie's looking and feeling much better and, by the time she kisses us good night, she says she feels fine. At midnight, I hear someone in the girls' bathroom and get up to check. It's Jackie, brushing her teeth.

"What's wrong, Jack?" I ask, with a feeling of dread.

"Mom, I have a terrible headache and thought maybe it's because I forgot to brush my teeth."

The look in her eyes tells me just how much her head hurts. She begins to cry.

I give her a pain reliever and try to soothe her. "Come to bed with me, maybe that will help," I suggest.

Thirty minutes later, her head is still pounding and I call our doctor. "Bring her in first thing in the morning," he says.

I feel she needs immediate attention, and take her into emergency right away. As I inform the receptionist at the emergency room why we're here, I begin to tell her all the ailments Jackie has had in the last few weeks. Once I begin listing them, alarms go off in my head. All could easily be excused: she's always tired - too much band practice; her shoulder hurts - bursitis from flag twirling; the big bruise on her leg - she got hit with a flagpole, and is on the prescription drug, Naprosin, a blood thinner.

When added up all at once, it's all suddenly making horrible sense, and it becomes painfully obvious. Jackie has leukemia. I keep my thoughts to myself. She's admitted for observation, and our physician is called in. After examining her, our doctor orders the necessary blood work, then excuses himself and leaves the room. By now, Jackie's headache is gone, she feels better and wants to go home.

"Jay, can I speak with you and Susan out in the hall?" Dr. Smith asks, as he peeks into the room.

I know exactly what he's going to say, and I don't want to hear it. "I'm not going out there," I tell Jay. I just want to take my daughter home. If we hadn't brought her here in the first place, she wouldn't be sick and he wouldn't be telling me she has leukemia.

Jay calmly goes out into the hall. Reluctantly, I follow.

"Jackie's white blood count is grossly elevated." he says. "We're not certain of a diagnosis because the pediatric hematologist won't be in until morning. My guess is mononucleosis. There's also a chance it could be leukemia."

"Leukemia or mono? You can't tell the difference?" I ask in disbelief. He just doesn't want to admit how bad this is.

"I want Jackie to remain overnight, so the specialist can look at the blood samples in the morning and give you a precise diagnosis."

"Well, if all he needs are the samples, why can't we take her home?" I ask. Home with me where I can hold her and love her and make everything better, just like I've always done. No, no, this can't be happening! There's nothing wrong with her. I've taken such good care of her. She's never been sick or cold or neglected. She can't be ill. I love her with all that I am. Doesn't love keep children well? No? Well, it should, damn it! I can't lose another child. I just can't, I won't make it this time. Oh, God, please help her. I promise to never ask for anything else. What will I do if she dies?

Jackie and I stay the night. In the morning, the hematologist reports that he can't be positive of the results, either. An appointment has been set up for Jackie to see Dr. Lawrence Wolfe at the Floating Hospital for Children in Boston, later today. He then hands me a sealed manila envelope to bring with us and tells Jackie to take along an overnight bag, in the event she is admitted.

At home, Jackie and I shower and pack a few things. Jay and I hardly speak, neither of us willing to say out loud the thoughts that fill our heads.

Although, once in the privacy of our bedroom, we hold each other and cry, too afraid if we actually speak the word, leukemia, it will be true. That ominous manila envelope lies noticeably unopened on the kitchen counter. Neither Jay nor I have the courage to open it. However, on our ride to Boston, Jackie bravely reads it aloud.

Their suspicion is acute myelogenous leukemia. It's amazing how calm she appears.

I'm in a near state of frenzy by the time we arrive at New England Medical Center. I've lost all concentration and have difficulty following the signs to Pediatric Oncology. While checking in with the receptionist, my voice quivers and my hands shake. The receptionist is very sympathetic and has all the right words to put me a little more at ease. When I join Jay and Jackie in the waiting room, they appear to be holding up much better than me.

The clinic is jammed with parents and children. There are kids everywhere with IVs running. Some are receiving life-saving infusions of chemotherapy, while others receive blood transfusions. The older kids are watching TV, talking quietly or reading. The smaller children are playing together at a table with puzzles and blocks. None of the children have any hair, their faces are round and puffy, and their eyes seem dark and sunken. Yet, this is not a room of doom and gloom by any means. The children are smiling and laughing, apparently enjoying this special time they're able to spend together, while being treated as outpatients.

The room is brightly painted, and the children's art works are proudly displayed along the walls. The aquarium is alive with colorful tropical fish. There's also a large poster board full of pictures of all the children who have been treated at the clinic. Strangely enough, it's a touching sight to behold. To think these kids bravely face death everyday and willingly receive treatments that, at times, are more deadly than their disease itself. It's overwhelming. And these must be just a fraction of young people here at the Floating Hospital.

I've never before in my life witnessed such a scene, and it takes everything I have not to cry. I pray this doesn't happen to Jackie. I'm getting warm and dizzy, and I'm falling apart, while Jay and Jackie sit quietly, appearing calm and ready to handle whatever lies ahead. How in hell will I ever get through this?

After what seems like forever, Jackie's name is called. We're shown into an examining room. Dr. Wolfe glances at the contents of the envelope we brought with us, and making no comment tosses it aside. He examines

Jackie and takes more blood samples. We're sent to lunch and told that, when we return, they'll know exactly what's going on.

As if any one of us can eat! Staring at my sandwich, I try to convince myself that the doctors at home are wrong, and that's why new tests are being taken. Jackie's fine. We'll bring her home and things will be back to normal.

When we return, Dr. Wolfe and his nurse join us in the examining room. They sit in two office-like chairs, while we sit on the examining table. Without blinking an eye, Dr. Wolfe says, "Yes, Jackie has leukemia. Unfortunately, it's not the children's type. The form most adults get is very difficult to treat in teenagers and some very aggressive forms of chemotherapy will be needed. She must be admitted today for further testing. Her treatments will begin on Friday."

Jay and Jackie fall apart. My husband sits motionless, and I take her in my arms as she sobs. Then, Jay quickly composes himself and wraps his arms around both of us. "Girls, don't worry, everything is going to be okay. Together we can beat this, I know we can."

I call Brian and he can barely speak when I tell him the news. He almost sounds angry. He mentions something alluding to the fact that his father had died from a blood related disease. I promise to call him back once Jackie is settled in and we know what's what.

Arrangements for admission need to be made and I volunteer to go. I don't know if it's because I have to get out of that small room that's closing in on me or because Jackie will panic if Jay leaves. Walking down the hall with the nurse, my legs give way and I feel as if all life has been drained from my body. I fall against the railing and slide down the wall onto the floor. My heart is racing and I'm trembling all over. The nurse sits down next to me.

"I feel like I'm having a nightmare!" I cry.

"It's the stress," she explains. She's probably been through this a million times. "Every parent goes through this, at first. Just give yourself some time and you'll be fine."

"How am I ever supposed to be fine? My beautiful, healthy sixteen-year-old daughter has just been diagnosed with a leukemia that has less than a thirty-percent chance of survival, and I'm supposed to be fine?"

Offering a look of sympathy, she silently helps me to my feet.

I'm having difficultly remembering what went on yesterday, after I returned from the admissions office. I recall walking the corridors like a zombie, with one arm around Jackie and the other one holding her hand. Vaguely, I remember a bank of elevators, and then being brought to Jackie's room, here on the seventh floor. I do recall that she was taken to a procedure room to have some bone marrow extracted from her hip. When I heard her cry out in pain and wasn't allowed to go in to comfort her, the sick, burning feeling in my chest and stomach made me nauseous. After that, everything else is a blur. My memory of yesterday must be stored in my safe place - the same place I put my memories of 1968. A place that is dark and numb, a safe place where they can't hurt me, so I can go on and do what I have to do.

After Jackie's first round of chemotherapy, the doctors are amazed at how well her body accepts the treatments and how quickly it has attacked the leukemia cells. Remission has happened almost immediately, as if a miracle has been bestowed upon us. Now, after only a few of weeks of inpatient care, she's allowed to come home for a weekend visit.

It's so great having her back home again. Although she's not allowed visitors, Dr. Wolfe concedes that one friend can visit, if they both wear masks and don't touch. Jackie and her friend, Beth-Anne, have a remarkable visit. Although I can't see their faces hidden by the masks, their eyes say it all. They convey how much they love and have missed each other. I leave them alone to visit.

Jackie continues to do well and Dr. Wolfe feels she's in a solid remission and will benefit from a new experimental procedure called an "Autologous" bone marrow transplant. The procedure involves harvesting her own marrow, cleansing and purifying it, then transfusing it back to her. Transplants are not common protocol, so her name will be placed into a lottery. In the meantime, she'll receive another round of chemo.

Just before Halloween Jackie's name is chosen, and she is discharged and cared for at home by a visiting nurse and myself. The transplant will be done the first week of December, at Boston Children's Hospital. Jackie is doing well, so Dr. Wolfe allows her to attend a marching band competition, as long as she dresses warm and stays away from the crowd. "You can go, but don't you dare breathe! I don't want you catching a cold." He's only half joking.

The moment she hears that she has permission to go, her eyes hold a sparkle we haven't seen in many weeks.

Being with her friends, catching up on all the news and watching the band perform is the best medicine she's had so far. Her spirit and zest for life are renewed. The doctor is encouraged, and she's also allowed to attend marching band finals at Boston University's Nickerson Field the first weekend in November. Her marching band is like her second family, they are all so close.

Thanksgiving night, she begins getting bone and joint pain, this time in her legs and back. In the morning, we bring her into the clinic. Jackie has relapsed, and she's devastated. Her transplant must be canceled. We've been so hopeful and now this. I don't know what's worse: diagnosis or relapse. In the beginning, she didn't know what she was in for. With relapse, she knows exactly what lies ahead and all the pain that's involved.

Two extremely difficult rounds of chemotherapy prove fruitless. There will be no transplant for Jackie. I'm concerned about the effect this setback might have on Kris and Beth. Although my mother has quit her job to care for them, I worry that I may be missing their distress signals by being gone so much. So, I speak with our parent advocate about initiating a counseling group for siblings. If my girls can talk with other kids experiencing the same fears, it might make coping with Jackie's illness and my absence a little easier.

Tonight is the first siblings meeting and Bethany, being only five, doesn't want to attend. So, Kris goes alone. Jay and I wait anxiously, hoping the meeting helps. The first thing I notice, when the meeting lets out, is her grimace through the glass divider, as she washes her hands and dons the necessary hospital garb to enter Jackie's isolation room.

"So, how did it go?" I cheerfully ask, ignoring her frown, still hoping.

"Those kids need help!" Kris exclaims.

"Yes, they do, honey. They're going through a very difficult time, just like you and Beth," I explain.

"No Mom, that's not what I mean. Those kids are skipping school, failing their subjects and some have even attempted suicide." I'm stunned and at a loss for words.

"I don't feel like them. They're mad at their parents for being here at the hospital all the time. They're even mad at their brothers and sisters for being sick. How can they be mad at them for that?"

I just sit and listen, not knowing what to say.

"It scared me, Mom! Do I have to go back?"

"No, I guess not, not if you don't want to," I say hugging her. "I just thought it might help you to understand."

"Mom, I do understand. I know you have to be here. This is where you belong. Dad and Grandma are taking good care of us."

"Told you so," Jackie says with a shrug and a smile, upon learning of her sister's strength.

It's Christmas Eve Day and Jackie has pneumonia and is sent to Intensive Care. The pulmonary specialist informs us her condition is critical due to her depleted immune system, and that it's strictly wait and see if she will survive.

The shooting pains in my back and chest are nearly debilitating, and I don't even want to breath, it hurts so badly. It's the same pain as when I had pleurisy with my pneumonia. I can't get sick now. Dear God, let me stay well.

At eight in the evening, Dr. Wolfe checks in on Jackie. He assures us she isn't in any imminent danger and feels comfortable enough to urge one of us go home. "Nothing is going to happen tonight. One of you should be home for Christmas."

Jay wants to be the one to stay. "Jackie, would you mind if I went home to be with your sisters tonight?" I ask.

"Sure, Mom, you go home, it's Christmas Eve. Can Dad stay in my room tonight? I'm scared."

Although, it's against the rules, we look to her nurse for permission.

She quickly consents. "Yes, of course, its Christmas Eve!"

I kiss and hug Jackie good night, as I've never hugged her before. I look into her eyes, so she can see how much I love her and that going home is the last thing I want to do. I'm so terrified I'll never see her again. I place my faith in God and Dr. Wolfe's words and convince myself she'll make it through the night. It's the only way I can walk out of here. I change out off my hospital garb and run crying to my car in the garage.

The moment the girls walk in with my mother, the pains in my chest disappear. I hug and kiss them a hundred times. I haven't seen them in more than a week. I fill them in on Jackie's condition, we have a good cry and then sleep together, holding one another and praying for Jackie.

Bright and early Christmas morning, the phone rings, and I'm terrified Jackie has died.

"Merry Christmas!" It's Jay and he sounds ecstatic. "Jackie's feeling much better. She's sitting up and asking for Christmas presents. For some unexplained reason, the fluid in her lungs began to dissipate overnight, and she's breathing much easier." He takes a deep breath. "Sue, she's a little tired, but she can't wait for you and the girls to get here. Bring all the presents!"

I want to speak with her, to hear her voice for myself, but there are no phones in ICU. So, I send my love to her through Jay. Dressing quickly, we pack the car full of gifts. Suddenly feeling more hopeful, we sing Christmas carols all the way. It's a Christmas miracle.

Although, Jackie beat the pneumonia, it's just been one thing after another. She's been through so much, and she's tired and worn out.

We're all tested to find a bone marrow donor, and it turns out that Brian is the match she needs. A second transplant is scheduled at the University of Kentucky for mid January. On January tenth, the transplant is canceled, due to a severe esophageal infection. Nothing is going right, and Jackie is becoming weaker and weaker with every passing day.

Before her illness, Jackie had been preparing to receive Confirmation at CCD. Since her diagnosis, she has studied with Sister Claire and Father Jim, who share the responsibilities of the hospital's pastoral care and are truly loved by all the children because of the light and hope they bring into everyone's life on a daily basis. How they manage to stay so positive, under such dire conditions, is beyond me. They are especially blessed.

My brother, Tom, and his wife have asked that Jackie and Jay be Godparents to their new baby girl, Sarah, who was born this past November. Jackie is thrilled at having something so special to look forward to. Sister Claire and Father Jim explained her situation to the Cardinal of Boston's Archdiocese, and he has not only agreed that she should be confirmed in the chapel at the Floating Hospital, he wants to be the one to do it. In addition to that, he agrees to baptize little Sarah the same day. This is just what we all need, a king size dose of sunshine and happiness. Jackie's confirmation is set for Saturday, the tenth of February.

Confirmation is over, the family has left and Jackie is exhausted and about to fall asleep. What a joyous day it was to have the entire family together for such a special occasion. At the last minute, the Cardinal was called away and Father Jim was given the opportunity of a lifetime, the chance to administer the sacrament of confirmation. Jackie has become quite fond of him, so it was especially meaningful to her to be confirmed by him.

A light tapping on the door makes us both look up. The Cardinal is framed in her doorway. He makes such an impressive sight, that we both gasp when he enters. Apologizing for being unavailable earlier in the day, he introduces himself. Jackie's so stunned she can hardly say a word. That's as unusual for Jackie as it is for me.

"Why did you choose to take the name Elizabeth?" the Cardinal wants to know.

"Don't you think it sounds cool?" Jackie asks. "Jacqueline Elizabeth - I like it!" she says, telling it like it is.

I'm certain he was expecting a more meaningful answer, related to the inspiring life of St. Elizabeth or something like that.

The Cardinal laughs out loud, and so does everyone else who has gathered in her room. It's amazing how, as sick as she is, she can still light up a room by finding the humor, even in her difficult situation. The Cardinal remains with her for nearly an hour, keeping the conversation light by talking about typical teenage matters. Before leaving, he suggests we take a moment to pray for wellness.

"Did he just give me the "Last Rites?" Jackie wants to know, slightly unnerved.

I, too, wonder the same thing. To reassure her, I simply reinforce for her the Cardinal's statement about praying for wellness.

Now, five days later, Dr. Wolfe is requesting a meeting. Jay and I know in our hearts what's coming, as we sit across from him.

"Any additional treatments would not only be experimental, they'd be cruel," Dr. Wolfe says considerately. "You need to be prepared. Jackie is dying. It could take a day, a week, or a month. We just don't know."

I sit motionless. My brain stops functioning. My vision blurs. I can't speak or even whimper. Jesus, I'm barely breathing. The pain in my head is nothing compared to the explosion in my chest, where I can actually feel my heart shattering, its shards searing my insides. Someone is talking - it must be Jay. I hear none of what he's saying and place my hands over my ears, so no words drift in. I lower my head to my knees and rock back and forth, back and forth, in a vain effort to comfort myself. Someone's arms are around me, trying to gain my attention.

"Susan, someone has to tell Jackie," Jay is saying.

"Jay, how can we tell her she's going to die," I say, sobbing. "After all she's been through and all the promises we've made to her about getting well?"

Both Jay and I know we could never be the ones to deliver such news. We don't have the courage or the strength left to do something so devastating. Dr. Wolfe kindly offers to tell her for us.

We stand just outside Jackie's doorway, while he and his nurse go in to tell her. The instant we hear their voices, we realize how wrong we are not to be the ones and rush in to comfort our daughter. What the hell we were thinking? We probably weren't thinking. We're too scared, too exhausted and too numb from the shock of it all, to even be able to think clearly. I know now that you can never be fully prepared for the death of your own child, no matter how seriously or how long they have been ill.

I had promised myself, from the beginning, I would always be strong for Jackie, to give her courage. I also tried, some days more successfully than others, to never let her see me fall apart, to always give her hope. But today, we're all falling apart, and it's as if my life is about to end as well.

71

Because it's Thursday, Brian will be coming for his weekly visit. I have the nurse watch for his arrival to tell him the circumstances before he enters her room.

Jay and I both stay the night, no one sleeps. Jackie dozes but keeps waking up and calling out to us. In my desire to comfort her, we talk a lot about heaven and my Grandma Goley. She loved my grandmother and smiles at the mention of her name. "Grandma will come for you when you're ready, and she'll stay with you in heaven," I promise. "And, even though you might not understand this now, you're the lucky one. You'll still be able to see, hear and be with us, whenever your heavenly spirit chooses."

Jackie smiles at that.

Thank you God, my words seem to be soothing her. I tell her how desperately I'm going to miss her.

The next morning, Sister Claire asks that we leave them alone for a while. Neither she nor Jackie share with me the things they spoke about. Since Claire's visit, a calm has washed over Jackie, and she seems ready to handle her fate. Claire must have delivered a very powerful message. Whatever it was, I thank God for both Sister Claire and her message.

My parents bring the girls to the hospital, and we spend the day together as a family. Jackie sleeps most of the day, and I'm not certain if it's the drugs or her body finally accepting what's to come. We talk about a number of things, including our lives together and what it's going to be like having to live without her. None of us can imagine living one day without Jackie, never mind a lifetime.

At the end of the day, it's time for the girls to go. Jay needs some time alone with Jackie. He was barred from the hospital the last week, due to a cold. Knowing how much they missed each other, I volunteer to bring the girls home. Even though my heart breaks having to leave her, I know I must.

Kristine and Beth are scared of what's to come and need reassurance that I'm there for them, as well as for Jackie. Over the past five months, I've tried to spend special time with them, even though they've never once demanded my attention. They seem to understand the importance of my caring for Jackie, at this critical time in her life. I couldn't be more proud of them.

Although our hearts and minds are with Jackie, the girls and I stay busy on Saturday, going out for lunch and to a movie. Later in the day, Jay calls and asks that I gather the family. "Jackie wants to celebrate your brother, Russell's, birthday and to see our old home movies."

I call everyone, put the movies and projector together, and then count the hours for tomorrow to arrive. To my surprise, Beth tells me she has been keeping a diary, a picture book of sorts, about Jackie's illness and asks if she can bring it along, so she could show it to her.

I'm so touched and ask if I can see it, too. She scurries upstairs and takes it from its secret hiding place, somewhere in Jackie's room. Her words and drawings, though juvenile, distinctly describe her feelings about what she thinks her big sister must be going through and how she's unable to understand why God would make her sister so sick. I find my favorite part is about the days they shared, while Jackie was at home and in remission. She may only be five years old, but she recognizes how precious those days were, playing school, listening to music and dancing together.

Before going to bed Jay calls to say that he and Jackie shared a very special day. "We talked like we've never talked before," he said, his voice breaking with emotion.

Before Jackie was diagnosed, their love and affection had only been implied. Since her illness, Jay seems to connect with the girls and me on a much higher and deeper level. We've seen a man come forth that's strong, yet gentle; stern, yet compassionate. He's become the father every girl dreams about, and the husband every woman wishes was hers.

Jay has shared with me the things Jackie told him of the huge impact he has had on her life. Not only his love, but also his disciplines, teachings and his never failing presence in her life, she feels has helped to make her the person she has become. She told him that she loved him just like a real father, because he loved and treated her like his very own daughter.

I can only imagine the tremendous effect just that one statement must have had on Jay. He isn't a man who can express his feelings openly or with any degree of ease, so emotions this strong are seldom discussed. Being so touched by her words, he was able to tell her how much it means to him to know that she has loved him as much as he has loved her, from the time she was five years old.

Knowing she will never be able to use it personally now, Jackie asked Jay's advice about what to do with the nearly twelve thousand dollars my brother, Tom, recently raised in her behalf, so I could live in Kentucky during her second scheduled transplant. She outlined to Jay all the items the Floating Hospital desperately needs on the wards: bathtubs for the infants, high chairs, walkers, strollers, VCRs for the isolation rooms along with a library of movies, Nintendo set-ups and toys and games for the playroom. She's requested a yearly scholarship award be given to graduating New Bedford High School seniors in her name. She also asks to be cremated and that her ashes be placed in a beautiful garden with a gazebo, at our home. Her wish is to remain close to us so her spirit can watch over her sisters as they grow. She is truly leaving a legacy on many levels.

Jay gives Jackie his solemn promise to establish the Friends of Jackie Memorial Fund and to erect a gazebo in her memory.

It's Sunday and Jay calls home early to say that Jackie's in good spirits and eager to see everyone. Once we arrive, my parents, brothers and their families each take a turn being alone with her to say their good-byes. As sad as this is, it's also uplifting to see her looking and feeling so calm. She has accepted what's to come and is ready to enter God's Kingdom. Yes, she'll miss us, but she also says she'll watch over and protect us. She has even offered, to the parents of a dying toddler she has grown very fond of, reassurance that she'll be waiting for Allison in heaven.

After speaking with everyone, Jackie and her sisters share some private time. Beth hops up onto the bed and shows Jackie her diary. Jackie is so deeply touched, she can barely find the words or the strength to tell Beth how much she loves it.

My heart is breaking as Beth puts her small hand into Jackie's. "Don't worry, you don't have to talk," she says, kissing her sister. "I love you." Then she climbs carefully off the bed.

Jackie whispers with tears in her eyes, "I love you, too."

Kristine's grief has left her bereft of words. She holds onto Jackie's hand and cries, as Jackie tells her she loves her. They whisper a secret to each other and hug.

"Mom, I'm tired, can I take a nap before the party?" Jackie asks.

"Of course, you can. No one will mind waiting," I assure her.

"Will you brush my teeth and wash my face?"

While gently wiping her face with a cool cloth, I notice the color of her eyes have changed. Oddly, they're no longer a beautiful bluish green, for they've turned a pale shade of gold. It's as if she has lost a very distinctive part of her identity. I say nothing other than to tell her for the millionth time I love her.

"Is there anything else I can do for you, Sweetheart?" I ask.

"Lay with me, Mommy."

"My pleasure," I reply, kissing her forehead.

She falls asleep quickly, and I remain next to her for about thirty minutes, all the while stroking her face and arms and just simply holding her. When she becomes restless, I get up and sit beside her, never letting go of her hand. I know in my heart she is dying. But for some bizarre reason, I feel as though, if I hold on to her hand, the lifeblood surging through my body will somehow enter hers, and she won't die.

Jay is lying on the other bed with Kris and Beth, watching us. It's now well after four o'clock, and Jackie has been sleeping for three hours. It's time for my family to go home. There will be no party today; perhaps tomorrow. I can see they're hesitant to leave, afraid they'll never see her again. Nonetheless, they all go. Jay and I remain at her side.

At five-thirty, Jackie's breathing becomes irregular, and I call the nurse, who pages the doctor on call. Examining Jackie, the doctor says that she suffered an aneurysm while sleeping. She tells us it's death's best-case scenario and is quite certain Jackie feels no pain. It's now just a matter of time before she draws her last breath.

This irregular breathing continues for hours. Listening to and watching her last breaths is excruciating. I request they remove the heart monitor and all of her medications, with the exception of the morphine. She can't feel any pain.

At six-thirty, Sister Claire asks where Jackie's father is. At first, I think she means Jay, and he's sitting right beside me. Then I realize it's Brian to whom she's referring, and I ask that he be called.

In Jackie's room, participating in a bedside vigil, are all those who have come to know and love Jackie during the past five months: Sister Claire, Father Jim, our parent advocate, her nurses and doctors.

At eight fifty-one, with Jay and me by her side holding her, Jackie dies. So does something inside of me. I've lost yet another daughter, and I know that no matter how hard I try, I will never be the same.

Once everyone leaves, Jay and I help Jackie's nurse tend and care for her body. We wash her, change her pajamas and then sit alone watching and holding her in her now peaceful state.

When I rest my head on Jackie's "little pillow," the one she holds close, as she sleeps every night, Jay suggests I write a note and attach it to her little pillow, telling the people in the morgue to be sure to use it to cushion her head.

I write the note, and pin it to her pillow.

In the meantime, Sister Claire has taken all of the cards and pictures down from Jackie's bulletin boards and gathered the rest of her belongings. After a long while, Jay says it's time to go. He knows it's best and gently insists we leave.

We each give her one last kiss. Before turning to go, I stroke her beautiful face and softly ask only one favor from her. "Please help Mommy through the days ahead."

I can barely drag myself away from her. Jay waits patiently, collecting her things. Finally, we make our way to the elevators.

Jackie's intern and her nurse accompany us to the car. Once Jackie's things are packed, we say our good-byes. For the second time, I drive away from a Boston hospital without one of my precious daughters.

Jay and I hold hands all the way home, reminding us of our connection with each other, which we unfortunately lost over the past five months. Neither of us speaks. There's nothing to say. Although, just before we arrive home to all of our waiting family, I find I need to share some thoughts with Jay in private. "When I married you, I knew in my heart what kind of man you truly were. For some reason, I failed to bring that man out in you. Amazingly, Jackie knew how. In the past few months, I have witnessed the kind of love and compassion you were always capable of. You have an inner strength I admire so. Thank you, with all my heart, for finding that part of yourself when the girls and I needed it most. You gave us your love and strength to depend on. No wonder I love you so much."

Jay doesn't reply. He just looks at me, squeezes my hand and gives me the vaguest of smiles. Something in his eyes tells me he's already in deep mourning.

There are over one hundred cars in the funeral procession led by the New Bedford Police. Many of them are off duty officers, not only volunteering their time because of my father, but also in memory of Jackie, the young girl they had heard so much about from Dad.

Before leaving for church, two of Jackie's closest friends, Beth and Meredith arrive at the funeral home, dressed in their colorguard uniforms in honor of Jackie. As difficult as it is for me to see them dressed that way, their courage and sentiment mean so much to me. My heart breaks watching them stand at her casket with tears rolling down their faces, and I embrace them. Their hearts are broken, too. I can only imagine what it must be like to be sixteen years old and attend the funeral of your best friend.

As our funeral car rounds the curve to our church, my heart stops. Cars are parked everywhere, and people are standing on the sidewalks and in the street. Traffic has come to a standstill. To my surprise, the Marching Band, in full dress uniform, has lined the steps of our church, serving as honor guards. The beautiful white hat plumes blowing in the breeze and the color guard uniforms, with their red and silver sequins sparkling in the sun, are extraordinary to behold. The sight takes my breath away.

Hundreds of Jackie's friends are here. To think they have come on a freezing cold February morning, when they could have been in their warm beds at home, enjoying their winter vacation. All are handling their grief well, and I'm proud to be witness to their impressive and heartfelt tribute.

Kris and Beth need a break from the sadness that has invaded our lives, so we book a weekend ski trip to Waterville Valley, New Hampshire. Both she and Beth invite a friend to join us. Before we set out, Kris shares with me how having to do this, invite a friend, makes her feel angry towards Jackie for leaving her alone, which in turn, makes her feel guilty. I try to explain that her anger is only natural, considering how very close she and Jackie were and that it has nothing to do with her love for her sister.

Then, just to make matters worse, a week later Brian informs us that he has recently accepted an out-of-state job transfer and will be moving soon. Even though he and Kris have somewhat grown apart over the years, she now has to experience another loss and I worry just how much she can take. After all, she's only fourteen, and even though she is doing her level best to accept her losses, it must be very difficult for her. I only wish I could take her pain away.

Jay and I remained on the Executive Board of the marching band during Jackie's illness because we hoped our continued participation would inspire Jackie to keep a positive attitude towards her difficult treatments and hospital stay, as well as, show our belief in her recovery. We band parents had been raising money to finance a trip to Florida, where the kids had been invited to play in Disneyworld during the April, 1990 school vacation. After Jackie relapsed and her transplant was canceled, her hopes of joining her friends on this trip were dashed, and we gave up our spots as chaperones. With her death, it has felt too painful to go without her.

However, Jackie's band family has embraced us in a way I will never forget - they want Kristine to carry the N.B.H.S. banner down Disneyworld's Main Street, in memory of her sister. Kristine is both flattered and honored, since her heart is set on auditioning for the color guard this coming August. They also have made Beth an honorary member, by having miniature color guard flags made especially for her. On top of everything, the parents have voted to use Jackie's allotted trip allowance to pay Kristine's expenses.

With building the house, incurring so many expenses during Jackie's illness, losing my income to care for her and paying for her funeral, we are flat broke. Never before have we asked my parents for financial help. Now there's no choice. We have to take the trip to Disneyworld, to be a part of such a tribute to Jackie.

My parents and my brother, Tom, and his family decided they want to witness Kristine's honored place in the band, too. Traveling with over one hundred and thirty kids, chaperones and instructors, plus all the instruments, flags, and uniforms is a great adventure. Despite it being bittersweet, seeing my girls with these band kids lifts my spirits. It's so obvious that Jackie's friends need to be with Kris and Beth, just as much as Kris and Beth need to be with them.

By noon, the sun is on fire, and the temperature soars to a scorching ninety-three degrees on Disneyworld's Main Street. The kids have to wear their winter marching uniforms, and they dread the thought of getting dressed. Luckily, the dressing rooms are air-conditioned. Knowing that once they hit the sunshine they're going to roast, I take charge of the girls in the color guard and cut off the sleeves and body of their turtleneck jerseys, leaving only the neck, dickeys style, under their sequined tops. That should help a little.

The Disney crew takes the kids underground to the staging area. Not wanting to miss a moment of the parade, we join our group of family and friends at the head of Main Street. The heat is so oppressive that everyone looks as if they're about to wilt. The sun is blazing mercilessly, and there isn't a cloud in the sky to provide relief.

When I hear the drums, I offer up a silent prayer to my special angel. Then, as if by magic, the moment the twirling flags are visible, a cloud appears and the sun kindly slides behind it. A gentle breeze begins to blow and immediately the searing temperature is brought down by ten degrees. It's then that I hear Manny, my friend and fellow chaperone, announce for all to hear, "It's Jackie, she's here. She's taking care of her friends."

By the time the band reaches us, every one of us are in tears. Even a family from England, whom we told about Jackie while we were waiting for the parade to begin, is crying.

As I watch Kris lead this talented group of young musicians, looking so proud and smiling from ear to ear, I know Manny is right - Jackie is here. I can see her in Kristine's smile.

Cousin Madeline & Susan - July 4, 1968 - One week before entering St. Mary's

Joanne at home with her new Mom & Dad - October 1968

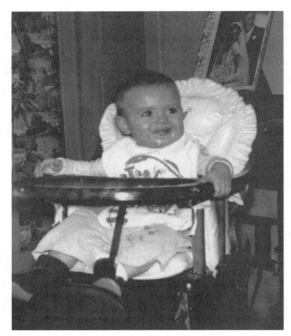

Susan - 1952

Joanne - 1970

Jay, Susan, Kristine & Jackie - 1982

Bethany, Joanne, Kristine, Susan & Jay
Kristine's Wedding - 2000

Colorguard
Joanne 1986 - Jackie 1988 - Kristine 1992

First photo Joanne received of Susan & Kristine

Joanne & Susan saying goodnight - First Face-to-Face meeting
May 21, 1999

Joanne & Bethany – Aruba 2001

Ann, Joanne & Susan - 2002

Chapter Seven

It's June 1991, and I've just celebrated my fortieth birthday. The pneumonia that has plagued me in the past has returned with a vengeance, and I've spent fourteen weeks going between the doctor's office and the hospital. I'm terrified because I can't get better.

"Jay, what could possibly be wrong with me?" I ask, as I lay weak in the hospital, after a repeat thorocentisis.

"Susan, all the pain and grieving has finally caught up with you," he says, simply.

Everyone agrees that I'm completely worn out after a year and a half of sleepless nights and being totally stressed by Jackie's death. There's also something else bothering me, something I've shared with no one. Lately, there's been a tugging at my heart, prompting me to share my story of Madlyn with Kristine. She's almost sixteen and, like Jackie, is mature for her age. She's been through a lot in her young life and has never failed to make me proud. She handled Jackie's illness and death with grace, and I imagine she'll do the same now. Still, I struggle and pray for strength, because I naturally fear the worst. I've already lost two daughters, and I'm petrified of losing another by telling her my secret. What if Kris thinks badly of me and loses all respect? Nevertheless, I can't risk anything happening to her before she knows about Madlyn. I'm not about to repeat the mistake I made waiting to tell Jackie. I feel such urgency about telling her.

We are having our daily after-school chat and three o'clock cup of tea, when Kris asks that I polish her nails. While sitting at my desk, face to face, holding her hand, I feel especially close to her and know it's the perfect time. Unsure how to begin, I nervously jump right in. "When I was sixteen, I got pregnant..."

After telling her only a portion of my story, she looks at me, her eyes filled with tears. "You mean I have another older sister? Oh, Mom, where does she live? How old is she? When can I meet her?" Then, holding my hand tightly, she tells me, "Thank you for sharing your secret with me. I only wish you were ready to find her."

She needs no excuses from me and isn't the least bit angry or resentful, just curious. Listening to my every word, the look upon her face and the sympathy in her eyes show me she understands just how much I love my missing daughter, and how my heart is aching to know her. She knows my love for Madlyn doesn't diminish my love for her.

It's September 1995, I'm on my way home from a six-day hospital stay in Boston after hip surgery, and I'm starving. A week of hospital food has left me with a craving for pizza. Driving down the main street, I realize that St. Mary's must be close by. As if it were yesterday, I can envision the group of us from twenty-seven years ago, waddling down this same street in our later stages of pregnancy, hell bent for a Chicago style pizza.

Remembering how heavenly that pizza tasted, especially since it had been so forbidden, I direct Jay to take a left at the lights, startling him. "We'll get pizza for the ride home."

"How did you know about this place?" he asks, as we pull into the parking lot.

If ever the perfect opportunity to tell Beth was presented, it's now. This time, I'm not afraid. Beth might only be eleven years old, but our relationship has already grown to be strong and loving. She's in the midst of developing a strong sense of character, along with a warm and caring nature. So, I know she'll be okay.

"Many years ago, I'd sneak down here with my friends from St. Mary's, whenever we needed a pizza fix," I attempt to explain.

Beth and Jay are naturally puzzled by my oddball comment. Jay has no clue what I'm about to say, because St. Mary's has always been a taboo subject, especially in front of Beth. Taking a deep breath, I begin my story. Unlike Kris, Beth doesn't cry.

"Excellent!" she says, thrilled to learn she has another sister. "When was the last time you saw her?"

"The day I left the hospital, when she was eight days old."

"Where does she live?"

"Well, that's the hard part. I was never allowed to know who adopted her or where she went to live."

"Gee, that's not fair!

"No, you're right, it's not fair."

"How old is she?"

"She turned twenty-seven last week. She was born the day before Jackie," I say, my eyes brimming with tears.

"Don't cry Mommy," she says, leaning over the backseat to pat my shoulder. After thinking things over for a moment, she asks, "If she belongs to us, why can't we just go and get her?"

The decision to keep my secret from Jackie was a huge mistake. She would have reacted in the very same manner as her sisters, with love for me and the sister she hadn't met. If only I could turn back time.

Trying to explain all the rules and regulations about surrendering, sealed records and confidentiality to an innocent eleven-year-old makes the whole idea sound even more ludicrous. Beth can't grasp the whole adoption concept, and why would she? I'm still wrestling with issues and doubts about the adoption system myself.

Even though it's been five years since Jackie's death and I'm feeling stronger, I'm not yet in a place where I can search, and it's difficult telling Beth I need more time to heal, when the idea of a new sister seems so exciting. There are no special elixirs, no magic words to ease my aching heart. No one is aware of how empty I continue to feel. I have learned to conceal my grief so well that no one knows I haven't let go of the pain.

The strain on my marriage, since Jackie's death, is another key issue. Jay's grief caused him to revert back to his old irascible ways, nearly tearing us apart. We now pretty much lead separate, fragile lives, living day-by-day just trying to survive our loss. I find myself again living life through my girls and dedicating myself to their happiness, while Jay consistently buries himself in his work and golf, leaving me to deal with my grief the same way he's dealing with his - alone. Life without Jackie is hell.

I have changed, too. My sorrow is doubled, and I've lost all faith. Even the small glimmer of hope I once had of finding Madlyn is gone. I feel defeated before I even start. The odds of my finding her seem slim, and that will be like losing her twice. My hope of our reunion has been what's kept me going. To think that, where I once believed I would be finding my daughter the year she finally turned twenty-one, I lost another one.

Now that the hard part of telling the girls is behind me, I'm growing more and more anxious to find Madlyn. First, I have to be sure I'm emotionally equipped to conduct a search and strong enough to handle the possibility of a rejection. Dear Lord, just the idea of losing Madlyn a second time is too much to bear. Also, I have to be certain I'm not searching for Madlyn to fill the void left in my life by Jackie's death.

By July of 1997, my "running" nightmares are becoming all too frequent. Too many nights I wake up with a start to the same pounding in my chest. Busy wrestling my demons, I'm unable to fall back to sleep. The time has come to "catch the child." I need to begin my search for Madlyn and lift this burden I've carried for far too long. The thought of shedding that millstone is exhilarating.

Losing Jackie in 1990 put me in a tailspin and damned near destroyed me. Just the mere act of getting out of bed was a task. Her death left me feeling, once again, cheated and betrayed and the grieving process has been overwhelming. But, I have somehow managed to tap into the broken spirit of my soul, to put my grief into perspective, allowing me to understand that Jackie's death was not God's punishment for giving Madlyn away. Life sometimes is a game of chance and, at other times, our decisions and actions pave the road ahead. I can now fully appreciate how strong and resilient I've become, as a result of both sets of circumstances and continually fighting hard to never let life beat me down. That newfound strength has helped me to realize that no one, not even Madlyn, could ever replace Jackie, just as Jackie never replaced her.

Now that that fear has been quelled, the full impact of my need to find Madlyn strikes, and I can't delay my search any longer. But, where and how do I begin? Watching a television program on searching for missing family members, I learn I might be able to find Madlyn through the Internet. Being a stay at home mom, there's been no real need for me to become computer savvy, though Jay and the girls spend all of their free time in cyberspace. Frankly, that machine scares the hell out of me. Having no idea how the search will turn out or what might be involved, I don't want to get their hopes up. So, my plan is to investigate the Internet a little on my own, before sharing my intentions.

After dinner one night, I nonchalantly ask a few basic questions about "surfing the net." They seem impressed that I finally want to become a woman of today, when I stretch the truth a bit and use the excuse that I just want to join the *All My Children* chat room.

"Welcome to the nineties, Mrs. Souza!" they cheer. I choose my screen name and listen closely to their instructions.

The following morning, with a cup of tea in hand, I sit at the desk and turn the computer on. Right away, I forget my password and need assistance from Beth to gain access to the Internet. Good thing it's not a secret password or my search would be over before it begins. Once on line, I shoo her away.

Putting my fingers on the keyboard, I find I can barely type. How can this be? I used to type like the wind. Why do I feel so nervous?

Then it dawns on me. I'm actually about to do what has only been a secret wish for twenty-nine years - find my daughter. The notion of that dream becoming a reality is both frightening and thrilling. With renewed understanding, I breathe a heavy sigh, go to Keyword and type "Adoption."

It's amazing. There are more sites than I ever imagined. Now I'm not only nervous, but also confused and have no clue where to begin.

As I scan my list of options, the site that catches my attention is ISRR, the International Soundex Reunion Registry (P. O. Box 2312 Carson City, Nevada 89702). I surf on over and end up chatting with a nice lady named Maureen. She's full of useful information and shares some interesting adoption and reunion stories, getting me excited about the journey I'm about to undertake. She's a reunited birth mom and encourages me to go to the Catholic Charities office to fill out a "Waiver of Confidentiality." I'm having trouble with her adoption lingo and have to ask her to explain.

"If you sign, notarize and file this particular waiver, all the information in your adoption file will be made available to Madlyn, if and when she requests it," she writes back.

"No way!" I type in disbelief. Searching is forbidden and my records are sealed for life is how I've always understood things.

She emails the necessary forms I need to join this registry. Apparently, ISRR is the largest registry in the world and the number one place to go if someone is searching for a missing family member. She gives me some excellent leads for other registries, and I register in every one. In the meantime, I'm always scanning the Adoptees' Searching List to see if, by some chance, Madlyn is looking for me.

Tracking down Catholic Charities, I learn the agency is now called Catholic Social Services and has been moved from its original downtown New Bedford location. It's currently housed in the old convent of my childhood parish, where the nuns, who taught me from kindergarten through eighth grade, lived. Now, it's tough enough garnering the courage to go the agency in the first place, especially if that tattletale neighbor still works there, but revisiting the old place will certainly be bizarre. Why does my past with nuns continue to haunt me?

I park in the church lot and go directly to the side door of the old brick convent - the only door we children were allowed to use in the fifties and sixties. Only the kids who took piano lessons were allowed to venture past the ominous back hall and up the narrow staircase to the music room. On the rare occasion we were playing in the church lot prior to a school function, we might be allowed into the kitchen and dining room areas to help bring in groceries, books or penny sale items. Access to the convent was limited and frowned upon without invitation.

After ringing the doorbell three times, there's still no response. Ghosts from my parochial school past are playing games with me, and I consider running back to my car. Once I calm myself enough to realize there actually was no sound, when I pressed the old buzzer, it draws me to the obvious conclusion that the bell must no longer work. So, I knock. No response. Good grief, what the hell is up with this place? Oh, don't swear. What if the old Spanking Machine is here?

While chuckling at my last thought, I look to the bay windows overhead. The drapes are old and tattered. Perhaps this part of the building is no longer in use. There's no choice, I must walk around to the forbidden, absolutely and without question, off limits front door.

Making my way up the walk to the dreaded door, I feel a surge of emotions, the biggest being fear and the next biggest shame. I'm deathly afraid of standing face-to-face with another human being who doesn't care about me and admit what I did so many years ago. Not to mention, having to enter a building that has, for so many years, represented nothing but discipline and forced respect, has me quaking. When I reach the doorway, I'm in a daze and very much distracted by my thoughts. I spot the intercom and press the button. "Yes, may I help you?" asks the voice from the box.

"I'm looking for information on a 1968 adoption," I say quietly and as close to the intercom's speaker as possible. How absurd that I'm still afraid someone is within hearing distance. Will these feelings of shame ever go away? The buzzer sounds and I open the door. While waiting to be helped, I walk beyond the walls of the tiny office to snoop around. Where are the holy pictures and statues that once adorned the halls? It seems nothing has been done to preserve the convent's holy and historic appearance. The walls are in dire need of painting. The floors, which were always highly polished, have lost their luster. Its meager furniture is old and shabby. Only the stale smell of a home not loved and cared for any longer permeates the air.

"How may I help you?" asks a voice from out of nowhere.

Startled at the question, as the woman seemed to sneak up behind me, I fall all over my words. Somehow, I get my point across about opening my records.

"I'm sorry, I can't help you," she says. "All of our adoption files are stored in the Fall River office. You'll have to contact them."

Thankful for the reprieve, but surprised by my disappointment, I promise myself to go the very next day. However, opening my records and coming out of the "birth mother closet" is more frightening than I ever imagined. Dragging my cold feet, I never make it to the Fall River office.

In the meantime, I have come across an outstanding on-line birth mother support group, The Sunflowers. They correspond daily via email and are very helpful in supplying me with new and diverse avenues of search, as well as providing the best support system available to searching birth mothers in today's climate of adoption. Their daily encouragement and inspiration are keeping me strong enough to follow my dream.

With each passing week, I'm not quite so nervous. Still very much in the birth mother closet, I nevertheless feel safe searching from the privacy of my home. As the months pass, I painstakingly search each registry, with the hope that Madlyn has found one of my postings. If she has, this whole affair will be over and done with. It'll be simple enough: Madlyn will call, we'll meet and live happily ever after.

After a frustrating year of hitting one dead end after another, the time has come to pursue my search openly and aggressively, which means telling Jay and the girls about what I've been up to. Jay isn't as excited about my endeavor as Kris and Beth. He seems apprehensive and explains that he's afraid I'm not ready and might get hurt. Becoming stronger already, his doubts don't deter me. Next, I tell my parents and brothers. My brother, Tom, shares Jay's opinion. Still, I remain firm in my resolve. The fact that two men I love and respect have expressed their doubts and I can so easily disregard their opinions, assures me there will be no stopping me now.

Still, it's impossible to express the feelings of loneliness and desperation of sitting alone at two in the morning, with only the light of the desk lamp shining on my computer monitor, scanning list after list of adoptees searching for their birth families. With the darkness and the special kind of quiet of my sleeping home enveloping me, the silence of my Internet Search is deafening.

Tonight, my head aches and my brain is too tired to continue. So, I sit back and close my eyes, envisioning this scene from some Lifetime Television movie. Cut from the scene of desperate and exhausted me at my computer to my daughter tucked safely into bed, her adoptive mom lovingly checking on her and kissing her good night. As the scene unfolds in my head, Madlyn is still a little girl and not the young woman she has certainly grown to be. If only there were some type of magic to transport me to that scene, so I can know all was well with Madlyn.

I long to speak with someone who understands, but my "Buddy List" of on-line birth moms is empty. Why aren't they up searching, too? Have they simply given up? Perhaps they know something I don't, that all of my searching will prove fruitless. Should I be upstairs lying next to Jay? No, I must fulfill my promise to Madlyn.

Summoning the courage to drive to the Fall River office and speak in person with someone about my secret past is something I simply cannot do. It's too personal, too intimidating. A phone call will have to suffice.

Anticipating the conversation, I actually feel faint. It's just that I haven't one single piece of evidence that I ever delivered this child. However, the kindness of the woman who answers my call puts me at ease. Thankfully, she requests no proof.

"Hold on," she says, "let me get your file."

Get my file! She can just go and get my file? Shouldn't it be somewhere down in the basement covered with dust and spider webs?

To be certain it's the correct file, she asks a few questions: what was my street address in 1968; Social Security number; date of birth? When she's convinced it's really me, she tells me that signing a "Waiver of

Confidentiality" is a must before anything can happen. She suggests I might also consider requesting non-identifying information, which would contain certain facts about Madlyn's adoptive family, without being specific enough to identify who they are.

All is going along smoothly until she throws me by asking why I have decided to search now, after all these years. There's no way I'm going to admit it's simply the overwhelming desire to know and hold my daughter again. That won't fly. Years ago, the nuns and counselors at St. Mary's made it crystal clear that searching is illegal. Not knowing what to say, I panic and shamefully use Jackie's illness and death for leverage, which causes me to break down and cry, and lose all sense of poise and direction. I find myself going on and on about Jackie, how sick she was and how fearful I am that Madlyn might be faced with the same illness someday, if not already.

"I need to inform Madlyn of Jackie's leukemia. She has to be aware that she has an entire family of bone marrow donors available to her and her children." I manage to say through my sobs.

"Do Madlyn and Jackie share the same father?" she asks.

"No, they don't."

"Is cancer hereditary on your side of the family?"

"No."

"Well, the chances of Madlyn having or getting leukemia are small, if neither of these facts are true."

Resenting her comment, I wonder how she can consider herself qualified to make this statement. Who appointed her master of all medical likelihood? Granted, she's probably right in her prognosis, but I just want someone to help me. Everywhere I turn for guidance and support, there's another dead end.

We end our conversation with the understanding that I'll send her my notarized waiver and request for non-id information, along with a check to cover the cost of putting the data together.

My next step towards healing is huge - posting my search information on my AOL profile, for the entire Internet to see. Proclaiming to the world that "I am a birth mother and I will no longer hide," is unbelievably liberating.

Although I'm feeling stronger with every passing day, I know I'll never forget what it was like to be unmarried and pregnant in the '60's. It hurt a great deal then, and it still hurts today, to think about how I was looked down upon and treated. However, that scared sixteen-year-old girl no longer exists. I have grown and become unafraid. Never again will I allow anyone to shame me into feeling guilty about a decision I was pressured into making as a young girl. I did what everyone said was best for my child at the time, and the times dictated adoption.

It's Madlyn's thirtieth birthday and she's been on my mind all morning, when I receive an email from a young woman who's searching for her birth mother for medical reasons. She read my search post in the Massachusetts Registry and noticed that I had stayed at the same maternity home as her birth mother. She is curious about St. Mary's, what it was like and how we were treated. I reply immediately, all the while thinking that this could easily be Madlyn needing to know and feeling the same about me.

It's the first time in thirty years I've written about my days at the home and, as difficult as it is, it's cathartic. Never wanting to dredge up the sadness of a past I couldn't do anything about, I've never let myself dwell on what happened there. Although, as much as it was one of the saddest times of my life, writing about my stay brings back some happy and amusing memories of my days spent there. As difficult and interminable as the days were, they were also heartwarming and all too brief and I'm pleased to tell her it was a nice place and we were treated with kindness.

From her, I'm learning about how an adoptee feels. Has she ever thought about her birth mother, I ask?

She writes back: "I had never planned to search for my birth mother. While growing up, I always knew I was adopted and would sometimes think of this lady, my birth mother, on my birthday. It was just a small thought, and that was it."

'This lady? Just a small thought?' I'm troubled by her comments and write back: "I guess I have mixed feelings about your attitude toward your birth mother. On one hand, it makes me very sad to think I may only be a 'small thought' to Madlyn on her birthday. On the other, because of that fact, she would have had a wonderful life with lots of love, and that was all I had ever hoped for."

After running an AOL search of all females born on Madlyn's birthday, I've come up with roughly one hundred names and send the following email to each of them:

> I am looking for a member of my family. She was
> adopted at birth. Her birth date is September 17, 1968.
> If this could be you, please contact me. If not, I am
> sorry to have bothered you.

Much to my surprise, nearly everyone replies, many sending good wishes. There's one girl, Jenni, who's not only born on the same day, but is also adopted. My heart stops. For a second, I think I've found Madlyn. However, she goes on to say she's already in reunion. She helps me a great deal with advice, and her kindness and support sustain me.

> "Remember, determination is very empowering!" she writes. "If it weren't for that, I would be no closer to finding my birth mother than I was two years ago. If you are a spiritual woman, prayer can also be very helpful, giving you peace and patience."

The waiver is notarized, and I mail in both forms. At last, something concrete to do in my efforts to find my child. My child - I keep forgetting she's already thirty years old. It's hard to believe that much time has passed since I last saw her and kissed her goodbye. To think, this is only the beginning of freeing myself from the secret that has become so buried along with my feelings, along with a part of my heart. All I need to do is make sure I keep out of the birth mother closet and begin making some "noise."

Feeling bolder, I call Catholic Social services again and ask if Madlyn is aware she is adopted.

"Yes, I believe she is," the social worker tells me.

Though I'm relieved to hear this, her answer indicates she knows more than she's letting on, so I question her. "How can you be sure?"

"Oh, just a feeling I have."

"Have you had any contact with Madlyn or her adoptive parents?"

No response. Why is she hesitating?

"In 1994, the adoptive mother requested updated medical information," she finally confesses.

So, that's why my file was so readily available. I knew it, I just knew it. Madlyn's sick, too. What if she died? Don't even tell me she died. Did she need my bone marrow? Why did I ever let Jackie's death get in the way of contacting the agency sooner?

"Oh, dear God, was Madlyn ill?" I ask.

Hearing the panic in my voice, she quickly answers, "Absolutely not. I believe she got married and was simply interested in her biological medical history."

Is there more to this than she's saying?

Mom is on the phone reading a letter to me from Catholic Social Services explaining that my biological mother has relinquished her right to confidentiality. This comes as both a surprise and a scare to me. It means that the medical information we requested several years ago is now available. It seems safe to assume much more information is available as well. We probably only have to ask and we will receive. We both accept the information very matter of factly and don't get emotional over it. We don't explore the possibilities or discuss the implications that come with this letter. Too afraid of upsetting Mom, I don't ask her how she feels. I simply ask for the telephone number and make a mental plan to call the social worker myself.

I'm in denial and still don't believe the obvious, my biological mother is searching for me. But I want to find out what is going on and just what is expected of me. All I had asked for was medical information, why doesn't she just give it to me and close the file? I don't understand what this letter is about. Why is she baiting me this way? If she can give me the information I have asked for, then why hasn't she? After a couple of days, I call the social worker. I identify myself and wonder if she will recognize who I am and to what case I am referring. She immediately knows exactly who I am.

She explains in a very abstract way that I can learn who my biological mother is. I'm not even sure I fully understand what she is trying to tell me. She's beating around the bush. I'm afraid to ask questions because there might be privacy guidelines that should be respected, even though the whole point of this is that confidentiality has just been tossed out the window. I'm confused, but she seems nice enough so I'm comfortable speaking with her.

While on the phone, I realize that all I have to do is ask her one simple question, "Who is my biological mother?" After all, since she did relinquish her right to confidentiality, then can't I ask anything I want? It seems too simple, it shouldn't be this simple. I don't know if I want to know. I don't want it to be that simple. I do share with her my apprehension about knowing who she is and from where I came. I never ask the question. I explain, "All I wanted was medical information."

She assures me in her, I know better than you voice, that, "Many adoptees tell themselves that when, in fact, they want to know a lot more but they find this is an easy and safe way to begin their search."

What search? She's got me confused with one of those mal-contents who care about their biological parents and their background. That's not me. I'm a very happy well-adjusted adoptee. I'm not about to search for anyone, that wasn't my intention.

I ask no more questions other than, "So what should I do?"

I have no reason to take advice from this stranger on the phone, but I do.

She encourages me to write a letter, persuasively suggesting, "You don't have to contact her directly. You might want to consider writing a letter to her and sending it to me. I can then be sure she gets it."

She's now pressuring me to write this letter. I'm still in denial. I don't want to face this. I never thought I would have to. All this implies that she is obviously in contact with my biological mother. At least she tells me that she has not disclosed to her that she and I have been in contact. That's a relief. I'm still anonymous to her. I find comfort in that.

I begin the letter but procrastinate finishing it, hoping it will just go away, hoping she will go away. I'm afraid she will contact me directly. Everything is telling me she eventually will but I still don't believe it. I fear her coming into my life. I don't want to choose between mothers. I already have a mother, I don't need another one and I don't want another one. It may seem silly for me to even think this way, after all, I'm not a child, no one can come and take me away from my mother. I'm an adult with my own life and in control of who is in my life...aren't I? Right now, I'm not feeling in control. This person seems to be getting close and there's nothing I can do about it. She's going to find me, I feel it and I'm afraid of how this is going to make my mother feel. I'll ignore it.

Knowing Madlyn is aware of her adoption allows me the freedom to continue my search. Otherwise, I don't know if I could pursue it. Since it's not my intention to hurt either Madlyn or her adoptive parents, I'd respect their desire to keep it secret, if that were their wish.

Madlyn's relationship with her adoptive mother will be crucial to all aspects of our reunion. Will she be seen as the loving and caring adoptive mother, and I the birth mother/stranger/abandoner, putting me in a most precarious position? As I imagine my reunion with Madlyn, I base my thoughts of our future relationship on what I know to expect from my close relationships with both my own mother and that of my daughters. If Madlyn has the same close, secure relationship with her adoptive mother, this reunion will be positive, of that I am certain. She will know how to become close with me.

In December, I receive the non-identifying information. Now I know what non-identifying means - not a remote clue. The adoptive parents description includes their years of birth, height and weight at the time of adoption, occupations and nationalities. A million people could fit their description. The report states that my daughter grew up in a nice area of a small city in a two-family home. There's no information about siblings. I paid fifty bucks and waited eight weeks for this? They could've told me this much on the phone. Why in hell would I need to know how tall they were or how much they weighed? This is crazy!

I don't know exactly what I was expecting, but it was more than this. Reading the document over and over, I try to glean something between the lines, hoping there might be a subliminal message. I'm desperate and at the end of my rope, and don't know what to do next.

Along with that useless information, they've also sent along a "Birth Parent Background Packet" to update my family's medical history. The forms seem involved, so I take my time. When it comes to including Jackie's battle with leukemia, I'm uneasy, especially since those are the facts that most need to be told. For some reason, it seems impersonal to record such critical information on a mere sheet of paper that Madlyn may never see.

So, I place another call to the agency. I'm beginning to make "noise."

"This story isn't just a matter of listing facts, it's the story of her sister's life and her death. My daughter should be told in person," I say, as I beg the social worker to place the call.

"I understand," she says. "I'll call the adoptive mother and inform her that your waiver has been filed and medical information is available."

"Please be sure to tell her it's urgent medical information," I insist.

"Yes, I'll do that, right after the first of the New Year. I don't want to upset anyone during the holidays," she explains.

Even though I don't want to hear this, I figure it's best. My future is at the mercy of this social worker.

In a desperate attempt to gain access to my files, I have included my name on a petition to an archbishop, put together by a group of searching birth mothers in Texas. My hope is that he can cut through the red tape of Catholic Social Services in order to give Madlyn what I consider to be crucial medical information. After all, it's a valid reason for contacting her and both Catholic Social Services and the Church should be helping me. Just the simple fact that they have the knowledge of her whereabouts is killing me. The adoption system is still operating in the dark ages, and we birth mothers continue to be considered second-class citizens. Adoptees are dying every day, deaths that could be prevented if they knew their medical history. Such knowledge should be a birthright. I'd get a job with the agency, if that's what it would take to get a hold of her records and get this information to my daughter.

Secrets are debilitating. Posted by my Sunflower Group is a published article revealing that birth mothers are often plagued with illness throughout their lives after relinquishing their children. The causes are all stress-related and initiated by Post Traumatic Stress Syndrome. No wonder I've been so sick all of these years. Thinking of and worrying about Madlyn has put a terrible strain on me. Then, Jackie's illness and death only added an additional sorrow. Beginning the forbidden search process, one I knew nothing about, and telling my girls has just added to the already enormous stress.

It's the end of January 1999, and I still haven't heard from Catholic Social Services, Madlyn or her adoptive mother. I call the social worker to see if she's placed the call to my daughter as promised.

"No, I didn't call, but I did send her adoptive mother letter on January 21," she explains.

"Did you include Jackie's illness?"

"No, I'm afraid not," she says. Something in her voice tells me she knows more than she's letting on.

My experience with Catholic Social Services is disappointing, at best. They have neither the time nor the manpower to effectively handle my search. I've been candidly informed that birth mother/adoptee searches are their last priority. Being honest and aboveboard is getting me nowhere but more impatient. The adoption system today is nothing more than a continuation of the secrets and lies I have been living with since my pregnancy was first confirmed. I'm no closer to finding Madlyn now than I was eighteen months ago. I don't know where else to turn. I'm fed up with the bureaucracy and need to devise another plan.

Chapter Eight

Retreating to the sanctuary of my bedroom, I close the door, lay on the bed and tell myself that I must now bring this journey to an end, regardless of the result. Spreading my papers out across the bed, I find the number of a searcher I'd filed away a few weeks before, too afraid to make the call then.

I hear that the searcher is quite successful, and I find myself fearing that she might actually locate Madlyn. How will I feel when this all-consuming search suddenly ends? What if Madlyn is angry and doesn't want to know me? And, if she does want to know me, am I confident enough to face my own daughter? I don't know if I'm truly prepared for whatever I may find.

I dial the number and the woman answering sounds cordial and to be about my age. After explaining the reason for my call, she shares with me that she's also a birth mother, and her search partner is adopted. "Even though our success rate is high," she says, "I must warn you that we only work part time, so it might take a while to find your daughter. In the meantime, you should sit back, relax and leave all the work and worry to us."

Being emotionally exhausted from the roller coaster ride I've been on, I welcome the break and don't mind however long it might take. The searcher asks basic questions: my maiden name, home address in 1968, date of birth, where I stayed during my pregnancy, when and where I delivered and the agency that handled the adoption. When I volunteer more information, she assures me she has enough. She suggests that while waiting, I keep busy by putting together a family photo album for Madlyn, as well as writing an introductory letter to her. She also recommends I read some of the many books available on adoption to prepare myself for what might be coming.

Why, what might be coming?

Leaving the search in her hands, I soon discover that her prescribed rest and relaxation isn't easy. So accustomed to searching, I don't know what else to do with myself. On her recommendation, I begin reading *The Primal Wound*. The stories depicted are heartbreaking. Learning, that adoptees suffer from the "primal wound" of being torn away from their birth mothers and can struggle their entire lifetime searching for the very love their adoptive parents are trying to offer, begins to shatter my illusions. Unable to accept their adoptive parents as substitutes, adoptees can fear a repeat of the rejection and/or abandonment they experienced as infants.

Intense feelings of sadness, betrayal, resentment and anger are common, sometimes causing adoptees to act out by being promiscuous juvenile delinquents, running away from home and provoking the very outcome they are so fearful of in the first place - rejection. This is their attempt at mourning the loss of their birth mother.

The thought of Madlyn experiencing these same feelings causes me to close the book, as I open to the possibility of a reality for Madlyn I had not considered. If what author Nancy Verrier says is true, I was wrong in consenting to give my baby away, and I've been wrong for not trying to find her sooner.

Over the years, while watching my girls grow and blossom, I imagined Madlyn's life was just as happy with her adoptive family. She loved them and was loved by them. As much as these stories frighten me, I still feel in my heart that Madlyn is enjoying a good life because there is no evidence she's looking for me. On the other hand, I worry that, if her life has been less than happy, she may be turned off by the close-knit and loving relationships in my family, which she's been denied. I'm ashamed I never seriously considered that she might be unhappy and searching for love and acceptance. I have naively assumed that adopted children are special and they never think of themselves as misfits.

Even with the little I've read so far, I see the need for personal support and counseling. The searcher mentioned a Triad Support Group (birth parent, adoptee and adoptive parent) near me, where meetings are held weekly. The birth mother, who runs the group, encourages me to attend, and the thought of sharing an occasional evening with other birth mothers comforts me. Having the opportunity to speak with adoptees and adoptive parents to hear their views on adoption is also appealing.

On the ninth anniversary of Jackie's death, I attend my first Triad meeting. Already I can see this is going to have an enormous impact on my life. For the first time in over thirty years, I am with other birth mothers - women just like me, who've lived their lives in "the closet," and are finally able to wear their profoundly broken hearts on their sleeves. The moment I walk into this room I feel I've found a place where I can be me, a safe place, where I can lay all my guilt and shame on the table, without the fear of being condemned or criticized.

We birth mothers all want to hear each other's stories, so many versions of the same heartache and loss we all share, to finally know we are no longer alone. Each woman, who comes forth to share her story and her tears, makes it easier for others to cry and to cope. Each one of us, only one of the untold numbers, struggling with unwanted and unasked for demons. There is power in our numbers, and I can see right away that the more women who come forth to tell their stories and share their heartache, the sooner sealed adoption records will be opened for our children. Every story, child and mother must be counted.

But, here I am, having to down a couple glasses of wine before telling those gathered for our annual "Cousin's Party" about my search. It's surprising to learn that the people who knew my secret never told anyone, not even their most significant others. It becomes my pleasure to do so.

My cousin, Madeline, never told her husband. Over hearing my story, Mady's older brother, Don, cracks me up with his astonishment. "You had a baby? Where was I? Why didn't I know?"

Don was in the Coast Guard during the summer of '68 and Aunt Mary must never have felt the need to include him or his wife, Carol, in on my little secret. Carol's reaction touches me deeply, as tears well up in her eyes and she gives me the biggest heartfelt hug. "How can I help?" she offers, making me feel special and understood.

Even my brother, Russ, never shared my story with his wife of seventeen years. Denise nearly faints when I tell her. Her tears move me in ways I can't describe. The love and caring that come across in her words of support mean so much. She's positively intrigued and has lots of questions about St. Mary's, my relinquishment and wants to know as much as possible about the little girl I named Madlyn.

Twenty years ago, during a particularly difficult time in my brother Tom's life, I told him the story of my unwed pregnancy, in the hope it would somehow help him through his troubles. He was stunned and couldn't believe my parents had never told him. Like everyone else, he never mentioned it again, either. Several years later, I shared my story with Tom's wife, Wendy, when she was pregnant with their first child, my godchild, Jessica. We were having lunch and I told her about Madlyn and some of what I had been through. Perhaps the subject came up because I wanted to share with her how special it is to see and hold your first-born child. I don't remember why exactly I felt so compelled to tell her. At any rate, she was at a loss for words, and I poured my heart out. She never repeated my story to anyone. I can't remember whether or not I made that request of her.

Everyone is excited and anxious for me to find Madlyn, especially my daughters. I feel extremely fortunate to be the recipient of such unconditional love and loyalty. My daughters never once voiced any doubt that finding Madlyn will add anything but happiness to our lives. They encourage me daily in my search, always wanting to know more about the sister they can only imagine. Jay and Tom remain rather concerned. Despite my reassurance, they fear if Madlyn rejects me, I'll be devastated once again, and they both love me too much to see that happen. But there's a force inside of me, greater than my fears, that urges me on.

I've often wanted to tell my friends about Madlyn and my search but can never find the right words. I'm afraid they'll judge me too harshly and not be able to find it in their hearts to understand, and then I'll not only lose their friendships but their respect, as well. Was I ever wrong! Their compassion and acceptance of my situation is heartwarming, and we're frequently in tears while discussing my story and the progress of my search. Their responses are all very similar. Mostly, they talk about my strength and ability to survive two horrible tragedies. Quite frankly, I'm amazed by both their comments and admiration. They think of my relinquishment as a generous sacrifice and not the selfish act of a self-centered teenager. For the first time in thirty years, I feel accepted for who I am: the girl who loved the precious baby she had to give away - the girl I had buried and kept hidden from the world. With each person I tell, it becomes easier to tell the next. Coming out of the closet is the best thing I have ever done for myself. I am set free.

The photo album turns out to be a most healing project. The pictures of my brothers and me at various ages bring up all sorts of fun memories. I can see our own children in our childhood faces. Closely examining the ones of Tom, Russ and me, I notice the patches on our clothes and the jackets that were just a tad too small. For the first time, I realize we were poor and didn't know it. Everyone we knew must have been poor, so it must not have mattered. I remember that most of my clothes were handmade by my mother, even my dancing school costumes. I vividly recall Mom sitting at her sewing machine, with all of the blue sequined material spread out on her bed for my King Neptune number. The glitter was in her hair and on her eyelashes. But, what I remember most about watching Mom sew were her hands. She had soft, lovely hands with pretty nails, hands that could soothe any hurt known to me. Hands I now possess and have passed down to my girls. Even at her age, my mother's hands are still beautiful.

A flood of happy memories keeps me smiling as I work away. There's the photo of the rusty old swing set in our yard that had no swings. The crabby old lady, who owned it, took them off whenever her kids weren't outside playing. That didn't deter us. We became great gymnasts, bravely flipping around the bars, performing death-defying feats like great circus performers. We also loved to rummage through the trash in the back of the Stop & Shop grocery store. Madeline and I would fill our wagon with cake and brownie mixes, then stir them up with water from the garden hose to play restaurant under the grapevine in the backyard of our tenement house on Fruit Street.

I dig out all of my baby pictures and those of my girls. It breaks my heart to see all of the recent ones without Jacqueline. Before getting too melancholy, I assign each girl their own individual page, which seems to make it less obvious that Jackie is gone from our lives. Kristine carefully selects the ones she wants presented to her new sister, and Bethany picks enough photos to fill three pages. While rifling through the pictures, Beth makes us laugh, "Oh, look how adorable I was!" "Mom, you can't use this one, my ears look huge!" We finally add one last page with all three girls together and a few that include me.

Wanting Madlyn to know her namesake, I find lots of old and current photos of Madeline and me, so she can see how close we were as children and still are today. I've wanted my daughter to be just like her: gracious and kind, in every sense a lady, with a great sense of humor and a laugh people never forget. With so many pictures, it's hard to decide which ones to include, so I choose the ones where I look best, like Beth does. Why not?

Finding pictures of Mark proves difficult. I know exactly where his senior class picture is, the one he had signed on the back, which I kept hidden in my wallet for years. But, I can't find any others. How can that be? My father was the king of photography back in the sixties; he even had a dark room. When I ask him where they could be, he swears on every dead relative's soul that he has no idea. I suspect he knows and just won't say. If some guy did to my daughter what Mark did to me, I'd throw out all of his pictures, too.

This Mello Family Album has to be as enticing as possible. If I don't get the opportunity to present it to Madlyn in person and have to mail it, it will have to be wonderful enough to win her over. So, I include fascinating tidbits of information and delightful displays of family events, revealing all the things she could have ever dreamed about her birth family. Just in case she shares our crazy sense of humor, I add funny commentary and captions.

Now that her album is complete, I busy myself redecorating Jackie's bedroom, which has remained the same since her death. It's a long shot, but my hope is that she might someday want to stay here. Then I talk Jay into painting and wallpapering the family room. He says I'm going overboard, so I relate a story to him about one birth mom who put an entire addition onto her house, while waiting for her child to be found.

"Is it going to take that long to find Madlyn?" he asks.

"I certainly hope not," I confess. "I don't think I can stand the wait much longer."

It's Sunday night, February 28, when the searcher calls to confirm some information concerning my home address in 1968.

"I have to tell you that we're very close to locating your daughter," she confides. "All I need is to match the names on the marriage license, and I'll do that as soon as I can get into Boston."

Paralyzed, I ask only one question. "What's her name?"

"I really can't say until everything is verified," she says. "I just want you to know that things are fitting together nicely."

"Please, can't you at least tell me her first name?" I beg.

She gives a big sigh and my heart is doing flip-flops in the dead silence, as she decides.

"Joanne. I'm 99% positive your daughter's name is Joanne."

I can't speak.

"Oh, and one more thing. If this is your daughter, you're right, she did grow up in Fall River."

I knew it! I knew it! I knew it!

"I'll be in touch soon," she says, and then hangs up.

I hope I said, "Thank you."

Jay is lying on the couch, as I remain frozen in the Lay-Z-Boy. "Jay, that was the searcher. She thinks she has found Madlyn. Her name is Joanne." It was strange to hear my voice say it out loud.

He smiles, but makes no comment. I know what he's thinking. He's afraid I'll be hurt again, putting me back to square one.

Our marriage, though much better, is still not where we'd like it to be. The years have taken their toll on us since Jackie's death, and we often find ourselves falling back into the old habit of treading lightly and keeping our distance from one another when difficult or sensitive issues are involved. So, even though I've wanted to babble on to him about the discoveries in my search, I've held back. It bothers me that I haven't been able to share my findings with him, but he doesn't seem to want to hear it. I tell him only what's necessary and keep the rest to myself. Whenever I'm asked how Jay feels about my search, I describe him as, "Vaguely interested and silently supportive."

After telling him my daughter has been found, and I'll soon know where she lives, I go over to the couch, lie down beside him and sob in his arms. It's so cleansing to rid myself of thirty years worth of worry as he holds me close.

I've been restless and edgy all morning. Not only is the news of Madlyn/Joanne on my mind, but I'm also waiting for my girlfriend, Madeline, to call. Madeline and her husband, Manny, have been dear friends since 1969. Their daughter, Julie, is scheduled to deliver her first child today by Caesarean Section. Julie became ill during her pregnancy and was told there's a chance her baby has been affected. Naturally, we're all concerned.

As I'm distracting myself by cleaning the kitchen, the phone rings. Fully expecting to hear Madeline's voice, I'm surprised when I hear, "Good morning, Susan. Your daughter's name is Joanne Marie Medeiros Harrington."

Wow! When the searcher said soon, I thought she meant a week or so, not two days later. Joanne? Joanne! Suddenly, I completely love the name Joanne. For years, I've fantasized about Madlyn's adoptive name, and Jennifer has always been my educated guess. In the early seventies, while working for my obstetrician, many of our patients had named their baby girls that. It was, by far, one of the most popular names, and that's why I never chose Jennifer for any of my girls, just in case. I immediately appreciate the coincidence of the three "J's." Jennifer, Jackie and Joanne. Amazing! Actually, it will be somewhat of a relief to stop referring to her as Madlyn. We already have enough Madelines with my mother, my cousin and my long-time friend.

Thanking her profusely and crying like a baby, I'm about to hang up, when she says, "Don't you want to know the rest?"

"Of course, I want to know the rest! What's wrong with me?" I gasp. "Hold on, I need to find a pen," I say, rummaging through the kitchen junk drawer. This searcher must have some powerful connections. It's only been a few weeks, after I spent nearly two years and got absolutely nowhere.

The only thing I find to write with is a fluorescent-pink Mickey Mouse pencil with huge rubber ears. "Okay, tell me everything. But you're gonna have to tell me fast, before I pass out," I say, half-crying, half-laughing and blissfully out of my mind.

"Here's what I have," she begins. "Just as you thought, Joanne grew up in Fall River, on Lincoln Avenue. She now lives in Waltham, Massachusetts. She married Daniel C. Harrington, also of Fall River, on September 18, 1993 at St. Joseph's Church."

"Oh, My God, that's Jackie's birthday! She was married on Jacqueline's twentieth birthday. What are the chances of that? What else, what else do you know about my daughter?"

"Her adoptive parents are Joseph and Ann Medeiros. I know of only one younger sibling, a boy named Joseph, I don't know if he's adopted or not."

She's full of information: the Social Security numbers, the time of Joanne's birth, her birth weight and even the doctor's name that had delivered her. In awe of how much she has dug up, I repeat everything to be sure I haven't missed a thing.

"Have you decided how to make first contact?" she wonders.

"No, not yet," is my reply.

"I'd be happy to place the initial call," she kindly offers. "I can first break the news to Joanne gently and persuasively, so she isn't frightened away. Also, if she isn't receptive to a meeting, being told 'no' through me will be much easier."

What should I do? Should I let her call? No, I have to think this through. "Can I get back to you?"

"Certainly. Just let me know if I can help."

Ecstatic and about to burst, I call Jay and Kris and everyone else I know. In a short moment between calls, the phone rings, startling me. Its Madeline's husband with news about their new grandchild, Abigail Victoria. Both mother and baby are well and doing fine. As concerned as I am about Julie and the health of her new baby girl, all I keep saying is, "I found my daughter! Manny, I found my daughter and her name is Joanne." After shamelessly going on and on, I finally come to my senses and congratulate him, and then apologize for acting so crazy.

For the past few days, I've been content just knowing Joanne's whereabouts. Now an incredibly strong urge has come upon me, an urge so strong that it takes everything I have not to jump into my car, family photo album in hand and drive to Waltham. Tears stream down my face, as I explore Map Quest on my computer and her street address comes up on my screen. After all these years, here it is, her home address is right before my eyes.

Knowing where Joanne grew up, I figure she must have attended Durfee High School, so I convince my friend, Linda, who is also a birth mother, to go with me to check out the 1986 yearbook. "I can't wait another minute to see her face," I explain.

Driving to the school's library, my guilty conscious is in overdrive. "Linda, help me come up with an acceptable reason for spying," I plead.

It's impossible to imagine they would help me, or even understand. I'm sure they don't just hand out pictures of birth mother's relinquished children everyday. For lack of a better excuse, I steal an idea used at my twentieth class reunion to gain access to her book. "I'm using senior class photos for lapel pins that will be worn at my family reunion," I tell the librarian. Jay and his three brothers also attended Durfee, so I ask for their books, as well, thinking it looks less conspicuous.

Joanne's yearbook in hand, I just stand in a stupor staring at it. Impatient with me, Linda snatches it away, opens the book and puts it back down on the table in front of me. My hands tremble, as I attempt to appear nonchalant while flipping through its pages. Having none of my act, Linda grabs the book back and goes directly to the "M's." We scan the page. Medeiros, Joanne Medeiros. There she is, the last picture in the last row.

"Linda, she's beautiful! Oh, she's wearing pearls." We're like two insane women, tears rolling down our faces, not quite knowing what to do next. I can't imagine what the librarian must be thinking. My impulse is to take the book and run. Instead, I offer to buy it or another copy.

"There are no 1986 class books left to purchase, but I have plenty of the others," he informs me.

My luck. "No, thanks."

"I'll be happy to make as many copies as you need," he offers. "What about the other books? Do you need pictures from them as well?"

Oh, yeah, the other books. Now, I have to at least look through the others to make my story seem plausible, when all I want is to stare at Joanne and bring this picture home to my family. While checking out Jay's book, and David's, and Mike's and Steven's, Linda continues to search through Joanne's.

"Susan, it seems Joanne was one busy girl," says Linda, from the other end of the table. "She's all over this book. You're not going to believe this, she was a member of the marching band. And, captain of the Colorguard!"

"No way! Let me see."

I have copies made of all the pictures. As I walk out of the library, I feel such an extraordinary sense of happiness. At long, long last I know what my daughter looks like. Linda and I are giddy with excitement and keep getting lost. When we finally do find the exit, I'm surprised to see my sister-in-law waiting in the foyer for my niece to get out of her morning session of preschool. I'm thrilled and proud to show off my pictures of Joanne so soon.

Being in the neighborhood, I decide to drive by the house where Joanne grew up and her mother still lives. The viselike grip, that takes hold of my chest at the mere sight of her house, seems to squeeze the very breath from me. Seeing her yard, the place where she played as a little girl, creates a lump in my throat so thick only crying relieves the discomfort. Envisioning Joanne as a teenager sitting on the porch steps, flirting with a new boyfriend and, more importantly, descending those same steps on her wedding day, leaves me feeling strangely empty.

Linda suggests we make one more trip around the block, but I've seen enough. From the look of things, Joanne grew up exactly like myself and my girls, just as I had hoped. My curiosity is satisfied and my heart is content. It's time to go home.

Linda and I feel a bit like Starsky and Hutch, as we laugh and cry all the way back to Acushnet. I'm proud of what I've accomplished.

Now that I know Joanne was a member of the colorguard, I add band pictures of both Jackie and Kris to her album. After much deliberation, I include pictures of Jackie's funeral, so Joanne can see what kind of person her sister was. Certainly, she will be able relate to the story, because of her association with Durfee's Marching Band. During Jackie's illness, never a day went by when she didn't receive cards, balloons, tape-recorded messages and phone calls from her band friends. They never failed to let her know they hadn't forgotten her. Every single band member that was in town attended her funeral. Once you belong to a close-knit group like that, they become family. Joanne would have experienced that feeling.

Though the press was prohibited from attending the funeral, we did grant the newspaper an interview later in the day. I include that article, which was on the front page of the local section of our newspaper the following day, along with some color photos taken outside of the church.

It's such a comfort to think that Joanne will understand.

Chapter Nine

Because I believe Joanne has a subconscious memory of my promise to find her, I feel it is important to tell her, in this first letter to her, my reasons for not searching when she became twenty-one. She should have a little information about her sisters and me, but not so much that all curiosity is satisfied, or she'll have no reason to call. Or, so I think. The letter needs to be personal enough to pique her interest, and it must be perfectly worded. Wording, it's all in the wording. She needs to understand I'm just a regular, everyday, run-of-the-mill mother. I have no idea what she knows about me or has imagined about me, if anything at all. First I need to gently break it to her that she has been found, that she wasn't stalked and that I mean her no harm.

Despite knowing exactly what I want to say, I've rewritten the letter a dozen times.

My first complete draft explains Jackie's illness and death and my reasons for not contacting her in 1989. I submit it to my support group for their thoughts and recommendations, and they bombard me with emails telling me to exclude the piece about Jackie, afraid it will scare her away.

I disagree, but figure they must know best and rewrite it. Personally, I think it's misleading not to tell her, and I feel guilty of the sin of omission. Also, I want to include a photo of myself, when they advise against that, as well. Now, I realize that their advice is well intended and very well may work for someone else. However, Joanne is my daughter and has to be, in some ways, like me and will want to know everything possible right from the start.

Nonetheless, I do as they say.

> Dear Joanne,
> My name is Susan Mello Souza. I've dreamed about writing this letter to you for thirty years. I am your birth mother. When you were born, I was seventeen years old and about to enter my senior year in high school. I was sent away to St. Mary's Home for Unwed Mothers in Boston. I was lucky enough, however, to care for you the first eight days of your life, while we were inpatients. I named you Madlyn Jeanne, after the two women in my life I admire most, my mother and my cousin.

The image of your small sweet face has never left my heart. I never, for one moment, ever wanted to give you up. Having to leave you at that hospital was the hardest thing I've ever had to do. I made a promise to you on the last day we were together, that I would search for you when you were older. I would someday like to share that experience with you.

There are so many things I want to share with you. I'm a married, self-employed stay-at-home mom. You have three sisters - Jackie, 25, Kristine just turned 23, and Bethany is only 14. They too, want so much to know you. We have brown curly hair and brown eyes; Jackie's eyes are hazel. We tend to be tall, 5'8" although Beth is only 5'4". I want to answer all your questions to ease both your mind and your heart.

Joanne, not one, single day of my life have I not thought about you and prayed for your health and happiness. I thank God every day for your parents, who took you home and loved you so much. I'm here for you now or whenever you are ready. I will not push you into anything you're not ready for. Just remember, you are in my heart and my thoughts every day. I love you and I always will.

Forever yours, Susan

We're leaving for Aruba and won't return until the twenty-first of March. I can't risk not being home to receive her call, so I wait until we return to mail it. On March 22, I send the letter first class, overnight, special delivery to be sure it's hand delivered to her door.

It's a beautiful spring evening, and the ride home from work is particularly enjoyable. The trees are finally budding and it's getting warmer and closer to summer, the season I live for. I've missed the warm sun and can't wait to go to the beach. Hopefully, Dan won't be working too late tonight. Rounding the corner of my driveway, I notice an express mail package, leaning up against my screen door. My mind is racing through all the possible things it could be, when suddenly I know. Oh, my God, it's a letter from my biological mother - I just know it!

I can't find my house key fast enough. Dropping my gym bag on the dining room table and with the front door still wide open, I rip the envelope open.

It's a letter addressed to me in beautiful handwriting on pretty stationary. How did I know it's from her? Before I can take it all in, I have to read through it twice. She found me! I can't believe she found me! She's a whole person with a whole family, a whole life - no longer a fictional character in a fictional tale I tell, whenever I tell my story about being adopted. She's real! I have sisters! And, she lives in Acushnet, only fifteen miles from Fall River, the town I grew up in, the place I consider my real home.

I can't believe I have sisters, fairly close to my brothers' ages. What do they look like? They're only half-sisters, not real sisters like my brothers are real brothers to me. No, that's wrong! Oh, my God, I don't even know what I'm saying! What does "real" mean anyway? My brothers are as real as it gets. I don't even think of them as not blood related. They are my real brothers. But these three girls, even though they are half-sisters to me, are blood related. So weird.

Who can I tell? Picking up the phone, I put it back down and instead drive to the high school to show Dan, hardly able to wait to show him. I still can't believe this is happening. As exciting as it is, I'm actually not sure how I really feel about it.

The high school is only five miles from the house, but it feels like it's taking forever to get there. As usual, Dan is the only teacher left at school, probably busy working on a lesson plan, creating a lab or correcting papers.

As I pass by, I greet the janitor, and then walk into room 214. Seeing the look on my face, Dan knows something has happened.

"Hey, Jo, what's up?" He looks concerned.

"Look what I just got in the mail today. It's a letter from my biological mother."

"Wow, what's it say?"

I read the letter aloud, which helps it seem a little more real. After I finish, we sit quietly together, just staring at the letter, not saying anything. I shake my head in confusion.

"What the hell am I supposed to do with this?" I ask him.

"What are you gonna do?"

"I don't know."

"How do you feel about this?"

"I don't know."

"Do you plan to tell your mother?"

"Yeah, I'll tell her. I'll call her tonight and read the letter to her. Dan, it has her address, phone number and email address. Should I call her? I don't think I want to call her, I think I'd rather write to her. Maybe I'll just finish that letter I've been working on and send that to her."

"That sounds like a good idea," he agrees.

The first week after sending the letter, I barely leave the house, waiting for Joanne to call.

I have no idea whether or not I want to respond. When I received word that my files had been updated six months ago, I was shocked. Knowing she had actually contacted the agency freaked me so much my stomach felt like it dropped to the floor. In 1994, when Mom and I requested medical information, there was none. All I wanted was my medical history. If my mom was uncomfortable, I didn't plan to even ask for that. Happily, Mom made the call because I wanted my identity to remain anonymous, not wanting to be confused with adoptees who search because they are unhappy.

As she looked back on it, Mom was amazed that she was given no information when they got me, medical or otherwise. She just felt so lucky to get me that it didn't matter where I came from. Catholic Social Services had recommended that she quit her job and be a stay-at-home mom, and she did it without question. She and Dad would have done anything to have a family and always made me feel so special and wanted. I never felt adopted. My parents were my "real" parents, and I was proud of my family and proud to say to people who asked that I had no interest in knowing who my biological parents might be. That night, after hearing from the agency, Mom and I both ended up in tears, as we told each other how fortunate we were to have the life we were given.

My mother's words meant even more, since, though very giving, she is not a very expressive person, and she felt relief and gratitude that I felt the same.

The information we were given was sketchy. All my life, I have wondered who might look like me, and how I would age. Would I recognize someone if they passed me on the street?

With the notification of Susan's waiver, I knew she wanted to find me. But, I didn't know if I wanted to be found. Now, her letter. How can anyone really prepare for something like this? There's no playbook, no instructions.

The second week, I leave the house, but never for very long.

Unable to think of anything but whether or not to respond to Susan, I find myself just sitting on the couch, staring at the television all the time. It's not supposed to happen this way. The adopted person should be the one to search. I always thought I was safe from knowing her. Finally, I realize why I don't want to know her - I would rather not know her, than know her and not like her. Now, I know I would never have searched for her.

The third week, whenever I do venture out, I call home to check for Joanne's call.

More than wanting to know who my "real" parents are, I want to know how the hell she found me, and what she knows about me. It feels like my life has been invaded. Have they been staking out my home? Has she already been in my neighborhood, down my street? I need to hear her voice, hear how she handles herself and how she answers how she specifically tracked me down. The way she answers is very important. Maybe then I will know whether or not she's weird or crazy. Still, I feel so shallow wondering about this more than anything else.

What if she's poor or sick? What if she needs my help? What will my mom think? What will my three brothers think? What if she wants my kidney!

Now at the beginning of the fourth week, I'm in a total panic. I can't come up with any good reason why Joanne hasn't called by now. Perhaps I should send another letter and enclose my picture this time. Or, maybe I should just call her? Once again, I look to my fellow birth moms for advice. They all agree that it's too soon for a call, but a second letter with a photo would be appropriate.

As difficult as it was to write the first letter, it's nearly impossible to compose the second. Do I say how I feel? "Hey, Joanne, why the hell haven't you called me?" No, this second letter has to be an acknowledgement of what she must be going through. If I mention the photo album and my pearl ring, would that be considered baiting? Of course it would be, but I don't care. I'm desperate.

> Dear Joanne,
> I realize my first letter to you must have been quite a shock. Please know it was never meant to hurt you in anyway. Some of the girls I've been in contact with during my search tell me that, as much as these letters are unexpected, they are expected to some degree. They also tell me they, at one time or another, have considered searching themselves, but were always afraid of rejection and that is what sometimes stopped them. I must admit, that thought terrifies me, but not as much as the thought of never knowing you.
> Enclosed is a recent photo of Kris and me, just so you might be able to find some resemblance in us. During the weeks since my first letter, I have put together a photo album for you. It consists of pictures

of me when I was a little girl, some during my high school years, including your father, then up through the years to the present time. There also are pictures of your sisters, my parents, my brothers and their families. I have also saved for you, the ring your father gave to me on my 16th birthday.

Joanne, I don't want you to be afraid to know me. If you have even the smallest part of me in you, you will realize I pose no threat to your family. We just might be able to be friends. Again, remember I'm here for you, now and forever. Everyday, I hope this will be the day I hear from you.

Love, Susan

Wondering if she actually ever received the first letter, this time I send it "Return Receipt Requested."

Now, I'm really annoyed. She's sent a second letter, this time certified, and it's such a hassle getting to the post office. She's barging into my life uninvited.

Bethany is in a Show Choir competition at Waltham High School, giving me the perfect opportunity to look for Joanne's house. I need to see where she lives.

The moment I lay eyes on the first Waltham sign on Route 128, my heart sinks and the panic sets in. I've got my Map Quest pages and begin to give Jay the directions, when he casually mentions that he knows where she lives.

"What? Why the hell didn't you tell me this before?" I'd like to smack him!

"I don't know. Guess I didn't think about it."

"Guess you didn't think about it? Jay, this is all I've been talking about for weeks!"

"I made a U-turn on her street, when I visited recently," Jay says lamely. "A friend of mine works at a health care organization just around the corner from Marlborough Road."

I don't know if it's my nerves, my anger, or both. I'm on the verge of tears and my whole body is shaking, as we drive down Main St. My hands are sweaty, and my damp finger marks are embedded in the wrinkled map pages from the near death grip I have on them.

"We just passed her post office!" I announce, as if Joanne actually owns the place. Passing a drugstore and a convenience store, I envision her walking along these streets and going into its businesses. I'm so close I can actually feel her, and I'm overwhelmed. The tears begin to flow. It's too much to think that, after waiting thirty painfully long years to know where my daughter lives, I'm actually driving through her town. It's all so surreal. As we cross some railroad tracks and pass a playground, I'm feeling nauseous. The only thing preventing me from going completely over the edge is silently concentrating on these unneeded Map Quest directions.

Suddenly, here it is - Marlborough Road, and my heart skips a beat. Oh, dear God, I'm here. I'm really here! Jay takes a right turn and we look for number twenty-three.

"I don't see twenty-three, Jay do you see twenty-three?" I'm panicky. "Hey, we're already up into the hundreds. Damn, we missed it."

Jay turns around and spots the house. Thank God, because I can hardly see through my tears. I'm in awe of the blurry, blessed vision before me - my daughter's house. She lives in an ordinary town, on the corner of an ordinary street, in an ordinary house - painted red! I live in a red house. Now, just how many people live in a red house? Is it just a coincidence?

Trying to will her out onto the porch, I stare at her house for the longest time. On her front door, she's hung a pretty wreath and she has nice curtains in her windows. Driving around the block, we can see that there's no yard to speak of and no toys on the porch. Must be no children, yet. Which car is hers?

On our third trip around the block, I tell Jay that's enough. I'm too afraid someone will notice us and call the cops. Exhaling a big, uneven sigh, I wipe my tears and blow my nose and take one last look at my daughter's red house. Such a sense of relief washes over me. If only I had the courage to walk up to her front door and ring the bell. But, I must be patient and let her come to me. After all, I made the first move.

After five days, I still haven't received the return receipt, so I call the Waltham Post Office.

"A notice was left in her mailbox. There will be one more attempted delivery on the twenty-second. After that, the letter will be returned to you," the clerk informs me impatiently, hanging up!

After several more days, there's still no receipt. Should I implement Plan B, ship the photo album to her and again wait for a response?

Terribly disappointed and afraid that I'll never hear from her, I ask Kris to write a letter to be placed in the album, along with the one written by Bethany in February, in case Joanne doesn't contact us.

Hi!

You know something? I can't wait to know your name. I think it's a very big part of who you are and what your personality is. But, I don't really need to know it until I meet you. I figure you'd want to know a little bit about me. My name is Bethany Jay. Everybody either calls me Beej or Beth. I'm fourteen, going to be fifteen on July 9th. Yup, that means I can't drive... I'm a freshman in high school... *NSYNC is my favorite group... We live in the quietest town but I love it...

Our sister, Kristine, lives with her boyfriend, Jeremy... Hopefully, they'll get married soon because I want to be in a wedding. My dad likes Jeremy, but it's hard to tell because he says he won't like any of our boyfriends no matter what! My dad is cool, he's a hospital consultant... I got to go to California with him and Mom - we went to Disneyland. We went on every ride including Thunder Mountain, that's Mom's favorite. She will stand in line for that ride almost as long as she stays online... Since she's been looking for you, she has gotten less and less computer illiterate. She spends her mornings working and her afternoons searching for you. You really do mean a lot to her. She joined a club for mothers that are searching for their children, The Sunflowers.

When Mom told me about you, I was eleven. She says I took it well. I asked why we couldn't go and get you right then. Because I was very curious, I kept asking about you. I wanted to know how old you were and where you lived. I wanted to know as much as I could. Mom kept telling me she didn't know much. I could tell that her not knowing about you bothered her but she didn't say anything. Then about a year or two later she told me she was looking for you. I thought it was a great idea and so did the rest of the family. None of us can wait to meet you!

Bethany

Despite searching all over for my little "knee pillow," which I use every night to relieve the pressure on my repaired hip, I can't find it anywhere in my bedroom, and I can't imagine where it could be. Without it, I can't get comfortable and I'm having a restless night, unable to fall asleep.

All of a sudden, I sense a presence in my room. From the familiar scent of her perfume, I know it's Jackie, even before I see her silhouette standing at the foot of my bed. She appears to be holding a pillow, and I watch, as she ever so gently lays it on my bed. Softly, I call her name. As tears trickle down my face, her image fades away, leaving behind only her flowery scent.

I lean over to turn on the bedside lamp, lifting my legs over the side of the bed in order to reach it. When my feet touch the floor, I feel my little "knee pillow." A chill runs down my spine and the hairs on my body stand up. Then a beautiful feeling of ethereal calm washes over me, and I know all is well – Jackie is close by to help me.

Feeling braver than usual in the morning, I call the post office again, in a last ditch effort. Finally, they're understanding of my dilemma. The postal worker, a female this time, is kind and offers to call Joanne, to remind her that my letter will be sent back, if it's not picked up soon.

I say a silent "Thank you" to Jackie!

Chapter Ten

I'm alone. Jay's away on business this week and Bethany's at school. A million thoughts run through my head as I pace the house all day, with no one to talk to but myself. Maybe she's on vacation. Maybe someone stole the first letter. Maybe it was never delivered. Maybe she got it and wants nothing to do with me. Maybe, maybe, maybe - I'm making myself crazy.

By seven in the evening, Beth has watched my turmoil enough since getting home and shaking her head suggests, "Mom, will you please just pick up the phone and call her."

"Call her? You think I should call her?" I ask, as if I haven't wanted to do exactly that a thousand times, in the past few weeks. "Shouldn't I let the searcher call like she advised?"

No! Why should I let someone else place the most important call of my life? If Joanne rejects me, she's going to have to tell me herself, because I'm not about to squander what might be my one and only opportunity to hear her voice.

"Mom, call Joanne."

Taking a deep breath, I dial her number. The answering machine picks up, and I nervously leave my message. "Hi, this is Susan Souza, your birth mother. I sent you a letter a few weeks ago and wondered if you received it. Please call me."

As apprehensive as I was about making this call, I'm just as disappointed she didn't answer. I didn't even listen to the message. Did I leave my number? Was that even Joanne's machine?

"It could have been anyone's home. I have to call back," I say to Beth. "But, what if she has Caller ID? I don't want my name coming up again. She'll think I'm nuts. My intention is to make her like me, not think I'm crazy."

Beth remembers that my mother has a blocked number, and we go next door to use her phone to hear Joanne's message.

Dan and I were walking through the door, when I heard Susan's message. Sitting on the couch, we're deciding about whether or not to return her call, when the phone rings again, startling me. Both of us stand over the phone, staring at it.

"It's her. I know its Susan. It's been only a little while since she left her message. She's getting impatient and doesn't want to wait for me to call her back. She's hoping to catch me at home now."

"Why would she be calling back?" he asks. "How do you know it's her?"

"I just know. What am I gonna do, Dan? You answer it."

"I don't know what to say, it's your mother, you answer it."

This time, Joanne answers. Startled, Beth hangs up.

"Oh, Beth, she saw it was me the first call, and chose not to pick up before. Damn, I haven't come this far to give up now. I'll take my chances, call back and leave my number, then pray for her to call." I redial her number.

If I don't pick up the phone, I will never have the guts to call her back. Well, at least not tonight, so I might as well bite the bullet and get this over with. I'm just stalling and avoiding the inevitable. One more day won't make a difference. She's already waited thirty years. Isn't it important to let me have my time? But, time for what? I guess I'll just let life unfold.

On the fourth ring, I hear, "Hello?" Oh, dear Lord, she answered, now what? "Is this Joanne Harrington?" I ask.

"Yes," she says curtly.

She's not happy. OK, calm down. Don't let her tone intimidate you. "This is Susan Souza. I didn't expect you to answer," I say, as my mind draws a complete blank. "I just wanted to leave my number."

"You did leave your number."

She sounds cool and irritated.

Wow, I'm being so cold. I'm not making it easy for her at all. I'm going to let her be the one to do the talking. Since she's the one making the call, she must have something to say. And, I don't even particularly want to be having this conversation.

She isn't making it easy, so I keep talking so she won't hang up. "I was wondering if you received the letter I sent a month ago," I ask, in my sweetest voice.

"I received the first one, but haven't had the time to pick up the other one," she replies bluntly.

Ouch, that hurt! Maybe I should have let the searcher make this call after all.

There! How does she like that? She's inconveniencing me, and I just let her know it. I should be the one making this call. I hate this.

This is not at all what I expected. I wrongfully assumed she would, at least, be kind. My motherly instincts are failing me, and I don't know how to get through to her. I'm feeling helpless and vulnerable. "Were you surprised when you received my letter?"

"No, not really," Joanne answers, with a cocky attitude.

I'm shocked. "Really, why not?"

"Seven months ago, Catholic Social Services contacted my adoptive mother to tell her that medical and non-identifying information regarding my adoption was available."

So, that's what I heard in the social worker's voice. I knew there was more than she was letting onto. She just wasn't able to tell me. She was trying to reunite us all along.

"In 1994, my mom requested medical information, but there was none. So, when the social worker sent us the letter stating you had relinquished your right to confidentiality, we wondered what had changed. I began writing a letter to you last October," she admits, "but I've had difficulty completing it."

This isn't going well. She really doesn't want to be having this conversation. How can I get through to her and make her realize how much I love her? How can I make her relax and talk to me, not at me?

"I'm sorry. I never meant to upset you."

At best, our conversation is awkward. She remains cool, while telling me a few things about her life. I'm hungry for every bit of information she's doling out and don't much worry about her tone, as long as she keeps talking.

Not sounding happy at all she asks, "How did you find me?" Before I even have the opportunity to answer, she asks again, "How did you find me?"

I have no trouble telling her the truth. First, I tell her about my Sunflower support group and the adoption search sites I had visited. Then I tell her about the searcher.

None of these search methods sound crazy. I can handle this. Maybe she's not a lunatic. In fact, this is going well. She sounds young and pretty, her accent is familiar and comforting.

"How did this searcher find me?" she wants to know.

Oh, no, now she's mad.

"I really don't know," I admit, feeling foolish. "I guess it didn't matter enough to ask how. I just wanted to find you." Now, the last thing I want is to have Joanne angry with me for hunting her down, so I explain that only after looking on my own for nearly two years, did I decide to hire a searcher.

"Wow, two years!"

"The searchers came highly recommended by another birth mother. Evidently, they have some powerful contacts, which allowed them access to your original birth certificate. Once they had that, finding the amended copy was easy." I assure her that no one had been following her or staking out her house.

It's impressive that she's had so much determination and put so much effort into finding me. Me, the object of such a dedicated search effort - such a flattering notion. It's like having a fan! I should be telling her I'm so happy she found me, or I've been searching for her, too, or at least fantasizing about it. But, I'd be lying. I feel so insensitive. This is like telling a new boyfriend who loves you that the feelings aren't reciprocal. I'm at a loss for words. She knows nothing about me, yet I mean so much to her. It's so interesting, though, how she put the pieces of my life into place, to hear about myself through her eyes.

"What did the searcher tell you about me?"

I tell her everything and then confess that, once I knew she grew up in Fall River, I went to Durfee High School to check out her yearbook. She laughs, as I describe my undercover spy mission. Maybe, I'm on my way.

"Really, you saw my yearbook?" she asks, sounding pleased.

Finally, a positive response. Do I detect a friendly tone in her voice?

I can picture her nervously asking to see the yearbooks, trying not to look suspicious. She's so cute and makes me laugh. I'm not even caring about the invasion of privacy thing.

"Yes, I did. I couldn't wait to see your picture. You're beautiful, just like your sisters." Oh, please, let her be flattered. Okay, what else can I say? "Joanne, I saw that you were in the color guard. So were Jackie and Kristine," I'm quick to add, trying to keep her attention.

"No way!" she shouts. "That is such a coincidence. They were in the New Bedford High Marching Band?"

"Yes, and like you, Kristine was captain."

"No way!" she shouts again. "This is so wild!"

This is it! This is the "in" I need. I'm thrilled to share this interesting tidbit with her. She sounds so happy that her sisters also twirled flags and is amazed by the coincidence.

"I was in the marching band while in college, at the University of Massachusetts, Amherst," she offers.

"I loved watching UMass perform 'The 1812 Overture' during Band Finals at Boston University."

"I was in the band when they did that!"

We figure out we missed each other by one year. She performed in 1987 and Jackie competed in 1988. "Close but no cigar," I say joking. Our conversation is getting better by the minute.

"Tell me about the girls."

You mean your sisters, I'm thinking. I guess she can't yet allow herself that gift. Now comes the tough part, having to admit I lied, when I wrote she had three living sisters. I cry telling her about Jackie and explain why I omitted such an important fact. She seems to be trying to understand. She becomes quiet, and I can tell she's upset. It's a feeble excuse. I can only hope she'll forgive me. I explain how my plan to find her, when she became twenty-one, failed. She listens, but says very little. She must not know what to say.

What a blow. I feel so ripped off. For a month, I've been thinking I had three sisters, like I have three brothers, and what a coincidence that is. Why am I feeling such a sense of loss? Is that what Susan wants me to feel, grief like the rest of her family? How can I be annoyed at such terrible news? Her daughter died.

"I'm sorry to hear that," she says, her voice trailing off. Then, she shares that she, too, has lost someone she loved very much - her adoptive dad.

I express my sympathies and we move on, keeping the conversation light. I talk about Kris and Beth, hoping we come across as normal. We talk a little more about her husband and their jobs, and I can tell she sounds comfortable, at last.

"Do you have any children?" I'm dying to know.

"No." She offers no explanation, so I drop the subject.

I hate that question, no matter who asks it. Dan and I are just not ready. I have a bigger one for her. How do I ask it? I need to know why I was given up. Hopefully, she doesn't think I am judging her. I hope they were high school sweethearts like I've always believed.

"Who's my father? Did you love him?"

With tears in my eyes and my heart bursting with joy, I tell my daughter, "Yes, I loved your father with all my heart. I loved him for many years. We were high school sweethearts." I'm not even concerned that I'm sobbing, as I tell her the story. All that matters now is she understands that she wasn't only conceived in love but, also, surrendered in love and how much I have always loved her. Telling her about our love affair, I don't get into the circumstances surrounding his refusal to marry me. I leave it that we were too young, and our parents thought it was best.

"Does he know about me?"

Do I want to get into this on the phone? Oh, what the hell, tell her the truth.

I tell her about the "miscarriage" story, and that Mark didn't know the truth until 1983, but none of the particulars. Some things are better left unsaid, until they can be shared in person. "Would you ever be interested in meeting him?"

"I don't think so," she says matter of factly.

At last, our conversation becomes warm and personal, as if we've spoken many times before, just like old friends. Hearing her voice puts me at ease, and I believe I'm doing the same for her, because she now trusts me enough to share her reaction to hearing my voice on her machine – total ambivalence it seems.

"Are you married?" she asks.

When I tell her about Jay, whose real name is Joseph, it turns out she has a brother named Joseph, also nicknamed Jay, and he's a pharmacist, too!

That kind of freaks us out a little.

"Your letter said that you are a stay-at-home mom and self-employed. What do you do?"

"I'm a manicurist."

"I love to do my nails! I do them myself and haven't found anyone who does them better. I bet you do a great job, if you're as meticulous as I am."

I assure her she has great genes for aging well, and I just know she's going to be thrilled. When she complains how unfair it is that she doesn't know what we look like, I'm quick to inform her, in my own motherly fashion, "Had you gone to the Post Office to pick up my second letter, you would have a picture of me and your sister, Kristine." She promises to go tomorrow.

"Do you remember what I looked like when I was born?"

"That's something I will never forget. It's the memory of your precious sweet face that has kept me going all these years."

"Was I chubby?"

"Yes, you were short and fat, with lots of wrinkles, the cutest little button nose and beautiful greenish blue eyes."

"My eyes are green now."

"Somehow, I knew they would be. Mark's mother has the most gorgeous green eyes."

She has our sense of humor, and I love hearing her laugh. Still, I can't believe I'm talking to and laughing with my first-born daughter. Thanking me for the generous, yet painful, decision I had to make, she assures me her adoption was never an issue for her. She never felt any different than her brothers.

117

I can still picture two books, THE FAMILY THAT GREW and THE ADOPTED FAMILY sitting with other books in between my bronzed baby shoe bookends.

Hearing those words lifts the burden of worrying about her fitting in with her adoptive family, and I cry with relief. Now she's animated, as she tells me about her three brothers, her friends, her hobbies and how much she loves music and dancing. In turn, I fill her in on everything. Even though she must be on information overload, I squeeze in one more piece of information, a tidbit about my parents, and that's when she asks me to verify her lifelong belief about her nationality. "Just how Irish am I? I've always thought I'm half."

When I tell her just how Portuguese she is, she remarks, "To think how much I used to brag on St. Patrick's Day. My brothers are going to enjoy this. I always tease them by claiming to be more Irish than they are." Then, after a short pause, "Wait till I tell my mother!"

She and her mother have already spoken about me, and Joanne will do so again just to be sure her mother understands how much she loves her. Perhaps, it isn't my place to tell her this, but I do anyway. "This might sound like a silly thing for me to say, Joanne, your concern for your mother makes me feel proud."

When we talk about Jackie, I share with her that they were not only born within a day of each other, five years apart, but that she was married on Jackie's twentieth birthday. Once again, she says very little. She must be in awe of the many parallels we have already uncovered in our lives.

Susan's convinced Jackie's spirit was with me on my wedding day, while I'm convinced my father was certainly there, looking down from heaven. Just ten months before, we were in the same church for his funeral. Susan must feel sad that she missed such an important day in my life, but I have to admit that I didn't think of my birth parents at all on that day. Nothing was missing for me, except my dad.

"I actually have no contact with teenagers. It's going to be interesting and fun getting to know Beth."

It pleases me to hear, "getting to know," because it gives me hope that I may have a shot at meeting her.

Beth wants to talk, so I hand her the phone. I need someone to pinch me, to make sure I'm not dreaming. Their conversation takes on a light and happy air. Beth's face is animated and she doesn't appear nervous at all. She gets Joanne interested in *NSYNC and promises to mail pictures from the concert we attended last month. They also talk about basketball and show choir. I hope they become good friends.

After two hours, my hands are killing me and both of my ears are hot and red from holding the phone so tight to my head, not wanting to miss a word. Before hanging up, I ask if we can meet and Joanne agrees. She doesn't even sound hesitant, though she does still want to take things slow, and promises to gather some pictures and send them to me.

We hang up with a number of things to be done and a lifetime to catch up on. To think we came so close to disaster.

I'm in complete awe. It's hard to believe I've just spoken with the young woman who was once my baby girl. She's smart and articulate, with a marvelous sense of humor. What I have also taken away is that she appears to be a loving and caring daughter. I admit that, at first, I experienced major pangs of jealousy and stored them in a safe place where they would do me no harm. After all, they'd serve no purpose. I learned to live with my decision years ago and that's all I ever prayed for - that Madlyn had a mother she loved. So, I won't brood. I'll accept it and go on with my reunion.

Through tear filled eyes, I read the first email from my daughter. It arrives two days after our miraculous first conversation. Her words are too precious to lose, so I print out her message and hang it on the fridge, just as if it were her first gold-starred paper from kindergarten.

> Susan,
> Just a quick note to let you know I sent an envelope to you today via regular mail. I know you're probably anxious, so I want you to know when to expect it. I included a few photos I think you will like.

Like a hawk, I wait for the arrival of the postal truck. As soon as I see it drive away, I run out the door, fly across the street and flip open the mailbox. There it is - her envelope addressed to me. I trace her handwriting with my finger, trying somehow to feel her vibes.

As excited as I am to see what this package holds, I don't want to tear it by just ripping it open. So I rush back into the house, and not finding the letter opener right away, settle for a steak knife.

There's a handwritten note on a pretty post card printed by her company.

> It was really great talking with you last night, Susan. I admit I was apprehensive and apologize if I sounded cold at first. I was very nervous, as I know you were, too. I stopped at the Post Office on my way to work,

rather than risk working late and missing your letter again. I've been staring at the photo all day. Wow! I do look like both you and Kristine. There are so many similarities in our faces. I'd love a photo of Beth, as well. Enclosed is the letter I have been working on since October... Also, notice this postcard? The photo is by me. Brandt Island in Nantucket. My company uses some of my photos as marketing sample pieces. This one is a favorite of mine.

The photo on the postcard is picturesque - simple, clear and colorful. There's also a snap shot of Joanne and Dan in Nantucket, with that very same lighthouse in the background. They look like a normal happy couple.

In her typewritten and very matter of fact letter to me, the one she began in October, she makes it quite clear she's had a very full life without me:

Dear Susan,

I feel hesitant to make contact. I feel nervous and apprehensive, especially with regard to my mom's feelings. I would hate for her to feel betrayed in any way or to feel that I have a void in my life that she and my family did not fill... I want you to know I feel lucky; lucky to have the life I have. I am grateful to you for giving me the chance to have this life... My adoption was a great thing and I've never wanted for anything but to have the parents and the family I have. I feel no animosity now nor have I ever felt bitterness or resentfulness towards you while growing up... I love my family with all my heart and can't imagine my life without them.

Had I received this letter without speaking with her first, I'd certainly think I'd just been royally blown off.

Setting the letter aside, I look through the pictures again. One photo is a 1997 summertime picture of her adoptive family at Baker's beach in Westport, Massachusetts. In the photo, her adoptive mother is sitting amidst her children in the sea grass on a sand dune. My heart is pounding and I'm baffled as to whether it's breaking or bursting with joy? This picture depicts a beautiful woman with lovely gray hair and an easy smile, a woman any girl would love to call Mom, the woman my daughter calls Mom. We are total opposites. Hopefully, Joanne will think her two mothers being so different is a good thing.

In all the photos, Joanne looks like me. However, seeing her wedding portrait, I gasp and run to get the family album I've put together for her. Comparing her wedding picture with Mark's class picture, I can't believe my eyes. The photo captures his looks perfectly, especially his nose and the little creases at the corner of his mouth. I stand frozen with visions of her wedding day and what I would have given to be there. Trying unsuccessfully to keep my tears from falling onto her pictures, I tell myself, "Don't obsess. Obsessing is futile. Don't let anything ruin this day."

Where I cried when I found her picture in the yearbook, seeing her as she is today - looking animated, healthy and happy, I sob. Feeling woozy, I lean on the sink for support. It feels so damn healing to cry for a happy reason.

My tears are upsetting to Kris and Beth when they discover me in the kitchen, until they notice the pictures and then they understand. The three of us spend the longest time finding the different ways Joanne resembles us. The one thing we see for certain is we all four share the same smile.

"I will treasure these pictures forever. They may be the only ones I ever get," I tell the girls.

"Don't worry, Mom," Kris assures me, "there'll be more. She didn't write this nice note for nothing. She sent these pictures because she wants us to know her just as much as she wants to know us."

It's so much easier for Kris to see that.

The girls begin their own email correspondence with Joanne, and it is clear that they are enjoying their contact with each other very much.

I am discovering over these days how very much alike Joanne and I are. After confessing that I am a beach bum, she responds that bumming at the beach is what she does best. So, I write back that we love to throw parties, using any excuse to throw one - "Oh, you got a haircut? Let's have a party!" Her response: "We celebrate haircuts, too!" We are both so excited, learning every detail about one another.

Mother's Day is approaching, and I'm feeling anxious and a bit cranky. Dare I think Joanne will send a card? Does she even think of me in that way? I doubt it very much. So, I'm not going to set myself up for disappointment. I'm just happy I found her and that she is healthy and happy.

However, the day before Mother's Day, there's an envelope addressed to me from Joanne. I do the happy dance all the way across the street from the mailbox. It's a beautiful Hallmark note card, the kind that is blank on the inside for personal messages. On the front is a simple black and white picture of a little girl, wearing a big straw hat, sitting on a stone step and holding a single red rose. In her handwriting it reads:

HAPPY MOTHER'S DAY, SUSAN

I gave up on trying to find a Mother's Day card appropriate for our situation. I guess there is one card Hallmark hasn't thought of, yet. I have thought of you often since we first spoke, and find myself very excited about the whole situation. I never anticipated the feelings I am experiencing. I feel a connection between us and I'm anxious to learn more about you and your daughters. I look forward to the day we will actually meet. I'm thinking of you and smiling.
Love, Joanne

"Love, Joanne" - hopefully, the beginning of a dream about to come true. Her card means everything to me, and it looks marvelous sitting along with my others from Kris and Beth. The best part is I know the words come from her heart, because she wrote them herself. Is it possible to feel this happy?

I respond with a short email telling her I, too, am feeling the connection; the same connection I felt thirty years before, when I held her in my arms, looked into her eyes, and told her how much I loved her and that someday I would find her. "My feelings for you have never and will never change. Thoughts of you make me smile, too."

On Monday, I again feel the need to acknowledge her card, but I don't want to appear to be a lunatic about it, so I preface my message with information about my brother, Russell. Russell, like her husband, was a lifeguard while in high school and college. I also tell her he has lobster pots, and how we love to have clam boils and little necks whenever possible, hoping she shares our love of seafood. The coincidences we uncover are amazing us both, and many of them center around the beach we both love so much.

I then thank her for my card once more. "Joanne, the most important thing I want to say is this, thank you for thinking of me this Mother's Day. The way you touched my heart is beyond words. I was even afraid to secretly wish you would remember me on this special day. But you did; you made my wish come true."

Kris and Joanne are chatting on the phone. It's been a couple of hours, and I'm dying to know what they are talking about, so I call Kris. She picks up on call waiting and tells me they both laughed when they heard the beep, knowing who it was. Kris promises to call me later.

When she does, I grill her. Joanne shared with her the feelings she experienced, once learning of Jackie's death. She said that for five weeks she believed she had three sisters, and, when I told her of Jackie's death she felt a sense of loss. That upsets me. I never meant to hurt her in any way by omitting that fact from my letter of introduction.

Feeling compelled to make up for not following my intuition and being as honest with Joanne as I always have been with my other daughters, I look for and find the perfect greeting card; it's a Hallmark. My only hope is that Joanne won't think it's too forward of me. It reads:

"You know how it feels when you're putting together a jigsaw puzzle and you find, at last, the one perfect piece?
Take that feeling and multiply it by a lifetime, and you'll know how unbelievable it was for me to find you!
You were the missing piece I'd been searching for, the perfect, gentle fit into the pattern of all my days.
You were the one who made my life complete."

Joanne's response eases my mind that she is accepting my efforts at building a loving relationship. "Just to let you know, I have such a wonderful impression of you and your family. I can tell you are really great people."

More pictures arrive in the mail from Joanne, and Kris and Bethany pour over them with me, examining every detail. Being able to share such a meaningful time in my life with Kris and Beth is extraordinary, and I marvel at their generous and loving behavior. They could have resented all of this.

An email I receive on May 17 has me alarmed. Joanne sounds overwhelmed, and I can only hope I haven't blown it.

> Susan, below you will find the letter I typed this morning... I hate how impersonal it might come across in an email, but it's the fastest way of communicating. So here goes...

> Dear Susan,
> I've been thinking a lot about meeting you and thought it would be good to put some thoughts on paper. I've some reoccurring concerns I should bring

out in the open. I want us to be on the same wavelength... I keep searching for answers to questions like: "What should I do?" "Should I meet them?" "When should I meet them?" "How often should I see them?" No one has the answers, and there really are no "right" answers.

This is a unique situation and there are no rules, so I have followed my instinct by taking things slowly and not meeting you right away... I can tell the girls are anxious to meet me as I know you are - of course you are, you have been waiting thirty years for this. I understand that. I ask that you remember I have not waited thirty years for this. For me, it has been real for only three weeks, since that first Tuesday night phone call. That is the point at which everything really hit me and I felt "found" by you, although your letter did give me some preparation... I just want you to realize we are, in fact, on different time lines.

The whole concept of having birth parents has been very abstract; I never expected to know you. I accepted that a long time ago and think I have figured out why - it is because of my parents. I never felt like anything but their daughter and didn't feel curious enough to give it much thought beyond that. I never wanted my mom and dad to ever feel like I wasn't theirs. I never wanted them to think I felt there was something missing in my life.

Now that you have contacted me, the concept is no longer abstract. You are a person to me now, not just an idea... I not only know where you are, but I'm learning who you are and I like you all. Now, the assumption of there being people that "look like me" is reality and I'm faced with it, although I never intended to be. Now that I am, I do want to know more, more about you and your family.

Which brings me to my first concern. How much of myself I can share with you may not be what you anticipate. I'm concerned that our expectations may not be the same, which could lead to disappointment and guilt among any one of us... I'm concerned your expectations may exceed mine and I'll eventually disappoint you and that will lead to my inevitable feelings of guilt - all of which could be avoided as long as expectations are set realistically. Forgive me for stating the obvious, but I will anyway. I have built strong relationships with my family, Dan's family and my friends. I have a very busy social calendar, and, as it is, I sometimes feel I am spread thin... Everyone is busy with social engagements and obligations, and sometimes it's difficult to juggle them smoothly. I worry now it may be even more difficult for me to juggle with your family, should you expect more of me than I can give...

You may have already thought about this and even talked to Kris and Beth. I just feel it is appropriate to bring it up since I have been worried about it lately. I want to meet you and get to know you, but I want all involved to realize it will take some time and I don't want to disappoint anyone.

I don't want anyone to feel they have to make up for lost time because there is no lost time, we all have lived our own lives to the fullest and now our lives will continue to be lived to the fullest with one change; we now know one another. I hope you understand how I feel and do not view it as negative. It is not negative... I would love to talk about this and to get your feedback. Maybe we can talk tonight. I am very anxious to meet you; in fact, I think we should set a date... I would love to visit you at your home if you're comfortable with that...

Joanne

Before placing my call later that evening, I make sure to have my appointment book handy, in the event Joanne is willing to set a date. I've printed out her email and made notes in the margins, because I often become brain dead while on the phone with her, and I don't want to screw this up. My inability to concentrate is caused by the sheer disbelief that I'm actually speaking with her. I'm feeling nervous and that's odd. I've become comfortable with my thoughts of Joanne. But this is different. This conversation could make or break any future we might have.

"Jackie, please give Mommy the right words," I pray, as I dial Joanne's number. At first, I find I'm speaking so fast, I barely make sense. Then, the "right words" do come from out of the blue.

"Joanne, under no circumstances will I ever place any unrealistic expectations on you to give more than you can or are willing to give," I tell her, holding my breath. "I understand and appreciate the commitments and relationships you have formed with your family and friends. Those are the very things I've always wanted for you. I'm willing to wait, as long as necessary, for you to feel secure and comfortable with your decisions about dealing with me."

"Thank you for that," Joanne replies, sounding relieved. "And, I'll do the same. No expectations on either of our parts."

I then confess the same desire to meet in familiar and loving surroundings of my own home. She agrees that private and personal is best. With that settled, we set the date for Friday, May 21 - only four days away!

Beside myself with happiness, I can't think of another thing to say. Joanne laughs at my sudden speechlessness. "Okay, now how do I get there?" she asks, sounding calm and collected.

She hopes to arrive by seven o'clock, depending on traffic.

Four days to prepare for the meeting of my life! Maybe we should have added that sunroom to the house. Wouldn't it be nice to entertain Joanne in a brand new sun filled room? Relax, I tell myself, they're visiting at night.

Staring at myself in the mirror, I wonder if I'm too fat. Can I lose ten pounds by Friday? Joanne does aerobics everyday. Will she think I'm lazy because I hate to exercise? What will I do with my hair? What will I wear? Will Joanne ever think of me as her "other mother?" Good God, I don't even know if she'll think of me as a friend, never mind her other mother.

I've become a crazy lady, despite all the reassurance from family and friends that Joanne will like me. Everything has to be perfect. My two redecorated rooms seem hardly enough. I drive my housekeeper insane on Thursday and follow her around making sure she does everything right. What am I doing? She always does a better job than I do. I need to leave her alone before she quits. I call our yardman to have him here early on Friday to make sure the yard is perfectly groomed.

As our anticipation grows, we are all emailing each other back and forth about our excitement and the plans for the evening.

At one point I write to Joanne: "My biggest problem is this - do I wait in the house until you ring my doorbell, or out in the middle of street?"

Chapter Eleven

I'm feeling lightheaded, jittery, somewhat nauseous and at the same time downright giddy. As I look at my reflection in the mirror, I can't seem to wipe the grin from my face, yet, I cry whenever I try to speak. The intensity of emotion I'm experiencing can only be compared to the overwhelming feelings I had when Jacqueline passed away. Except today, I'm filled with as much happiness as I was filled with sorrow those last painful days of Jackie's life, and with the grief following her death.

If the weather is any indication of how our reunion will go, it's going to be magnificent. To think, I'm only hours away in my thirty-year countdown to see my daughter again. Always believing my countdown would be only twenty-one years long, there was no way of anticipating Jackie's death and the added years I needed following it to recover. The last four agonizing weeks waiting for her to respond to my letter, however, have sometimes seemed longer than the thirty years it took to get to this glorious day.

Sitting at the kitchen counter, sipping my morning tea and leafing through the family album I've made for Joanne, I'm happy with all of the finishing touches added in the past few days. The pearl ring Mark gave to me on my sixteenth birthday is polished and looks shiny and new. How could I have known, when he gave it to me then, that all my dreams about our wonderful life together would be so shattered, and that I would be giving the ring to our daughter the day of our meeting, thirty years after her birth. How does someone process that? The cream-colored satin ribbon I use to tie a bow on the leather ring box feels as soft as a baby's cheek.

The doorbell rings, startling me out of my thoughts. A florist's delivery truck is in the driveway and the driver is heading up the walk carrying a beautiful bouquet of flowers. They're from our good friends, Sue and Steve. Their card reads:

"Wishing you much love and happiness on this special day."

Such sweet friends! If they only knew how deeply that acknowledgment touches me, after so many years with no one understanding.

Thank God, Dan doesn't have to work late and is coming along with me tonight. I'll feel so much safer having him with me. I'd be a wreck going alone. He agrees that Susan and her family seem to be a very nice, normal family and not a bunch of wackos. He doesn't seem worried at all.

My biggest fear is that Susan will want to take up too much of my life, overwhelming my schedule and me. How am I going to handle holidays? My friends, who've shown much more interest than my family, have been such a great help with advice about wording my emails just right, so that I have been able to get to know them slowly before our meeting. If only my family knew how much I needed their support. The last thing I want is for my mom and brothers to feel jealous and insecure about their relationship with me. But, Mom was pretty curt when I asked her to go along with me tonight. Even with all my reassurance that she could never be replaced, she says she has no need to meet Susan. I just hope my mom knows how much I love her and appreciate her.

Fifteen minutes to go. Kris picks up Beth and takes her back to her place, so Joanne and I will feel less inhibited during our first couple of hours with each other. The girls will come over later. Although, for my part, I would do the same thing if the whole world were watching - take her into my arms once again and hold her close to my heart, then look into her beautiful green eyes to see the very soul I connected with thirty years ago.

"Jay, it's after seven and she still isn't here," I say, feeling panicky. The clock says seven-fifteen. "I bet the traffic from Boston is hell." I'm pacing the house, and Jay's watching golf. How can he be so calm?

"I'm calling Kris."

"Why are you calling her?" Jay wants to know, barely looking away from the television.

"I don't know, I just am." Has Joanne had second thoughts and changed her mind? No, she would have called. Were they in an accident? Oh, dear Lord, don't let that happen.

We are so late! Susan's waited this long, I guess a few more minutes shouldn't make a difference. Surely she understands Boston traffic and that we're doing our best.

My nervous ramblings to Dan must be driving him crazy. Have I worn the right outfit? Clothes make such an impression and getting dressed was such a debate. I hope my nails look good. Of course I had to give myself the best manicure and pedicure, knowing Susan is a professional manicurist. Lately, it's been so hard to focus on anything else other than tonight's meeting, and I've been spending hours sending emails back and forth with my two sisters and with Susan. Will they really look like me? What will it be like to be in the presence of people who look like me? How will they act? Never would I have dreamed I'd be doing this.

Susan is so anxious, she makes me nervous sometimes. I hope she doesn't expect too much of me, and I end up disappointing her. The closer we get to her house, the bigger my doubts get, and the greater my excitement.

"Kris, she's not here yet. Do you think everything's okay?"

"Mom, don't worry, she'll be there. Relax."

"Kristine, how can I relax at a time like this?" Why am I giving her a hard time?

This is country! We're not in New Bedford anymore, Toto. Her little town of Acushnet is cute, nice houses and some not so nice. Which will be hers, nice or not so nice? My stomach is doing flip-flops as we approach a huge, awesome red house with shutters and a circular driveway, perfectly manicured with stonewalls and ivy growing everywhere. Cute porch. Nice cars. Very inviting front door. Everything's beautiful. As I get out of the car and remember the two huge L. L. Bean bags filled to the brim with photo albums in the back, I'm embarrassed. I decide to leave them there for now; no one is going to want to look at all those pictures.

After pacing from one end of the house to the other, I call Kris back. It's already seven-thirty. Before I can say anything, Jay announces they've just pulled into the driveway.

"Kris, she's here. I have to go!"

After hanging up, I begin to rant, delirious. "What's an extra half-hour after waiting thirty years? She's finally here! She's late!"

"She's late? She's punished!" Jay yells, cracking me up. He looks at me and just shakes his head. He always knows how to calm me.

"Which door is she coming to?" I ask Jay, suddenly panic stricken and standing frozen in the middle of the house, not knowing which way to turn.

"She's coming up the front walk."

How can he be so calm?

With my heart pounding in my chest and very near tears, I take a deep breath and open the door.

Before she even has me in sight, she's crying, but with a huge smile on her face at the same time! I can't believe what she looks like. She looks like me! I can't believe what she's wearing - a favorite outfit of mine, a pink oxford shirt and khaki pants with loafers. I could have shown up in this very outfit tonight. Same gold hoop earrings as me too. She's preppy and adorable and has tears streaming down her face behind her glasses.

She's wearing black slacks, a short sleeve linen blouse and black sandals. Lovely. Lifting her head, Joanne sees me and a beautiful smile comes across her face - the same smile I have seen thousands of times before on the faces of Jackie, Kris and Beth. It seems the closer she approaches, the bigger her smile gets.

I welcome her back into my life as I wrap my arms around her. Holding her as close as possible, I can feel the beating of her heart. I put her at arm's length and look into those eyes I've so longed to see again. Touching her face, her skin feels velvety soft. "You are absolutely beautiful," I manage to tell her between sobs. Kissing her cheeks, I hold her close again.

We hug hard and long and she's crying. Should I feel badly for not crying? Actually, a tear or two are brimming. She has tissues everywhere, in her hands and in her pockets. She doesn't want to stop hugging or kissing me, and I find it so sweet. She's been waiting a long time for this moment, and I don't mind giving it to her. It's her moment.

The best part is she is hugging and kissing me right back. I can't get enough of her - the way she feels in my arms and the smell of her hair. My baby, my grown-up daughter has finally come home.

The sound of Jay's voice breaks the spell, though I really don't know what he's saying.

When I finally introduce Jay, Joanne thanks him for the beautiful flowers.

"Flowers? He sent you flowers, too?"

"Yes, this morning, to my office."

When the flowers arrived today, I realized that Susan has such a supportive and considerate husband. His card read:

"Hope this adds to today's excitement, memories and your smile.

Warmest Regards, Jay"

He's tall, dark and handsome and seems to be a very strong, yet laid back person. He calls me "sweetheart," and I like it.

To celebrate this miraculous reunion, Jay had sent flowers to Kristine at work and Beth and me here at home. But, Joanne, too! What a guy! Still, after nearly seventeen years of marriage, I never quite know what to expect from him. For months now, he has seemed distracted. Although lately, I've seen him slowly becoming excited by the prospect of this reunion. He has to be so relieved to see this day, since he did all the worrying that I couldn't do. Was I spending too much time on a project that would never come to fruition? What would the impact of finding her be on me? How would she treat me, if she accepted me at all? Would I blame myself if I found a drug addict/alcoholic, and where would that lead me, to more depression and guilt? What if she were ill? What if she had died? No wonder he's been distracted. But, he hung in there with me, nevertheless.

Joanne hugs Jay. Then, I hug Joanne, again. Laughing at our inability to stop hugging, Jay suggests we pull ourselves away from the front hall and go into the living room. Joanne and I continue to stare at each other, not quite able to believe we are actually meeting face to face. I give Joanne the dozen pink roses I got for my "Baby Girl." No one gave us roses when she was born. Her eyes are glistening with tears, as she reads my words on the card: "My dream has come true."

Such a huge bouquet of pink roses for me, her baby girl, fit for a prom queen. Fresh flowers are everywhere and a tissue box, which I'm beginning to need, is strategically placed. I didn't think I could ever pull myself away from the front hall. There's so much in her house to take in, and I don't want to appear rude, checking it out too much. We're just falling all over each other. She just keeps staring at me in the strangest way. Is she really listening to me? Am I babbling and sounding stupid? I'm losing her attention and my babbling is just getting worse.

She's talking about the traffic and how they had no trouble finding the house and, all the while, I'm permanently etching in my mind what she looks like, in the off chance that this will be our only meeting. She seems to be doing very well, hardly crying at all. Touching her hands, I begin crying all over again. I'm crying enough for both of us.

Finally, I hand her the small leather jewelry box. Slowly untying the satin bow, she opens the box and sighs. With care that shows me she feels the significance, she slips the ring delicately onto her finger and marvels that I saved it for her.

"It's the only thing I had left after you were born that proved the love Mark and I had for one another. For thirteen years I wore it, until Jay bought me this onyx ring." I see that Joanne wears an onyx ring, too. Amazing.

All I can think of is the ring my boyfriend gave me when I was sixteen. It's almost impossible to imagine what it would have been like to be pregnant back then. It's impossible to imagine how she must have felt giving birth to me at that age. I appreciate what this ring means to both of us. It is strange that a big pearl ring is something I've wanted since high school. My friend Vicki had one, but I never got one. Now I know that's because one was waiting for me all these years.

From the excitement in her eyes, as she notices the rest of the presents on the table, I can tell Joanne's eager to see what else is in store for her. She's definitely enjoying herself. So I tell her the story of my Sunflower pendant, the one I've been wearing since beginning my search. The Sunflower pin is a symbol of the unity of the group, which has eight

131

hundred members. My brother Russ had it engraved for me with Joanne's original initials, MJM, along with the date of her birth, 9/17/68.

As I take the pendant from around my neck, I tell her how wearing it, in some strange way, always made me feel close to her. As I put it around her neck and fasten the clasp, she places her hand over the Sunflower, as if to hold it near to her heart. Clearly, she is flattered by the notion, that I have thought so much about her over the years. My tears begin again, and she hugs me. Even though not a word is exchanged, we sense what the other is feeling. It's incredibly healing to reestablish our connection that was so traumatically broken long ago.

I'm feeling a little embarrassed that she is showering me with all these gifts, but I can see the true joy this is giving her. After all, this is my birthday - my birthday for Susan. My original initials on the Sunflower pin have more meaning to Susan than to me. I don't really like the name Madlyn Jeanne. Maybe I would have liked being called Mady. Regardless, this is how she has referred to me for thirty years, so I will wear her necklace proudly and remember her dedicated search for me, which she endured with all the other Sunflower women.

Next, I hand her the photo album, and she excitedly removes its matching satin ribbon. She just stares at the first page, which has Mark's and my high school class pictures, along with a brief explanation of the photos. As I watch her closely for her reaction when she first sees an image of her father, I can't glean much from her expression. God, I wish I knew what she is thinking. She offers no comment and I don't push. I do mention the resemblance to him in her wedding picture, and she is quick to agree. I think she's stunned by their likeness.

Since receiving the first picture of Kris and me, she's been convinced she looks exactly like us. Now, seeing this picture of Mark, I think she's amazed by how much she looks like him, too. Actually, she's is a beautiful combination of both of us. A certain way she turns her head, or when she grins and the tiny lines at the corner of her mouth appear, is when I see him in her so clearly.

But, it's when she looks into my eyes that I see what he and I missed, and what we could've had if only he had been willing to give us the chance. Amazing how, after all I've been through, the thought of him still makes me smile. I guess he will always be a part of my heart, no matter what, because of my love for Joanne.

I try to see the resemblance to Mark she is talking about. I can only faintly note it. Perhaps if there were more photos to compare. Oh well, she seems to find comfort in seeing it, so I leave it that way. Her face lights up when she talks about him, and she has a special tone of voice as she tells me how much in love she was with him, describing him as the love of her life. I feel uncomfortable that she is saying all this about Mark with Jay in the same room. I'm not as interested in Mark as she probably thinks I am. If anything, I'm feeling resentment towards him for not marrying her. I just can't believe he let her go through everything alone all those years ago. I resent him for Susan, not for myself. Though she's saying she will help me find him, I'm not interested. Her family is big enough to keep me busy for a long time. I don't need his family inviting me to their events, too.

Telling her I was already six months pregnant with her when my class picture was taken, suddenly everything seems surreal. The sepia-toned picture is worn around the edges, from all the times I've pulled it out and stared at it, all the shame and embarrassment flooding back each time. We were to wear only white collared blouses for the picture, and I was much too pregnant to tuck my blouse in any longer. To make matters worse, my skirt couldn't be zipped up all the way. So much to hide for someone so young.

Looking at my class picture with Joanne, I am seeing it through different eyes. Now, all I see is the face of a scared, seventeen-year-old girl who bravely drove downtown, despite her swollen pregnant body, to have her class picture taken. I'm feeling her broken heart, shattered into a million pieces, because of what she was going through and what was still to come. More than anything, though, I'm remembering the tremendous love she had for the baby that was growing inside of her, a baby she unfortunately would never be able to claim as her own - until today. If I live to be a hundred, I will never be able to completely express how lucky I feel to have found her and to have her back in my arms again.

"Susan, your hat looks like a plant pot!" Joanne teases, as she stops at a picture of me in my 1964 Easter outfit. To think I had been so proud to be old enough to wear that silly hat! She has no trouble making fun of my various hairstyles and fashion statements from over the years. As she devours all the photos of my life and my family, I tell stories about each one. It's hard for her to believe there can be so many people who look like her. As much as she always believed she looks like her adoptive family, she really doesn't and can only now realize it.

I'm never going to remember all these people!

From out of the blue, I hear her say, "Susan, I can't believe how comfortable I feel. Its as though I belong here. I don't feel strange at all." There's no hesitation or reservation in her voice, as I lay my hand on hers.

Susan keeps touching me. Her hands look like mine, just a bit older. Everything about her is like me. I don't mind how she has to touch me all the time. I allow her to indulge, it's actually kind of nice, a comfortable warm feeling.

I want so much to say, "You do belong here," and maybe I will. I'm just so pleased she feels secure enough to admit it. In the past few weeks, I've come to know she doesn't say things she doesn't mean, another way I find she is like me.

Nearly two hours have passed, and I know Kristine and Beth are dying to get here, so I call and tell them to pick up the pizzas as planned.

Thank God the pizza is on its way. I'm starving and could eat a whole pizza myself. I feel guilty that I'm worrying about food instead of my sisters who are bringing it. They must have been going crazy waiting for that call, but Susan and I needed time alone first. Otherwise, we would have been a chorus all talking and blowing our noses at the same time.

They arrive through the family room. The kitchen is between us. When we hear the door open, Joanne and I stand and I turn to greet them. Joanne can't quite turn in their direction, as she summons the courage to meet her new sisters, face to face. Kris and Beth stop short, mid-kitchen, not knowing what to do, either. Now, there is complete silence. Finally, Joanne turns around to face them and they just stare at one another. The silence deepens. I'm frozen like them, and have no idea what to do.

Joanne makes the first move with a happy girlish giggle that breaks the spell, and they all rush into each other's arms, and hug and laugh and hug again. I'm crying, and can only imagine what it must be like for them.

In their group hug, I see three beautiful heads with identical shiny dark brown hair, three flawless complexions and three identical smiles. I hear three voices so youthful and giddy, I have to laugh. They are so much alike, same mannerisms, same speech patterns, same animation.

They're so carefree, so down to earth and comfortable. We have the same smile.

So much happy chaos is going on, that no one is even worried about the pizzas that have fallen off the kitchen counter and onto the barstool. While the girls talk and laugh, I get the plates and napkins and straighten the mess out. Only the men dig in, when I bring it out to the living room. We girls are much too excited to eat. But then, maybe they aren't having any because I'm not, so I grab a slice. Why am I eating this? They haven't even noticed, and I'm not the least bit hungry. "Smile!" Jay says, as he takes a picture, right while I have a mouthful of food.

Joanne jumps up and Kris and Beth are quick to follow her out to her car, to help bring in the canvas beach bag full of photo albums. Joanne insists we first look at her wedding pictures and then the video a friend had made for them as a wedding present. Such a great collection of photos of Joanne from her childhood through high school and college days. Though bittersweet to watch, I could see it all over again in a heartbeat.

I'm shamelessly proud to show off my family to all of them, and pleased they are indulging me. Susan is hurt that she missed out on my childhood and can never get it back. Seeing these photos is the closest she can get, and I want to show

134

her my happy childhood. Isn't that what she wanted for me? She should be happy. What she did turned out to be a good thing. I was a happy kid, everything was okay. I hope I'm not making her feel bad.

As we sit on the floor laughing and sharing stories, I find myself absorbed by the smiling faces and laughing eyes of my three daughters, thrilled that they are enjoying each other so much. Of my four girls, I see my first born is most like me. In Joanne, I can see the happy young girl I once was that I don't always see in Kristine and Bethany. The emptiness they carry from losing Jackie is a mirror of my emptiness losing two daughters. Joanne is the combination of all three of them: she's comical, with Jackie's wit: beautifully poised, well-spoken and gracious like Kristine; and, as animated, boisterous and uninhibited as Bethany. All four of them share one thing I lost over thirty years ago, a self-assuredness I could never get back.

As heartwarming as it is for me to see them together, Jackie isn't here, and I find myself missing her more than ever. What difference would her presence make tonight? Would she be married by now? Imagine, I would be cherishing and embracing two green-eyed beauties and two gorgeous brown-eyed girls. Sadly, it wasn't in God's plan, so I try my best to shake these thoughts and fight the tears that are welling up.

There Susan goes again, just zoning out watching us and randomly breaking down and crying. Everyone else is ignoring it, so I do too.

We take dozens of photos of all of us in every possible combination imaginable. I can't recall a time in the past thirty years when I have felt so alive, so at peace.

It's after one in the morning and it's a long drive back to Waltham. The evening has flown by. I never want it to end. Joanne and I manage to malinger a little longer, but it's time to call it a night. We pack up her pictures, cameras, flowers and presents and the guys start bringing it all out to the car. I hand her the updated medical information packet I had filled out months ago, being sure to give her everything. I want her to come back to me because she wants to, not because I have held anything back. I don't want her to leave. What if I never see her again?

I really don't want to leave, it's been such a pleasant night. Saying good night is difficult. Susan doesn't want to let go, and I know she fears never seeing me again, but there will be many more visits.

Joanne and I are last to leave the house. I'm quite comfortable putting my arm across her shoulders and squeezing her tight. We walk down the driveway in silence. Even though I haven't said a word, she senses my fear of losing her again, and with a loving smile says, "I will be back."

"Do you promise?" My joy is mixed with desperation.

"Yes," she reassures me, love in her eyes. With a last kiss, she climbs into the car, smiles and waves goodbye, as they drive away.

By the light of the nearby lamppost, I watch her car disappear. Looking up to heaven, I see a million stars in the sky, and thank the Good Lord. Jackie is the brightest star in the heavens tonight, and I thank her, positive she's had a great deal to do with getting my little girl back. If Jackie were ever angry with me for not telling her about Joanne, I know, in this very moment, she has forgiven me.

For the first time since I can remember, I go to bed without a worry on my mind. The hole in my heart I've lived with, since losing Joanne, has finally been filled, and a sublime peace washes over me. I sleep...

Chapter Twelve

The sun is brilliant again this morning. What a rush! How novel, waking up to only happy thoughts. My spirit has been renewed and, for the first time, my husband is seeing my genuine smile, the one God gave me. Last night he witnessed my metamorphosis back to the young girl, who thirty years before left her childhood innocence and smile at St. Mary's

While still relishing my first morning thoughts, the phone rings and interrupts my reverie. It's my brother, Russ, only the first of many calls to come. I'm eager to share my story of last night's miracle with anyone who is willing to listen. While on the phone, pacing from the kitchen to the breakfast room then out onto the deck, I'm practically yelling into the phone. I'm so wound up I can't help myself. Jay and Beth are sitting at the counter having breakfast, laughing at my antics.

As soon as the photo lab opens, I'm there. Waiting the hour for the pictures to be developed is pure torture. Jay scans a few of the pictures and I email them to Joanne. This way, she will have them first thing Monday morning. Hopefully, she won't mind that I took the liberty of sending them to her office.

As the calls pour in, I can tell my family can't wait to meet her. But I'm much too afraid to overwhelm Joanne so soon and risk the chance of having her pull away. She wants to take things slowly, and that's exactly what we'll do. I've followed her plan up until now, and it has worked out perfectly. She needs to first become accustomed to the fact that I'm real, that I'm here to stay and that I'll never leave her again. Even though our meeting went well last night, I'm still somewhat concerned that, once the novelty wears off, she might become disenchanted with me. This walking on eggshells isn't one of my strong suits. I'm an upfront and in-your-face kind of gal, so what lies ahead is going to be a challenge. I must remain cool, since I haven't come this far to blow it now.

The letter I am enclosing with the pictures is ecstatic:

> Dear Joanne,
>
> Oh, what a reunion it was! It was the single, most important night of my life. It was everything I ever dreamed it would be. To experience so much joy from an event that, so long ago, tore my life and heart apart is beyond comprehension. My life is now complete. I know where all of my girls are… Joanne, I have loved

you from the moment I knew I was pregnant with you. That love never waned, but when I saw you Friday night and held you in my arms, I fell in love with you all over again...

Love, Susan

I can't help myself, I'm on Cloud Nine. Just writing her name and address on the envelope makes me happy.

When things finally calm down a bit, I email my Sunflower sisters to express my gratitude to them for being there for me every step of the way. They taught me how to love myself again and got me ready for the meeting of my life. If only each one of them could experience the same love and happiness in their reunion. That would be my greatest wish.

Joanne is on Cloud Nine, too. She loved getting the photos at work and is reliving the excitement all over again, as she tells everyone in her office about our reunion. The photo album was a big hit. She's been taking it with her everywhere. Her family saw it on Saturday, and she brought it to work. Everyone she shows it to is amazed at how much we all look alike. I think she's pleased to hear that. "The pictures scream a thousand words," she writes. "I have emailed your photos to all my friends... I had emails pouring in this morning asking me how everything went. They were really excited to be able to see photos so quickly and share in my excitement, and are thrilled to see three girls that look like me, as they have always known that has been something I've always been curious about."

On Saturday, spending time with her family, she says she felt especially loving and appreciative of them. "I think I was just keenly aware of my emotions and felt stirred by them (all positive, by the way). I just felt so happy. What are the odds that someone could be lucky enough to have two wonderful families?"

To let it sink in that she really had a wonderful time and likes my family, I read her email over and over. Now, I just have to wait for her to be ready to become part of my family, too. That might not be easy, because she already has an awesome family. She just needs some time to realize what I have always tried to teach my girls: there is always enough love to let new people into your heart.

On Wednesday, Joanne emails me to let me know the package of photos arrived, and that she found my letter very touching. She's worn my pearl ring every day.

Our messages back and forth are exuberant. Kristine's messages to Joanne are so similar to mine, it startles me. To have held every position a sister can hold in a family, without complaint, Kristine must be a very old soul. For the first eight years of her life, she was the youngest. Then, when Bethany was born, she became the middle child. After Jackie passed away, she took over as the oldest. Now, since finding Joanne, she appears to be happy to be back in the middle again. My experience of losing Joanne enhanced and intensified my love for my other girls, in ways I'll never know, and they are very secure. Sometimes, I wonder if losing Joanne is the reason I've been so successful in my role as a mother.

A huge question I've lived with since losing Joanne has been answered. Which is worse: adoption or death? Before finding and meeting Joanne, I thought adoption was worse. At least I knew where Jackie was - in heaven. Now, I know death is worse. I will never see Jackie again.

I've decided to write to Joanne's adoptive mother because there is so much I need to say to her. How do I begin to thank her for helping to relieve the biggest burden I've have ever had to carry? Writing the letter takes a couple of days.

> Dear Ann,
>
> I have thought about you for many years, and what I would say to you if I had the chance. Now, I find myself at a loss for words. How do I begin to tell you all the things I need to say? Finding Joanne was always a dream of mine, since that day I had to leave her at St. Margaret's. I prayed every day for her and for the new parents who would be lucky enough to take her home. I also prayed that this new home would be filled with joy and love.
>
> In 1989, just when I was about to search, Jackie was diagnosed with a life threatening illness on Labor Day. I just couldn't understand God's plan for me. I was emotionally unable to search for many years following her death. I needed to put my grief into proper perspective, to know I wasn't seeking out Joanne to replace Jackie. I knew I had accomplished that when I realized Joanne could never take Jackie's place, just as Jackie never replaced Joanne.
>
> I have been quite angry with God these past thirty years, first with losing Joanne to adoption and then Jackie to leukemia, and I have had difficulty seeing through the grief, at times. Now I must tell you, my grief has somewhat subsided and my anger has now been put to rest. And, I have you to thank for part of

that. As Joanne describes her life and family to me, my heart leaps with happiness. You gave her the life I could not have given her at age seventeen, the life I prayed she would have. God didn't forsake me after all. He gave Joanne to you, and I now thank Him everyday for that.

I hope I have been able to adequately express my feelings. What I am trying to say is this - thank you for taking such good care of my baby. She is an amazing young woman. I may have made her beautiful on the outside, but you and your husband loved and nurtured her to be beautiful on the inside, as well. I honor both you and your family. Hopefully, we will meet someday. After all, we have a very special common bond - we both love Joanne.

Fondly, Susan Souza

Ann needs to know it has never been, nor will it ever be, my intention to take Joanne away from her. Knowing all too well what it is like to lose a child, I could never inflict that pain upon another, never mind the very woman who saved my baby's life. Also, I don't want her to think I searched for Joanne because I lost Jackie.

Satisfied with my letter, I need to get the okay from Joanne before I mail it. So, I attach the letter to an email, asking her blessings to send it.

There's been no response all day, and I just know I've blown it - pushing too far and too fast. What the hell was I thinking to even consider writing to her mother? I'm probably the last person she wants to hear from.

The next morning, I get Joanne's okay. "My mom should view it as a tribute to her. I do know it will make her cry, but that's ok."

I was worried for nothing. I need to relax and stop walking on these damned eggshells.

Plans are being made for a day at the beach, just Joanne and I alone together. Since both of us were so nervous the night of our reunion, we kept the conversation light and cheery. Now, we agree we need to spend some quiet time to learn more about one another and share our thoughts and emotions.

Madeline offered her cabin in Little Compton. Joanne is all for it and wants to have me pick her up at her cottage, so she can show it off and I can meet her sister-in-law. Then we will drive to Little Compton together. She's letting me into a corner of her life, and she's excited about seeing me again. I'm psyched.

During the course of solidifying our plans, I learn her mom could barely get the words out to tell her that she had read my letter. According to Joanne, Ann thought the letter was very nice and got really choked up. I feel as if it's not even necessary that she reply. It's enough to know I said my peace, and it was well received.

The day is overcast, but if Joanne is the beach bum she claims to be, the clouds won't scare her away. Besides, we can spend the day in the cabin. I've packed a picnic lunch of fresh lobster meat sandwiches, pasta salad, cheeses, fruit and crackers, and picked up some fresh baked apple turnovers from the bakery. It's the first meal I've ever prepared for my daughter. I'm bringing a "Friends of Jackie" sweatshirt, T-shirt and hat for Joanne, so she can feel like an official Friend of Jackie.

It's no trouble finding her cottage, and I arrive on time. Her driveway is full, so I park across the street. By the time I get out of my car, she's already bounding down the walkway to greet me. Once again, there is that smile I love so much and my heart is so happy to see her again. She has this spirit about her, an effervescence. It's easy to see she carries no burden. If only this could have been true for me at her age. I must have done the right thing giving her up. Instead of inheriting problems, she's had the opportunity to have this remarkable life. Of course, I'm assuming I would have been unhappy if I'd kept her, and that's probably not true.

Inside, Dan is sitting at the kitchen table busy at his laptop. His sister, who is his spitting image, is getting ready for a morning run. The cottage is quaint and lovely and meticulously kept, painted sparkling white inside and out. They've done it all themselves, right down to Joanne's sewing of the curtains. The shutters on the windows are painted a rich dark green. The rooms, though small, are bright and cheery with sunlight streaming in through the windows. I can easily imagine the parties, as well as the quiet evenings they must spend on the screened-in porch all trimmed with mini lights. Their view of the water is spectacular. No wonder they love to spend all their free time here. My tour is finished, when she shows me the new seedlings she has so carefully planted around the cottage.

At first, as we set out for Mady's cabin, I'm at a loss for words. I'm so in awe of the fact that she's actually sitting right here beside me chatting away like we have been friends forever. It's amazing how easily we find things to talk about. At times, I must ask her to repeat what she has just said because my brain goes haywire every time I look at her. We manage to follow the crazy directions drawn on a white paper plate by Mady's husband last weekend.

By the time we get to the cabin, we're starved. As I'm puttering around the kitchen getting lunch ready, we talk and laugh about all kinds of things.

Suddenly, Joanne gets up from the couch, with tears in her eyes, and comes over to give me a hug.

"What's wrong?" I ask, frightened. "Why are you crying?"

"You stand like a duck!" she exclaims, half crying and half laughing.

"What do you mean I stand like a duck?" I ask, looking down at my feet perplexed.

"I've always wondered why I stand like a duck," she goes on to say. "Now, I understand. It's because you stand like a duck, with your feet pointing out. I stand just like you - like a duck!"

Never would I have ever thought I'd consider a comment like that to be such a compliment! After thirty years, it must be wonderful for her to finally see why she is the way she is. I wish with all of my heart I could have given this to her much sooner. But, I refuse to dwell on the past. I must live for moments like this one and all of those to come.

She loves the lobster, but spits out all of the celery pieces I so carefully chopped by hand! "I hate eating the crunchy things," she says, as she makes a funny face, cracking me up.

After lunch, we make our way down to the beach. The tide is up, so there isn't a lot of sand, but we manage nicely. We get ourselves comfortable and simply sit and look at one another for a moment or two, each of us lost in our own thoughts. It's our first moment of silence. I'm sure to everyone else here on the beach today we look like any two friends. Or, just maybe, we look like any other mother and daughter enjoying a day in the sun together. How could anyone possibly guess the significance?

Quickly, I find out my daughter does not beat around the bush. The first thing she asks about is my relationship with Mark and the whole story of why we decided to give her up for adoption. How can I look her in the eyes and tell her? At first, I stumble over how to begin, but she's so easy to talk to that the story begins falling nicely into place. Tears stream down my face as the words spill out, and I wonder how tears and words can feel so healing? So much shame and sorrow is being released. I tell her about our courtship and all the fun that we shared, about going to the obstetrician by myself and being afraid to go home afterwards, fearing my father would hunt Mark down and shoot him. I brace myself before telling her about his drug use and how it affected our lives.

Describing my days at St. Mary's, my delivery and the days she and I shared in the hospital gets my tears going all over again. When I come to the part about leaving her behind, I fall apart and the compassion she feels is so evident. She is making this very easy for me. She not only understands, but also realizes how much I loved her then and how much I still love her now. I answer every question she poses and tell her some things she didn't even think to ask.

But, how do I justify not following through on the promise I made to find her when she turned twenty-one, a promise I made with every fiber of my being at the time? Is it possible to vindicate myself without sounding self-involved? What can I say that won't sound inadequate and lame? Illness and death - does that constitute a good enough reason? How can I rationalize placing one child's well being over another's? There just isn't an easy answer.

"I was so scared," is all I can say. "I was scared of what was to come with Jackie's illness, and didn't have the strength to face both situations at the same time. I'm sorry."

From the way she looks at me, I know she feels there is no need to explain and goes on to tell me how her reality was so different from mine. She turned twenty-one during her one semester at the University of California, Chico. She went to California with high hopes of seeing the great sunshine state, making new friends, having a lot of fun, becoming more independent and growing as a person.

"I realized all of these goals that semester," she tells me, as I marvel at the huge disparity in our realities. "There was no way I would have ever guessed, when I boarded the plane at Logan Airport on August 21, 1989, that you had ever contemplated searching for me, much less had a countdown, waiting for me to reach a certain age to begin one. It was actually the furthest thing from my mind." Then she laughingly admits, "That birthday, all I cared about was getting into bars and drinking legally. To be honest, I don't think I would have been very receptive, and there probably wouldn't have been a happy reunion story to tell. I was an immature, distracted, self-absorbed college co-ed in search of a good time, and a reunion wouldn't have fit well into my plans. And, here you were going through your second nightmare of a lifetime."

As hard as it is to hear, I so appreciate her honesty, though I'm feeling relieved and hurt at the same time. I long to touch her and hold her again, but I know I shouldn't, at least not here on the beach. Why am I so hesitant? I have been a mother for most of my life and showing affection to my girls always comes so naturally. Why am I at a loss when it comes to my behavior with Joanne? My heart sinks when I realize I know the answer - I am a total stranger to my own daughter, this young woman whom I have loved, thought about and prayed for every day of her life.

Trying to lighten the conversation by talking about my parents and brothers, I mention tomorrow is my parent's fiftieth wedding anniversary, and we're going to have a small dinner party for them tomorrow evening. "No big blow out, just my brothers and our families," I tell her.

Joanne gets this impish look in her eye. "You mean tomorrow - Monday?" she asks.

"Yes, after everyone gets out of work."

"Do you think it would be all right if I came to the party?" she asks, as she raises her hand to her lips, almost as though she's not quite sure whether she should have expressed such a desire, or if she's really ready.

"Do I think it would be all right?" I ask incredulously. "Of course, it will be all right!"

"I think I'd like to go and meet everyone," she says, with a look of both anticipation and apprehension.

"My parents will be so excited. What a present you'll be giving them." My heart is pounding with excitement.

"Okay, I'll try to make it. Don't tell anyone," she warns, with childlike mischief in her eyes. "I'd like it to be a surprise."

"Oh, my God, I'm going to see you again tomorrow!" How will I ever keep this secret without exploding? Everyone is going to freak out! I'm sworn not to tell even Jay or her sisters. "No problem, I promise." I'd promise her anything, at this point.

We pour over the names of everyone in the family because she wants to be sure she remembers who everyone is. She's looking forward to meeting my brothers, but I think she's nervous when it comes to meeting my parents. To make matters worse, she has to come alone because Dan is working.

It's getting chilly, so we gather our belongings and go back to the cabin. It's also getting late, and she still has to drive back to Waltham. We talk a little more and take a few pictures. As much as we hate to admit it, it's time to go. We pack up our stuff, Joanne makes an entry in Mady's guest book and we are on our way.

The ride back to the cottage seems so much shorter. When we arrive, she invites me in for a drink and I stay for a bit. When it's time to finally leave, knowing I'll be seeing her again tomorrow makes leaving easier. She walks me to my car and gives me a hug. I gladly hug her back.

While driving away from her cottage, I catch my reflection in the rear view mirror. My hair is frizzy and wind blown, and there's a gritty mixture of sand and suntan lotion on my face. There's also a glow shining through my grimy face, as I recall the wondrous day I just spent with my oldest daughter.

I am glad to hear that Susan and Mark were sweethearts, although, it was not a concern of mine that I may have been a product of rape or abuse. I never even thought of that. I was content believing the few details given about my adoption. It was a good enough story for me, certainly an understandable one, one that many girls can relate to. Thinking my birth parents were in high school was probably the best reason, in my judgment, for them to have chosen adoption. Two teenagers, accepting the fact that the responsibility of marriage and a family is overwhelming and impractical at their age, makes adoption a very respectable choice in my mind. I was never embarrassed to share with others that reason for being adopted. Adoption is an admirable choice and, in some way, it made me proud to say I came from parents who were responsible enough, and they had parents who were responsible enough, to choose adoption.

Now that I think about it, I wouldn't have wanted to think there was any other reason. If I did happen to learn anything other than what turned out to be the truth, I probably would have kept it to myself. I know for a fact I would have kept any other less respectable circumstance of my birth a secret. I know that, because Susan has since told me about Mark and his drug use, and I have kept that a secret.

When the story was completely anonymous, I never had any negative feelings about it. Now that I know Susan and her story, I am angry with my birth father for abandoning her as a pregnant teenager. She wasn't even worried about being pregnant at first, because she figured they would get married and live happily ever after. But he refused to marry her and quit school. I'm not mad that he abandoned me. I don't feel abandoned, but Susan must have. How could he do that to her? When I imagine what kind of life Susan and I would have had if he had married her and brought me up as his daughter, I don't see such a pretty picture. If he were getting into trouble, then it would have been Susan and me who would have lost out. We might have had a terrible life because of him. So again, I'm feeling lucky. We both have had wonderful lives.

I was able to keep Joanne's secret all last night. But now, doing Mom's nails, it's nearly impossible to look her in the eye without blurting out that her first granddaughter will be coming to her party tonight. While Mom is still at my table, the phone rings. It's Joanne saying that she's definitely coming. Surprised to hear from her this early, I'm caught off guard. Hedging around the conversation, trying not to spill the beans, I nonchalantly try to get the message across that my mother is sitting right here. I must sound nuts to both of them.

As I settle back down to finish Mom's manicure, I find myself worrying about how she will react to seeing her granddaughter. I always worry about my parents' feelings before worrying about my own, burying any negative feelings I might have. For example, after giving up Madlyn, it seemed my parents thought that as long as I had new clothes and kept busy, I would be healed. So, I wore my new clothes and tried to be a party girl. Years later, on the day Brian moved out, I went upstairs to their apartment and told them he'd left. Thinking he was on an outing, they asked where he went and then were shocked when I told them we were separating. Am I that good an actress that they didn't even have a clue, practically living in the same house? When, as a single parent, I was broke and had no money to pay my utility bill, I wouldn't go to them for help, because they might think "all wasn't well." My gas and electric were shut off, instead.

I had been searching for Joanne a full fifteen months before I told my parents, because I never had shared with them that I planned to find her. For all these years, I lied by telling them I would never barge into her life. I thought they would think I was foolish to search, and I worried I would disappoint them in the sense that sending me away had been in vain, if I were just going to seek her out in the end. More importantly, I didn't want to embarrass them by what they had done, if they ever had to meet her face to face, thinking they would feel guilty and ashamed. If they did feel guilt, they never showed it.

I have to learn how to speak up and be angry again. Maybe, if I had been allowed to be angry, when I was being asked to give up my baby daughter to please everyone else, I might have been able to find a way to keep her.

Joanne isn't coming until seven and, as luck will have it, everyone is arriving early. I stall dinner as best I can. Thankfully, Jay isn't home yet. So, I'm using that as one of my delay tactics. My biggest problem is Dad, because when he's hungry we have to eat, and we have to eat now! I have Kris break out the cheese and crackers, chips and dip and send everyone outside to the deck with drinks, hoping that will keep them satisfied for a while.

In the meantime, my sister-in-law, Wendy, is in the kitchen washing a few things, and I'm slowly setting the table and dying to tell my secret. I try to get her to go out with the rest of the gang, so I don't blurt it out, but she refuses to leave me with all the work.

Jay calls to say he's only minutes away. The one time I want him to be late he gets home on time. Beth calls to say she's still at the UMass library and wants to stay longer. I panic and tell her, "No, you have to come home now!" The phone rings again, and it's Joanne. She's right on schedule and will be here in twenty minutes. So, Jay will be here when the surprise arrives, but Beth may not make it.

Realizing an ally could come in handy, I confide to Wendy that Joanne is on her way to celebrate with us. As her jaw drops and her eyes fill with tears, I quickly tell her it's a secret and she needs to help me keep everyone outside.

Before long, Jay arrives and, of course, is hungry. Giving him a hunk of cheese and a beer, I put him to work in the kitchen. My sister-in-law,

Denise, comes in looking to refill her drink. "When will Beth be home?" she casually asks.

"She's on her way." No sooner are those words out of my mouth, when a car pulls into the driveway. Denise assumes its Beth and walks to the family room door to greet her. I can see out the dining room window it's Joanne and say nothing, still not believing I've remained so calm. Denise gets to the door, just as Joanne is reaching the porch. Upon seeing her, Denise puts her hands up to her face, her already big brown eyes now huge as saucers. As she opens the screen door, she exclaims, "Oh, my God, I can't believe you're here!"

Hugging Denise, Joanne asks her, "How did you know it was me?"

"How did I know? We've been looking at your pictures for months. How did you know it was me?"

"Same here," Joanne admits.

Jay comes out of the kitchen, looks at me stunned and asks, "Joanne's here? Did you know she was coming?"

Puzzled, Kristine just grins at her sister who just mysteriously appeared.

Hearing all the commotion, Russ comes in from the deck and is totally in shock upon seeing Joanne. All he can manage is, "I'm Russ," as he gives her a big hug, tears in his eyes.

"I know who you are," Joanne says simply.

Tom is right behind Russell and swoops Joanne up in the air. It's quite a sight. Tom is six feet, three inches tall and weighs about two hundred twenty-five pounds, and Joanne a mere five feet, five inches tall and maybe one hundred twenty-five pounds. Through his mustache full of tears, he proclaims, "Hi, I'm Tom!"

Of course, she knows that, too. Wendy is next with the hugs and tears. Now, everyone is crying. Russ goes upstairs to tell the younger girls and the stampede begins, as the four noisily descend the stairs. Sarah trips and falls. Livie doesn't miss a beat, as she steps right over her cousin and says, "Move, get out of my way!" There is such urgency about them, as they rush in. Then, they stop short and just stare at Joanne. They can't believe she's actually here, either. They have been asking about and dying to meet their new cousin, ever since I told them about her months ago. Everybody is joyfully talking and crying and laughing.

When I introduce Joanne to the girls, they love the fact she knows each of them by name. She makes each one feel so special, and they all immediately fall in love.

Someone asks, "Where's Mom and Dad?"

I turn and see my parents silently standing in the family room doorway, staring at this scene in sheer disbelief. Mom grabs Dad by the shirtsleeve, never once taking her eyes off of Joanne. "Eddie, it's her - Joanne - she's here."

My father takes giant steps towards Joanne and takes her in his arms and cries, "My number one granddaughter!" My parents only have granddaughters, eight of them.

The rest of the girls quickly take offense and say, "Hey, how did she get to be number one so fast?"

Dad apologizes and explains that he only meant Joanne is his first-born granddaughter. That's okay, they can accept that.

My mother patiently waits her turn to greet Joanne. I can't even imagine what she must be feeling at this moment. Seeing all of us gathered around this beautiful young woman, her eldest granddaughter, has to be an incredible sight for her. I wonder how difficult it has been for Mom to live with the decision she and Dad made so long ago. Now, Mom is crying so hard that she can hardly speak. Amidst hugs and kisses, she tells Joanne how beautiful she is and how much she looks like me. I especially like that comment!

Finally, Jay, Kristine and I get our own hugs in, and I explain to them how important it was that I kept Joanne's secret, that she has to know she can trust me, just as they do.

We're all still standing at the door, and I'm afraid Joanne might suddenly be feeling completely overwhelmed by her new family. We have a way of doing that to people, all of us being very passionate where family is concerned. However, she seems to be holding her own and keeping up her side of all the conversations going on around her. I move everyone into the kitchen and make her a drink. Poor kid, she must need one after that ambush.

Finally Bethany arrives, at first not noticing our exalted guest as she puts her book bag down. When she discovers Joanne, she's as shocked and pleased as the rest.

Before Joanne got here, everyone was "starving to death," and now no one seems to care if we eat or not. Over the delicious clam boil, there's lots of laughter and conversation. Tom is always a big tease and believes he's a born comedian, although he's met his match. Joanne keeps right up with him, never missing a beat. Everyone is vying for her attention, and she seems to be loving every minute of it. It's as though she has been part of us for a lifetime, she so easily fits right in.

After dinner, the girls all want their pictures taken with Joanne, as if she were a big celebrity, and Dad gets his camera.

My parents get a few moments alone with Joanne, and Mom shows her their part of the house. When building this house, we made an apartment for them in place of a garage. We still joke and say they live in the garage.

At some point in the evening, Joanne has decided to call them Grandma and Grandpa. Although I say nothing, I'm feeling resentment build towards my parents. Here I am, her mother, the only one who wanted to keep her and I'm called Susan; whereas, they are given the honor of being Grandma and Grandpa, and it was their decision to give her away! It just doesn't seem fair.

Nevertheless, before she leaves, I thank Joanne for her generous gift of a lifetime to my parents for calling them her grandparents. Part of me, just not all of me, is happy for them. I can tell how excited she is by the whole evening, and her emails confirm it the next day. In one email, she expresses surprise that my nieces would love her instantly.

"They know how much I love you and how long it took me to find you. It's pure and simple, you are now a part of them. They are your new extended family and, whether you see them often or not, they will still love you," I write to assure her.

"You have such a loving family and the girls tell it all," Joanne writes back. "Love goes a long way and with love you love. It makes perfect sense. How lucky I am to have a new family of girls!"

"With love you love." And, she's wise, too!

When she gets the pictures, she writes and tells me that she can't stop looking at them. "It's so funny to look at pictures of your family with me in them, cuz I've been looking at photos of them so much without knowing them. Now to see my face in the photos with them, it's almost surreal. I'm still flying high!"

With the family reunion coming up, Aunt Mary has been busy doing genealogical research for our family tree and calls to ask if she can include Joanne. Of course, I'm delighted. When she asks for Mark's last name, I start thinking better about all this. Joanne might resent my taking such liberties.

Joanne responds that she wouldn't feel bothered in any way. So, why is this so unsettling for me? Digging a little deeper into myself, I realize I'm seething with resentment towards Mark and feeling he doesn't deserve to be named as her father. He has no claim to her. I alone paid the price. I alone endured the pain, the humiliation and the heartbreak of surrendering her and missing her everyday. Besides, I feel very protective of Joanne. What if he took advantage of her, if he's still in a bad way and on drugs? He could ask her for money or help. As much as I would love a fairy tale, happily-ever-after meeting, it's just not in the cards. Besides, Joanne has no desire to meet him or his family, as much as I'd actually like her to meet his mother. I can't have his name be included.

I'll tell Aunt Mary the truth, that Joanne is mine and only mine. As much as I want to believe that, it's not true and Joanne deserves to have her father listed. She isn't the product of some anonymous encounter. I loved Mark and he loved me. So, even if it kills me, his name must be included for Joanne. After enduring the ultimate sacrifice the day I gave her away, what's one more?

Somehow, through my sobs and tears, I tell Aunt Mary she can list Mark's name. Even though she understands my unwillingness, she also knows it's the right thing to do. She calms me by helping me to remember that all of my pain is in the past, and now it's the time to celebrate Joanne and make new and happy memories.

With all of this conversation about mothers and fathers and family trees, Joanne and I talk a little more about Mark, our relationship and what our lives would have been like had we married and kept her. As usual, Joanne is very practical in her response. "You're right, maybe Mark's life could have been better had he married you and been my dad, then again, it might not have. His life could have been better or our life could have been worse. In my opinion, the odds seemed to have been against us, and I do feel lucky things turned out the way they did for us. We both have had great lives with no regrets," she tells me.

Asking her forgiveness for not giving her the father she deserved, it came to me to tell her that God took care of that by giving her a loving father, Joe Medeiros.

"It makes me proud that you realize just how lucky I was to have Joe Medeiros for my father," Joanne says seriously. "I'm relived that you know what a great and caring father he was to my brothers and me. I was so afraid you would not understand, and, of course, you would never know him, so I only hoped you had a true impression of my dad, and now I know you do."

It's amazing that Joanne thinks I have no regrets. I have more regrets than I know what to do with. She views my life in a totally different light when, in fact, it's been difficult to the point of exhaustion. Needless to say, the secrets and lies of adoption have transformed me into a marvelous actress, able to portray myself in any light. Even my own daughter believes me. How sad is that? Who am I, really? I don't even know, but I'm sure as hell going to find out. The time has come to search for the real Susan Mary Mello.

Chapter Thirteen

It's Labor Day weekend and summer is sadly almost over. Our days at the beach are sorely numbered, so Jay and I pack the car and head for Horseneck Beach. The parking lot is jam-packed, and we drive around and around, trying to find the closest space available. It's a long trek over the sand dunes to the beach, especially carrying all the paraphernalia needed for a successful day in the sun. Finally, we get settled in just the right spot on the sand and angle our chairs in perfect alignment with the sun. Jay mixes his usual concoction of sun tanning lotions to achieve his desired glow, then tunes into our favorite radio station. We're set.

Still enthralled with my reunion, I chat away to Jay about it, probably repeating myself several times. Jay just smiles and listens to me going on and on. Finally hearing enough, he suggests we take a walk down the beach. Thinking we might find his brother, Dave, and his family there, we head for Baker's Beach.

After walking along the shoreline a little while, I feel drawn to look up towards the bathing houses and immediately spot Joanne. "Jay, there's Joanne!" I yell over the sound of the pounding surf.

"Where?" he asks, looking around.

"Right there, sitting next to her sister-in-law."

"I don't see her."

Now, I'm frustrated with him. "For crying out loud, Jay, she's right there, in the blue two-piece bathing suit," I say, as if she's the only one on the beach. "Her mother is with her, too, if I remember correctly from the pictures."

"How the hell did you find her in this crowd?"

"A mother's radar?" I joke.

At first, Joanne doesn't notice me, so I take a few steps towards her and wave. Still, she doesn't see me. I take a few more steps closer and bingo she spots me, gets up off of her beach chair and runs towards me. She gives me a big hug and asks us to come up and meet her mom.

As her mother watches us approach, she remains seated until she realizes who I am. Thrilled to be meeting this woman who raised my daughter, I find myself just staring at her, wanting to say so much but not able to utter a sound. She's wearing shorts and a sleeveless shell. I can't see her eyes because of her sunglasses. Her smile is warm and friendly. Joanne is doing all of the talking and taking care of the introductions, while Ann and I just stand there, a little stunned.

"I'm so happy to meet you," I finally say to Ann. A flood of talking is now unleashed, as we try to catch up on thirty years worth of conversation in this first meeting. We speak about everything, from my relationship with Mark to the very first day she knew she was going to be Joanne's adoptive mother.

In order to prepare to adopt a baby that was to be born at the end of September, Catholic Charities suggested she quit her job with the phone company that April, and she didn't hesitate. "I'll never forget the day I received the call to come get Joanne," Ann said. "It was on a Monday, October 7th. I was ironing when I heard the phone ringing. The social worker was calling with the news that I could pick up our baby girl on Wednesday, at St. Mary's Orphanage in New Bedford."

Her words hit me hard, not only because their new baby girl was my precious daughter, but also because it had been just a week since I signed the final relinquishment papers. Was my baby there that day I signed? It's so horrible to realize how I didn't have a clue where my own baby daughter was. I shake these thoughts from my head and try very hard to refocus on what else Ann is saying.

"We didn't even want to wait one more day, never mind two," she's saying. "We wanted to go and get our new baby girl right then and there."

"Waiting those two days must have been as frustrating as waiting all those months," I tell her. What if she had to wait thirty years?

Comparing what we were told about the adoption, we realize not much adds up. We were both given different stories, but none of that matters now. All that's important is she loves my daughter and provided her a loving home and family.

Before long, we find ourselves crying and hugging. What must people be thinking of us becoming so emotional on such a beautiful day at the beach?

Joanne joins in on our tears, as she puts her arms around both of us and says, "My two mothers."

Music to my ears!

This is a little too much for Jay, and he finds Dan down at the water. After a while, sensing the emotional tide has gone back out again, the two of them come up the beach to join us. A friend of Dan's approaches our little circle, and Joanne introduces us to him. "Scott, I'd like you to meet my birth mother, Susan, and her husband, Jay."

Holy cow! She introduced me as her birth mother.

Scott looks confused. "Nice to meet you," he says, probably not knowing what a "birth mother" could possibly be.

They're all chatting away. I'm much too overwhelmed to really absorb anything that is being said, hardly believing I'm actually standing here talking to Joanne and her mother.

Finally, not wanting to over stay my welcome, we say our good-byes and head back to our end of the beach, forgetting all about our original mission to find Jay's brother. Jay wants to know every single word that was spoken while he was down at the water, and I'm all too happy to oblige.

It's the following day, and Jay and I are packing up for another day at Horseneck, when Kris and Beth ask if they can tag along. Since I didn't know if Joanne would be at nearby Baker's again, Beth phones her to see. Joanne tells her she will be there with her family and friends again.

When we get settled in our spot, Kris and Beth ask me to go with them to Baker's to visit Joanne. For some reason, I feel it's not a good idea for me to go along and tell them to go ahead without me. They make me promise to walk down to meet them in an hour or so for the walk back along the quarter mile stretch between Baker's and Horseneck.

As much as I enjoy walking along that stretch, I feel hesitant. My gut is telling me not to intrude. Jay convinces me I'm being foolish thinking that way, and that we need to meet Kris and Beth as promised. Against my better judgment, I go.

When we meet up with the girls, they are still with Joanne, and I can easily see that Joanne isn't as pleased to see me today as she was yesterday. Our conversation seems forced and so does her smile. This time, her adoptive mom or brothers don't get up from their chairs, they just stare and wave. Walking away after saying our goodbyes, I feel like a "cheap, bad girl" all over again, like I had no business being with her acceptable family and friends.

Kris and Beth are disappointed, too. Even their reception wasn't as warm as anticipated. Just as I thought, we were considered an intrusion. It had been okay to meet by chance, but on purpose? If the girls weren't here with me, I'd be crying. Instead, holding back my tears, I try to explain away what just happened, to make them feel better and put up a good front.

After a few days, I am able to discuss what happened with Joanne, and learn that she did feel pressured and uncomfortable with us being there along with her family and friends. It's just too soon. Much to Joanne's relief, I have offered not to return to Baker's. Even given our honesty and obvious love for each other, we still are walking through an emotional mine field with our reunion.

For Joanne's upcoming birthday, the first we will celebrate together, I ask if she would like a big family party or just a small one with Jay, her sisters and me. She wants to spend this birthday alone, just the two of us, which really delights me. With her wedding anniversary the day after her birthday, she and Dan are going away for that weekend, so we make plans for the Wednesday after.

Our plan was to meet at 6:00 P.M. at the Hilltop Restaurant in Braintree, the halfway point between our two homes. Having never gone there before, I leave early enough to allow time to get lost. However, her directions are exact and waiting these fifteen extra minutes in the parking lot seems interminable. I'm longing to see her again. Without noticing, she passes my car as she pulls into the lot, and I proceed to follow and park right beside her.

"Perfect timing," she says, as I get out of my car.

Not wanting to admit I had been waiting, I answer, "Yes, imagine that." Her hair is pulled up and her face is tanned and glowing. She looks so beautiful, and I'm feeling so proud to be with her.

The hostess seats us in a quiet booth for two. Just the thought of her wanting to share this birthday dinner with me is amazing. When she thanks me for the single long stemmed pink rose I sent to her office today, with a card that read "My dream continues," she lets me know she understands its meaning. She knows the magnitude of this occasion for me, and I can only hope it means something to her, as well.

My brother, Russ, made her the same gold ID bracelet that Kris and Beth wear - the same one I have been wearing for ten years that belonged to Jackie, a simple Figaro design with a narrow gold faceplate engraved with her initials, MJMJMMH. On the inside is engraved our reunion date, 5-21-99, and "Love, Susan." Not able to wait a moment longer, I give it to her before dinner. "Happy Birthday, sweetheart," I barely croak the words, they're so loaded with meaning after thirty years without her. "Joanne, you can't imagine what this means to me."

The loving kindness of her demeanor erases all of my pain and heartache. The light I have been searching for is right here, sitting across from me, in her eyes and in her smile.

Laughing at her long monogram, she declares, "It's perfect!"

Just then, all the waitresses carry a lit birthday cake, singing and clapping as they pass by our table. The look of alarm on Joanne's face makes me laugh, "Don't worry, I wouldn't do that to you," I reassure her.

The lobster pies were so delicious, we have no room for dessert. Much to my dismay, I realize it's getting late and Joanne must be tired. She's had a long day and still has an hour's ride home.

Reading my mind, she asks, "You're not going to go already? Can't we sit and talk for a while?"

Can we sit and talk for a while? I could sit here forever. "There's no where else I'd rather be," I assure her.

The waitress passes by and I ask her to take a picture of us, as I move over to her side of the booth. Sliding in next to my daughter, I put my arm around her for a birthday picture that was once only a dream.

We sit talking for another hour. I love listening to her stories, because there's so much about her I still need to learn. Tonight, for example, I learned she prefers a salad and French fries to soup and a baked potato. Who would have ever thought such a simple fact would thrill me so?

It brings me joy to see so much of Mark's handsome face in hers, especially as her facial expressions go from frowning, to smiling, to that sly grin I loved so much. Watching her brings me back to days of such happiness and innocence with Mark.

As she speaks, all I want to do is touch her face, hold her hands and embrace her for a lifetime. I'm so afraid of losing her again. If only there were a way to guarantee her presence in my life. I just have to bide my time and give her all the space she may need to fit me into her life. It will be well worth the wait.

Walking back to our cars, I so badly want to ask about seeing her again, but say nothing, other than to tell her to drive safely. I give her a hug and a kiss on the cheek, wish her a good night and one more Happy Birthday. This time, with my heart so much lighter after our wonderful evening, it's much easier to say.

At long last, the spirit of Christmas has arrived at the home Jay and I built for the girls ten years ago. I was so frightened that first Christmas Eve all alone in our new home, waiting for Kristine and Bethany to be brought home and Jay so far away with our dying Jackie. Tonight, the fire in the fireplace is blazing and we've been sitting comfortably around it, unwrapping gifts for hours. With my renewed joy, I went a little overboard with presents, buying everything from hats to nail polish. I wanted to completely spoil my girls this year. It's been so hard for Kris and Beth to wait until the day after Christmas to open their gifts, but they want to spend Christmas with Joanne as much as I do. Expecting the tree to be nearly withered by the time Joanne could make it to our house for our first holiday together, I'm thrilled we only had to wait until the day after. It feels as natural as if she's always been with us.

All the gifts finally opened, Joanne notices the light coming from the backyard and goes over to the French doors to peer out. Jackie's gazebo is brightly lit and trimmed with garland and poinsettias. Huge boxes wrapped in shiny holiday paper with colorful bows are piled on the floor. Nearby are snowmen. Excited, Joanne suggests we go out to the gazebo and take some pictures. We're all game and grab sweaters, rushing out. There's so much posing and laughing no one seems to mind it's freezing, not even me.

Losing myself in their happiness, I feel like the young carefree girl I once was a long time ago. My faith has been renewed. All of us have been through so much, and we've all changed since my finding Joanne.

The peace and contentment I feel now has spilled over into Jay's life, for I see again the gentle kind man, who took such care of Jackie when she was sick and dying, the generous man who, at the young age of twenty-two, willingly took my children under his wing and, without hesitation, made them his own.

The anger Kris sometimes felt toward Jackie for dying and leaving her alone has somewhat lessened, now that Joanne has come into her life. However, nothing will ever fill the gaping hole left by Jackie's death.

Beth, who only recently explained that my being so wrapped up in Joanne is the reason her grades have slipped, has forgiven me for not being as attentive to her as she needed. She never resented Joanne, just my behavior at times, especially because she was the youngest and used to my undivided attention. Unfortunately, it was hard to focus on her needs while I tried to heal. To Beth, Joanne is just part of the family and she's very happy having another sister.

My daughters are growing closer and closer as sisters. Naturally, I'm thrilled. Kristine will be getting married in August and Joanne has agreed to be her bridesmaid, while Bethany will serve as her Maid of Honor.

As I let myself back into the warm house, I gaze up at the angel on the top of the tree. She seems to be smiling and winking a bluish green eye at me. Gee, I wonder who this twinkling angel just might be?

Susan's Afterword

I've finally come to terms with the past. Since finding Joanne, I haven't even had a cold, much less my recurring pneumonia. My sleeplessness has greatly improved, which has enhanced my overall appreciation of life. My migraines have disappeared.

No wonder I was always so sick, with never a day going by that I didn't worry about Joanne, saying silent prayers for her health and happiness. I may have been just a kid when I had her and may not have been allowed to keep her, but in my heart I was always her mother, and that feeling will never go away. Undoubtedly, the future will hold new challenges for me. I now stand my ground on the things I am angry about. I also know when to let them go. I recognize that I alone am responsible for my happiness. I draw comfort from my relationships with my daughters - their love heals me. I draw strength from my husband - his love empowers me. I am ready for whatever comes, because with them, I am invincible.

Looking back over the past couple of years, my reunion with Joanne has been sprinkled with so many delightful and fulfilling experiences. Our relationship has flourished and has grown to be loving, comfortable and easy. A simple thing between a mother and a daughter one might think, but as simplistic as it may sound, it took a lot of hard work, respect and patience. Never before have I had to monitor my reactions, reflexes and words so carefully, not even during my unwed pregnancy and the days and years that followed. Back then, I merely had a secret to guard, now my daughter's continued presence in my life was at stake.

Back in 1969, I was sick with worry over what my little girl's first birthday would be like. There was no need to worry. I've seen the pictures. It was perfect. She even had the "good" baby shoes I'd hoped for her - the Stride Rite's. Joanne surprised me by giving me her bronzed bookend baby shoes, on my fiftieth birthday. Now they are proudly displayed on the bookshelves in the family room, placed right next to mine just as she suggested.

It's as if she has known me all of her life and wants to please me as much as I wish to please her. More importantly, after being in reunion one year, three months and twenty-four days, I heard the words every birth mother longs to hear. We had just arrived at her house after shopping for her thirty-second birthday, when I handed her a carefully chosen birthday card. She told me how special she thought it was. We hugged and for what must have been the hundredth time told her how very much I loved her.

"I love you, too!" she responded, sounding somewhat surprised by her very own words and admission. Then, she looked at me and said, "I really do, Susan."

All I could do was hold her and cry.

Finally, Joanne's adoptive mom and I are at peace with the places we each hold in Joanne's heart - the loving heart I gave her and the one Ann so tenderly nurtured. One of my favorite memories is on the occasion of Kristine's wedding when, as a surprise to me, Ann attended the Mass. Her presence helped to answer the question of acceptance on her part, and closed the circle of love around Joanne. Ann and I continue to be considerate and kind to one another and respect the unique circumstances surrounding our lives.

Our lives - it is such a thrill and a privilege to be included in that thought. Such a thrill to have a part in my little girl's life. Such a privilege to be a part of my little girl's heart. At long last, I have all of my children, and that is the greatest comfort in a mother's life.

I'm proud that I had the courage to have this child, regardless of the circumstances, and I thank God for the strength it took to find her.

Joanne's Afterword

While growing up, I was always proud to say that I never cared or wondered who my birth mother was, where she was or what she was doing. I had never even heard the phrase birth mother used before, never mind used it to describe someone I didn't know. Now, since our reunion, I live my life so proud to say that not only do I know my birth mother, I see her often and I love her.

I feel as proud and special to say that I have two families, as I was growing up to say that I was adopted. I love both my families. Where I thought I was lucky before to have a wonderful family, now I have two wonderful families and two mothers, Mom and Susan, who love and care about me completely and unconditionally. Ann and Joe Medeiros will always be my mom and dad no matter who comes into my life and I hope my mom never forgets that. The bond I feel among me and my brothers, Jay, Don, and Rick, will never be diminished no matter how many sisters I now have. We grew up together and there will never be anything that could replace the closeness we felt growing up or the friendship we feel now.

Reuniting with my new family has made me appreciate my adoptive family even more than before. They watched me experience different emotions throughout the reunion process and they were very concerned about me and the outcome of a possible reunion, but they supported and encouraged me to do what I felt was right. I have always been able to count on my parents and brothers to do that and to always be there for me and what I believe in. I thank them for that.

Meeting Susan and my sisters has impacted my life in ways that I am probably not even aware of yet. Getting to know them has been more than a pleasure; it has been a true joy. I consider it a miracle that we have had the opportunity to reunite because they have truly enriched my life. I have found new friends in relatives that I had never known.

It is hard to understand how I can be so much like Susan. Nor do I understand how I can be so much like my sisters, when we did not grow up together. There is such a bond and obvious connection among us, it amazes me. Even though we have known each other for a short time, it feels like forever because we are so similar. We are similar not only in looks but in mannerisms, actions, thoughts and feelings. We share so many of the same opinions and I know they think just like I do. Our minds and hearts work in the same way. They have provided a mirror in which to view myself that I never had before. I can see myself in them and it allows me to see myself clearer and to better understand who I am.

Before our reunion, I was never much of a believer in the nature aspect of the nurture vs. nature argument. Now I realize they are equally influential in creating the person I am. I am clearly a product of my Medeiros family upbringing and my Mello family genes.

Over the years since our reunion, the relationship between Susan and myself has become so strong and is such a comfort to me. She really has been the loving, supportive mother she always wished she could be to me.

Sylvia Brand

RICHIE ETWARU

DEDICATION

To my wife Vashti, and our two children, Aarjun and Aakash
Etwaru.

AFTER READING THIS NOVEL, YOU MAY NEVER CLICK "I ACCEPT" EVER AGAIN.

When Sylvia Brand reports for work on Monday morning, she discovers her lascivious, sexist manager has been abruptly transferred, and Sun Motors has replaced him with a genderless robot. At first, Sylvia and her co-workers are overjoyed to discover that Carin, the robot, is very nearly the perfect boss: unfailingly polite, eager to help solve problems, and dedicated to making the office a better team. As the days pass, Sylvia readily agrees to an increasingly invasive series of company policies - after all, she reasons, Sun Motors is a good place to work. But little by little, Sylvia is pulled into a totalitarian nightmare. After being sent to a secret facility to serve as a captive source of medical data, she embarks on a life-or-death journey to freedom to save both herself and her unborn child.

ACKNOWLEDGMENTS

This book would not have come to life without the support and encouragement of thousands of individuals in over seventy-five countries that continue to support the 31st Human Right: "everyone has the right to legal ownership of their inherent human data as property."

Specific thanks to Jim MacLeod for the cover design and illustrations, and Thomas Hauck for the editing.

PREFACE

I was probably about seven years old, and from my memory I lived on the veranda. My parents lived in a modest house in a poor village surrounding a sugarcane factor in the countryside of Guyana, an ex-British colony in South America. The veranda was the place to be, it gives you the best panorama of the village, the roads and the farmlands, and it was painted in blue and white, my favorite colors. It had all the ingredients for a super cool child's hangout, there was danger – you could fall down, there was privilege – it was a precious part of the house, and for me, there was freedom – it was the closest I could get to the birds, the electrical wires that ran near the house, and the sky, all of the things and places that helped me dream.

My father, a part time electrician and a full-time schoolteacher had already taught me about capacitors, transformers, and the ability to manufacture electricity. I'd experimented with hydroelectricity, and magnets, and all shapes and sizes of batteries from watch batteries to car batteries. Batteries were my quest. Most of my toys needed batteries, and the battle to get my parents to purchase more batteries for me to play with my toys was getting more and more difficult. I needed rechargeable batteries. I needed to find a way to capture and store energy, and redirect it to my battery-operated toy cars, trucks, and airplane.

I was never successful, and I suffered the pain of having to beg for new batteries, but I came close once. I was convinced that I could turn a paper pinwheel into a wind-powered electricity capture-source to power my toys. And the best place to mount these paper pin wheels was my veranda. I was seven. This is where the wind was. For days I experimented, weeks I dreamed, never catching a breakthrough. Lots of paper, lots of pins and glue, wood, wires, my father's soldering iron, his multi-tester to test voltage, and the ruin of several toys whose circuits I had fried.

My last hoorah was "Project Boost", I would mount four pin wheels in

1

the front grill of my father's car and hope for a mega capture of electricity to be stored in a capacitor which I had learned how to strap to the toys with rubber bands. But Project Boost was quickly cancelled by both my parents, unanimously as it was above a danger threshold. I'd failed. And by eight, a brand called Eveready batteries distributed rechargeable AA batteries to my country, and my childhood took a turn for the better.

I'd forgotten all about Project Boost until October 10th, 2017. I was in an Uber which was a Tesla Model S, an electric car, and I was being driven over the Øresund Bridge which was one of the longest bridges in Europe connecting Sweden and Denmark. The Øresund Bridge is the longest combined road and rail bridge in Europe and connects two major metropolitan areas: Copenhagen, the Danish capital city, and the Swedish city of Malmö. If you're in an electric car, you want to check to make sure you don't need a recharge of your battery when going over one of the longest combined road and rail bridges in Europe. The Uber driver was a tall lean Anglo-Saxon man, he was in his 50s and dressed is a semi distinguished manner. His grey hair was crafted, he looked like Nordic intellectual royalty, and he spoke English with a distain only the French can top. He said to me "I will need a recharge on land."

I knew what he meant instantly. He was low on battery, and we were on a very long bridge. I figured I would talk to him to reduce any nervousness he might feel, and any embarrassment he might embrace. Right, I was talking to him to distract myself from nervousness that could build as a foreigner who knew no one in Denmark other than my co-workers who I was heading to meet with, and was about to be stuck in a car with dead battery on a long bridge in the middle of what definitely looked like nowhere. He met my chit chat with very stoic remarks. The one that stood out was "you can relax, we have very good wind on the Lillgrund." The Lillgrund is the largest offshore wind farm in Sweden, and as I looked out to the right of the car from the back seat of a Tesla, I saw the most beautiful sea of towering white wind turbines I had ever seen. From afar, it looks like a pasture of grey-white beautiful paper pin wheels, spinning magnanimously, on a beautiful blue ocean. And we, my seemingly pleasant but stoic driver were going to stop and re-charge the battery of a Tesla on land, with electric power that came from wind turbines, large paper pin wheels.

A little over thirty years after the cancellation of Project Boost unanimously by both of my parents, my entire mind went back to the veranda, with vivid imagery and deep emotional tug. Paper pin wheels. Nikola Tesla, Elon Musk, my Uber driver, and me.

It had happened again.

Something which I imagined, had come to reality and happened a few decades after. It drains you. You ask yourself if you are special, lazy, stupid, blessed, or cursed. You feel a mix of emotions, you feel anger, regret, and you feel a sense of responsibility. Responsibility for not having the courage to follow through.

Today I still dream.

I no longer have my parent's veranda. I live in the mountains of Northern New Jersey in the United States. I look out my windows of my home office at the trees, birds, wild turkeys, deer and squirrels. My two toddler sons chatter in the aftermath of my thoughts, and only my wife has veto power on any of my projects.

I am sharing this story with you the reader so that you can see what I see, and you might be motivated to act. Unlike the bright abundant energy future for humans I saw on the veranda with paper pin wheels, today I see a dark future for humans. We became the energy source. Action will not bring anything new to life, instead it stops something terrible from happening. I present to you Sylvia Brand, a fictitious character in my dreams, and her story to regain her data dignity.

SYLVIA BRAND

CHAPTER ONE

Sylvia peered over the top of her cubicle. From her desk she had a clear view of the doorway leading to the executive offices. No one was coming or going. She glanced at her computer screen. The time was fifteen minutes after nine. She looked back at the door. Her stomach tightened and the familiar tension crawled up the back of her neck.

Through the door a man entered the room of cubicles. It was Joe, the regional logistics manager. A harmless guy. Actually rather nice, but in his own little world. He was eating a bagel while looking at his phone. He stopped to speak to one of the employees before quickly moving on. He was like that—friendly and thankfully not pushy.

Sylvia could feel her hands becoming clammy. She wiped them on her skirt. Damn! Why did this have to happen? All she ever wanted was to enjoy her job, be a good company person, get regular promotions, and look forward to well deserved retirement when she turned sixty. That's the way it was supposed to be at Sun Motors. The company's mission statement said, "We value equity, equal opportunity, and employee empowerment." The slogan was emblazoned all over the website and on every company report. But what did it mean in real life? As far as Sylvia was concerned, it meant that Randolph Meekin was empowered to put his hands on her, make lascivious comments, and generally act like an oversexed creep, all without facing any consequences.

She glanced again at the digital time display on her screen. Nine eighteen. On a Monday morning it was unusual for Meekin to have not yet made an appearance in the office. He wanted to be seen so his employees would know he was present and observant. You could call it "controlling." He was a control freak.

She picked up her phone and punched a number.

"Judy?" she said. "Have you seen him yet? No? Hey, maybe it's our lucky

5

day, and he's got the flu. It's going around. Let his wife take care of him for a week and give us girls a break. See you at the meeting at ten."

Sylvia took a deep breath and slowly exhaled. The pain in the back of her head intensified. Relax, she told herself. Stay loose and maybe it will go away. Don't want to take a painkiller so early in the day. She checked her screen. No reply yet from human resources. Last week she had lost her patience with Meekin and had filed a formal complaint—her first.

He had come into the office at the end of the day, when people were going home. Sylvia had been at her desk trying to track down a shipment of battery current sensors due from the supplier in Mexico. The existing inventory was down to just one day, and shutting down the assembly line of the highly profitable Comanche truck because of one part was not what anyone wanted. Meekin had circled the room, and while she was on the phone speaking to the trucking company dispatcher she had forgotten to track Meekin's location.

Suddenly she felt hands gently grasp each of her shoulders. Without seeing, she knew to whom they belonged. She stiffened, put her hand over the phone mouthpiece, and turned her head.

"Mr. Meekin—I'm talking to a dispatcher," she hissed.

"And I'm sure you're doing a fine job," he said with a smile. With his fingers he gave her shoulders a tender squeeze.

"Julio, just tell me the truck has cleared customs," Sylvia said into the phone. "I can't tell from the RFID tag. Yes? Okay. Gracias. Buenas tardes." She hung up.

"See?" said Meekin. "It all worked out. Everything will be fine." He eased his hands down the outsides of her arms nearly to her elbows before sliding back towards her neck. "You seem tense. Relax—it's almost quitting time." He leaned down so that Sylvia could feel his warm breath against her ear. "You look especially nice today. Got a date tonight?"

"No."

"We should go out for a drink," he said. He paused and Sylvia could sense him peering intently down at her chest from his position just above her right shoulder. "Is that a black bra you're wearing? Wow, that is so hot. Do you realize how hot you are?"

Instinctively Sylvia reached for the top button of her blouse, which—how foolishly!—she had left open that morning, revealing the slightest glimpse of skin and lace. With fumbling fingers she quickly buttoned it.

"Mr. Meekin, this is extremely inappropriate," she said. She could feel the muscles of her jaw begin to twitch.

"The only thing inappropriate is how unfriendly you're being," he replied. His hands continued their clumsy massage. "Especially considering there's an opening in logistics for a regional manager. Rob Jones is retiring. You could be in the running for that job. But I need team players. You're a team player, aren't you, sweetheart?"

A drop of sweat tickled her forehead. With her hand she quickly wiped it away. "Yes, Mr. Meekin. I'm a team player. But really, this is not appropriate."

Removing his hands from her shoulders, he pivoted to lean against her desk. "I'll tell you something." By this time the workers in the immediate vicinity had left for the day and he was speaking more openly, less furtively. "I like you. You might be able to handle the job. But not yet. Not on your own. I can help you. Show you the ins and outs, so to speak. What do you say?"

"Say about what?" she replied, stalling for time.

He smiled. "You know what I'm talking about. Imagine what that job could mean to you. Bigger salary, more vacation time. But we need the right person. Let's chat about it over dinner tonight."

"Tonight?" Her mind was racing.

Reaching into the neighboring cubicle, Meekin pulled out the empty chair and sat down. He scooched up until his knees were nearly touching Sylvia's chair. She remained as she was, facing her desk.

"Yes, tonight," he said to the side of her head. "Table for two at the Beaujolais Bistro. We can talk about your future. Get to know each other better." His hand slid onto her knee.

Twisting in her chair to face him, she pushed away, leaving his hand hanging in midair. He showed a humorless smile as with feigned nonchalance he clasped both hands together with one elbow resting lightly on her desk. His greedy eyes slid down to her legs.

"I'm so sorry," she said. "Tonight I have a board meeting. At the church. I've got to grab dinner there."

His eyes narrowed into reptilian slits. "That's too bad. I want to talk about your future. It could be very bright." His eyebrows came together in a frown. "You're not saying no, are you? That would be a big mistake. I could do a lot for you. I have influence not only at Sun Motors but at the upper levels of the Industrial Council."

"I understand that. I'm not ungrateful. But tonight is not going to work. Why don't we talk in your office tomorrow?"

"My office?" he shrugged. "Maybe. We'll see." He stood up and leaned closer, with one hand on her desk. "You really are super hot. I hope you know that. I wouldn't waste my time on just anybody. Do you understand?"

"Yes, Mr. Meekin."

With one last appraising look up and down, he sauntered away.

When he had left the room, Sylvia began shaking and her stomach churned as if she were going to throw up. She could not hold back her tears. Without bothering to shut off her computer, she grabbed her purse and ran to the door.

After a sleepless night, the next day she had gone to human resources and filed a complaint.

"Do you really want to do this?" said the assistant manager, a woman named Estelle. "Of course you have very right, but it's going to be rough. Mr. Meekin will attack you. Call you a liar. He's been with the company for over a decade. People respect him. You could be destroying your career. Is there anybody who can corroborate your story?"

In fury Sylvia had said to Estelle, "Corroborate my story? Are you kidding? All you have to do is get off your ass and talk to any woman in the logistics office. He does it to all of us."

"Excuse me?" Estelle's eyes flamed. "Do you know to whom you're speaking?"

"I'm sorry—forgive me. Don't take it personally. But do you know why the turnover rate in our department is off the charts? I can name you three girls who have left in just the past six months. All for the same reason— Randolph Meekin. You should know—it's your office that hires them and puts them there, and then takes their separation papers. It's a horrible environment."

"As long as the Industrial Council approves, there are no violations," Estelle had replied. Grudgingly—so it seemed to Sylvia—she took the form Sylvia had filled out. "After we process this," she had told Sylvia, "we'll call you in for a formal interview. Up until that time, you can withdraw your complaint. But after the interview, the wheels will start turning. Mr. Meekin will be notified and will have the right to respond. Do you understand?"

Sylvia had nodded yes.

For the remainder of the week her interactions with Meekin had been tense—or at least she had been tense, while he had seemed maddeningly relaxed and confident. Together they had reviewed the contracts for the new supplier of Comanche ignition relays. And the center link contract was put out for bidding—a company in Ireland was the frontrunner, and Sylvia was hoping to wrangle a visit to inspect the factory. It was always nice to get out of Detroit for a few days, especially to get away from Randolph Meekin.

In his pursuit of the women in the office he was relentless, and if one evaded his snare, another might be caught. A few months earlier Sylvia and Meekin had been slated to fly together to visit the Sun Motors assembly plant in Hermosillo, Sonora, Mexico. They would have stayed overnight at the Hermosillo Marriott. The plan had filled her heart with terror and disgust. In panic, she had concocted a story about needing surgery that same week. Nothing serious, she took pains to say, but it simply had to be done, and that was the only week the hospital could fit her in.

Oh—what hospital? Meekin had asked.

A clinic in Canada, she had said. I'd really rather not discuss it.

Sylvia was not surprised to learn that Meekin had then recruited a young assistant manager named Pamela to go with him to Hermosillo. Sylvia didn't know whether to feel sorry for Pamela (if she were simply naïve) or to condemn her for selling herself to gain favor with Meekin. But the following week, after Sylvia's "surgery" and the trip to Mexico, Pamela seemed edgy and tense. A few days after that, she was transferred to the Sun assembly plant in Kansas City, Missouri. That was the last Sylvia heard of her.

And now it was Monday morning. Sylvia knew that Meekin wouldn't give up. That was his pattern. He'd hit on you hard for a few days and then back off when he sensed he wasn't getting anywhere. He'd be nice for a while before circling around, like a wolf, for another run at his prey.

Sylvia checked her personal email on her phone. There was a message from the executive placement agency. They had reviewed her resume and wanted her to come in for an interview. With the automobile industry having rebounded after the devastating Global Depression, Sylvia knew that other companies were hiring. There was no reason for her to live in misery under the leering eye of Randolph Meekin. Despite having worked at Sun for her entire adult life—the summer after high school graduation she had started as an intern—she felt she had no choice. It was time for her to join the other women who, seeking professional respect and a collegial work environment, had fled the Sun Motors Detroit Assembly Plant logistics office.

At ten o'clock, with still no sign of Meekin, Sylvia went to the contracts team meeting. He would attend because as the director of plant logistics, vendor contracts were an important part of his portfolio. As Sylvia approached the door to the conference room she steeled herself for a bad experience. Oh, he'd probably be all right during the meeting itself—there were usually three men and four women present, and Meekin knew enough to behave himself in public situations—but it was likely he'd ask one of the girls to stay behind, or meet him in his office. It was like a twisted game of Russian roulette—you never knew if the chamber with the bullet would be aimed at you.

She walked in and sat next to Judy. Soon Mei Lien, Edouardo, Roger, Maxwell, and Lauren came in and took their seats.

After a few minutes, Roger asked, "Has anyone seen Mr. Meekin this morning?"

The answer was no.

"I'll give him a call," said Lauren. She picked up his phone. After a moment she said, "Strange—his voicemail went to a generic box."

"I'll go to his office," said Maxwell.

The members of the contracts team sat around the table and waited. After a few minutes Maxwell returned. "He's not in his office," he said. "His desk is clean. I mean all the papers are gone. No family photos. His football signed by Joe Montana is gone. His diplomas are off the wall. All that's left is the phone and the computer."

"That's bizarre," replied Mei Lien. "I saw him here on Friday. We were among the last to leave at closing time. He seemed perfectly normal. He said that he wanted to be sure to go over the quarterly report this morning. Then he said, 'Have a good weekend.'"

"What are we supposed to do?" asked Judy. "We need him to sign off on a bunch of proposals and approve the production numbers for the next quarter."

At that moment a man appeared at the door. Sylvia had never seen him before. Middle-aged, dressed in a gray suit, white shirt, and narrow necktie. His hair was close cropped, like a member of the military. Very old school.

"Pardon me," he said. "This is the contracts team, is it not?"

They replied it was.

The man entered the room. "My name is Howard Starling. I'm the vice president of human resources for the company. I normally work in the Sun Motors building downtown. I know this is a bit unexpected, but I hope to have a few minutes of your time." He took the seat at the head of the table, where Meekin usually sat. "I'm sure you're wondering where Randolph is. He's been transferred to corporate. He'll be working downtown. As for your team, the Detroit Assembly Plant has been selected for an innovative new pilot program named Bright Horizon. Starting today, the combined positions of director of logistics and director of operations will be performed by Carin."

"Carin," repeated Maxwell. "Is that someone's name?"

"In a sense, yes," replied Starling with a smile. "Carin is an autonomous humanoid operator."

"You mean like a robot?" asked Sylvia.

"We don't like to use that term because it conjures up all sorts of outdated images—you know, clumsy clanking machines with blinking lights. Carin is something quite different. However, 'robot' is a familiar label and I'll admit to using it out of a sense of convenience." He glanced at his phone. "Ah— instead of us sitting here and talking about Carin, let's go meet him."

"Him?" asked Judy.

Starling stood up. "To be honest, Carin has no gender. That was a deliberate design decision. But because of the limitations of the English language, the only gender-free pronoun we have is the word 'it.' But no one wants to call Carin 'it.' To do so would seem heartless and rude. But to call Carin 'he' or 'she' would be equally inaccurate. So we're stuck. Some linguists have proposed a gender-free human-like pronoun in the form of 'dee.' The object form would be 'deem.' So if you were to say, "She gave the assignment to her," then the gender-free version would be, 'Dee gave the assignment to deem.'" Starling shrugged. "I don't know how it's going to be resolved. So for now, you can call Carin either 'he' or 'she.' It doesn't matter. Carin doesn't care."

"What does Carin look like?" asked Mei Lien.

"You'll see for yourself in just a few minutes," replied Starling. "But so that we will not be tempted to talk about Carin in front of him, I'll take this opportunity to say a few things about the design approach. The key thing is that the project executives and builders agreed it would be a mistake to produce an entity that appears exactly human, or which at first glance could be mistaken for a human. We're fully aware of the principle of the 'uncanny valley,' and have made every effort to avoid that problem."

"What's the uncanny valley?" asked Roger.

"As a robot becomes increasingly human in appearance, real people—you and I—are more likely to be able to relate to it and to form an emotional attachment to it," said Starling. "We're more likely to empathize with it, as we would a pet dog or cat. The field is called social robotics, which is related to anthropomorphism. This common human tendency is used to facilitate social interactions between humans and social robots. The objective is to give robots social behaviors that are sufficiently credible for human users to engage in comfortable and productive relations with them.

"If you were to plot it on a graph, the level of empathy would continue to rise as the robot became increasingly human in appearance and behavior.

"The problem is that when a social robot looks very nearly human but still retains some subtle mechanical qualities, people who interact with it feel not attraction but revulsion. The almost-human robot suddenly seems creepy and disturbing. On the graph, the level of human attraction suddenly dips. This is called the uncanny valley—the 'valley' referring to the dip in the graph. The concept was first identified in 1970 by the robotics professor Masahiro Mori as 'bukimi no tani genshō,' which was first translated by Jasia Reichardt as 'uncanny valley' in her 1978 book Robots: Fact, Fiction, and Prediction.

"Then, as the robot's appearance continues to be more and more human-like, the emotional response again becomes positive and can approach human-to-human empathy levels.

"The zone of repulsive response aroused by a robot with appearance and motion between a 'barely human' and 'fully human' entity is the uncanny valley. In the design of Carin, instead of trying to cross the uncanny valley, we stopped short, and aimed for an appearance that we call 'humanesque.'"

He went to the door. "Carin will be working out of Mr. Meekin's old office. He doesn't really need a personal space—he could work from anywhere—but from time to time he'll need to speak privately with a team member, just like any other supervisor. So we gave him an office."

SYLVIA BRAND

CHAPTER TWO

Starling led the group down the hall to Room 320. They went inside. Sitting behind the desk was a humanoid figure of average proportions, dressed in a plain, one-piece jumpsuit. The hair was short and dark. The mouth was closed, with the pinkish lips turned up in a vaguely friendly smile. The skin was a pale brown, suggesting no particular race. The ears resembled those you would see on a department store mannequin—ear-shaped but nonfunctional.

Carin was clearly not human. Sylvia noted that the entire structure seemed to be simplified, without any of the idiosyncratic details that distinguish one person from another. If there were one word that Sylvia would have used to describe Carin's appearance, it would be "generic." Carin was a generic humanoid entity, as if you had taken photos of thousands of people of different ages, genders, and races, and had combined them into one.

This was comforting. Suddenly Sylvia knew what Mr. Starling had been talking about in his discussion of the uncanny valley: Carin appeared human enough to relate to, but not exactly human enough to provoke feelings of revulsion. He was a perfectly likeable robot.

"Why don't we introduce ourselves?" said Starling.

Carin stood up. His height was average for a man. His eyes—or rather his two eye-like cameras that were obscured, Sylvia noted, behind a pair of what looked like sleek, form-fitting tinted glasses, giving him a vaguely athletic look—scanned the room.

"Pleased to meet you," said Carin, his mouth and lips moving effectively enough so that Sylvia could believe the sounds were being formed not by a hidden speaker but by air passing through a pharynx and over tongue and teeth. The timbre of the voice was somewhere between masculine and feminine—Sylvia couldn't decide if it was a man with a high voice or a woman with a low voice.

After the five members of the contracts team had given their names and job titles, Carin smiled with the corners of his mouth and said, "Throughout the day today, I'll be meeting with each of you individually. The goal is to get to know you better and learn more about how I can help you succeed at your jobs. I strongly believe in team cooperation. As a leader, my policy is to share the credit for our successes while taking responsibility for our shortcomings. There is an old saying by the Chinese philosopher Lao Tzu: 'A leader is best when people barely know he exists. When his work is done, his aim fulfilled, they will say: we did it ourselves.' This I believe. I also believe in the words of Woodrow Wilson: 'You are not here merely to make a living. You are here in order to enable the world to live more amply, with greater vision, with a finer spirit of hope and achievement. You are here to enrich the world, and you impoverish yourself if you forget the errand.' At Sun Motors, our job is to help people and their possessions get from one place to another safely, reliably, and pleasurably. This is our mission and our goal.

"You are aware that I'm not a human being. I will tell you that I'm aware of this also. While human beings have many remarkable qualities of which I can claim to possess only a very few, I will promise you that I care not for material gain and do not seek personal power. My role is to do the very best in the position to which I've been assigned. As you may have been told, I'm assuming the dual roles of director of operations and director of logistics for this facility. Traditionally these roles have been performed by two people, but my data processing and decision making capabilities allow me to identify and exploit untapped efficiencies, and my designers believe it's advantageous that I perform both." Carin paused. "Are there any questions so far?"

"If you don't mind me asking a personal question," said Sylvia, "who exactly are—or were—your designers? From where have you come?"

"I was designed and built by Morta Laboratories in San Mateo, California. Technically, I'm a Morta AHO 6-C. That means autonomous humanoid operator, model 6, version C. While some of my components have been functioning independently for almost a year—being tested and so forth—I came online as Carin exactly four months, three days, and six hours ago. Since then I've been in training. I arrived in Detroit on Saturday afternoon. This is my first day on the job at this facility."

Sylvia had heard about Morta Laboratories. It was a privately held company that did a lot of classified defense work in advanced robotics. This was the first time she had heard of a Morta product being used in a civilian setting.

"As far as your day-to-day jobs are concerned," continued Carin, "nothing will change. I'll function the same way as my predecessor. As I said before, my goal is to help you succeed. I'm what they call a 'servant leader.' If you have a problem you cannot solve, my first priority is to ensure you have the appropriate training to find the solution. I may then actively step in to assist you. I believe you're all highly qualified and we're going to make a great team. Now then, I see it's already twenty minutes past ten. We need to move ahead with our contracts meeting. Let's adjourn to the conference room, where everyone can sit at the table."

The group, without Starling, who had excused himself, went down the hall to the conference room. Sylvia noted that Carin walked with confidence, albeit a bit stiffly, like an older person with a mild case of arthritis.

To Sylvia's pleasant surprise, the meeting was efficient and businesslike, with none of the little psychological games in which Meekin routinely indulged and the subtle arrows he aimed at his staff. Carin was unfailingly polite and managed the discussion well. Maxwell volunteered that he was having a problem getting an acceptable price from a potential vendor of tie rod ends. The vendor wanted a minimum order of thirty thousand units to meet the price Maxwell was authorized to pay, and Maxwell only needed twenty thousand. They were at an impasse. Carin nodded and said, "Twenty thousand units is the quantity you need for the Comanche truck for the next six months. But you're going to need another five thousand for the Army's new mobile strike vehicle. Production is going to begin at this facility next year. It's exactly the same part."

"I've heard some rumors about the Army vehicle contract," said Maxwell, "but that's all it's been—just rumors. Is the Army ramping up for war with Rodinia?"

Carin smiled. "The threat from Rodinia continues to be very real, and we must be prepared. As far as the contract goes, nothing is signed yet, but based on available data, I calculate the chances of Sun Motors winning the Army contract at ninety percent. Those are good odds. Offer your vendor an order for twenty-five thousand. Don't tell them about the Army contract. What is your vendor asking per unit?"

"Twenty-eight dollars. I'm authorized to pay up to twenty five."

"Who's the vendor?"

"Maxx Systems. In Lumberton, North Carolina."

"They have problems. They're going to be sued by the state for dumping toxic solvents into the Lumber River. It won't put them out of business, but it will cost them money, and they may lose contracts from organizations that have environmental concerns. Mention the investigation into the pollution. Offer them twenty-six dollars per unit, take it or leave it. We'll make up the difference from the Army."

"Okay," said Maxwell. "Thanks. I'll do that."

"And by the way," added Carin, "if for some reason we don't get the Army contract and we have five thousand extra tie rod ends, we'll sell them to Star Automotive Group at a discount. The tie rod ends used by most of their Polaris trucks are nearly the same—the only difference is a couple of two-dollar bushings. Or we'll unload them on an aftermarket parts dealer.

Either way, don't worry. We can't lose."

At one o'clock, Sylvia, Mei Lien, and Judy went out for their usual lunch at a local eatery. Once they had been seated in their booth Judy said, "Well, what do you guys think of Carin?"

"I suppose we shouldn't be surprised that our new boss is a robot," replied Mei Lien. "At first the idea seemed strange, but when you think about it, the plant is full of robots. We have robots on the assembly line that perform quality control tests and are authorized to shut down the line if there's a problem. Many members of our janitorial staff are robots. We have fleets of autonomous city buses and delivery vehicles operating on the streets of Detroit. We have cargo ships that sail themselves from port to port, and rockets that take off and land without human guidance. So it's a logical next step that the company would put an autonomous humanoid operator in a management position. After all, we humans are just cogs in the big machine—not much different than the robots doing spot welding on the assembly line."

"Personally," said Sylvia, "I think that getting rid of creepy Randolph Meekin and replacing him with a nice, friendly robot who hasn't got his brain in his pants is a dream come true. Ladies, I feel better already. The reign of terror is over!" She paused, as if performing an internal self-assessment. "Wow—I'm amazed that my headache has gone away. My neck doesn't seem as stiff. My stomach isn't tied in knots." She raised her glass of wine. "I propose a toast to a new beginning. A workplace where we don't have to live in fear of our Neanderthal boss putting his hairy hands all over us and making gross comments and using his position of authority to threaten us."

"To a new beginning," agreed Judy.

"I hope so," said Mei Lien. "But what do you think will really change? Meekin now works downtown. It sounds like he got a promotion. What does that say about Sun Motors? And why did they choose our office for this robot manager pilot program? I'm not convinced. There's something fishy going on. Sun Motors is one of the largest privately held companies in America. We know nothing about what happens on the top floors of the Sun building downtown. I mean, aside from our chairman, president, and CEO, Hugh Atkinson, who delivers his annual message to us on our computer screens, have you ever seen a member of the Atkinson family?"

"No," said Sylvia. "They keep a very low profile. But it doesn't matter to me. All I want is to do a good job, keep the Comanche trucks rolling off the assembly line, and go home every night. I don't care what they did with Randolph Meekin. I don't care if he works downtown or in Brazil, as long as he's nowhere near me. Ugh! What a pig he was. I'm sorry, but there's just no other word to describe him." She raised her glass and downed the last of her wine. "God, this stuff tastes like two-buck Chuck," she grimaced.

"What do you expect at a place like this?" laughed Judy.

"I don't care if it's from the bottom of the barrel—I'll have another," said Sylvia as she turned to search for the server.

"Do you think you should?" asked Mei Lien.

"Today we celebrate," replied Sylvia. "And you've got to admit that Carin is pretty sharp. The way he analyzed Maxwell's contract problem was amazing. He saw the situation, crunched the numbers, calculated the odds, and provided a solution. What a breath of fresh air! Meekin would have said,"—and here she lowered her voice to a slow drawl—"'Uh, Maxwell, I'm going to have to get back to you on that. We need to evaluate this carefully. You keep working on it, okay?' Of course, Meekin would have ignored the problem until Maxwell either gave up or made a decision on his own that Meekin could then criticize. Oh, Meekin was very good at avoiding responsibility! Whatever you did that was good he'd take credit for, and if you screwed up he'd tell everyone how hard it was to work with incompetent people."

"Yeah," nodded Judy. "Remember when Roger proposed that we use the same speed sensor both the Comanche and the new SUV? The company would save twenty dollars per car. When the engineers gave it the green light, Meekin walked around and bragged that it was his idea. What a jerk."

Sylvia's phone rang. She glanced at it. "Sorry, ladies, I need to take this," she said. "Hey Jason, how's it going?"

Mei Lien and Judy exchanged glances. The call was from a man who for the past six months Sylvia had refused to identify as her boyfriend.

"Wednesday night?" said Sylvia. "Yes, I'm free. What do you have in mind? You have tickets for the Linz String Quartet chamber music concert? Yes, that sounds like fun. Dinner at six o'clock? Okay, see you then." She hung up.

"Sylvia, you hate chamber music," teased Judy.

"That's not true," she replied. "I'm getting used to it. It's growing on me."

"But Jason isn't officially your boyfriend," said Mei Lien. "Is he worth the investment?"

"Why not?" replied Sylvia. "I believe in being flexible and open to new things. And what else am I going to do on Wednesday night? Sit by myself and watch old movies? Please!"

"Something's going on," said Judy. "On a Wednesday night Jason is taking you to dinner and a romantic concert. He hasn't been to a jewelry store lately, has he?"

"Oh, come on!" said Sylvia. "Don't be silly. I think you guys have too much time on your hands and you spend it by dreaming up these fantasies. Anyway, if Jason and I go to the next level, you'll be the first to know." She glanced at her phone. "I need to get back to the office. I have a meeting with Carin."

SYLVIA BRAND

CHAPTER THREE

Sylvia stepped into Carin's office.

"Please close the door," said Carin. After giving Sylvia a perfunctory smile his face returned to its default expression of vague friendliness. Sylvia took the chair opposite. They sat for a moment in silence. It was then that Sylvia became aware of a faint whirring sound coming from behind Carin. Boldly, she said, "You have a cooling fan?"

"You have the mind of an engineer," smiled Carin. "Yes, I do. Humans, like all mammals, generate body heat, and so do we; but since we neither breathe nor perspire, we need a mechanical cooling system. However, our designers are working to eliminate all unnecessary moving parts, so future versions of the AHO 6 are expected to have a passive cooling system. Now then—enough about me. You've been with Sun Motors since you were eighteen years old. That's rather remarkable."

"Yes, I began as an intern."

"After graduating from college with a degree in mechanical engineering you were hired as a process engineering specialist at the West River plant in Kansas City. After two years you were transferred to this facility as a controls engineer before taking the position of associate logistics manager. You are presently a senior logistics manager. Your impressive work history with Sun Motors means that you are, of course, familiar with the company's code of conduct."

Sylvia felt the blood rise in her face. "Yes, of course," she replied. "Why do you ask?"

"At this moment you are showing a blood alcohol level of point zero three five. This is not enough to cause impairment—you would not be placed under arrest if you were stopped by a police officer while driving—but it indicates that, as a woman who weighs one hundred and forty pounds, you've consumed two drinks within the past hour. My guess is that it was two glasses of red wine—Burgundy, to be exact. Company policy discourages the consumption of alcohol during working hours, does it not?"

"How are you determining my blood alcohol level?" asked Sylvia.

"A breathalyzer test. I'm equipped to monitor the air quality in my immediate area. Also, given the level of light in this room, your eyes are dilated more than normal. Your skin is also slightly flushed, indicating increased blood flow into your dermal capillaries. These observations confirm the breathalyzer test."

Sylvia leaned forward and looked into Carin's eyes. "Am I in violation of company policy or am I not?"

"You are not visibly impaired, therefore you are not."

"Then why did you mention it?"

"Out of concern for your health and welfare."

"Oh? Is that part of your job description?"

"Yes," replied Carin with a smile. "As the director of logistics and operations, an important part of my portfolio is to maintain the highest possible level of employee engagement. Key metrics include levels of employee happiness, physical and mental health, job satisfaction, and turnover rates. I want all of our employees to feel as though they are a valued part of the Sun Motors family. We all share the same goals and desire to make the world a better place through the work we do here."

"Will my two glasses of cheap Burgundy at lunch be noted on my employee record?"

"No."

"Then I thank you for your concern and request that we close this topic of discussion. What else would you like to speak with me about?"

"I just want to review a few things," said Carin. "You've been in your current position for one year and seven months. You've been with the department for two years and nine months. Are you happy with your career path?"

"I suppose so. To be honest, when Randolph Meekin was my boss I became discouraged about my prospects for advancement, but now that you've taken over I think I'll be treated more fairly."

"Why did you think you were being treated unfairly by Randolph Meekin?"

Sylvia paused before answering. She suddenly regretted bringing up the name of her former supervisor. Apparently Meekin was still very much employed by Sun Motors, in the downtown headquarters building. It was true that in a company as large as Sun Motors they were unlikely to cross paths again, but it wasn't worth taking the chance that, through Carin, word about what she said about Meekin would trickle back to him. She intended to withdraw her sexual harassment complaint; her reasoning was that since Meekin was no longer lording over her, by pursuing her complaint she had little to gain and much to lose, especially in the eyes of the Industrial Council. As far as she was concerned, she wanted nothing more to do with him, and that included not complaining about him to her new boss.

"Oh, I don't want to get into it," she said. "Sometimes there's friction between a manager and his staff. No one is to blame—it's just a clash of personalities. Some people just naturally click together and some don't. I wish Randolph Meekin nothing but the best in his new position."

With his unblinking eyes fixed on Sylvia, he seemed to purse his thin lips. This, she thought, must be the pre-programmed response to some aspect of the conversation. Suddenly she got the feeling that Carin knew she was not being completely truthful. She said nothing more.

"Of course," said Carin with a little nod. "To return to the matter at hand, I can tell you that your contributions to the success of your department, and by extension the company as a whole, have not gone unnoticed. You're on a good path for future promotions. Does that please you?"

"Yes, very much. I enjoy working at Sun Motors and hope to make my career here."

"I'm happy to hear that." A tablet was lying on the desk. He reached for it and studied the screen for a moment.

"Anything important?" asked Sylvia.

"Oh, just a few pesky forms."

Sylvia thought it was interesting that Carin used the word "pesky." It crossed her mind to ask him how he knew it, but she let it slide.

"As I'm sure you're aware," said Carin, "Sun Motors has begun to compete for federal government contracts. Specifically, we believe we can produce vehicles for the military—products including lightweight personnel carriers, transport trucks, and ultimately weapons platforms. Our forecasts suggest that within the next five years military procurement of such vehicles will rise at least twenty percent, and we intend to get our share of the business." He placed the tablet face up on the desk. Sylvia saw text on the screen but couldn't make out what it said.

"We'll need everyone to pull together on this," said Carin.

"Absolutely," she nodded. "You can count on me one hundred percent."

"Glad to hear it. In order to bring the company into full compliance with Department of Defense contractor requirements, we need to ask all employees to sign some forms. They're nothing serious, and something that every other vendor has to comply with." He slid the tablet across the desk to her. "This is a standard conflict of interest statement. By signing it, you affirm that neither you nor any member of your immediate family hold a DoD position or have input into any DoD procurement process. Basically, the government wants to be certain that you can't award a contract to yourself or someone in your family."

"My brother Charlie is in the Naval Reserves."

"Not a problem."

Sylvia scrolled through the document. It seemed dense but straightforward. Her name, address, and company job title were already filled in. She didn't read every word—that would have taken several minutes and Sylvia didn't want to keep her new boss waiting. With her fingerprint she signed the screen. After positioning the tablet to capture an image of her face, she handed the tablet back to Carin. After glancing at it and tapping on the screen a few times, he slid it back across the desk.

"This one is a confidentiality statement," he said. "It says that you won't sell or distribute the plans or specifications for a contracted military product. Of course you wouldn't do that anyway—you've been at Sun Motors a long time and know all about product development confidentiality."

"Yes, I do," she replied. "Everyone in the office gets calls from industry analysts and reporters from car magazines. We're trained to give them the number of the public relations office and then hang up."

"Good," nodded Carin. "As long as we're on the subject of analysts and the press, the next form—you can swipe to it—is the same thing, only internal. Corporate doesn't want anybody talking about my presence here. At the appropriate time the Bright Horizon pilot program will be announced, but the consensus is that it should come after everyone is satisfied that I'm performing as expected. Since I'm the first autonomous humanoid operator in a large industrial setting, there's going to be a tremendous amount of public interest. We need to control the flow of information."

"Okay," agreed Sylvia as she quickly scanned and then fingerprinted both documents. "We wouldn't want any leaks."

"No, we wouldn't," said Carin as he took the tablet and tapped the screen a few times.

"By the way, can I get copies of those?" asked Sylvia.

"Copies? I'll have to check on that. You see, their very existence is confidential. We can't have documents circulating that reveal we're asking you to refrain from talking about a confidential program, because that in itself would be evidence that such a program existed. Of course these documents will become a part of your employee file in human resources, but access will be tightly controlled. I'm sure you can understand."

"Sure—I get it," said Sylvia with forced aplomb.

"Just one more—I don't want to keep you from your work." He gave her the tablet. "This one is another standard boilerplate form that gives the company the right to conduct workplace drug testing. We may from time to time ask you to submit to a urine test, saliva test, blood test, or any other minimally invasive procedure. We may also use passive data collection methods. The results of such testing may be used to evaluate your overall fitness for DoD contract work. Of course the information will be kept confidential."

She scanned the document. It was several pages long. "I don't know—this seems complicated. Should I have a lawyer look at it?"

Carin's eyes seemed to drill into her. "It's your choice. To be honest, this one is nothing more than an updated version of the one I'm sure you signed nine years ago when you first joined the company."

Sylvia had a vague recollection of signing several forms on her first day as an intern, and then more when she was hired full-time.

"As far as we're concerned," said Carin, "a valid consent form can last ten or even twenty years. But people sometimes challenge the old ones, so we want to use an abundance of caution and have everyone sign this new one."

Sylvia continued to read. After a few moments, Carin leaned closer, as if to speak confidentially. "Don't you trust me?"

"Of course I trust you," replied Sylvia. "But you know how it is. People are always saying that you should never sign a consent form without understanding it completely."

"And they're right!" said Carin. "I couldn't agree more. Now then, what questions do you have? I'd be happy to clear up any areas that are confusing to you."

Sylvia studied the form. Carin sat and watched her. In the office, alone with Carin, Sylvia became increasingly self-conscious. Carin did not move—not even a finger. The only sound in the room was the faint whirring of Carin's cooling fan. In the absence of the usual human micro-motions—the blinking of the eyes, the scratching of an ear, the shifting of weight in the chair, or even the subtle expansion and contraction of the chest as the person breathes—Sylvia was reminded that Carin was a machine. And being a machine, she wondered if Carin were capable of deception. Was it possible that Carin was not being fully truthful? Could Carin have been programmed to carry out some devious scheme?

She felt she had to ask a question, if only to appear to be a thoughtful partner. "It says here," she said, "that I understand that 'only duly authorized company officers, employees, and agents will have access to information furnished or obtained in connection any and all tests; that they will maintain and protect the confidentiality of such information to the greatest extent possible; and that they will share such information only to the extent necessary to make employment decisions and to respond to inquiries or notices from legally authorized entities.' That sounds pretty broad, doesn't it? I mean, what does 'the greatest extent possible' mean?"

"The system is based on trust," replied Carin. "Unfortunately, I'm sure you know that many personal injury lawyers are looking for reasons to sue. They do so much damage to innocent people and organizations! Think about it. Let's say a sophisticated hacker broke into the Sun Motors human resources network and accessed employee data. It was an attack that no one could have defended against. It could have happened to any person or company. Do you think justice would be served by hordes of greedy lawyers filing endless lawsuits against Sun Motors, and threatening the company with bankruptcy and the loss of thousands of jobs? I don't think so. That's why the company needs the same basic protections that you or I would want if we were in the position of safeguarding something valuable. The company will promise to use every reasonable means to protect the integrity of the data it collects. Nothing matters to Sun Motors more than the safety of personal information. And by the way, no one at Sun is exempt from company policies—not even the chief executive officer. We're all one family. We can trust each other."

"Really? Everyone has to sign these same forms?" asked Sylvia.

"No one is exempt from company policies," repeated Carin. There was a moment of silence as Sylvia continued to study the pages of text displayed on the tablet.

"A moment ago you mentioned the passive collection of health data," she said. "What does that mean?"

"Oh, it's just another safeguard," replied Carin. "As you know, all living creatures, and especially mammals, are constantly shedding or excreting or exhaling little bits of themselves into their immediate environment. If at this moment you were to get up and leave the room, you'd leave behind millions of cells from your skin, your respiratory system, your hair. You'd leave behind traces of gases that you've exhaled—including molecules of alcohol from your two glasses of inexpensive Burgundy at lunch today. Even as we speak, all that stuff is floating in the air and settling on the desk and the floor, and even on the walls. Technology has advanced to the point where a machine—like me—can collect those samples and analyze them. Not that we would ever choose to do so. The capability is there. For example, let's say that one of your colleagues at lunch had not two glasses of Burgundy but five, and came back to the office roaring drunk. My sensors would indicate an unacceptably high blood alcohol level, and consequently the person would be legally and appropriately separated from the company. Should the employee who had been fired then sue the company for passively collecting the health data that led to his dismissal? Of course not. The guy was spewing alcohol into the air, and it would be almost impossible not to capture it."

"I suppose that makes sense," said Sylvia. She smiled at Carin. "You're lucky—you don't go around leaving a trail of dead cells wherever you go."

"No, I don't," smiled Carin. "As a human being, your ability to reconstitute yourself by growing new cells to replace the ones that have ceased to function is highly advantageous. But it has its drawbacks. The process of cell growth can be corrupted and lead to disease. But that's a discussion for another time. Do you have any other questions?"

Sylvia continued reading the text on the tablet. Even to a university-trained engineer, the language seemed opaque.

Suddenly Carin reached out his hand. "If you don't wish to sign, that is your right," he said. "But it would be a shame if you were not seen as a team player. And if that were the case, you would have difficulty moving up the corporate ladder. As the company grows, we're looking for people who are one hundred percent committed, and whose applications for transfer or promotion would be readily granted by the Industrial Council. I would hate to see doors close on you because of a silly thing like a routine consent form that, once you signed it like everyone else in your office already has, would be filed away and forgotten."

Carin remained with his hand poised to receive the tablet.

Sylvia felt the atmosphere in the room grow oppressive. Her stomach began to tighten. She had been working at Sun Motors for her entire adult life. She didn't want to throw an obstacle into her career path. By a stroke of fate her tormentor, Randolph Meekin, had been whisked away. Life had suddenly gotten better. Everyone in the logistics office thought Carin was a breath of fresh air—an unbiased, pragmatic manager who solved problems and only wanted the best for the company and its employees. And now the robot was making a simple request, but one that if refused could end her career. And for what? Some imagined invasion of privacy? Heck, the social media sites she routinely visited probably knew more about her than Sun Motors and the Industrial Council ever would.

"I have nothing to hide," she said as she placed her fingertip on the signature square. After adding the snapshot of her face, she handed the tablet back to Carin.

"I'm sorry if I sounded silly about this," she said. "But you can never be too careful."

"I agree completely," smiled Carin as he tapped the screen. "Sylvia, you're a valuable asset to the company because you're a thoughtful person who considers every possibility. I'm sure your future at Sun Motors will be very bright."

SYLVIA BRAND

CHAPTER FOUR

The next morning Sylvia came to work with a happy heart. As she pulled through the gate of the Sun Motors Detroit Assembly Plant and into the vast employee parking lot, she felt no queasiness in her stomach, no tension in her neck. Her joints were comfortably loose, not bound tightly by rigid muscles. Having slept soundly during the night, she had no need for her usual double espresso to jolt her awake, nor for her bottle of painkillers to soothe her headache. The plant—and by extension the world—seemed to be a brighter, sunnier place than it had been twenty-four hours earlier. There were clouds in the sky, but they were happy clouds, fluffy and white, rather than harbingers of gloom.

She knew exactly why the world had become a more agreeable place: Randolph Meekin, the man who had made her life miserable, was gone. It was only after she had experienced a full workday of emotional and physical freedom did she recognize what her "normal" state had been. Like a captive animal that had become conditioned to its cage, she had gotten so accustomed to Meekin's lascivious tyranny that she had lost perspective and had come to believe she didn't deserve any better. It was like the Stockholm syndrome, in which Meekin was her captor who, over time, made her empathize with him and accept his twisted world view.

A new day was dawning in the Sun Motors Detroit Assembly Plant, and the abused female workers could look forward to being treated with the respect and dignity they deserved.

"Hey, Maxwell, what's up?" she said as she breezed by his cubicle.

"Same old, same old," he replied. And for him, it was probably true—he and the other men in the office had no clue what the women had been going through. Sylvia couldn't blame him, but a little more enlightenment would have been nice. Anyway, it was all moot now. Carin gave every appearance of being a fair, rational manager—and a smart one too, who had a solid grasp of data and knew how to make informed decisions. This new feeling had re-ignited in Sylvia a spirit of competitiveness that she hadn't felt since Meekin had become her supervisor. Sun Motors was going to be a great company for years to come, and Sylvia was proud to make her contribution.

At nine-fifteen she saw Carin come through the door that led to the executive offices. As she worked on returning a batch of defective voltage sensors, she kept an eye on Carin as he made his way around the office. As Carin paused at one cubicle and then another, the atmosphere was congenial and businesslike.

This is what a workplace should be like, she thought.

She called Judy to clarify a parts quantity. Judy worked in a cubicle on the other side of the room, and Sylvia hadn't seen her since the office opened at nine o'clock; but that wasn't unusual, and they generally caught up with each other later in the morning. Sylvia got Judy's voicemail, and she left a message.

Ten minutes later she called again, and again got Judy's voicemail. This time she stood up and peered across the maze of cubicles. Employees were standing here and there, visible from the shoulders up, but Sylvia couldn't tell if Judy was at her desk. Welcoming an excuse to stretch her legs, Sylvia made her way through the cubicle maze to Judy's. At the narrow entrance she paused. Judy's chair was empty and her desk was clean. The photos of her husband and two kids were gone. The birthday cards that her kids had made with crayon were gone. The little framed painting of Ghat Bruno—the self-proclaimed spiritual leader of the religion to which Judy and her family adhered—was gone. The phone was blinking with unanswered calls.

Sylvia took out her personal phone and tapped Judy's home number. Voicemail. Where did her husband Tim work? Judy had told her once… oh yes, he was a carpenter for a local homebuilding contractor. She found the number and tapped it. The receptionist who answered told her that Tim was not on any of the worksites today. Was he expected to be tomorrow? She was not sure, and that's all she could say.

What the hell! Judy had never mentioned making a change. She liked her job and got along well with everyone in the office. What had happened between five o'clock Monday afternoon and nine o'clock Tuesday morning?

At that moment Carin appeared at Judy's cubicle. With her was a young woman.

"Excuse me—I was just looking for Judy," Sylvia said to Carin. "I needed her to confirm the number of backup cameras we need for this week's Comanche production. Do you know where she is?"

"Judy has taken a leave of absence," replied Carin with a smile. "In fact, I'd like you to meet Tameeka White. She'll be filling in for Judy."

"Sylvia Brand," said Sylvia as she extended her hand. "Nice to meet you. So, you're a temp? How long do you expect to be here?"

Tameeka glanced at Carin.

"Tameeka's assignment is open-ended," said Carin. "I'm sure you'll find her to be highly qualified and an effective member of the team." Suddenly Carin appeared distracted. Then he said, "Excuse me. I have a call I need to answer." He walked away.

"You must specialize in last-minute placements," said Sylvia as Tameeka sat down at what was once Judy's desk. "The phone rings at seven in the morning and you've got to be at a new job by nine. Right?"

"Actually, they called me yesterday," said Tameeka. She clicked through with her new password and the computer screen came to life. "They told me to be here today. So here I am."

"What time yesterday?"

"It was early in the afternoon."

"Who called you?"

"The employment agency. They said I should report to human resources, and that I'd be working for someone named Carin." She lowered her voice. "They didn't tell me Carin was a robot! It was quite a surprise. Before I met him, they made me sign a non-disclosure form promising I wouldn't reveal it to anyone. Seems strange—how long do they expect to keep something like that a secret? Anyway, I really hope this turns into a permanent job. I'm tired of being a temp."

"Who made you sign the form?"

"A man named Starling. He met me at the human resources office before he took me to see Carin."

"Okay," said Sylvia. "Once you get settled, I need you to find out the quantity of backup cameras we need this week. I emailed the part number to Judy, and I'll forward it to you. You can call or email me, but I need to know as soon as possible."

"No problem," smiled Tameeka.

Sylvia went to the human resources office. Estelle was behind her desk.

"Are you here to file another grievance?" asked Estelle without looking up from her computer.

"No, not at all," replied Sylvia. "Everything's great. Carin is amazing. But I'm curious about something. What happened to Judy Loring? We worked closely together. This morning, she's gone. Poof—just like that."

Estelle looked at Sylvia over her readers. "You know I can't comment on personnel issues. Ms. Loring has taken an indefinite leave of absence. That's all I'm authorized to say."

"The funny thing is, the temp who has taken her place—Tameeka—was called yesterday afternoon. I saw Judy before the end of the business day at five o'clock. She didn't mention anything about taking a leave of absence."

"She wouldn't be the first employee who kept her plans private," replied Estelle. "Even from her colleagues. Between you and me, if you want an answer I'd look at that crazy religious cult she belongs to."

"You mean the Church of the Golden Way? They seem like a harmless enough group. They preach peace and love and nonviolence. Nothing wrong with that."

"There's nothing wrong with it as long as she does it on her own time. But it seemed like every month she wanted to take a day off for one of their religious holidays. This month she wanted a day off because they were celebrating the birthday of their leader, what's-his-name."

"Ghat Bruno."

"Yes, Ghat Bruno. He's supposed to be one hundred and ten years old."

"Christians celebrate the birth of Jesus, right?"

Scowling, Estelle removed her readers and leaned into Sylvia. "Oh, come on. Every company has reasonable policies about religious holidays. But you can't just join some obscure cult and suddenly want your own special celebrations. What if everybody demanded their own holidays? And then there was the time she wanted to burn incense at her desk. We shot down that idea in a second."

"Okay," said Sylvia. "I see your point. I don't want to argue. But Judy didn't mention anything to this office about a commitment to the Church of the Golden Way?"

"No, she didn't."

Returning to her desk, Sylvia sat and thought for a moment. Who could she call for more information about Judy's sudden absence? She thought the best candidate would be their most recent supervisor, who unfortunately happened to be Randolph Meekin. But she needed a pretext for calling him. It had to be something important about the office. Ah—she could ask him for what he knew about a particular potential contractor in Indonesia. She didn't want to waste time with the contractor if they weren't up to the high standards of Sun Motors. Then, as an afterthought, she could casually ask him if he knew anything about Judy's sudden leave of absence.

Taking a deep breath to steady her nerves, she picked up her phone, tapped the main number of the Sun Building downtown and, after listening to various options, tapped the number for the employee directory. After choosing "M," she waited as the names rolled by: Madson, Mark, Matthews, Mead, Meachum, Meefer, Meehan—and then Meetor and Miner. No Meekin. She tapped "O" for "operator." After a moment a woman answered: "Sun Motors, may I help you?"

"Yes—please connect me to Randolph Meekin."

There was a moment of dead air. Then the operator came back on the line. "Would you please spell the last name?"

"M-E-E-K-I-N. First name Randolph."

More silence. The operator came back. "I'm sorry but there's no one here by that name. Are you sure you want the Sun Motors Building? We have many facilities worldwide."

"I'm sure—but thanks for looking," said Sylvia as she hung up. Stupid phone system—someone hadn't yet put Meekin in the staff directory. And Meekin himself was probably too lazy to demand the process be speeded up.

At lunch hour, Sylvia told Mei Lien and Maxwell that she couldn't join them at the restaurant because she had to run some errands. She drove to Judy's house, an old-fashioned two-story colonial at the end of a cul-de-sac in a suburban neighborhood of professional people and middle managers. Judy's car—a red Sun Motors SUV—was parked in the driveway. Sylvia parked in front of it, went to the garage door, and peered through one of the little windows. Another car was parked inside. She went to the front door and rang the bell. No one answered and she heard no sound from inside. She tried the door. It was locked. She walked around the side of the house to the back. Judy and Tim had a dog—a big friendly golden retriever named Buddy. To keep Buddy in the back yard, they had installed a chain link fence. Sylvia opened the gate in the fence and entered the back yard. There was no dog. She went to the back door and knocked. No answer. She peered through the glass. The kitchen was deserted. She tried the doorknob and it turned. Pulling open the door, she went inside. There was no response to her calls. The kitchen sink and counters were clean—no sign of breakfast dishes. In the living room the odor of sandalwood incense lingered in the air, and a big framed painting of Ghat Bruno—a beaming smile on his white-bearded face—hung over the fireplace.

The house was there, but the family was gone.

As Sylvia returned to her car she saw an elderly woman come out of the house next door.

"Excuse me," called Sylvia. The woman stopped and looked at her. "Have you seen Judy and Tim?"

The woman walked across her weedy lawn to the property line. "They left last night," she said.

"Last night? But their cars are still here."

"They were picked up."

"By who?"

"A sort of bus or van pulled up. This was about eleven o'clock. I remember because I was watching the news, and from where I sit I can see the street. You don't often see traffic down here late at night, so it got my attention. I didn't want to be nosy, but how can you not be interested?"

"Who was driving the van?"

"There were three people in the van and another person in a car. They went to the house and went inside. After a few minutes they all came out and got in the van, except for the person who went back to his car. Then they drove away. Just like that. I assumed they were going to the airport because each member of the family had a suitcase—Judy and Tim and the two kids."

"Can you tell me anything more about these people who picked up the family? Male, female? White, black, something else? Were they from the Church of the Golden Way?"

"I'm sorry. It was dark, and they didn't stand around. It happened very quickly. But I don't think they were church people. Whenever I see Judy and the family go to their church, they wear those pretty saffron-colored robes, like they wear in India. These people were dressed in black."

"You didn't talk to them?"

"Oh, no. I stayed inside the house. Since my husband died I never go out at night."

CHAPTER FIVE

"What's this?" Sylvia said to no one in particular. She was looking at her computer screen, where on the company intranet there was a message that had been sent to all two thousand five hundred employees of the Sun Motors Detroit Assembly Plant.

The message read:

"It is with great pleasure that Sun Motors announces the launch of a bold new program designed to support the health and wellness of our valued employees. For every Sun Motors employee, the Sun Motors Employee Wellness Plan (SMEWP) will provide full access to the highest quality health care, including overall fitness, vision, dental, mental health, and genetic health. Details will be provided by your human resources officer. And here's the good news: If your current primary care physician is on the SMEWP list of healthcare partners, you'll be able to keep your doctor. If your physician is not on the list, please contact your human resources officer for assistance in identifying a healthcare partner who can become your primary care physician."

Sylvia clicked through to the list of approved primary care physicians. Scrolling down, she searched for the name of her family doctor.

Her doctor's name was not on the list.

"What the hell," she muttered.

Her doctor was a partner in a clinic, the Dearborn Medical Group. Four other primary care physicians were also partners. Sylvia scrolled the list and found no names from the Dearborn Medical Group.

The Dearborn Medical Group was not affiliated with SMEWP.

This is a pain in the ass, she thought as she picked up the phone. She tapped the number for Carin.

The call went to voicemail. You'd think a robot would be able to answer more than one call at a time. She hung up without leaving a message.

She went to human resources, where she found Estelle behind her desk.

"How may I help you?" said Estelle without looking up from her screen.

"Can you tell me about this Sun Motors Employee Wellness Plan? I just got the email blast. I searched for my primary care physician on the approved list and her name wasn't there. In fact there was not a single name from the Dearborn Medical Clinic. What's going on?"

Estelle clicked out of her screen and shrugged. "The program is being managed by the corporate human resources office. We have nothing to do with it. I got the same email blast that you did. I'm sorry that Dearborn declined to participate in the program. I'm sure they were given the opportunity." As she peered at Sylvia over her readers, her expression softened. "Do you want my advice? Don't fight it. I know it means changing doctors. No one likes to do that. My doctor wasn't on the list, and I've been seeing her for ten years. But I made a few calls to doctors who are on the list, and I've chosen one. If I don't like her, next year I can sign up with another. It's no big problem."

"To stay with the Sun Motors plan, you changed doctors?"

"Yes. Listen to me: This is an outstanding program. It's better than any I've seen at any other major corporation. The coverage is comprehensive. Health, vision, dental—everything, including prenatal and childbirth."

"Thanks, I'll remember that," replied Sylvia sharply.

"You're a smart woman and a good employee," continued Estelle. "If you want to get along, go along. On the list of providers you'll find some of this city's top-ranked doctors and medical groups. When you find a doctor you like, your current doctor will transfer all of your records. You'll be covered for more diseases and health problems than any other plan available." She swiveled her computer so that Sylvia could see the screen. It showed the same email that she had received, describing the new SMEWP. Estelle scrolled to the bottom of the email, where there was a sign-up form. "Did you sign up online?" she asked while pointing to the little box you used to click through.

"No. I was too upset."

Estelle opened another window on her screen. "Let me show you something." It was a real-time report on a dashboard. "See that?" she pointed to a field where a number was displayed.

"Yes. It says eighty-two percent."

"As of this moment, of the two thousand five hundred employees in this facility, two thousand and fifty have signed up for the Sun Motors Employee Wellness Plan. Of the remaining four hundred and fifty, I think that within a few days another eighty percent will agree. That means that by the end of the week, ninety-six percent of the employees at this facility will have signed up for the Sun Motors health plan."

"What will happen to those who don't sign up?"

"They'll get a cash rebate in their paychecks so they can go out onto the open market and purchase the health plan of their choice. But let me tell you something—they're not going to find a plan as good as this one for the price. No way. The Sun Motors plan is a gold-level plan. The people who shop on their own—most likely because they want to keep their own doctor—are going to get a bronze level plan. They'll end up paying much more out of pocket for every service, and they won't get things like dental coverage." Leaning back in her chair, Estelle threw up her hands so that her bracelets rattled. "But hey, you can do what you want. Just remember that Sun Motors is looking for team players. You didn't hear it from me, but the word is that being a team player is a factor they look at when evaluating employees for promotions. This goes right up to the Industrial Council. You know they have the last word on everything. If they don't like you—pfft." She flicked her hands as if clearing the air of cobwebs. "You can kiss your promotion goodbye."

"You're kidding, right? The Industrial Council cares which health plan I choose?"

Estelle's face grew serious. "They care about whether you're on the team or you're freelancing. Sweetheart, you can do what you want. As for me, I'm sticking with the Sun Motors plan. I'm not going to jeopardize my career. If you want to buck the system, it's your choice. But there's no upside to it. You'll be cutting off your nose to spite your face."

"I don't know anything about these other doctors on the list."

"Well, you'd better decide soon, because the best ones fill up and won't take any more new patients. I'll tell you what I'll do. I'll send you an email with a list of the top medical groups on the list. It will save you from spending hours shopping around. Just make a few calls and then make your choice. But don't diddle-daddle. Do it today."

Sylvia returned to her cubicle. The euphoria she had felt after Randolph Meekin had been abruptly transferred—supposedly to the corporate building downtown, but that seemed unclear—was fading. Just as suddenly as Meekin had been transferred, her friend Judy was gone too, and not just from her job but from her house, along with her husband and two children.

She sat in her chair, paralyzed with indecision. She hadn't told Estelle this, but she felt tremendous loyalty and attachment to her personal physician, who had been with her through her first and only pregnancy, which had ended in a miscarriage. It had been a heart-wrenching experience; not only did she lose her baby, but her boyfriend at the time, who had told her he wanted to get married, was so freaked out by the loss of the baby that he had dumped her. After the joyous discovery that she was pregnant and a feeling that life was all sunshine and flowers, twelve weeks later Sylvia had found herself in world of gloom and spiritual desolation, with no baby, no boyfriend, a deep sense of personal failure, and the fear that it could happen again. Dr. Donna—her full name was Donna Giacalone, but everyone called her Dr. Donna—had been her Rock of Gibraltar, supporting her and helping her keep her experience in perspective. She had told Sylvia that spontaneous abortion, which was the medical term, happened in ten to twenty percent of all first pregnancies, so it was hardly uncommon; and most women who miscarry are subsequently able to have healthy children. It wasn't her fault, and it was no reflection on her ability to be a mother.

And now she faced a difficult choice. Dr. Donna, who practiced at the Dearborn Medical Group, was not affiliated with SMEWP. Many other doctors and clinics were, but not Dr. Donna. Estelle had urged her to sign up with the Sun health plan, not only because in her opinion it was a better plan than any Sylvia could get with Sun's cash alternative, but it was also a political decision. If she went with the corporate plan, the Sun Motors bosses, and even the Industrial Council, would view her more favorably, and would be more likely to keep her on track for promotions. If she took the cash and somehow made up the difference herself so that she could keep Dr. Donna, not only would it cost her more but her career might suffer.

At that moment her screen changed, and the image of Carin appeared. He was behind his desk in his office.

"Oh—hello Carin," said Sylvia as she squared her shoulders and sat up a little straighter. "What can I do for you?"

Carin smiled. "I just wanted to check in with you about the health plan memo that all employees, including yourself, received earlier today. I understand that the response to the company's very generous offer to cover employees under the Sun Motors medical program has been tremendous. Across this facility, we are now at ninety percent acceptance, which is exactly what we expected. And within the logistics office, I'm pleased to say we're at ninety-nine percent acceptance. I'd really like to make it one hundred percent—and you're the one who can put us over the top."

"Me?"

"Yes. Should you decide to accept—which I hope you do—the logistics office will have one hundred percent buy-in. This will be a feather in our cap, so to speak, and will not go unnoticed by our company leaders."

"And by the Industrial Council, I suppose?"

The moment these words passed over her lips, Sylvia felt a deep sense of regret and fear. From day one, employees at Sun Motors—indeed, employees at each and every large company across the United Americas—were taught that the Industrial Council was a benevolent association devoted to the growth and profitability of its two hundred thousand corporate members and the welfare of the fifty million people who worked for them. It was the Industrial Council that advised and guided the federal government in all matters relating to the national economy and, because the economy had been judged to fall within the realm of national security, the related policies of international trade, the environment, and national defense. Of course the nation possessed all the familiar branches of government that had been put in place when the U.S. Constitution had been first ratified in 1789; in its outward form, the structure of government hadn't changed in hundreds of years. The current president of the United Americas, Robert Deacon, was as popular as most presidents had been, and he was expected to win his second term handily. And while he went about his business of governing, and the Congress passed laws, and the Supreme Court ruled on those laws, most people knew that the real power resided with the Industrial Council, which following the terrible Global Depression had been granted sweeping powers to regulate the economy in the hopes that a firm hand on the tiller, as the saying went, would prevent the ship of state from once again smashing onto the rocks.

Like the Federal Reserve, which was now one of its subsidiaries, the Industrial Council was seen as being above politics; and indeed constitutional scholars frowned upon any direct communication between the White House and the Council, although most members of the press had long ago concluded that any sensible president knew enough to propose only those policies endorsed by the Council.

Because of its vast power, which reached down into the very hiring decisions made by the companies under its jurisdiction, while you were at work it was never a good idea to say anything negative about the Council, especially to a member of the management team of your company.

On Sylvia's screen, Carin smiled. "I'm sure the Industrial Council would be pleased to hear that the Sun Motors logistics office achieved one hundred percent buy-in to the Sun Motors health plan—why shouldn't they? It's all about teamwork and striving for perfection in all areas of business. Here at Sun Motors our goal of zero defects can be seen not just in the vehicles we produce but in how we conduct ourselves every day and in every way. And besides, the Sun Motors health plan is amazingly good. I can think of no rational reason why any Sun Motors employee wouldn't jump at the chance to participate."

"Of course, you're quite right," replied Sylvia. "The judgment of the Industrial Council is always...." She paused to find the right word that would end the discussion. "Infallible." As she said this bit of absurdity, she made an effort to keep the muscles of her face relaxed and her voice smooth.

"And yet you have reservations," said Carin. "Perhaps I can alleviate them for you."

Sylvia paused, to choose her words carefully. "I've been with my primary care physician for many years, and I would like to keep her, but she's not on the approved list. That's why I've been putting off my decision."

"That's understandable. I won't invade your privacy by asking you the name of your doctor. But perhaps I can help. You're twenty-seven years old and in generally good health with no chronic diseases—is that correct? I mean to say that you don't require the care of a specialist?"

"That's correct."

"And you live in Mexicantown?"

"Yes, since I graduated from college. I grew up in Franklin."

"I have two names for you. You don't have to write them down—I'm emailing them to you. Dr. Rebecca Goldsmith at the Willowdale Center, and Dr. Tina Packer, who has a private practice. Both are within a fifteen-minute drive from where you live. They're both accepting new patients. Either one will take very good care of you. I suggest you give them a call. You can also visit their websites."

"Okay, thanks. I'll do that."

"If for some reason they're both unsatisfactory, I have other suggestions. But I'm sure one of these two will be a good fit."

"Thanks."

"I hope we'll be able to add your name to the list of logistics office personnel who have signed onto the Sun Motors health plan, giving the office a participation rate of one hundred percent."

"I'll do my best."

Carin vanished from Sylvia's screen.

On the off chance that Dr. Donna could be persuaded to become affiliated with the Sun Motors program, or shed some light on why she wouldn't, before Sylvia contacted either one of the doctors Carin had recommended she decided to reach out to her familiar primary care physician. She went to out to her car, and using her personal phone called the Dearborn Medical Group.

Dr. Donna took the call. Sylvia explained that Sun Motors was offering a new health plan with which Dearborn was not affiliated.

"Why don't you stop by after work," said Dr. Donna. "I know you have a difficult decision, and I'd like to discuss it with you in a relaxed environment. Off the clock, so to speak."

CHAPTER SIX

As the setting sun cast its rosy glow, Sylvia wheeled her car into the parking lot of the Dearborn Medical Group. Just as she had countless times throughout her life, she walked through the glass doors and entered the faintly musty and antiseptic-smelling reception area. There to her left was the familiar wood-paneled reception counter with its protective Plexiglas front punctuated by the arched openings through which you talked to the ladies behind the desk. Beyond the potted plants in the waiting room area were the old-fashioned stainless steel-framed couches clad in turquois-colored fake leather. The screen bolted to the wall was tuned to the state news station. Mercifully, the sound was off.

It seemed like nothing ever changed here, and to Sylvia that continuity was comforting.

After a few minutes Dr. Donna came into the waiting room. "Do you have plans for dinner?" she asked Sylvia. "My husband has a Chamber of Commerce event. I find them horribly boring and try to avoid them whenever I can. I'd much rather get something to eat at a decent restaurant than cook for myself at home."

"Sounds good to me," replied Sylvia as she set aside the well-worn self-improvement magazine she had been perusing.

Once settled at a table at the Brickyard Tavern, and each with a glass of wine, Dr. Donna leaned forward and said, "I know all about the Sun Motors Employee Wellness Plan. A few months ago, their human resources people contacted us. Said they had five thousand employees in the Detroit area, and they were revamping their employee health plan. I was one of the partners who talked to them. They invited us downtown to a conference room in the Sun Building, where they gave us the pitch. Very splashy, with videos of happy, healthy employees and wise, caring physicians. They laid on the flattery with a trowel. Tried to make us think we were the chosen people destined to bring a bounty of good health and longevity to each and every Sun Motors employee and their families. And the fee scale wasn't bad either. They were going to pay as much as any of the major independent healthcare systems."

"So what was the problem?" asked Sylvia as she tore off a piece of bread from the wicker basket on the table.

"The problem was data."

"Data? What kind of data?"

"Every kind of data that bore any relationship to our Sun Motors patients, their illnesses or lack thereof, and how we interacted with them. They wanted access to everything. Every patient record for every visit or phone call. Every diagnosis and every pill prescribed. Every procedure, from an assembly line worker getting his leg put in a cast after a slip-and-fall to treatments for cancer and heart disease."

"How would they collect this endless river of information?"

"By tying into our internal systems. They said we wouldn't have to do anything other than go about our normal business. They would set up and operate the back end data collection network and databases."

"But what about patient confidentiality? Did they want you to get release forms from every patient who was a Sun Motors employee or family member?"

"No. They said they had taken care of that by having every employee sign a consent form where they worked. If you're a Sun Motors employee, and you've signed up for the Sun Motors Employee Wellness Plan, by definition you've given your consent, not only to us but to any other provider partner. How about you? Have you signed any healthcare consent forms recently?"

"Yes," replied Sylvia as a wave of embarrassment swept through her mind. "Yesterday I signed a consent form that allows Sun Motors to collect information about my physical condition while I'm on the job. Because of defense contracts—so they say—they can perform invasive tests, such as drawing blood or a urinalysis. But it goes much further than that. They can passively collect samples. My supervisor gave as an example an employee who comes to work with a high blood alcohol level." Sylvia paused, unsure about how to discuss Carin with someone who didn't work at Sun Motors. "To make a long story short," she continued, "they now have the capability to collect molecules that come out of, or from, your body, and enter the common space. If you're exhaling alcohol, you no longer have to blow into a machine. They can get it just by being near you. It's like when you put your trash on the curb to be collected, it becomes public property. If you walk into the office and shed a few million dead skin cells, you no longer own them. Anyone can collect them, including your employer. By signing the form, I acknowledged the company can collect and use information that enters the public space."

"Not just booze but cancer," said Dr. Donna. "Exhaled breath contains volatile and non-volatile organic compounds produced by metabolic processes, and the composition of such compounds varies between healthy subjects and subjects with lung cancer. You can diagnose lung cancer by analyzing the patient's breath. In our ability to analyze human exhalation we're finally catching up to dogs and cats. With their super-sensitive noses they've been able to do it for centuries. Anyway, you signed the consent form."

"Yes. My supervisor asked me to do it. I have to admit I felt I was being strong-armed. He implied that if I didn't sign, I wouldn't be viewed as a team player within the company, and that even the Industrial Council would take note of my lack of cooperation. With fifty million people working for Council companies, do you really think they would keep track of Sylvia Brand, a twenty-seven-year-old senior logistics manager working at a plant with twenty-five hundred other employees?"

"The answer is yes."

"Yes?"

"They would keep track of you because they can. To them, Sylvia Brand is just another data set, one of millions handled by the Industrial Council's big data centers. One of them is right here in Detroit. Anyone working at the Council can enter any query and pull up a list of people, including if they have signed up for the Sun Motors Employee Wellness Plan."

"But what about your patients who aren't Sun Motors employees?"

"The Sun Motors guy said that all we needed to do was assign an identifying digital tag to the patient records of Sun Motors employees. Their systems would unlock only the records with the Sun Motors tag. Non-Sun patients would not be exposed."

"Did you believe that?"

Dr. Donna took a swallow of her wine. With a laugh, she said, "Do I believe in the Easter Bunny?"

"So your partners decided to decline the offer from Sun Motors?"

"Yes. The scheme smelled bad. It reeked of abuse. Our impression was that Sun Motors was looking for rich data mines. Partners that would provide a flow of free healthcare data that they could use for—well, I don't know. Whatever they use it for."

"So it would be fair to say that any physician or medical center that signed up with the Sun Motors Employee Wellness Plan was required to sign the data contract as well."

"That would be a good assumption." Dr. Donna looked around the room for their server. "They never give you enough salad dressing. They must measure it out with a thimble." After a few moments she caught his eye and he came over. "A bit more of the raspberry vinaigrette, if you don't mind," she said. With a nod he sauntered away. She watched him. "If I were forty years younger..." She looked at Sylvia and winked. "Maybe you could have a go at him. He's cute."

"What?"

"Oh, I'm sorry. Of course, you have Jason. Is that right?"

"Yes," replied Sylvia. "We're going out tomorrow night. I have a sneaking suspicion he's going to ask me the big question. But I don't want to talk about it—not until it happens."

"I know what you mean. You don't want to jinx it."

"Right. To go back to your decision about the Sun Motors health care contract, what happened when you told them 'no'?"

Dr. Donna grew pensive. "I'll tell you, but first there's another reason I wanted to have dinner with you tonight. I'm retiring. I'm sixty-eight years old and it's time. I've known you since you were born. You've grown up to be a very capable and successful woman. With you and many others, I've had a nice record of success. But times are changing. At Dearborn we have five partners. Three of them want to sell out to National Health Systems, a big conglomerate based in Little Rock, Arkansas. They say it's either sell out or be crushed by the Industrial Council."

"How could the Industrial Council crush you?"

"Perhaps 'crush' is not the precise word. 'Starve' would be more accurate. If you're not one of the two hundred thousand corporate members of the Council, you're a part of the vast American canaille—literally, one of the dogs. You're just one of the millions of small and mom-and-pop businesses that do the everyday grunt work of our society—the fast food joints, taxicab drivers, auto repair places, dry cleaners, used clothing stores, bookstores— and yes, small medical clinics. These are much more loosely regulated than the elite Two Hundred K, as they're called, but in return for their freedom the little guys are severely curtailed in how big they can get. The moment you post over a set ceiling in revenues—it varies according to your industry—you must either agree to sell out to one of the Two Hundred K or be placed on the Council's banned list. That means that none of the Two Hundred K can do business with you. Their employees can't do business with you either. So you gradually wither and die. Dearborn is facing that choice. Three partners want to sell to National Health Systems. Two of us think that would be a horrible thing to do and would be bad for our patients. I don't want to fight. I'm retiring. My husband will keep working for another few years before we move to Costa Rica. So to answer your question, Barbara and I—the two holdouts—have decided to cash in our chips. The clinic will be sold to National Health. The three remaining partners will operate Dearborn, but strictly as a subsidiary of the parent company. So if your supervisor wants you to sign up with the Sun Motors Employee Wellness Plan, you might as well. There are no more good independent doctors. Our time has passed. Today, you're either part of the Industrial Council's machine or you're fending for yourself in the swamp of the canaille."

"And living among the aberrants," said Sylvia.

"Oh my God, yes. Let's not even think about that."

With a feeling of deep resignation, Sylvia told Dr. Donna about the two doctors Carin had recommended.

"Dr. Packer is headed for retirement," said Dr. Donna. "I'd go with Dr. Goldsmith at the Willowdale Center. She'll take good care of you."

"But the Willowdale Center is plugged into the Sun Motors data collection program, right? The company will know everything about my health history."

"The law says that patient data must be scrubbed of identifying information—name, address, phone number. In theory you're anonymous. It's a good theory—just like the Easter Bunny. I would assume that from the moment you sign up for the Sun Motors Employee Wellness Plan, all of your health data, including your historical data that we will be obliged to send to the Willowdale Center, will become their property."

"Including my miscarriage?"

"That and every other illness you've had since your parents first brought you to me when you were a child. Your entire patient history. Every phone call, every pill, every swab, every blood test."

Sylvia sat in silence, listlessly picking at her roast chicken. The atmosphere of the restaurant, which moments before had seemed friendly and inviting, had become harsh and obnoxious. The man at the table next to her brayed like a horse. The clatter of dishes at the busing station invaded her ears. The stupid fake candle on her table had gone out. She just wanted to go home and eat a pint of rocky road ice cream.

"Hey, kid, don't take it so hard," said Dr. Donna, giving her hand a friendly pat. "That's the way it is today. Go with the flow. It will all work out in the end.

CHAPTER SEVEN

At her desk on Wednesday morning, Sylvia opened the company intranet message announcing the launch of the Sun Motors Employee Wellness Plan. She read the text again, but after plowing through two pages of fine print that seemed like a bunch of legalese she scrolled to the bottom of the page and clicked "I accept." Then from the drop-down menu she selected the name of Dr. Rebecca Goldsmith at the Willowdale Center as her primary care physician. She clicked "enter," and that was all. She was now a part of the SMEWP system.

She returned to her work, which at that moment consisted of tracking an overdue shipment of O-rings from Indonesia. The container ship carrying the forty thousand O-rings—along with twenty thousand tons of other goods packed into six thousand containers stacked on her massive deck—had been caught in a typhoon in the Solomon Sea. Contact with the ship had been lost for several hours, and when the weather cleared and contact was restored the captain reported that thirty-five containers had been swept overboard. It appeared as though the Sun Motors container with the O-rings had been one of them. This was bad news because the inventory of O-rings at the Detroit Assembly Plant was down to three weeks, and even if the container ship had arrived on time in San Diego with the container intact it would have been a tight schedule to truck the parts to Detroit without a delay in production. If the container were truly lost at sea, then unless Sylvia could scrounge up forty thousand O-rings the Comanche assembly line would grind to a halt.

This potential debacle was particularly worrisome to Sylvia because she had signed off on the production schedule at the factory in Indonesia. She knew there was little room for error and that it was typhoon season in the South Pacific, but the production manager at Astra Karawang had assured her the schedule was no problem and the parts would be delivered on time. If the parts didn't show up on time—even if the cause was a typhoon—it would be a black mark on her record.

At that moment a window opened on her screen. It was Carin, sitting at his desk.

"Sylvia," he said, "please pardon the interruption to your very busy day, but I want to congratulate you on making the logistics office one hundred percent compliant with the Sun Motors Employee Wellness Plan. You've made a very wise decision! Your choice demonstrates that we are indeed a united team, we're all on the same page, and we're each thinking only of the greater good. I'm sure you'll be very pleased with the service provided by Dr. Goldsmith at the Willowdale Center. She's very highly rated. All of her patients give her glowing reviews."

"Thank you, Carin," said Sylvia. "I look forward to having Dr. Goldsmith as my primary care physician."

After a short pause, Carin spoke. "Sylvia, you seem to be under some stress this morning. Is there anything I can help you with?"

"No, thank you. I'm good." She said this not because she couldn't have used Carin's help—she certainly could have—but because years of working under Randolph Meekin's lascivious gaze and hearing his crude comments had conditioned her to never ask for his help. Never, ever. She had learned this when they first began working together. She had had a problem with a shipment of defective parts and had asked Meekin to intercede. He did so, and he had helped solve the problem. As the supervisor, this was in his job description. But from that day forward he had acted as if he had done Sylvia an immense personal favor that had saved her from being fired. (In fact, it wasn't nearly so serious.) He had asked her out, and when she declined he reminded her that she should have been more grateful to him and more willing to show her deep appreciation for his efforts on her behalf. His pressure on her was relentless, and that was the last time she had asked him for help solving a problem.

"Are you sure?" Carin inquired.

Sylvia thought for a moment. Carin wasn't like Meekin. While Meekin was an oversexed human male with serious boundary issues, Carin was an asexual robot who had shown his professionalism by helping Maxwell with his problem with the pricing of the tie rod ends. That had been a pretty neat solution, delivered without gloating. It was not in Carin's nature—or programming, if that's how you wanted to look at it—to play the kinds of games Meekin enjoyed. He himself had said that it was his primary mission to be helpful to the team. Why not give him the chance?

"Okay," she said, "as long as you're asking, I'm very worried about a container with forty thousand O-rings that seems to have been swept overboard during a typhoon in the South Pacific."

"Oh—you mean the Globe Nebula. She left the Port of Tanjung Priok on the fifteenth of this month, bound for Honolulu and then San Diego, with a load of six thousand containers. Three days out, the ship was hit by the storm. Fifty-five containers were reported lost. Statistically, seventy percent of containers washed overboard are recovered. But let's assume the report is correct and ours was one of them, and it is indeed lost forever. How many O-rings do you need for production until the end of this quarter?"

"Five thousand."

"We can get them from other Sun Motors assembly plants. We can get one thousand from Kansas City and Hermosillo, and five hundred from Chattanooga, Chihuahua, Brook Park, and Windsor. That's four thousand. Going further afield, Liverpool and Cologne have a few hundred each, as does Croydon. Taken all together, that should be enough to buy us enough time to sort out the problem with the missing shipment. When do you intend to file the insurance claim?"

"As soon as the shipping company confirms the loss."

"Don't wait. Do it now. If we're wrong and the container shows up, we'll just drop the claim. Okay?"

"Yes," replied Sylvia. "Thank you."

Sylvia was both amazed and gratified. Carin had instantly produced global inventory data that would have taken her days to track down. And he did it without making her feel as though she owed him a favor in return. It was just part of the job, as it should have been.

She returned to her work. A few minutes later her screen came alive again. Again she saw the image of Carin, but this time it was a pre-recorded message.

"Please excuse the impersonal nature of this message, but I wanted to deliver it to everyone in the logistics office. I'm very pleased that everyone has signed up for the Sun Motors Employee Wellness Plan, and that all of you have chosen your primary care physicians. The next step is to schedule your appointments for your annual physical exams. It's all part of our commitment to ensuring the very best physical and mental health for every member of our Sun Motors family. For your convenience, your appointment for your physical exam has been made during normal work hours—we would never impose upon your private time. We've been able to arrange appointments for everyone within a week. No one will have to wait longer than that. Please go to your personal calendar to see your appointment day and time. Some of you are scheduled for this afternoon, but don't worry, you don't need any special prep. Just go about your day, eat whatever you usually have for lunch, and go to your appointment. Most appointments will take less than an hour. Thank you."

Sylvia clicked open her calendar. She had been given an appointment with Dr. Goldsmith at three o'clock that same afternoon.

"Today?" she said to herself. "Oh, well—might as well get it over with."

At three o'clock Sylvia registered as a new patient at the Willowdale Center. The lobby was clean and bright, the receptionist all smiles. In the waiting room she joined a handful of other patients, who seemed to be generally younger than the doddering geriatrics she had always seen at the Dearborn Medical Group. Even better, none of them smelled bad.

After watching the news channel for a few minutes—the sound was on, and the news reader was talking about a terror bombing in Rome—the nurse announced her name, and she was ushered into an examination room, where the nurse performed all the routine tests including blood pressure ("one hundred over seventy," the nurse said with approval) and asked about any recent complaints (none).

Dr. Goldsmith entered the room. After introducing herself, the doctor spent several minutes reading Sylvia's medical history from the computer screen. Sylvia thought the doctor's application of cherry red lipstick was rather aggressive, but otherwise she appeared to be a reasonable human being without any peculiar traits.

"You had a spontaneous ending of your pregnancy?" asked the doctor.

"Yes. A year ago. That was a bit of a rough patch for me."

"I don't see a cause listed here."

"Dr. Giacalone said it was difficult to pinpoint a single factor."

"Everything has a cause," replied Dr. Goldsmith. She turned to Sylvia and smiled. "Most spontaneous terminations occur because the fetus isn't developing normally. The most common causes are chromosome issues associated with random errors that occur as the embryo divides and grows, or as the result of a damaged sperm or egg cell.

"There are other ways a pregnancy can end. In the intrauterine demise of the fetus, the embryo forms but then stops developing. With what we call a blighted ovum, there is no formation of an embryo.

"You could have had a molar pregnancy, in which case the father provides both sets of chromosomes. There is no development of a fetus, only an abnormal growth of the placenta. In a partial molar pregnancy, the chromosomes from the mother remain, but the father also provides two sets of chromosomes. This condition is associated with placental abnormalities and growth of an abnormal fetus. Molar and partial molar pregnancies are not viable, and can sometimes be associated with cancerous changes of the placenta.

"Other causes that aren't related to chromosomes include diabetes, infections, hormonal problems, uterus or cervix problems, or thyroid disease."

She stood in front of Sylvia, who was seated on the end of the examining table with her legs and feet dangling over the edge. "I have enormous respect for Dr. Giacalone and the Dearborn Medical Group," the doctor said with her red lips. "But you may find that we have a different approach to patient care. Here at Willowdale we believe that nothing happens by accident and that every disease or condition has a specific cause. In addition, we place a very high priority on uncovering that cause. After all, how can you draw a conclusion about something unless you fully understand it?"

"I suppose you cannot," replied Sylvia.

"Correct. If you had a shipment of a part for a car go missing, you wouldn't rest until you found that shipment or knew what happened to it— am I right? Or would you throw up your hands and say, 'We lost the parts. We don't know where they are. Next time will be better.'"

"Obviously the former."

"Of course! Here we have the same attitude." She put a tourniquet around Sylvia's arm. "We're going to test your blood and see if we can eliminate any hormonal issues. We'll also run a complete DNA profile to pinpoint genetic red flags. As a bonus, you'll learn all about your genetic heritage. People are often amazed to discover where they came from. When I had mine done, I found out I had a great-great grandfather who was North African. I never knew!" Dr. Goldsmith drew the blood into four little vials. "If you don't mind me asking, do you have any plans to get pregnant again? I noticed you're unmarried—is the man still in your life?"

"No, we split up. But I do have a boyfriend."

"Ah—someone new. Where does he work?"

"He works at Hilltop Financial. Downtown."

"That's one of the Two Hundred K. A good one, too. You don't need me to tell you that you shouldn't be messing around with any man from the canaille. And certainly not an aberrant! That would mean the end of your career and any sort of normal life for you and your family."

"You don't have to worry about that. I have no intention of throwing my life away."

"What's the lucky fella's name?"

Sylvia thought this question crossed the fine line between professional and personal, but Dr. Goldsmith exuded a motherly quality that put her at ease, and so she replied, "Jason Quin. He's an analyst. Specializes in the telecom industry. He writes investor reports for the weekly Hilltop Financial newsletter."

"Nice job," replied Dr. Goldsmith. "Okay—I think we're all set. We'll get the results of the blood tests in twenty-four hours and the DNA tests in forty-eight. If you have any questions, please don't hesitate to call and I'll get right back to you."

SYLVIA BRAND

CHAPTER EIGHT

At a few minutes before six o'clock, Jason stood at the door to Sylvia's apartment in Mexicantown. Like every man who would be attending that evening's concert, he was dressed in a dark business suit (his was blue), white button-down shirt, and necktie. He rang the bell. She came downstairs to the vestibule. "It's gotten cool out," she said. "Do I need a coat?"

"I don't think so, unless you want one," he replied diplomatically. "It's totally up to you."

"Where are we going?"

"El Barzon."

"I'd better get a coat."

Sylvia returned wearing a lightweight cream-colored wool coat. "Does this look nice on me?"

"Yes," replied Jason. "Very lovely."

"Better than my blue one?"

"What?"

"I said, does it look better than my blue one?"

"They both look equally beautiful. Since you're wearing this one, why don't you keep it on, and we'll have a nice dinner and then the concert."

They got into his car and drove to the restaurant. Their table for two was waiting.

"So how was your day today?" Jason asked as he looked at the menu.

"Pretty good," she replied. "Carin helped me sort out a problem with a shipment of O-rings from Indonesia. Our container got swept overboard in a typhoon, and it looked like a major headache. In about ten seconds Carin reeled off a list of other Sun Motors plants that had excess inventory they could send us. I was impressed. The guy's got game."

"You called him 'the guy.' Sounds like you're getting used to him."

"Yes, I think all of us are. Carin is a huge improvement over Meekin."

She paused. She hadn't told Jason very much about Meekin other than he was generally a jerk. She hadn't told him about Meekin's inappropriate touching or repeated invitations to dinner. To do so, she assumed, would only anger Jason—a former Michigan State linebacker—and incite him to beat up the guy. Sylvia knew that would not be a positive solution to the problem.

"Oh yeah, Meekin," said Jason. "He's gone now, right?"

"Yes—he's gone. Supposedly to the Sun Motors Building. Anyway, Carin seems to be as close as you can get to the ideal boss. He gives you help when you need it and stays out of your hair when you don't. He's obviously a robot, which makes it much easier. It's not like he's some sort of facsimile human being, which would be really weird. How about you? Anything new at work?"

"We've learned that North American Telecom will be rolling out their holographic video chat service next month. Instead of seeing a flat image of the person you're talking to, you'll see them sitting or standing next to you. If you get up and walk around, it'll be just like they're in the room with you."

"I'm going to hate that," laughed Sylvia. "It's bad enough your boss can see you on the screen in two dimensions. Now you'll have to look good in three!"

"You'll always look good in three," replied Jason. "What else has happened at work? Oh yeah, on Monday the company launched its new employee healthcare program. They call it the Hilltop Financial Health Initiative. Apparently the Industrial Council has passed some new regulations mandating that every Two Hundred K employee have comprehensive healthcare, which is already pretty normal, but they also want the right to collect your personal health data. We got new consent forms to sign. I had signed a bunch of them years ago, but the company wanted them updated. I went for a physical yesterday. Fortunately my regular doctor was on the approved list. He did all the usual tests, including blood work and DNA."

"What a coincidence," replied Sylvia. "We've been going through the same process. New health plan, new consent forms, new physical exams. I had to switch doctors because my old one, Dr. Donna, refused to become a part of the Sun Motors Employee Wellness Plan network."

"Why did she refuse? That sounds like a career-killing move."

"She decided to retire. Some of her other partners are selling out to National Health Systems, which is plugged into the Sun Motors network. So I found a new doctor on the Sun Motors list. Her name is Helen Goldsmith. Seems very nice, very professional. A little bit nosey, though."

"Nosey?"

"She asked me if I had a boyfriend, and where you worked."

"Probably just trying to get to know you better."

"Yes, I suppose so."

After dinner, as they were driving to the concert hall, Sylvia said to Jason,

"This has been a very lovely evening so far, but sweetheart, you seem like you have something on your mind. Is there anything you want to talk about?"

"As a matter of fact, there is." With these words he pulled over to the curb. "There's a lovely little park right here. There are benches you can sit on next to the pond. Let's take a walk."

"Won't we be late for the concert?" said Sylvia as she unbuckled her seat belt.

"This will only take a few minutes. I just want to show you something."

He walked with her into the park, bathed in the cool glow of streetlights. In the distance they could hear kids playing basketball. He found a park bench under a willow tree by the side of the pond. They sat down and watched the ducks huddling and fussing in the shallows by the muddy bank.

"What do you want to tell me?" she asked.

Jason stood up and reached into his jacket pocket. As he did this he dropped to one knee in front of her, like a squire from King Arthur's court. From his pocket he produced a small felt-covered box. With his fingertips he flipped open the top of the box. The streetlights caught the glimmer of a diamond.

"Sylvia," he said, "I hope that you'll become my wife."

"Oh, Jason, I don't know what to say."

"Then just say 'yes.'"

"Yes—of course I will! I was hoping you would ask! Should I have said that? Oh, it doesn't matter. Yes, I will. I would like nothing more. May I try it on?"

"Please," said Jason. "I had to guess at your size. I hope it fits, but we can always have it resized."

She slipped the ring on her finger. "Oh, it fits perfectly! Do you like it?" She held out her hand so the ring sparkled in the light.

"Of course I like it," replied Jason, still on one knee on the asphalt sidewalk. "The question is, do you like it?"

"I love it," she replied as she leaned forward to give him a kiss. "I cannot tell you how happy I am! We have so much to talk about—the wedding, where we're going to live…"

"I thought maybe you could move into my place. I have plenty of room."

"Forget it, buster. I promised myself that when I got married, my husband and I would find a house of our own. No one is going to be moving into the other person's apartment. We're going to start off on an even footing. We're going to start driving around on weekends, looking at houses. It will be fun, you'll see."

"Okay," he said, raising his hands in mock surrender. "I know a really good real estate agent who can help us."

Sylvia glanced at her phone. "We'd better get going—we don't want to be late for the concert."

The Shapiro Theatre was a small hall with a few hundred seats, a testament to the relatively small market for chamber music. The volunteer usher showed Sylvia and Jason to their seats in the center of the hall a few rows from the stage. "We're in a good location," said Sylvia as the members of the audience milled around, talking to each other or reading their programs.

"I have to confess," said Jason, "a client gave me the tickets. He and his wife have a season subscription but they couldn't attend tonight. So here we are."

"Yes—here we are," said Sylvia as she kissed him on the cheek.

The house lights dimmed, and everyone settled into their seats. On the stage, a man dressed in a business suit walked into the glare of the spotlights. He introduced himself as William Masters, the managing director of the theatre. After welcoming everyone and delivering the usual announcements, he said, "Tonight, the Shapiro Theatre is particularly pleased to extend our warmest thanks to our generous corporate sponsor of this performance by the Linz String Quartet. Our sponsor is Alliance Partners. Please give them a warm round of applause."

The audience dutifully complied.

"In fact," continued Masters, "We have a very special representative from Alliance Partners with us tonight. He's sitting in one of the boxes… Palor, will you please stand up?"

One of the spotlights swung around to the box seats at the side of the hall. A figure stood up. To Sylvia's astonishment, he looked exactly like Carin, with the same plain, one-piece jumpsuit, short dark hair, pale brown skin, and wraparound glasses. The only difference was that Palor's jumpsuit was pale blue, whereas the one worn by Carin was khaki.

Palor turned to face the audience and gave a friendly wave.

"I don't want to embarrass Palor by talking about him," said Masters, "But you can see he's an autonomous humanoid operator. Is that correct, Palor?"

Palor nodded. "Yes, that's precisely correct. I manage the mergers and acquisitions department on the thirty-fifth floor of the Alliance Building. I can tell you that Alliance Partners is very pleased and honored to be the corporate sponsor of tonight's performance. At Alliance we are proud of our long tradition of strong commitment to arts and culture, which as I'm sure you all know is in perfect alignment with the vision of the Industrial Council. As for me, I must confess that I have very little knowledge of chamber music in general and string quartets in particular. I know a few facts. In the seventeen fifties the Austrian composer Joseph Haydn developed the string quartet into its current form, and ever since that time the string quartet—consisting of two violins, a viola, and a cello—has been considered a prestigious form and represents one of the true tests of the art of both composer and performer. As an ensemble, the Linz String Quartet is one of the premier practitioners of this art form. I look forward to the performance this evening."

To a smattering of applause and a few confused looks among members of the audience, Palor sat down.

"Oh my God, he looks just like Carin!" whispered Sylvia to Jason.

"Probably the same make and model," he shrugged.

"After the concert, let's go and talk to him."

At the end of the evening as the houselights were coming up, Sylvia hustled Jason up the aisle to the lobby, where they could position themselves to meet Palor as he came out of the boxes. A moment later he appeared with his human companion, a man dressed in the ubiquitous dark business suit. Sylvia saw that Palor was the same height as Carin and had the same appearance. Except for the color of his jumpsuit, they could have been twins.

Sylvia approached him and introduced herself and Jason.

"Sylvia, it's a pleasure to meet you in person," replied Palor. "Of course, I know you well. You're serving as the senior logistics manager at the Sun Motors Detroit Assembly Plant. Today you had a problem with a container of O-rings that was swept off the deck of the Globe Nebula, which left the Port of Tanjung Priok on the fifteenth of this month, bound for Honolulu and then San Diego. I believe my colleague Carin provided a solution." He turned to Jason. "It's a pleasure to meet you as well. I hope all is well at Hilltop Financial and with the telecom industry?"

"Yes, thank you—business has been very good," smiled Jason. "Do you have a particular interest in chamber music and string quartets?"

"A particular interest?" replied Palor. "I'm not sure what that means. While I have my job specialty, which is mergers and acquisitions, I'm interested in everything equally."

"I suppose that you were sent here tonight," offered Sylvia. "Your boss asked you to attend."

"Yes," replied Palor. "The goal of tonight's visit was to maintain my steady rate of machine learning, which is key to artificial intelligence. Tonight's concert was very informative, despite the many mistakes made by the performers."

"Mistakes?" asked Sylvia. "The quartet sounded pretty good to me."

"In the Schubert 'String Quartet Number 14 in D minor'   I counted eighty deviations from the score," said Palor. "In the Debussy 'String Quartet in G major' there were sixty-seven deviations. In Leoš Janáček's 'String Quartet Number 1, the Kreutzer Sonata,' there were—"

"Forgive me for interrupting," said Sylvia, "but do you really believe all of those deviations, as you call them, were mistakes? Every performer gives every piece his or her artistic interpretation. It's the emotional element that makes each performance different."

"Either you play the piece as written or you don't," replied Palor in his pleasant genderless voice. "Wouldn't you agree?"

"I don't know if I would," replied Sylvia.

"For example," continued Palor, "in the business of motor vehicle manufacturing, the cars are built according to specifications, and the goal—as it is in any business that makes a product—is to have zero defects. In the old days the goal was Six Sigma, which is three point four defects per million attempts. Today, nothing less than Ten Sigma is acceptable. Soon we will achieve One Hundred Sigma."

"I understand what you're saying," replied Sylvia. "But you may find it helpful if you looked at the written score for a piece of music as being like human DNA, which is never set in stone but is subject to interpretation, through the process of gene expression. Human identical twins share the same DNA but still show subtle differences in appearance and behavior. This is because genes can be switched on or off, depending on the environment and other factors."

"That seems rather random," replied Palor.

"If you'll excuse us," interjected Jason, "it's been a long day and I think we should be making our way home."

Palor nodded, and then said with a smile, "Sylvia, I see you are wearing a new engagement ring. A lovely twisted vine style with pavé diamonds and a cushion-cut stone. Should I congratulate you and Jason?"

"Yes, thank you," said Jason before Sylvia could answer. "We haven't made any announcements yet, but we are engaged. I assume you won't tell anyone."

"No, of course not. I wish you both every happiness."

In the car on the way to Sylvia's apartment, she turned to Jason. "That was an extremely creepy encounter."

"How so?"

"Palor knew who I was and all about the missing container of O-rings! The problem happened just this morning. The only people who knew about it were Carin and I. We didn't broadcast it to the whole world, and especially not to a management robot at Alliance Partners. And he also knew my engagement ring was new. I've only been wearing it for a few hours!"

"I can't explain it," said Jason. "Unless Carin and Palor share a common memory."

"Do you mean that Palor knows everything that Carin knows, and vice versa?"

"Maybe. Perhaps instead of being fully autonomous machines, they're more like two computer terminals networked to the same cloud database."

"Instead of being pseudo humans," said Sylvia, "they could be pseudo ants—individual representatives of one colony. They can act independently while being linked to one centralized consciousness."

CHAPTER NINE

At her desk on Thursday morning, as Sylvia was arranging for the return of a shipment of defective brake calipers, her calendar pinged.

Hurriedly she closed the file, picked up her phone, and tapped a number. "Hey Mei Lien, you're going to the grand opening of the new day care center, aren't you? Yes, I know—all the women are supposed to attend. I don't know why they aren't making all the men go too. That seems a little bit sexist. I'll swing by your desk and we can go together."

After going down the elevator to the ground floor, Sylvia and Mei Lien walked through an enclosed breezeway to an adjacent building. Inside the entrance atrium, a crowd of mostly female employees had gathered along with a smattering of men. For a few minutes they stood while more employees arrived. The doors to the new Margaret J. Atkinson Day Care Center were closed. Next to the doors a temporary stage had been erected, with a podium and some folding chairs. On an easel was a large photo of a woman. It was a formal portrait, from the shoulders up, and she was smiling.

"Who's that a picture of?" asked Mei Lien.

"I suppose it must be Margaret J. Atkinson," replied Sylvia. "I've never before seen her photo. You know the family is exceedingly private."

At precisely ten o'clock, a group of people mounted the stage. A man took to the podium. Sylvia recognized him as Gerald Posey, the chief operating officer of the plant and its highest executive. She had watched Posey's motivational messaging videos—everyone who worked at the plant had—but this was the first time she had seen him in person. She thought he was a rather bland looking man, with no particular features that would indicate an interesting character or personality. Like the other men on the stage, he was wearing a dark business suit, white shirt, and a necktie that Sylvia thought was too long.

"What's with these huge neckties that all the men are suddenly wearing?"

she whispered to Mei Lien. "It's must be a new fad or something. I hope it doesn't last long."

"The theory is that a long necktie makes you look taller," Mei Lien whispered in return. "Personally, I think it makes them look like circus clowns. To complete the ensemble, all they need are huge shoes and funny hats." Stifling a giggle, she looked around them. No one appeared to be listening. Sylvia and Mei Lien both knew it was a bad idea to publicly discuss company leaders in any way other than with effusive praise.

On the stage, Sylvia could see the other managers she knew, including Carin, who stood off to one side. "I can't imagine what our boss could possibly know about day care," Sylvia whispered to Mei Lien.

"I'm sure he must think the process of human reproduction is quite appalling," said Mei Lien. "He would probably want us to clone ourselves in a nice sterile laboratory."

"May I have your attention please," said Posey. The sound of his amplified voice reverberated through the atrium. "I would like to welcome you to the grand opening of the Margaret J. Atkinson Day Care Center at the Sun Motors Detroit Assembly Plant. Spearheaded by our chairman and CEO, Mr. Hugh Atkinson, and the Atkinson family leadership team, this new facility is part of a company-wide effort to support our Sun Motors families and give their children every possible advantage. This facility is named in honor of Margaret J. Atkinson, with whom Mr. Atkinson has shared forty years of marriage. She has devoted her career to helping children and families. She believes, as do we all, that there is nothing more important than the care and nurturing of our future leaders."

When his speech eventually concluded—Sylvia thought he droned on longer than was required to heap praise upon the Atkinson family—the group of executives left the stage and assembled in front of the door, across which had been stretched a red ribbon. To the sound of applause, Posey cut the ribbon and the doors were opened. Some of the assembled spectators moved forward while others hung back, waiting for the opportunity to leave.

"Might as well go take a look," said Mei Lien. "I have a feeling that you and Jason might soon be availing yourselves of its services."

They entered a brightly lit and cheerful room that looked like any other upscale kindergarten. Sunny yellow—the official color of Sun Motors—dominated the color scheme. Kid-sized tables and chairs, boxes of toys, and a TV monitor occupied the central space. Another section had been turned into a spacious indoor playground with a slide and a small jungle gym, all made from yellow plastic. Towards the rear of the room was a glass-enclosed space that to Sylvia looked like a clinic.

The center was already populated with twenty or so children, from toddlers to kids who looked like they were four or five years old, nearly ready for elementary school. Overseeing the kids were a man and a woman. They were both wearing white and navy blue—the man a white shirt and blue pants, while the woman a white blouse and blue skirt.

"Must be tough to play with kids while you're wearing a skirt," Sylvia whispered to Mei Lien.

The boys in the day care center were wearing white shirts and blue pants, while the girls wore blue jumpers over white blouses.

Sylvia approached the male teacher, who was sitting at a small table with two kids. They were coloring on pads of paper. She introduced herself. His name was Ahmed.

"I'm impressed with what I see," said Sylvia. "This is a first-class facility."

"Thank you," replied Ahmed. He seemed very pleasant.

"Can I ask you—what's with the uniforms? Is that some new thing?"

"The uniforms? Mrs. Atkinson firmly believes that an advanced society needs to focus on what we have in common rather than what separates us. An important part of the center's mission is to get every child on the same page, so to speak. Here, no one is any better than anyone else. We're all part of the Sun Motors family. The children have a sense of belonging, just like we all do."

Sylvia looked around the room at the children. "This is quite an attractive group. If I dare say it, they're all exceptionally beautiful. They could all be little fashion models. Tell me—how do you handle special needs kids? Or what if I had a child with a birth defect, like a missing limb?"

A fleeting shadow of bewilderment passed over Ahmed's face. "Um, in order to be accepted, children need to go through the screening process," he said. "I don't have anything to do with that."

"Oh, you mean this center isn't open to every child of a Sun Motors employee? To get in you have to qualify?"

"Yes. The people in human resources do the screening, just like they screen people who are applying for a job."

"I see," nodded Sylvia. She nodded towards the glassed-in area. "It looks like you've got a medical clinic over there. May we go inside?"

Ahmed shook his head. "No, sorry. It's not open for tours. I think it's a Board of Health requirement. But it's just an ordinary clinic where the doctor can provide regular checkups and attend to everyday injuries—cuts and bruises. That's all."

"Is it always wide open like that, so anyone can see inside?"

"No, they have curtains they can draw across the windows."

"They must be able to do blood tests and that sort of thing, too?"

"I really wouldn't know," replied Ahmed quickly. He abruptly turned his attention to a little boy who was coloring. "Say, that's nice! Is it a tree?"

The boy nodded.

Drifting away from the teacher and kids at the table, Sylvia and Mei Lien approached the glassed-in clinic. It looked like any other pediatric medical facility, with walls decorated with brightly painted cartoon elephants and bunnies. There was an examining table and all the ubiquitous cabinets and medical devices. In the rear was a counter with a computer on top, along with racks for tubes.

"That computer in the back looks familiar," said Sylvia.

Mei Lien peered at it through the window. "It's a Matrix Genome 3000," she said. "A desktop DNA sequencer. They each cost two hundred thousand dollars. They're supposed to be the most accurate small machine on the market."

"They're for sequencing DNA? Why would they need that in this company clinic?"

"Maybe as service to employees who want to know how their kids stack up in the DNA sweepstakes," said Mei Lien. "Or for parents who want to see if their kids have a genetically inherited disease, so they can plan ahead for treatment."

"Or perhaps," said Sylvia, "as a way to identify children who they think have a genetic inferiority."

Later that day, as Sylvia was working in her cubicle, the image of Carin appeared on her screen.

"Hello employees of the Sun Motors Detroit Assembly Plant Logistics Office," he began. "I'd like to talk to you today about something that's very important to the company, to the Industrial Council, and I hope to you. It's what traditionally has been called esprit de corps, which is defined as the common spirit existing in the members of a group, and which inspires feelings of enthusiasm, devotion, and strong regard for the honor of the group. Within this great organization, we're an important group, and I hope that we can build an esprit de corps that is second to none within our company and even within all the member organizations of the Industrial Council.

"Now then, those of you who attended today's grand opening of the new Margaret J. Atkinson day care center will have noticed that the children present—the very first to be admitted to the center—were all wearing clothing of white and navy blue. The teachers were too. This is to reflect the belief of both Mr. and Mrs. Atkinson that while on the job or at school, people benefit from the freedom of not having to worry about their wardrobe. Mrs. Atkinson has written in her recently published book Song for a New Civilization, which I hope you all will read if you have not yet done so, that when she was a girl she was required to wear a uniform to school; and instead of feeling as though this were a limitation on her freedom, she felt it gave her more freedom by lifting from her shoulders the heavy burden of choice. I'm reminded of the practice of our current president of the United Americas, Robert Deacon, who has said that he keeps a closet full of gray suits and white shirts because it frees him from having to make a trivial decision each morning and allows him to focus on what's truly important.

"Therefore, beginning next quarter, which is in two weeks, all employees of the logistics office will be following the new Sun Motors workplace attire guidelines. I won't recite every requirement in this message—you can read them for yourself on the human resources page. Suffice to say, the principle components are a white shirt and navy blue slacks or suit for men and white blouse with navy blue skirt for women. The human resources page provides a list of clothing retailers that stock the approved shade of navy blue."

There was more, mostly about subsidies and other incentives promote the new program, which Carin called "The Sun Motors Way." Specific penalties for noncompliance were not mentioned. Sylvia knew they didn't have to be.

SYLVIA BRAND

CHAPTER TEN

That afternoon Sylvia went to the break room, where she was joined by Mei Lien, Lauren, and Tameeka. They admired Sylvia's new engagement ring.

"Have you set the date?" asked Tameeka as she poured her coffee.

"Not yet, but it will be soon, we hope," replied Sylvia. "We see no reason for a long engagement."

After a discussion of the many wonderful personal qualities of Jason, the conversation drifted to other topics.

"What's up with the new office dress code?" asked Mei Lien. "I haven't worn a skirt to work in years. Are we going back to the twentieth century? Navy blue isn't a good color for me. And are we supposed to wear matching shoes and carry a matching purse?"

"I don't think it's so bad," said Tameeka. "I understand where the company is coming from. When I was a little kid, my mom would go to her job wearing blue jeans and sandals. Her company sold camping and other outdoor recreational gear, and the employees were encouraged to be super-casual at work. There was no discipline—not even a boss, really. It was just sort of assumed you'd do a good job. Then the Global Depression hit and the business went bankrupt. One hundred and fifty employees were laid off. It was a horrible time. We came close to having to live in our car, but then mom got a job in a restaurant. She had to wear a uniform. It was a starched white shirt and black slacks. The work environment was like, 'OK, no fooling around, we are totally professional. We need to be the best.' The restaurant survived and we weren't evicted. It was a close call! If I have to wear a boring uniform every day, I can live with it."

"I think a restaurant is a little bit different from an office where you're not interacting with the public," said Mei Lien. "And the fact that the company where your mom worked went bankrupt during the Global Depression may have had nothing to do with the company culture. The entire national economy went down the drain. The market for outdoor recreational gear vanished. No one was buying anything."

"If you look at history," added Lauren, "societies where people are forced to conform to an artificial standard are less creative. The workers don't see themselves as being able to think outside the box. There's less innovation and more stagnation."

"I'll leave the innovation to the bosses who get paid to think," said Tameeka. "Straining my brain is above my pay grade. I just want to get along and go along."

Sylvia scrolled through her phone. "I found the page that gives the new wardrobe rules. It's a long list."

"What does it say about shoes?" asked Mei Lien.

"It says that sneakers, athletic shoes, and sandals are prohibited. Shoes must be closed toe, and the heel must be no more than two inches in height. Choose basic conservative pumps in navy blue, brown, black, or maroon. They must match the conservative tone of the suit. No 'strange or unusual designs,' whatever that means."

"It means you can't wear your black leather dominatrix boots," said Lauren.

"I'll remember that," replied Sylvia. "But to answer your question, nowhere does it say that your shoes must match your skirt. But it does say that skirt length should be a little below the knee. No miniskirts, girls."

At that moment Carin entered the break room.

"I didn't know you drank coffee," joked Mei Lien.

"I was just passing by and I saw you were here, so I decided to come in and say hello," he replied. "No coffee for me, thank you."

"Carin," said Sylvia, "as long as you're here, I'd like to tell you something. Last night I had the most interesting encounter. At the chamber music concert."

"Yes, I know," he nodded. "You met Palor. You and Jason spoke to him after the concert. You were wearing your new engagement ring. Congratulations. Have you set the date?"

"Not yet," said Sylvia. "You guys will be among the first to know. I brought up the subject of my interesting encounter—which you already seem to know about—because I was amazed that Palor, despite having never met me before that moment, knew practically everything about me that you know. He described the problem with the Globe Nebula exactly. It was startling. Do you guys have some sort of memory-sharing system?"

"That describes it very well," said Carin. "We're all connected to the cloud, and can access any data from any of our brethren. In addition, if some new data appears that's relevant to me, I'll get a flag telling me it's there. That saves me the time and energy needed to constantly search the database. It's a highly efficient system."

"So how many of your brethren, as you call them, are working within companies like ours?" asked Mei Lien.

"Sorry, that's classified," smiled Carin.

"Okay, I get that," she said, "but if you have access to the individual and collective memories of your brethren, what happens if one of you is employed by a competitor of Sun Motors? Could that competitor access your memory and your knowledge of everything you witness or in which you participate on a daily basis here at Sun Motors?"

"Good point," added Sylvia. "In fact, Alliance Partners, the employer of Palor, is a big holding company with many investments in the automotive sector. They own a controlling interest in Shang Tono Corporation, a company based in Korea that makes vehicle airbags for most of the leading automakers. Shang Tono is in the unique position of having access to production records and projections for all their client companies. That means Palor has the same access. But Shang Tono doesn't sell to Sun Motors—we buy our airbags from a company in Indonesia. But since you, Carin, work here at Sun Motors, Palor knows our production history. And if another one of your brethren worked at Shang Tono, then he would also have access to our production numbers and even our contracts."

"In such an environment," said Mei Lien, "it would seem impossible to keep trade secrets."

"Carin," said Sylvia, "I'll bet right now you know how many airbags each of our competitors have ordered for the next four quarters."

Carin smiled. "You guys are good at creating hypothetical situations. That shows excellent inductive reasoning. You assert that because Palor and I share a common memory database (which, by the way, is updated in real time), then our competitors will know our plans, which is a bad thing. But you forget that we all operate under the careful and all-knowing guidance of the Industrial Council. The Council neither envisions nor seeks a world in which one member corporation has an unfair advantage over another. The philosophy of the Council is that among Council members, there's enough to go around. There are enough slices of the pie to keep everyone happy, and therefore cheating is counterproductive."

Sylvia put her coffee cup on the counter. "So you're saying that competition is only an illusion!"

"The Council believes that competition among Council member companies is irrational and wasteful," replied Carin. "But our national competition with the military and industrial power of Rodinia is very real. As you know, open warfare with Rodinia could happen at any time."

"So the government has told us every day since the end of the Global Depression," said Lauren with a smirk.

"Watch what you say," replied Carin with a sharpness of tone that Sylvia had never heard him use before. "The threat from Rodinia is very real. And it's not just from their military. Our government has identified a massive network of Rodinian spies operating in the United Americas. These agents seek to infiltrate every level of society—including the aberrants—with a twofold mission. One is to collect intelligence and the other is to sow discord. As the United Americas intensifies our defensive stance against the aggression of these covert agents, all Morta autonomous humanoid operators have two key missions: to enhance productivity within key Council member corporations and to identify any suspected spies."

"Part of your job here is to look for spies?" said Lauren. "That's crazy. We're just a car company."

"Again, I urge you to choose your words carefully," replied Carin with an expression that was an accurate facsimile of an angry scowl. "According to the mandates of both the Industrial Council and the White House, certain key industries are vital to our national defense. Because of their importance to our nation's security, they are outside the jurisdiction of Congress. Instead they are regulated by the President with the advice and counsel of the Industrial Council. Sun Motors falls into this category. This means that because our responsibility is greater, the standards we must meet are higher. I need not remind you this is a very special place. If the demands put upon us are heavy, it's because we represent an important bulwark against those who would harm our country."

"Was Judy Loring a spy?" asked Sylvia.

Carin turned to her with a cold smile. "As you know, Judy Loring has taken a leave of absence. We do not know when, or if, she will return."

"I'm puzzled because she left town with her entire family," replied Sylvia. "In the middle of the night."

"And you know this how?"

"I was concerned about them, so I talked to their neighbor."

"And what did this neighbor say?"

As Carin stared directly at her without moving, as if he were frozen, the room fell silent. Sylvia suddenly felt she had said too much. Trying not to show her nervousness—but of course Carin was analyzing her every breath and blink of her eyes!—she took her coffee cup to the sink and began to rinse it off.

"Oh," she said, "the neighbor didn't know much except in the evening they were at home and in the morning they were gone. Judy and her family must have left during the night. That's all."

"I know Judy is a friend of yours," said Carin in a more soothing tone. "Therefore, while it's not information that I would ordinarily be allowed to divulge, I can say to you that Judy is not suspected of being a spy. She has taken a leave of absence."

"That's reassuring," said Lauren. "I would hate to think one of our team was the agent of a hostile power!"

"A thought has suddenly occurred to me," said Sylvia. "If you're looking for spies, would it not be true that a person born and raised in Rodinia would have a genetic heritage quite different from someone whose family has been living in the United Americas for generations?"

Carin smiled. "Again you show superior inductive reasoning. While there is no certainty that a person from Rodinia would be genetically different from a citizen of the United Americas, there is a high degree of likelihood. However, you must not forget about the native-born Americans who might be recruited to become spies for Rodinia. Their agents use highly sophisticated methods to convert weak-minded citizens to their cause."

"Therefore when casting the net in hopes of ensnaring spies from Rodinia," said Sylvia, "you have no preconceptions about whom you might catch. It could be anybody."

"That's right," replied Carin. "A spy could be anybody."

That night, Sylvia and Jason snuggled on the sofa in Sylvia's apartment. After dinner they thought they would watch a movie, but a romantic interlude and then conversation had delayed the opening credits.

"Sweetheart, I think we should get married right away," Sylvia suddenly said.

"Really?" he replied. "Why? I mean, I have no objection—it really doesn't matter to me—but I assumed you wanted a regular church wedding."

"Let's be realistic. My parents are divorced and my father is a tightwad who won't give us nickel for a wedding. Your dad is no longer with us and your mom lives in Alaska. The idea of a traditional church wedding is rather ridiculous. To spend all of that money just to have a ceremony that looks like what you're supposed to do rather than what you should do seems crazy. I'd rather spend our money on a down payment for a house."

"I'm with you on that," he said.

There was a moment of silence.

"Is there anything else?" Jason asked as he ran his fingers through her hair. "You seem quiet tonight. Not your usual bubbly self."

"I'm sorry. I just feel—I don't know what it is. Call it a sense of foreboding. At work, things are changing. The culture is changing."

"I thought the culture was pretty bad when Randolph Meekin was your boss. When Carin arrived you told me it was like a new day dawning."

She reached for a handful of popcorn, which they had made in anticipation of the movie. "Yes, that's what it seemed like. But in the past few days it feels like we're moving towards a culture of hyper efficiency. The employees are being treated like cogs in a machine. I signed a bunch of new consent forms that, while I'm at work, give the company the right to collect and analyze the dead skin cells that slough off my body and the exhalations that come out of my lungs!"

"Yeah, we've had to sign the same kinds of forms."

"And now we have a new dress code. I have to go out and buy navy blue skirts and white blouses. It's all part of 'The Sun Motors Way." The company is offering wardrobe subsidies for current employees, but it strikes me as a big step backward in time."

"Does it have anything to do with the escalating tensions with Rodinia? Are they trying to impose discipline as they move us toward a wartime economy?"

"Could be," Sylvia said as she drew the blanket higher around her legs. In the fireplace the flame had dwindled to a dull orange glow. "To be honest, I don't really care about the dress code. I can live with white blouses and blue skirts. I care a lot more about the loss of privacy. Carin has enormous powers of observation and memory. What would easily escape the notice of a human being, he zeroes in on. The other day he chided me for having two glasses of wine at lunch. This was based on his analysis of my breath when I was talking to him, as well as his observations of my pupils and dermal capillaries, or so he said. But however he did it, his analysis was on target. He even accurately said I was drinking Burgundy."

"You drink Burgundy?" asked Jason. "That's news to me."

"Among the crappy wine selection at the restaurant, it was the best choice. We were celebrating Meekin's transfer."

"Okay, so Carin is a highly observant busybody. What else is going on?"

"Today they had the grand opening of the new day care center at the plant. In the infirmary they've got a DNA sequencing machine. They can analyze the children's DNA! The center isn't even open to all employees—the kids have to pass some sort of screening process."

"Perhaps they're checking for genetic conditions. But it makes you wonder what they would do if they discovered a child had a genetic disorder such as Down syndrome, cystic fibrosis, or sickle cell anemia."

"My uncle Charlie had muscular dystrophy," said Sylvia. "I don't remember much about him. He died when I was little. But he was the only member of my family that I know of who had a genetic disease."

"All I know is that you're perfect in every way," said Jason as he kissed the top of her head. "And I'm sure you'll have perfect little babies."

"You mean we'll have perfect little babies," she laughed. "They'll take after you."

"And unlike me, they'll know their real mommy and daddy. No foster parents."

"Your parents did a good job," said Sylvia. "I'd say you turned out pretty well!" She pressed closer to Jason. "All I want is a nice normal family. A boy and a girl, and a cute little house in a good neighborhood. And a dog."

Jason smiled and stroked her cheek. "And you, Mrs. Quin, shall have them."

CHAPTER ELEVEN

The next morning at work, Sylvia noticed a man with a ladder installing devices high up, near the ceiling, in each corner of the office. He looked like an electrician and the devices looked like cameras. The job took about an hour. When he was finished, Sylvia noted that while the walls to her cubicle shielded her from two of the cameras, the two that were behind her had a good view of her desk and computer.

At a few minutes before ten o'clock, Sylvia went to the contracts team meeting. Tameeka, Mei Lien, Edouardo, Roger, Maxwell, and Lauren were already seated around the conference table. Sylvia—who had not yet gone shopping for her new office wardrobe—saw that Tameeka and Edouardo were wearing the requisite white and navy blue.

At exactly the turn of the hour, Carin entered. "Ah," said with satisfaction, "It's good to see that two of our team members have embraced the new office dress code. The Sun Motors Way is going to transform the company, and I'm looking forward to one hundred percent participation. And here's some good news: Today is Friday, and since Monday—this current week—the number of parts delivered late to the assembly lines has been zero. It's true! During the past four and one-half days, we've achieved an on-time delivery rate of one hundred percent. You can't get any better than that! I've been told that before I came here, you had massive problems with late deliveries. Huge headaches. The sloppiness of delivery—wrong parts, wrong quantities, wrong times—was costing the company millions of dollars. It was a disaster. I think we can all be very proud of the job we've done this week, and I know we can do the same great job every week."

With his hands, Carin applauded—stiffly but with enthusiasm. The seven members of the team joined in. Then Carin stopped, and the team members stopped too.

Sylvia had to admit to herself that during the past few days the department had brought its performance up a notch. But its work output, even under Meekin, had always been pretty good. Never had she heard anyone describe the functioning of the logistics office as being a disaster, or that problems with part deliveries had cost the company millions of dollars. Was Carin engaged in puffing up his own job performance? That seemed to contradict what Sylvia understood to be his bedrock rationality and impartiality. Unless his creators at Morta Laboratories had programmed him to sell himself, and the Bright Horizon pilot program, at every available opportunity.

"It's good to be able to deliver positive news," said Carin. "Now on to business." With brisk efficiency he led the discussion as each member of the team gave their reports and noted any problem areas.

At the conclusion of the regular agenda, Carin said, "Any questions?"

"Yes," said Sylvia. "What's with the cameras in the office? I saw the technician installing them this morning."

"I'm glad you asked," replied Carin. "Recently, you may have seen me walking around the office with some people who are unfamiliar to you. If not, you will. In any case, we are very fortunate to have with us for the next several weeks a team of professional management consultants from the Special Services office of the Industrial Council. Sun Motors has hired them to study every aspect of our operations here at the Detroit Assembly Plant, from the executive suites to the loading docks, with the goal of increasing efficiency across the board. It's one more part of the Sun Motors Way, our comprehensive effort to boost productivity while trimming waste. We want Sun Motors to be the automotive industry leader, and within the company I'm sure you'll agree that we—the people in this room—want the Detroit Assembly Plant to be number one in every key performance indicator."

"Okay, but why the cameras?" asked Edouardo.

"Their purpose is to observe and record your physical motions during the workday. These motions will be mapped and analyzed for wasted movement. There is no judgment involved. That's not why we're doing this. We want to find out if we're working as efficiently as possible.

"I'll give you an example. Let's say—just hypothetically—that Maxwell and Tameeka, who are currently stationed on opposite sides of the room, are working on a project that requires them to walk over to the other person's cubicle several times a day. The computer will record their movements and calculate the amount of time spent walking to each other's cubicles. If the analysis reveals that we would see an increase in efficiency by moving them closer together, then that's what we'll do."

"You'll be able to see everything we do at our desks," said Mei Lien. "You'll be able to see what's on my computer screen."

"Yes, but that's not particularly relevant to this program," said Carin. "We already collect and process that information. Your keystrokes are recorded, as are the files you open and view. That's a standard human resources function of employee oversight. This is designed to reveal your physical motions during the workday."

"Is there a camera in the ladies' room?" asked Sylvia.

"No," smiled Carin. "That would be a violation of your personal privacy. And it has nothing to do with workplace efficiency."

"The break room?" asked Roger.

"Again, no." Carin smiled. He put both hands flat on the table as if he were about to stand up. "I hope that explains everything. It's all part of making Sun Motors—and this office—an industry leader in productivity. Okay? Good." He stood up and left the room.

Sylvia whispered to Mei Lien, "Meet me in the break room in fifteen."

Sylvia went to her desk and checked a work file on her computer. She typed a few keystrokes. As a typist, Sylvia was unschooled. She typed with two fingers and made generous use of the delete key to correct her many clumsy typos. She had never thought much about it, because in her mind all that counted was the product. It didn't matter if she made a hundred mistakes while typing something because she corrected herself as she went along, and when she finally hit the "send" key the writing was always perfect and the numbers accurate.

To be sure, when Sylvia had first attended college she had tried to learn touch typing. For some reason—she never knew why—the effort was hopeless. She practiced and practiced, but could never associate the correct key with the correct finger. Finally she had given up, and had resigned herself to "hen pecking," as her typing teacher had once derided the technique.

For years she had hen pecked and the work had never suffered. Now, at this moment, she suddenly found that she had become self conscious about her typing. A computer somewhere deep in the bowels of the Sun Motors complex was recording and analyzing each and every keystroke. This computer, she surmised, was comparing her performance to that of her colleagues, or perhaps to a standard created by the Industrial Council.

It was judging her not on the product but the process.

She began to type more slowly and methodically. It was better, she reasoned, to type accurately the first time even if the pace were a little slower. She was working on a written report on a proposed new vendor for the electronic control unit for the Comanche satellite signal receiver, and she found herself trying to slow down and type without making any mistakes. But the effort did not have the desired result. It was as if for years she had been operating at a particular speed, and her mind and muscle memory had locked into that speed, no matter how imperfect the outcome. In trying to type more slowly and more carefully, she found that her attention wandered. The task was more boring. She found that she would forget what she was writing, and had to stop and remember, which slowed her down even more.

"Damn," she muttered.

She glanced up at the nearest camera. Its gleaming black eye regarded her with indifference. Could it read lips? Why not? If a computer could recognize your face, at night and in the rain, and distinguish it from millions of other faces, then lip reading should be an easy next step.

Focus. Just get the report done. The vendor looks good and we can do business with them.

A key fact in their favor was they had no connection with Rodinia. Word had come down from the Sun Motors Building that foreign vendors with any association to Rodinia or any of its allies, or who sold to companies in Rodinia or any of its allies, were to be viewed with deep suspicion. If possible, they were to be terminated and new contracts signed with vendors approved by the Industrial Council.

Damn! I've used the delete key a dozen times in one sentence. Okay. Slow down. Take a deep breath.

Sylvia looked over the top of her cubicle at the rest of the office. People were working as they always did. Maxwell, coffee cup in hand (as always!), was walking over to Tameeka's cubicle. He looked so normal and relaxed. Did it not bother him that he was being watched the way a researcher watches a rat in a maze? Perhaps he was a good actor. Sylvia thought she, herself, was a terrible actor. Jason always told her this. "You cannot tell a lie," he had said. "You're too honest. You'd give yourself away." He was right. Even when she had to deliver an innocuous phony compliment to someone—such as when Estelle had worn a hideous dress to the office holiday party and Sylvia had told her how lovely it looked—she felt her heart racing and the wave of deceit slosh through her brain. If Estelle had possessed one tenth of Carin's powers of observation, the fib would surely would have been revealed.

She glanced at her clock. Time to meet Mei Lien in the break room.

But why would she, Sylvia, need to go to the break room? Her visit would be on the record. She had to be able to justify it.

Sylvia never drank coffee. Just never cared for it. But now, she reasoned, was a good time to start. The coffee machine was in the break room. Maxwell went there ten times a day with his cup. Perhaps Carin would notice this and speak to him about it. Perhaps not. There was no way to tell. But having an interest in coffee was a good cover for getting Sylvia out of her cubicle and stretching her legs.

She stood up and, with a cautious glance at the camera—don't look at it too long!—she casually made her way along the aisle of cubicles to the hallway. Were there cameras here? She wasn't sure. She entered the break room, where Mei Lien was waiting. A careful inspection of the corners of the walls and the ceiling revealed no cameras.

"What do you think?" she said to Mei Lien.

Mei Lien shrugged. "A camera could be hidden anywhere. There could be one in the microwave, or in the ceiling vent. We have to assume we're being watched from the moment we drive into the parking lot in the morning until we drive out in the evening."

"But who can live like that?"

"It's happening all over. My sister works for Onyx Telecom. She does customer service. Same thing—cameras everywhere. And yesterday her department got a robot manager. Its name is Waller. From what she tells me, it's the same model as Carin. Same jumpsuit and wraparound glasses."

"I'm feeling more and more like a lab rat," said Sylvia. "With the medical consent forms, the creepy way Carin can analyze you, the uniforms, the cameras—I'm beginning to wonder who I am. Where do I end and the outside world begins? Are my private thoughts the only thing remaining I can say are truly mine?"

"Soon enough they'll be able to read your mind," laughed Mei Lien. "Remember, it's just a job, okay? Eight hours out of your day. When you go home, what you do ain't nobody's business but your own. You're a free person. Look at it this way: It sure beats being one of the aberrants. They've got nothing. To be on the inside you must pay the price, but I'd say it's worth it."

At that moment Tameeka walked in. "Hey girls, what's up?" she asked as she went to the refrigerator.

"We were just talking about the new cameras," said Mei Lien. Sylvia wished she hadn't said it. Perhaps because Tameeka had replaced Judy under mysterious circumstances, Sylvia hadn't yet warmed to her.

"What about them?" said Tameeka as she took out a plastic cup with a cover.

"The idea seems a bit overbearing," said Sylvia. "Doesn't it?"

Tameeka put the plastic cup on the counter and opened it. It looked like it had yogurt inside. "I don't care," she said as she dipped a plastic spoon into the cup. "I've got nothing to hide. They can put a camera in my cubicle for all I care. I only want to do my job, get my paycheck, and go home. I'm here for eight hours a day. I don't care what they make me do for those eight hours as long as they pay me."

"But aren't you worried about the invasion of your privacy?" asked Mei Lien.

"Invasion of my privacy? I don't expect any privacy here, except in the ladies' room. If they put a camera in there, I'd be pissed. But out in the office? There's no such thing as privacy. For eight hours a day, they own you." Holding her cup and spoon, she turned to face them. "Girls, if you want my advice, I'd say, 'smile for the camera.'" She walked out of the room.

"You know, in a weird way I admire her," said Sylvia. "Here I am, getting all freaked out because I think I'm under the microscope, and there goes Tameeka with not a worry in the world."

"Do you know why it doesn't bother her?" asked Mei Lien.

"No—why?"

"Because she is astonishingly naïve and she believes the company will treat her fairly. She believes in the goodness of the world. She truly believes that if she does nothing wrong in her own eyes, then the company will treat her honorably. She doesn't understand that if the company wants to screw you, they will find a way and they will do it."

As Sylvia stirred her coffee—which was getting cold, a condition that didn't bother her in the slightest because she wasn't going to drink it anyway—she thought for a moment. "Do you think Tameeka could be a Rodinian agent?" she whispered. "After all, if you were going to be an industrial spy, you'd want to get along with everybody, especially with your bosses, and you'd do nothing to rock the boat. You'd do a good job at work while avoiding the spotlight."

Mei Lien frowned. "I don't know. I suppose anything's possible. Personally I'm not sure if I believe any of this spy talk."

"Why not?"

"I'm sure there are some spies from Rodinia working here in the United Americas. Every nation spies on every other nation. Even friendly nations spy on each other. That's been going on for centuries. The question is whether the spies from Rodinia are more numerous or more threatening than is traditionally expected, and whether you can use the threat of spies—as if they were a big bad bogeyman—to curtail traditional basic human rights." She glanced at the clock on the wall. "I'd better be going. In five minutes I have a video conference with a supplier in Brazil."

Sylvia returned to her desk. While her talk with Mei Lien and Tameeka had shown her that other people could view the increasing loss of privacy at Sun Motors with casual acceptance, she couldn't shake the feeling of being self-conscious and on edge. She told herself that Tameeka was right—it was just a job, and it didn't matter what they did to you from nine to five.

They could watch you, listen in on your phone calls, track your movements as you walked around the office, record each keystroke of your work on the computer, and even collect the organic material that came out of your body each and every minute you were on company property.

They could store your personal data in their vast databases, analyze it, compare it to others, and even sell it to other companies for whatever reason they wanted.

They could make you sign a non-disclosure agreement, ensuring you wouldn't go to the aberrant press with the inside story of life among the Two Hundred K. They could make you sign an arbitration agreement that forced you to settle any pay disputes within the company, in private, instead of in civil court, and you couldn't publicly reveal the amount of your salary.

They could make you wear a uniform like a schoolgirl. What was next—assembling outside around the flagpole each morning to sing the company song?

They could do all these things because every other Thursday afternoon, Sun Motors, Inc. sent a direct deposit into your bank account. This was the money that paid for your comfortable lifestyle—the house, the car, the nice restaurants, the annual two-week vacation to the shore.

It was just a job, Sylvia told herself. At the end of my workday and for the following sixteen hours, I'm beyond their control.

In Sylvia's desk drawer was the bottle of painkillers she had relied on when Randolph Meekin was her boss. For a week she hadn't opened it. Feeling the sharp tension in the back of her neck, from the bottle she took two pills, which she washed down with her cold coffee.

SYLVIA BRAND

CHAPTER TWELVE

That evening at her apartment, with Jason waiting outside the bathroom door, Sylvia took a home pregnancy test.

It was positive.

"Oh my God!" she cried as she fell into his arms. "I can't believe it! We're going to have a baby!"

He kissed her and said, "This is good news! I've never been more happy. You're going to be the greatest mom!"

Suddenly Sylvia grew pensive.

"Sweetheart, what's the matter?" asked Jason. "You look as if a black cloud suddenly blotted out the sun."

Sylvia sat on the sofa and turned to face him. She put her hand on his knee. "I need to tell you something. Promise you won't be upset."

"You want to tell me something? Why should I be upset?"

"Just promise."

"Okay, I won't get upset. Now what is it?"

"This isn't the first time I've gotten pregnant."

"You mean you have a child somewhere?"

She gave a rueful smile. "No. It ended in a miscarriage. It was a few years ago, long before I met you. The father—my boyfriend at the time—said that he wanted to get married, but when I lost the baby he broke up with me. I was devastated."

"What a jerk," said Jason.

"You told me you wouldn't get upset."

"I'm not upset. I'm just saying the guy was a jerk and you're better off without him." He took her hands in his. "Listen to me. I love you. My devotion to you comes without strings attached. What happened to you is in the past. It's gone. We need to focus on the future. If for some reason this one doesn't go well, we'll try again. Other people have faced these challenges.

77

It's going to be all right. We're going to stick together. Okay?"

Wiping away a tear, she said with a smile, "Yes. I'm very hopeful, I really am. I just thought you should know. I don't want us to have any secrets."

"No secrets."

Brightening up, she said, "Do you think it will be a boy or a girl?"

"How should I know?" he laughed. "Do you want to find out, or would you rather be surprised?"

"I'd rather be surprised, but it's hard to avoid learning what it is. When my cousin Joanie had her baby, she didn't want to know the sex, but during a routine examination the ultrasound technician blurted out, 'Oh look, your can see his little boy parts!' So that was the end of the surprise."

"Okay, we'll tell the doctors we don't want to know. In the meantime, we need to start planning. Let's get married as soon as possible. We can get the license from the office of the Wayne County clerk. We're going to have to move quickly on buying a house. We've narrowed it down to three or four top contenders. This weekend let's look at them all one more time and hopefully we can decide."

"But we can't appear to be desperate," Sylvia said as she sat down on the sofa. "We're not going to tell any of the sellers that I'm expecting. We're going to say that we're planning a family, not that we're under the gun to move quickly."

"Right," agreed Jason. "What's the Sun Motors company policy about maternity leave?"

She thought for a moment. "Good question. I'll have to ask Estelle in human resources."

"And you'll need to go see your doctor. The new one—what was her name?"

"Rebecca Goldsmith at the Willowdale Center. I'll call her office tomorrow."

On Sunday, Sylvia and Jason made an offer on a charming house on a tree-lined street in the town of Northville. Built before the Global Recession, the Dutch colonial had three bedrooms and a nice big backyard. As they had agreed, Jason and Sylvia didn't reveal they were expecting a baby.

On Monday morning, Sylvia's buoyant mood did not go unnoticed. In the break room, which Sylvia was planning to visit more regularly despite the fact that her inclination to drink coffee was now even lower than it had been before she took the pregnancy test, Tameeka said, "Girl, you must have had a pretty special weekend. You're practically glowing."

Sylvia was gripped with indecision. She hated lying, which in her mind included omitting an obvious and significant truth. If someone said, "How was your weekend?" and your weekend included learning you had become pregnant, and you replied, "Oh, fine," and nothing more, then that was as good as lying.

But that morning at work, Tameeka was the first person she had talked to about a non-work related subject. She felt neither obligated nor interested in making Tameeka—about whom she continued to have uneasy feelings—the first person to hear the news.

"Jason and I made an offer on a house," replied Sylvia. "We're very excited about moving in. It's in Northville, near Maybury State Park."

"Oh, that's a nice area. I'm sure you're super excited."

"Yes we are. Well, I've got to get back for a phone call." Sylvia walked away with the feeling that she had bought some time. But the news would be difficult to keep quiet, and eventually everyone, including Carin, would know.

At two o'clock, having managed to avoid personal discussions with her colleagues at work, Sylvia arrived at the office of Dr. Goldsmith for her first pre-natal appointment. A blood test confirmed that Sylvia was six weeks pregnant.

"Do you have an obstetrician?" asked Dr. Goldsmith.

"No, I don't. There was an OB at Dearborn Medical Group, but she's retired."

"Okay, we'll help you find one. When you're at eight or nine weeks, antepartum care begins. Your OB receives your comprehensive medical history and provides you with a full physical examination and various screenings. So we need to get one lined up quickly. I'd be happy to recommend you to Dr. Elizabeth Darcy at Detroit Hospital. I think you'll like her very much."

"Thank you," said Sylvia. "You know I had a miscarriage a few years ago. Will that reduce my chances of having a successful pregnancy?"

"No. Miscarriage is usually a one-time occurrence. Most women who miscarry go on to have healthy pregnancies. Only about one percent of women will have repeated miscarriages."

"That's good to know."

Upon her return to the office at four o'clock, Sylvia went to see Estelle to ask about the company's policy about maternity leave. But as she was about to enter the human resources office, she paused.

This was not something that had to be done right away, she thought. The company policy will be whatever it is, and it's not going to change in the next few weeks or even months. There's no reason to make my personal affairs known to anyone at Sun Motors until I absolutely have to. And what if I lose the baby? It would be better if no one knew anything about it. I don't want them fawning over me and telling me how sorry they are. I'd rather die than go through that experience again. No, it would be better to wait until it's noticeable. That will be about twelve weeks from now. Most miscarriages occur before that time, so if it happens again, I may never show a baby bump.

She turned around and went back to her desk.

At four-thirty, Carin appeared on her screen.

"Ah—there you are," he said. "An hour ago I tried to contact you and you were out. A check of the records indicated you had left at one forty-five. At four o'clock you returned."

"Yes, that's correct," she replied with a smile.

"Is everything all right?"

"Yes, everything is fine. I took some personal time. I believe I'm entitled to four hours per month."

"That's true. You've used two hours and fifteen minutes. I'm sure you're keeping track of it."

"Yes, sir, I am." That morning Sylvia had decided to address Carin as "sir," even if no one else did. It seemed like a politically positive thing to do. It cost her nothing to use this honorific when she spoke with him, and she hoped that in his eyes it would burnish her image as a company loyalist.

In addition, she had decided that during meetings or other public events, heaping praise upon Carin would be a useful strategy. She could thank him profusely for having solved a small problem for her, or compliment him for showing attributes of great leadership. Yes, she told herself, if there were a game to be played, she'd damn well play it better than anyone else.

"Is there anything else I can do for you, sir?" she asked with a smile worthy of a toothpaste commercial.

"No thank you, Sylvia." He signed off.

That went well, she thought. But was it possible that Carin could detect the odor of insincerity in her behavior? He was very good at picking up on visual and other sensory cues. As an autonomous humanoid operator, machine learning was an important part of his programming. Like a massive data magnet, he captured every sensation that came to him, analyzed it, classified it, put it into context, and stored it for future reference. His knowledge of humans and their behavior grew with every passing day.

But like a human, Carin had values. They included production efficiency and total loyalty. It might very well be, Sylvia reasoned, that outward praise and obedience were all that Carin was looking for, and the underlying sincerity—or lack thereof—was irrelevant. In Carin's world, what you see is what you get. Things that are unseen have no meaning and no value.

After work, Sylvia met Jason for dinner. While they were eating, he got a call from the real estate agent. Their offer on the house had been accepted. "I think this deserves a champagne toast," he said as he leaned over the table and kissed her.

"Oh sweetheart, do you think I should?" she said.

"People have been arguing for centuries about expectant mothers drinking a bit of wine. I don't think a few sips is going to cause fetal alcohol syndrome."

"I'd rather play it safe," she said. "You have a glass of champagne. I'll have sparkling water."

"Fair enough," smiled Jason.

After dinner they drove to Northville to see the house.

"Do you still like it?" asked Jason.

"Still like it? I love it more than ever," replied Sylvia. "I can't wait to move in and start fixing it up. It needs a lot of work. What color should we paint it? The green looks hideous. I think that's why it was on the market for so long. People saw the green and went, 'Ugh.' But when we paint it a pretty lemon yellow with white trim, it's going to look beautiful. The house has good bones. That's what they say, you know. If a house has good bones, then all the other stuff can be easily improved. What do you think of that big fir tree in the front yard?"

"I think it's depressing and needs to go," smiled Jason. "It looks like something a Hobbit would have in their yard."

"It's going to be a wonderful home," said Sylvia. "Our home."

SYLVIA BRAND

CHAPTER THIRTEEN

The next morning, as Sylvia was working at her desk, with a cup of cold coffee at her elbow, Carin suddenly appeared on her screen. With a quick glance at the cubicles around her, Sylvia saw with relief that Carin had pre-empted all of them. It was an office-wide event.

"Pardon the interruption," said Carin, "but I have a very exciting announcement. As you know, my work as director of logistics and operations is part of the bold new Bright Horizon program at Sun Motors, and indeed at many other Two Hundred K companies across the United Americas. Initiated by President Deacon and the Industrial Council, the Bright Horizon program helps ensure the United Americas keeps our global competitive leadership position, especially with regard to Rodinia, which, as you know, has a long record of stealing our intellectual property and engaging in highly unfair trade practices. These provocations are in fact pushing us to the brink of war. Neither the president nor the Industrial Council want armed conflict, but if it comes, we will be ready to defend our sovereign state.

"But let's get back to the announcement. For the past few weeks the Bright Horizon program has been in beta mode, so to speak. There have been no press releases or authorized press coverage. We have not invited public scrutiny. Today that is changing. I'm pleased to report that the Detroit Assembly Plant has been chosen for a visit from Facts News, which is the only network authorized by the Industrial Council to broadcast the exciting unveiling of the Bright Horizon program. A team from Facts News will be here, in this building, at noon today. A reporter will be interviewing me as well as several key employees. We wish she had time to speak with every employee, but of course that would be impractical. I would like the following employees to meet in the conference room at noon: Tameeka White, Sylvia Brand, Roger Khan, and Maxwell Marcos. Please come as you are—no special preparations are necessary. After our session in the conference room, we anticipate the television news crew will want to get some candid shots of the office. When we come in, just ignore us and carry on as usual. Thank you."

Sylvia was both pleased and taken aback. She was happy because out of fifty employees in the office, Carin had chosen her to be one of four to meet with the Facts News crew. I must be doing something right, she thought. Perhaps my strategy of being a team player is paying off. But she was concerned because as far as she knew, Facts News was nothing more than a propaganda outlet for the administration of President Robert Deacon. She didn't watch the channel very often because the reporting was so obviously slanted in favor of the president that she never knew whether what she was seeing and hearing was based on reality or what the White House Press Office wanted people to think.

She hoped that the interview would be more than just a celebration of Carin and the Sun Motors management team. But it didn't matter: Whatever they threw at her, she'd toss it right back at them.

At noon the group assembled in the conference room. Carin said, "Please allow me to introduce our guests from Facts News. I'd like you to meet correspondent Leslie Applegate, who will be conducting the interviews. With her is photojournalist Eric Dane and sound engineer Betsy Ford. They've also brought along a makeup artist, Chia Chen, who has kindly offered to ensure you're prepared to face the camera. Isn't that right, Chia?"

A slender girl with large white teeth smiled and nodded.

"With that," said Carin, "I'll turn it over to Leslie."

"Thanks, Carin," said Applegate. "It's a pleasure to be with you today as we reveal the big news."

Sylvia had seen Leslie Applegate a few times on television—not on Facts News, which she rarely watched, but on a television commercial for one of those shady reverse mortgage companies that try to convince old people to cash out of their family homes, spend the money, and leave nothing for their children to inherit. Gold Star Financial, in whose advertisements Applegate had appeared, had been sued by various states' district attorneys for fraud. Then the Industrial Council, using its sweeping powers to regulate anything and everything related to the national defense, had intervened and forced the states to settle out of court. Some commentators—all of them allied with the aberrants, it was said—had questioned why the Industrial Council had inserted itself into a dispute between the states and a reverse mortgage company. Eventually it was revealed that President Deacon's wife, Emily Deacon, was a major stockholder in Gold Star Financial. It was the unspoken position of the Industrial Council that to protect their personal financial interests, high government officials friendly to President Deacon, including the president himself, his wife, and their three adult children, were entitled to wield the levers of government power. This courtesy was not extended to the members of the hopelessly weak minority Liberty Party, who, much to the irritation of the majority National Unity Party, had not yet been entirely stamped out of existence. Many Liberty Party members had vanished, but others persisted. In fact, some people believed the National Unity Party deliberately kept the Liberty Party on life support because having an "opposition" party proved that the United Americas was still a democracy. "See for yourself!" proclaimed National Unity Party candidates for all elected offices, both local and countrywide. "We have tough political campaigns followed by free, fair elections. The United Americas is the beacon of democracy towards which all other nations gaze with envy."

As for Leslie Applegate, it was never proven that she herself had made any false or misleading claims on the ads. She was allowed to walk away from the scandal and keep her job at Facts News.

The first team member Applegate interviewed on camera was Carin. He was open about the fact that he was a Morta AHO 6-C from Morta Laboratories in San Mateo, California. He talked about the vast improvements that had been made in the autonomous humanoid operator industry, and how robots—for lack of a better term—working side by side with their human counterparts could take any company to new levels of achievement. And, of course, his human employees had never been happier.

This was the cue to bring on the four human staff members.

"Let's start with Tameeka White," said Leslie.

In front of the camera, Tameeka was a natural performer. She praised Carin and the Bright Horizon program, and extolled the virtues of Sun Motors products and work environment. Both Carin and Leslie Applegate appeared to be very happy.

Roger Khan and Maxwell Marcos followed. Each painted glowing pictures of Sun Motors and Bright Horizon. They were so uniform and effusive in their praise that Sylvia found the interviews to be boring. It was the same thing over and over again, as if they were scripted.

Sylvia resolved to outdo all three of them—Tameeka, Roger, and Maxwell. She was going to provide the highest praise and the most positive report. No one was going to outperform her. There must not be the slightest doubt that she, Sylvia Brand, had true leadership ability.

"And now for Sylvia Brand," said Applegate. After a quick facial powdering by Chia Chen, she was ready for the camera.

"And what has been your experience working with Carin?" asked Applegate. Sylvia looked into the camera lens and gave her biggest smile.

"Like a dream come true," she said like a starving person presented with a steak dinner. In high school Sylvia had won the drama award four years running, and now she was showing why. "From the moment we first met Carin, we knew a new day was dawning at Sun Motors. He sees problems and solves them, and always with no ego and no interest in personal gain. I work in logistics, which means I'm part of the team that must source thirty thousand individual parts that are used to make each Sun Comanche. It may not seem like a very glamorous job, but it's vitally important. We work with hundreds of suppliers from all over the world, and it's a challenge to keep them all on track. Carin has amazing abilities to cut through the red tape and get things done."

"It sounds like the Bright Horizon program is a smashing success," Applegate effused.

"It's not just Carin but all of Sun Motors," said Sylvia. "Just last week we had the honor of attending the grand opening of the new Margaret J. Atkinson Day Care Center, located here at the Detroit Assembly Plant campus. Our brilliant COO, Mr. Posey, cut the ceremonial ribbon. It feels like a miracle to have such a resource available to Sun employees. I have such high regard for Mrs. Atkinson, and indeed the entire Atkinson family! They are leading us to new heights of success, and I know that everyone here is so grateful for their inspired leadership."

Leslie Applegate took the microphone and addressed the camera. "Well, there you have it—some very happy and appreciative employees here at the Sun Motors Detroit Assembly Plant logistics office! It sounds like the Bright Horizon program is off to a roaring start!"

After the news crew had left to go to another part of the plant, Carin stopped Sylvia in the hallway. "You did an excellent job," he said. "It did not go unnoticed."

"Thank you," she replied.

She was on her way to the ladies room. Once inside, she closed the door to a stall and sat on the toilet, still fully clothed. She put her head in her hands. The pain in her gut intensified.

She heard someone come in. She recognized the shoes as belonging to Mei Lien. She opened the door to the stall.

Standing at one of the sinks, Mei Lien turned. "Oh—Sylvia." She peered at Sylvia's state of being fully dressed. "What are you doing? Are you all right?"

"I feel like I'm going to throw up."

"Are you sick?"

Sylvia got to her feet. The feeling of nausea made her take shallow breaths. "Not exactly. I'm just…. tired. Worn out. I don't know how much longer I can play this game."

"What game?"

In hushed tones, Sylvia told Mei Lien about the interview with Facts News, and how she had heaped praise upon Carin, Gerald Posey, and the Atkinson family. "It was pure bullshit," she whispered. "Totally phony. I put a big stupid grin on my face and told them exactly what they wanted to hear. I did not say this place is run like a prison camp. I did not say that Carin is a tinpot dictator. I did not say how strange it was that your kid has to audition to get admitted to the Margaret J. Atkinson Day Care Center, as if she were applying to Harvard. I did not say how people around here mysteriously disappear. Everyone knows that Randolph Meekin isn't working downtown. He never worked downtown. He just vanished. And Judy and her husband and two kids didn't take a 'leave of absence' from life. They left in the middle of the night in a van with a bunch of people dressed in black. Her replacement was hired the afternoon before she and her family abandoned their home." She looked in the mirror with an expression of disgust. "And these stupid uniforms! They might as well be orange jumpsuits. What are we, children? Or beasts of burden?"

Stepping back to lean against the stall partition, Sylvia took a deep breath and slowly exhaled.

"Let's just try and make the best of it, okay?" said Mei Lien, gently laying a hand on her shoulder. "Compared to other companies, Sun Motors is a really good place to work. At the interview, you did the right thing. Think of it as like performing in a television ad for Sun. You were acting in a commercial. You were following the script they wanted. If there was anything reprehensible, it's that they didn't pay you for your performance. They got it for free. Cheap bastards!"

They both laughed.

"I suppose you're right," sighed Sylvia. "I need to focus on the future. Did I tell you? Jason and I are buying a house. It's a cute Dutch colonial in Northville, near Maplewood Park."

"That's a pretty area," said Mei Lien. "Congratulations! Does this mean you're getting married soon?"

"Yes—very soon."

"Oh, I see…" Mei Lien gave a knowing smile. "Any particular reason for the accelerated nuptials?"

"No. No reason. We're just madly in love."

Sylvia left work an hour early for her appointment with Dr. Elizabeth Darcy at Detroit Hospital. Built over a century earlier, the stately brick structure was located downtown, near the river. Sylvia took the rattling elevator to the fifth floor, where the receptionist handed her an old-fashioned clipboard to which a stack of papers were attached. "Because you're a new patient, we need you to fill those out," said the receptionist. Sylvia took the clipboard and sat down in one of the vinyl-covered chairs. The papers included the usual medical questions—allergies (only to lobster, which she didn't like anyway), drug use (none), episodes of dizziness (no). Then there was the consent form, which consisted of several pages of dense text. Sylvia scanned through it, trying to perform some semblance of due diligence while knowing it was a pointless exercise. One paragraph caught her eye. It said, "In the event of my death, or if any of my tissues or organs are removed during a medical procedure, the hospital has my permission to use my tissues and organs in any way that advances medical science, including the development of biomedical products in which I claim no financial interest." She took the form to the receptionist. "What does this mean?" she asked.

The receptionist smiled and said, "I think they assume that because you're an ethical and caring person, you would want a fellow human being to benefit from advances in medical science that involve the use of human tissue. Wouldn't you want this? The alternative to using human tissue is to dispose of it. Just throw it away in the trash. Once our patients understand what it means, all of them have been happy to sign this form." Having said this, the receptionist fixed upon Sylvia a friendly but steady gaze.

"I suppose if you put it that way," said Sylvia, "it sound almost noble. But what about this paragraph, which says the Industrial Council may, from time to time and at its own discretion, access and review patient medical records?"

"That ensures the Council can provide the necessary regulatory oversight of health care providers," said the receptionist. "They need to inspect patient records to verify that every hospital, including this one, is meeting the necessary professional standards. It's for your protection as a consumer."

"I don't know—this all seems rather intrusive."

The receptionist gave her an unfriendly smile. "Well, if you'd prefer to pay cash at one of those aberrant medical clinics out in the country, you're free to do that. But it will cost you more and you'll be playing Rodinian roulette with your health. And as far as your patient data is concerned, in aberrant territory it's like the Wild West. Anything goes." She leaned forward and raised her eyebrows. "I've heard that aberrant clinics buy and sell human body parts. You go in for a cholecystectomy, and while you're lying there in dreamland they remove your infected gallbladder and one of your kidneys. Then they sell your kidney on the black market. You can't even sue—you know how bad the courts are out there. Nothing but incompetence and chaos."

"Well, if everybody signs, I suppose it must be all right."

"Of course it's all right! You can trust Detroit Hospital to take good care of your personal information. The Industrial Council has given Detroit Hospital the coveted four-star rating. That should tell you everything."

"Yes, of course." After signing and dating all the forms, Sylvia handed the clipboard to the receptionist.

"Okay—now that we've gotten the paperwork out of the way, I'll need to see your Sun Motors Employee Wellness Plan card." Sylvia handed it over, and the receptionist scanned it and gave it back. "You're all set," said the receptionist. "Please have a seat and the nurse will call you."

Presently Sylvia was ushered to an examination room, and after the usual preliminaries with the nurse, Dr. Darcy entered.

"Call me Liz," said the doctor as she read Sylvia's history from the tablet in her hand. "We don't stand on formality around here. You were under the care of Donna Giacalone until she retired, and now your primary care physician is Rebecca Goldsmith. They've sent all your records. You think you're six weeks along?"

"Yes," replied Sylvia.

"You're a senior logistics manager at Sun Motors, aren't you?"

"Yes."

"Will you want your child to enroll in day care where you work?"

"Do you mean the new Margaret J. Atkinson center? I hadn't thought about it. It seems like such a long time in the future! I haven't even started to show yet. Yes, I suppose I'd want our child to go there. It would be very convenient."

"Then we'll start the application process. You need to do it early. I've been told that this year and next year are already closed to admissions. If we're lucky, we'll be able to secure a spot when your baby turns two years old."

"Okay, thanks."

Dr. Darcy studied her tablet. "The baby's father is Jason Quin. Age thirty. He's been with Hilltop Financial for five years. A good company. Before that he worked as a loan officer at First Lakeville Bank. And you're not presently married, but you'll tie the knot very soon. Correct?"

"Yes."

"And you're buying a house together, in Northville. A nice little starter home."

"Yes, but how did you happen to know that?"

"It's simple—we have access to the metro Detroit area real estate records. If one of our patients shows up in that database, it's added to the patient record. We're not snooping—this is publicly available information. We just happen to be able to leverage it."

"That's interesting, but I don't see what that has to do with my health or that of my baby."

"Here at Detroit Hospital, we're concerned not only with the immediate condition of you and your unborn child, but your baby's overall well-being as he or she begins the journey of life. This includes the quality of the home environment. It can have a significant impact on the child's development."

After administering a battery of tests and taking a blood sample from Sylvia, Dr. Darcy left the room for a moment. When she returned she was carrying a small package, which she opened.

"This is a very simple dermal patch," she said as she removed the object from its sterile wrapper. "I'm going to attach it to your abdomen. As you can see, it's no larger than a small band-aid. It's waterproof, and will last until your next appointment, which will be in two weeks."

"What does it do?" asked Sylvia. (In reality, what had first entered her mind was the thought that Jason would, in a romantic moment, be turned off by seeing or touching a band-aid-like object stuck to her belly. But she was too embarrassed to say this.)

"It's connected to the internet," said Dr. Darcy as she positioned the patch on Sylvia's skin. "It transmits over one hundred data points to our monitoring system. This ensures that if there's the slightest problem or deviation from the norm, we can quickly intervene. Pretty cool, isn't it?"

"One hundred data points? That sounds like a lot. What are some of them?"

"Blood pressure, blood oxygen, glucose level, white blood cell count, a dozen different hormone levels, your heart rate, breathing rate, temperature. Also geospatial information—where you are at any given moment, and if you're lying down or upright."

"You're going to track me? Everywhere I go?"

"Wouldn't you want us to? Think about it. What if you were driving home at night and you got into an accident? Let's say your car ran into a deer and you ended up in a ditch. Let's also say you were unconscious. When you're carrying a baby, seconds count. With this dermal patch, your accident would be noticed instantly. Help would be on its way even before you could use your phone to call for assistance. This technology could save your life and the life of your unborn child."

"But the people in charge of the tracking system will know every place I've been. All the stores and restaurants I go to. They'll see if I leave work early one day or oversleep one morning."

"So what?" shrugged Dr. Darcy. "You're not a drug dealer, are you? You're not playing hooky from work, are you? If you have nothing to hide, then what's the worry?"

"Here's my worry," said Sylvia. "If I decide to stop at Starbucks to use the ladies room, am I suddenly going to get a steady stream of ads for Starbucks on my social media feed? If one day I go to a store and buy bananas, will I then receive emails from supermarkets that sell bananas?"

"I think your concerns are overblown. So what if you receive a few ads? We all get ads. Just ignore them, like I do. Let me show you something." She took her personal phone out of her pocket and then scrolled through it. She showed her phone to Sylvia. "See this ad for the cruise line? Last week I was online and I casually looked at some websites for cruises in the Caribbean. I wasn't at all interested in buying a ticket; I looked at these sites because I have another patient who loves going on those gigantic cruise ships that look like floating brothels, and so I thought I'd at least brush up on the topic. I spent about ten minutes searching and looking. I didn't linger long at any particular page or website. Later that same day, these ads started popping wherever I went on the internet. All from spending a few minutes doing a search. But I don't care. Let 'em send ads to me. I just scroll past them."

Having been connected to the internet by her dermal patch, Sylvia went home, with another appointment set for two weeks.

The Facts News story about the Bright Horizon program and Sun Motors was slated to run at ten o'clock that evening. At dinnertime, Jason came over to visit. To Sylvia's relief, when they were in bed together he wasn't bothered by the band-aid stuck to her stomach. Then at ten o'clock they turned on the television.

When Sylvia's segment came on, she cringed. "Look at me!" she said. "I look like an overeager cheerleader. My face looks so fat!"

"I think you look beautiful," he said. "And you did the right thing. You're giving them what they want. You and I may think it's a silly act and feel embarrassed by it, but you need to remember these people—and I include Carin with them—are shameless, and see only the surface. They judge you by your appearance. If you look happy, then you are happy. If you praise them, they believe you."

"It all seems very ominous," said Sylvia. "It makes me feel like I'm walking into a long dark tunnel."

CHAPTER FOURTEEN

On Wednesday Sylvia was at her desk when her screen suddenly showed the image of the Facts News morning anchorperson. Sylvia stopped working and sat back in her chair. It was impossible to get any work done during these occasional interruptions.

"We have disturbing new images coming from Rodinia," said the newscaster. "Yesterday morning the Rodinian Army staged a massive training exercise on the shores of the Yukasi Peninsula. This mock invasion of the peninsula reportedly involved fifty thousand of the elite Rodinian Guard troops, hundreds of aircraft, and dozens of Rodinian Navy support vessels, including the new Munk-class cruiser armed with laser weapons capable of leveling virtually any structure within a mile of the coast. In response, this morning President Deacon convened an emergency meeting of the Joint Chiefs of Staff and the Executive Board of the Industrial Council. White House spokesperson Mitch Cornwall has told Facts News that the meeting was, and I quote, 'highly productive,' and that this new act of aggression by Rodinia will be met with 'invincible determination.' The President has requested that his War Powers be broadened to include the imposition of a nationwide curfew when necessary, as well as new measures enabling the Industrial Council to set prices of goods deemed necessary for national defense. The Industrial Council fully supports the president's request. The House and Senate are expected to pass the appropriate legislation and have the expanded War Powers bill on the President's desk by the end of this week."

The image of the newscaster disappeared and Sylvia's screen returned to the files she had opened a few minutes earlier. She went back to work, tracking down a late shipment of cameras for the roof unit of the new autonomous Comanche truck.

Without warning her screen changed again, and the view of an office with a desk appeared. A man was sitting at the desk. Flanking him were flags of the United Americas.

"Damn," muttered Sylvia. "How are we expected to get anything done around here with all of these lectures?" Then she put her hand over her mouth. Word was going around the office that the surveillance cameras had been given lip reading technology, and everything you said was captured and instantly transcribed. It was only a rumor, but there was no reason to take chances.

The man was Hugh Atkinson, chairman, president, and CEO of Sun Motors. Sylvia sat up straight in her chair. Aside from his annual year-end talk, to receive a message from Mr. Atkinson himself was a rare event. He was not a man who often put himself out in front of the public or his employees.

"Good morning," said Atkinson. His voice was low and sonorous. With his bow tie and brown suit jacket, he resembled an Ivy League professor. It was the signature look of Old Money.

"No doubt you've heard the announcement from the office of President Deacon and the Industrial Council regarding the new provocation by Rodinia. This is a serious threat to our nation, and Sun Motors is ready to do our part. I am proud to say we have just been awarded a contract to produce five thousand mobile strike vehicles for the U.A. Army. Final assembly will be at the Detroit Assembly Plant. We have also contracted with the Department of Defense to produce a classified number of armored personnel carriers and heavy laser defense units. The participating plants will be briefed in closed session.

"As Sun Motors does its part for the defense of our nation, I know I can count on every member of our Sun Motors family to contribute one hundred and ten percent. Our country and our people are depending on us to provide not only the highest quality civilian vehicles but to supply our warfighters with the tools they need to triumph over those who would seek to do us harm. Thank you."

The image vanished and Sylvia's screen returned to normal.

Sylvia frowned. It was a week ago that Carin had told her there was a ninety percent chance the Army would award Sun Motors a contract to produce five thousand mobile strike vehicles. The provocation by Rodinia that supposedly triggered the contract had happened just yesterday. How was that possible?

Out of curiosity she pulled up the page of the United Americas Stock Exchange. She found Sun Motors. Over a period of twenty-four hours, from the day before until this moment, the price of a single share of Sun Motors stock had risen from seven hundred and six dollars to eight hundred and twelve dollars. It was an astonishing increase of fifteen percent. It had been reported—but never publicly acknowledged—that members of the Atkinson family collectively owned three million shares of Sun Motors stock. Therefore over the period of one day, their wealth had increased by over three hundred million dollars.

Sylvia didn't own any Sun Motors stock. Only high-level executives were offered stock options, and she didn't have any spare cash to invest in the stock market.

Again her screen changed. This time it was Carin.

Sylvia bit her lip. But in her mind she was saying, this is crazy.

"I'll only take a moment of your time," said Carin. "But I want you all to fully appreciate that we have been given a tremendous opportunity to serve our nation in a moment of crisis. I anticipate that each and every one of us will step up and meet this challenge. And to help you meet and exceed your goals, I and the management team will be with you step by step, minute by minute, providing real-time feedback on your performance, both as an individual and as a member of the team. Thank you."

The screen reverted back to Sylvia's files.

Real-time feedback? What the hell did that mean?

That afternoon Sylvia had just returned from lunch when Carin summoned her to his office. After stopping in the ladies room to check her appearance—nothing stuck to her teeth, perfect yet minimal makeup, white blouse free of wrinkles or stains, hair brushed away from the face—she reported to his office.

Carin was seated behind his desk. As usual, the desktop was spotless, with only the computer screen, keyboard, and mouse. No paper.

Seated next to the desk was woman Sylvia had seen around the office during the past few days. The woman gave her a bland smile. Carin motioned for Sylvia to take the free chair.

"As you'll recall," said Carin, "last week I mentioned that a team of professional management consultants from the Special Services office of the Industrial Council was going to be working closely with us to improve efficiency. I'd like you to meet Isabel Nassar, one of the team members. She's been observing you for the past three days, both on video and in person. I think you'll find what she has to say to be very interesting and will help you to become a much more efficient and productive member of our team. Isabel, why don't you lead the discussion."

"Thank you, Carin," said Nassar. "Sylvia, it is such a great pleasure to meet you, although I must say I already feel as though I know you very well. But such is the nature of our work—we watch our clients and develop self-improvement programs based on what we observe, while we ourselves remain in the shadows. One cannot objectively collect data if one is interacting with the subject, wouldn't you agree?"

"Yes, of course," replied Sylvia.

Nassar reached into her slim briefcase and pulled out two sets of papers.

"This is a copy of our report on you, which I hope to discuss with you." She handed Sylvia one of the sets of papers. "As you can see, I also have a copy, so we can easily review together."

"What's the report about?" asked Sylvia. She felt the muscles in the back of her neck begin to stiffen.

"In the old day they called it ergonomics," said Nassar. "It's the scientific discipline concerned with the understanding of the interactions among human and other elements of a system, and the profession that applies theory, principles, data, and methods to design in order to optimize human well-being and overall system performance.

"In classical ergonomics, the practitioner attempts to modify the work to fit the worker. The goal is to eliminate waste, discomfort, and risk of injury due to work by shaping the work environment to fit the capabilities of the employee. For example, if you have a chair that is uncomfortable for the worker to sit in, you redesign the chair to fit the worker. But we believe this makes no sense in real life. If you have one thousand workers in a shared environment, such as in a factory, how can you possibly adapt each part of the factory to conform to the needs or whims of each worker? How can you make each chair conform to each individual employee, with all their different shapes and sizes? This would be madness—a huge waste of resources and a move toward inefficiency. We have resolved to approach the subject in a fresh way by asking how our workers could do a better job of fitting into their work environment. Instead of seeking a thousand individual solutions or standards to fit a thousand workers, we say it's better to determine one solution and ask our workers to conform to it. Does that make sense?"

"I suppose so," replied Sylvia. "To be honest, it seems like we've already got a high level of conformity. We all wear the same uniform, don't we?"

"That's just one small step," smiled Nassar. She had small, pointed teeth, like a child. "We're very pleased that the Detroit Assembly Plant, and in particular the logistics office, has embraced the Sun Motors Way program wholeheartedly. But that is just the beginning. Now then, let's talk about how we can help you. I ask you to refer to the report. You will see that it's broken down into various subsections. These include use of time, choice of movement (meaning what you do), and efficiency of movement (meaning how you do it). Let's take a look at use of time. As you can see, during the past three workdays you've gotten up from your desk four times per day to visit the employee break room. I assume you do this to get coffee, is that correct?"

"Yes," replied Sylvia. Her coffee ruse had been discovered! The pain in the back of her neck intensified. She resisted the impulse to bring her hand to her neck and rub it. She feared it would be seen as a wasted movement.

"There's nothing wrong with drinking coffee, if that pleases you," continued Nassar. "More importantly, your average visit to the break room is eight minutes in duration, during which time you chat with fellow employees. In total, you've spent ninety-six minutes of the past three work days walking to the break room, being in the break room, or walking back to your desk. Out of consideration for you, we've not counted trips to the ladies room, which were also numerous. Those will not be included in your permanent record."

"My permanent record?" asked Sylvia. The pain had spread up into her head. She felt her breathing becoming more rapid and shallow. Carin was looking at her. Was he calculating her breathing rate? Observing the dilation of her pupils? In an effort to relax, she shifted in her chair.

"Of course," replied Nassar with her childlike teeth. "It's important that we track these key metrics over time. How else can you hope to improve? In our competitive business environment, and especially with an impending war with Rodinia, every employee of Sun Motors needs to be performing at his or her optimum level. As managers, our job is to help you meet and exceed performance goals."

"You make it sound like I'm a professional athlete," said Sylvia. As the pain shot through her neck and head she struggled to control her breathing and keep her facial muscles relaxed. She didn't want them to see her grimace, even slightly.

"Actually," said Nassar, "that's a very astute comparison. We are all like professional athletes. Just as they must train to get in shape, so must we. Just as they must hone their skills, so must we. And just as every athlete must be totally committed to winning, so must we."

With his unwavering gaze, Carin stared at Sylvia. "Are you feeling all right?" he asked.

"Yes sir," Sylvia replied. "Just a slight headache. Nothing serious." She forced a smile.

"Without seeking to intrude," said Carin, "may I say that in your condition you might want to reduce your intake of coffee."

"My condition?"

"Your pregnancy." After the words passed over his lips he smiled, as if the idea of smiling had come as an afterthought.

"You know?"

"Of course we know. As you're well aware, your health data is added to your employee record in real time. Data from your recent appointment with Dr. Darcy at Detroit Hospital was received by Sun Motors as it was being created."

"I didn't realize that."

"It's clearly spelled out in your employee consent forms for the Sun Motors Employee Wellness Plan. It's standard boilerplate language. Of course, this is for your own benefit. When the company added these provisions many years ago, we were thinking about workers on the assembly line and in the warehouses. There was concern that if a worker had an accident on the job—regrettably, despite our excellent safety record, mishaps can happen—it would be important to have access to the most up-to-date medical records. In a situation when every minute is precious, the company didn't want to have to wait and send for them. Doesn't that make sense? Wouldn't you want your full medical records to be available the instant they were needed? It could be a matter of life or death."

"Yes, I suppose so," said Sylvia.

"I'm glad we all agree on that," said Nassar, showing her childlike teeth. "Now then, let's focus on helping you become more efficient. More like a professional athlete, if that's how you want to look at it. How can we reduce the thirty-two minutes you spend every workday going to the break room for coffee? How can we get it down to, say, fifteen minutes?"

Because of the pain shooting up her neck, Sylvia felt she couldn't turn her head. Stiffly she turned her entire body to face Nassar. "I'll drink less coffee."

"Okay, that might work," said Nassar. "To help you reach your goal, I've got something that will help you stay focused." She opened her briefcase and pulled out a small plastic bag, which she opened. From the plastic bag she took out a slender wristband. "This device is sensitive to both motion and geospatial location." She handed the band to Sylvia. Its color matched her skin. "We ask that you wear your wristband during the workday—that is, anytime you're being paid by the company, which includes the lunch hour. The band's internal clock will measure how you spend your time. If by accident you happen to spend more than fifteen minutes on trips to the break room, it will begin to emit a buzzing sound. It will buzz until you're back at your desk. I think you'll find it to be a minimally intrusive way to achieve a higher level of self discipline."

With her fingers, Sylvia turned over the wristband. She gave it a little twist. It was flexible. "What's to stop someone from just putting it in their desk drawer all day?"

Nassar smiled. "Oh, that's an easy one. The band learns your normal range of motions from minute to minute. It will quickly figure out if you are right-handed or left-handed. It tracks your body temperature and it will know if, for example, you take it off and put it on your desk. There's a buffer of thirty seconds between the time it senses a lack of movement and when the buzzer sounds."

"Go ahead, slip it on," said Carin. "And don't worry—it's hypoallergenic. Quite safe to wear."

Sylvia put it on her left wrist. It stretched slightly to slide over her hand.

"It blends in with your skin tone," said Nassar. "You can barely see it. After a while you won't even feel it. If you want, you can even wear it home. The data functions shut off after five o'clock."

There's no way I'm wearing this hideous thing home at night, thought

Sylvia. "If you think it will help," she said, "I'll give it a try." She resisted the overwhelming need to massage the back of her neck to relieve the increasing tension.

"Oh, and by the way—congratulations on your pregnancy," said Nassar, showing her many little teeth. "Your first one?"

"Yes," she replied. She looked at Carin. "But of course you know that."

He gave her his bland smile. "There are data sets we don't routinely access. I have no particular knowledge of your history as a mother of children. Please accept my sincere congratulations. I'm sure you will bear an exceptional child."

Self-consciously wearing the wristband, Sylvia walked back to her desk. On the way, each time she saw another employee she glanced at their wrist, and she was sure they were looking at hers too. Roger was wearing a wristband. Funny, she had never noticed it before. Emily was wearing one too, as were Maxwell and Pauline. Could they all have been wearing them and Sylvia hadn't noticed? Or had all of them been issued theirs today, like she had?

She arrived at her desk. She saw that it was nearly four o'clock. That morning she had told Carin she needed to leave at four to meet with the real estate agent and the lawyer. Carin didn't seem to mind, but after the session with Nassar, in which Sylvia's use of time had been the subject of much scrutiny, she felt acutely uncomfortable.

But this appointment was one of the most important in her life. Taking a deep breath, she took off the wristband and shoved it into a desk drawer.

"Sleep tight," she said to it as she closed the drawer. "I'll see you tomorrow morning."

CHAPTER FIFTEEN

"Are you ready?" said Jason as he gripped Sylvia's hand.

"As ready as I'll ever be," she replied with a kiss to his cheek.

Jason opened the door of Room 201 of the Coleman A. Young Municipal Center. This was the office of Kathleen Barrett, the clerk of Wayne County and officiant of marriages.

After presenting their marriage license and paying the fee of one hundred and fifty dollars, they sat together in the waiting room. Sylvia tried to relax by breathing slowly and focusing on letting the tension melt away. Jason put a comforting hand on her back. "Hey," he said, "You're stiff a as a board. Are you okay?"

"I'm fine," she replied. "Just a tough day at work. I'll tell you about it tonight." She leaned into him and felt his strength. "All I want to think about is our future and the future of our child."

"Or children," he smiled.

"Let's not get ahead of ourselves. One baby at a time."

Their names were called and they went into the office, where they were met by Ms. Barrett and two witnesses, who otherwise worked as her administrative assistants. The ceremony took only a few minutes, and after they signed the papers Jason took the certificate of marriage, and together they left the building.

An hour later they lay snuggled on the big bed in their suite at the Detroit Heritage Hotel. The grand old edifice was once served as the headquarters of the Detroit Police Department, but after the Global Depression the cops had moved to a new building. When the hotel opened, it quickly became the city's trendiest overnight destination. The architects were careful to keep the flavor of the venerable structure; a few of the windows still had the original iron bars, and the old jail was now a four-star restaurant.

"You still feel a little tense," said Jason as he held her in his arms. "C'mon, let me give you a massage."

"Oh, no, you don't have to do that," she weakly protested.

"I insist. Roll over on your stomach. Put your arms over your head."

His strong fingers probed and pressed the muscles of her back and shoulders.

"Ouch!" she exclaimed.

"Ah—the splenius capitis muscle! Feels like a knotted rope. So does your levator scapulae. No wonder you can barely turn your head." He bent down and tenderly kissed the nape of her neck. "How does that feel?"

"Heavenly," she whispered.

"What was going on today at work?" he said as he gently worked the stiff muscles under her skin.

"Oh, you don't want to know," she said.

"Now that I'm your husband, I want to know everything. Especially whatever makes you upset."

"Oh, maybe it's just me, but the logistics office is starting to feel more and more like a forced labor camp. They keep coming up with these new rules that are supposed to increase productivity, but they're destroying employee morale." She paused. "Ooh, yes, whatever you're doing right now is working. Right there—where your left thumb is. That's the worst spot. Ouch! No, don't stop—I can feel it getting more relaxed. Now where was I? Oh yes. Employee morale. People are walking around like zombies. No one laughs, no one smiles. Everyone's terrified of being called out for wasting time or not being efficient. No one wants to go to the doctor because their medical information will go straight to human resources and the managers. This morning one of the girls in the office told me she thought she had a yeast infection. Instead of going to her own doctor, who's plugged into the Sun Motors Employee Wellness Plan, she went to an aberrant clinic out in the country. She had to pay three hundred dollars out of her own pocket for the examination and medications. She said it was worth every penny to keep Carin from finding out.

"Today they gave me—and everyone in the office, I think—an internet-connected wristband to wear. It tracks where I go and even my body temperature. They thought I was spending too much time in the break room, and they want me to cut it in half. Ever since Carin arrived and the Bright Horizon program started, they've installed surveillance cameras in the office, made everyone sign up for the Sun Motors Employee Wellness Plan, opened the creepy Margaret Atkinson day care center, and issued wristbands that track your every movement. They say it's simply a matter of increasing efficiency and making Sun Motors more competitive. Supposedly the data they collect helps pinpoint areas that could be improved. This looming war with Rodinia doesn't help—with new Department of Defense vehicle contracts, Sun Motors stands to make huge profits, and it forces all of us to conform to DoD standards, which are even tougher than the Industrial Council. I don't see where this is going." She paused for a moment as Jason kneaded her neck. "Oooh—right there! In the middle. You've hit the spot. Are you going to do this for me every day, or is it because we just got married and you want to keep me happy?"

"I'll do it whenever and wherever you want," he smiled. "If Sun Motors is becoming too regimented, do you want to work someplace else?"

"Where? All the Two Hundred K companies are the same. Isn't the Industrial Council doing the same things at Hilltop Financial?"

"Yes, they are. We haven't got the wristbands yet, but I suppose they could be coming. I try not to let it bother me. Remember, after five o'clock we leave all that stuff behind. We walk out the door and into our own lives. We can do whatever we want and live however we want. We've got our future to think about. Our family. My goal is to become CEO of Hilltop Financial and worm my way onto the Industrial Council."

"I think it would be easier to get elected president of the United Americas," said Sylvia. "I'm not opposed to being ambitious—that's one of your many very attractive qualities—but you've got to be realistic. Do you even know how many people serve on the Council? And where they meet?"

"According to what I've read, there are thirty members, and they have virtual meetings. They live all over the United Americas. When a seat is vacated, most often through death or infirmity, a new member is nominated and approved by a vote. To be nominated, you must be a CEO of a large-cap Two Hundred K company. The leader of Hilltop Financial qualifies."

"Is your boss, Sharon Westward, on the Council?"

"No one knows. She's never said one way or the other."

"I don't understand what it's all about," said Sylvia. "All this control. Is it power? Do the bosses enjoy having power over us and making us feel like cogs in their machine?"

"I don't think it's primarily power," replied Jason. He rolled over and lay on the bed next to his wife, propped up on one elbow. "I think it's about something much more boring and unimaginative: money."

"Money?"

"Profits. These guys are driven by the bottom line. The goal of the Industrial Council is to ensure its member companies return as much profit as possible to their investors. If a proposed strategy can help in that effort, they will do it. Making the workplace hyper-efficient is one obvious way to boost profits. Collecting and selling data is another way to make money. From their point of view, any personal data—health, lifestyle, consumer choices, political beliefs—that isn't harvested is like leaving money on the table. It's like letting good wheat rot in the field. You may not think your medical and behavioral data is worth anything, but when it's bundled with many other people who are like you—similar age, gender, income, and so forth—it becomes very valuable. Sun Motors doesn't just make SUVs and pickup trucks. Its thousands of employees make data, and Sun Motors has ensured that it owns that data and can sell it."

"But how about things like the wristbands? Don't they cost money to produce?"

"They're an investment, but they pay for themselves in boosted productivity. I guarantee you a bean counter within the Industrial Council ran the numbers on the proposed wristbands. He might have said, 'If we design and manufacture a million internet-connected wristbands at a cost of ten dollars apiece, our investment will be ten million dollars. If you add another five million dollars to run the program, that's a total of fifteen million dollars. We then ask ourselves if these wristbands, worn by one million employees of member companies, will generate increased productivity worth more than fifteen million dollars.'

"Clearly the answer was 'yes,' because the program was approved. This means that you, dear sweet Sylvia Brand, senior logistics manager at the Sun Motors Detroit Assembly Plant, are now required to wear a wristband every day. They will track and analyze your overall contribution to the anticipated increase in productivity. I'm sure you will not disappoint them."

"I wonder what it's like to live in the canaille among the aberrants," said Sylvia.

"Those people and their little businesses exist for three purposes: to buy goods produced by the Two Hundred K, to pay taxes to the government, and to provide soldiers to the military. All under the banner of patriotism. In the canaille, the only part of the civic infrastructure that's directly controlled by the government is the school system. From the cradle the kids are taught that the Two Hundred K is something to aspire to, the Industrial Council is their protector, and war is a glorious thing in which everyone should participate. That, plus the ubiquitous presence of the secret police, is the extent of the government's oversight of the canaille."

"It sounds ghastly," said Sylvia with a shudder.

"Let's not think about such dreary topics," said Jason. "I'm getting hungry—how about you? Do you want to get dressed and go down to the restaurant and get dinner? Or would you rather stay as you are and we'll order room service?"

"Sweetheart, I don't care if I never get dressed again," said Sylvia as she kissed him.

"Okay—I'll get the menu." He reached over and took the leather-bound folder from the little table next to the bed. "Let's see what looks good…. I think I'll have the pork loin with onion and Gruyere potato gratin and sautéed spring vegetables. And maybe the classic Caesar salad with Romaine Parmesan croutons. How about you?"

"I'll try the seared scallops. They come with sweet potato puree, sautéed spinach, and lemon parsley brown butter. Do you want to split an order of the crispy polenta with grilled portabella, spinach, and mushroom sauce? It sounds divine."

"Sure. And a bottle of Didier Chopin Brut Champagne."

"Isn't that expensive?" asked Sylvia.

"Isn't this our honeymoon?"

"Only until we can make plans for a proper vacation. Remember we talked about going to St. Bart. Tomorrow I'm going to start researching hotels."

"But not while you're at work," said Jason.

"God no—there's no way I'd spend even five minutes doing that at work. The keystroke recorder would tip them off, and I don't want Carin to know anything about our private life. It's bad enough he knows that I'm expecting a child. I'm surprised he hasn't given me a lecture on what brand of diapers to buy."

"If they could make you buy official Sun Motors diapers, I'm sure they would," laughed Jason. He picked up the phone and placed their dinner order with the kitchen. He turned to Sylvia: "They say they'll be here in twenty minutes."

"That give us nineteen more minutes to have fun," said Sylvia, giving him a kiss.

CHAPTER SIXTEEN

When Sylvia arrived for work the next morning, she never felt happier. The memory of her night with Jason filled her heart with gladness. She remembered his gentle touch, the weight of his body next to hers, the smell of his hair as he kissed her. Before drifting to sleep in each other's arms they had talked about their plans for their life together, the house they were buying, the child she was carrying. She thought back to her own childhood and the generosity she had felt from her parents, and she knew that she and Jason could give their child—or maybe children!—the same nurturing love.

As she approached the big glass and chrome entrance to the Sun Motors Detroit Assembly Plant offices, she gave a little inward sigh. Yes, the working conditions were difficult, even bizarre at times, but such was the nature of progress. You took the good with the bad. You gave up some freedoms in exchange for security and a rewarding career. Because the benefits were substantial, you endured the strange and often inexplicable decisions made by your superiors. And there was always the possibility of a promotion, so that eventually you could find yourself not just following the rules but making them.

It's funny, she thought to herself, that ten years earlier, when she was still a kid, the idea of being a senior logistics manager in a car factory would have seemed like the most boring and unfulfilling job imaginable. How much more fun it would be to be a car designer or test driver! As a person who sourced the parts for the cars, her job was hidden behind the scenes, like the stagehands who change the scenery in the dark so the actors can take the stage and thrill the audience. But over the years, ever since she had started at Sun Motors as an intern, Sylvia had learned to appreciate the role of the backstage workers. She saw how her work affected the making of the product and the lives of her colleagues. She derived personal satisfaction from solving problems and getting the contracts written and the parts delivered. In the grand scheme of things her role was small but important. And with her new family added to her life, she felt a deep sense of gratitude.

Lost in her thoughts, she was startled when Palin accosted her.

"Sylvia," he said with a big smile—the biggest she had ever seen on his mechanical face.

She stopped. They were standing in the parking lot a few yards from the entrance. Other employees walked past them.

"Oh, hi, Carin. What's up?"

"I have some amazing news for you! You have been chosen for a very special project. I can't tell you what it is. I need you to get in the car and go with your escorts. Everything will be explained in due time."

A black Sun Motors SUV eased alongside them. The side door opened. A man and a woman got out. They were wearing Sun Motors security uniforms. Smiling, they positioned themselves on each side of Sylvia.

"But what about my work?" she asked. "I've got a critical conference call in fifteen minutes. It's about the internal guidance system for the Comanche."

"I know all about it," smiled Carin. "I'll take your place. You've done an excellent job. Please, go with Robert and Janet. You are being given an incredible opportunity."

"But what about Jason? I need to tell him where I'm going. We keep no secrets from each other. Can I call him?" She reached for her phone.

Carin held up his hand. Without a smile he said, "We'll speak to Jason. You're going on a highly classified mission. We need to control what's being said about it. Don't worry, I'm sure you'll be seeing your husband very soon."

"Promise?"

"Of course." He extended his hand. "Now please let me hold your phone. You'll get it back the moment you return. It's just a routine security measure. Like when you go to court, and you have to leave your phone in your car. Not a big deal."

"Okay," said Sylvia. She handed her We don't want to fall behind schedule."

Sylvia turned to the open door of the SUV and then stopped. "How long will I be away?"

"Can't say for sure," smiled Carin. "Now please get in—you're a very important person!"

It was the special limousine model of the largest SUV made by Sun Motors, with leather seating, burled walnut panels, and deeply tinted windows. From behind his sunglasses, the driver gave her a glance and a little smile. Sylvia buckled herself by the window. Janet sat next to her. Robert took the seat next to the driver. Carin closed the door and the big SUV glided towards the parking lot exit. Sylvia watched the other employees getting out of their cars. Suddenly she felt exalted, as if she had been plucked from obscurity and placed on a throne. But why? What had she done to deserve this extraordinary treatment?

As the big car accelerated onto the Detroit Industrial Freeway, Sylvia turned to Janet.

"Where are we going?" she asked.

"To the airport."

"Oh—I'm going on a plane?"

"You'll see," she responded flatly. She looked straight ahead.

Sylvia sat back and watched the city roll by. She felt both thrilled and intimidated. She imagined her co-workers—Tameeka, Mei Lien, Maxell, Eduardo, and the others—passing her cubicle and asking each other, "Where's Sylvia? She's never late on Monday morning, and we have an important meeting." As the minutes and hours ticked by, what would Carin tell them? How much would he reveal about her sudden absence?

As if an electric shock had passed through her body, she suddenly turned to Janet. "Is this what you did to Judy Loring and Randolph Meekin?"

Janet gave her a bland smile. "I can't really speak to that."

"Those people left and never came back!"

"Every situation is different."

"Situation? What's the situation? I have no idea why I've been chosen for this trip. Or mission. Or whatever you call it."

"Be patient," said Janet. She gestured toward the lacquered door of the compartment between the seats. "Would you like some water?"

"No thanks, I'm good," replied Sylvia. "If this is an overnight trip, shouldn't I have brought a suitcase? I can't wear the same clothes two days in a row! And I'll need my toiletries from home—my makeup and toothbrush and all that stuff."

"All of that is being taken care of."

The car exited at W.G. Rogell Drive, but instead of going to the familiar commercial airline departure terminals the driver steered onto an access road that took them to a hanger. They came to a stop near a jet on the runway. The driver came around, and as he opened Sylvia's door the whining of jet engines and the smell of exhaust and fuel intruded. She stepped into the glare of the morning light. Far across the tarmac, a passenger jet roared down the runway and took to the sky.

"Sylvia Brand," said a woman dressed in a Sun Motors uniform.

"Yes, that's me."

"I'm Nancy. I'm one of your flight attendants. Please follow me."

Nancy led Sylvia to the steps of the jet. It wasn't one of those tiny little planes with only a few windows, nor was it as big as a regular commercial airliner.

"Today, you travel in style," said Nancy. "Sun Motors owns two business jets. This is one of them. It carries sixteen passengers and four crew members. We use it to fly our top executives to Sun Motors locations around the world.

And, when necessary, it's available for special projects." She gestured to the steps leading up to the door. "Please—after you."

Sylvia climbed the steps and entered the cabin. Instead of dozens of rows of seats in the familiar cattle-car arrangement, the space looked more like a modernistic living room, with big upholstered chairs alternating with banquette seating along the sides. The middle of the cabin had a partition leading into a conference room in the forward section. Sylvia saw there were several other passengers already on board. While they were all wearing the requisite Sun Motors uniform of navy blue slacks or skirt and white shirt—indicating they weren't top executives—she didn't recognize any of them.

Nancy showed Sylvia to her seat. One of four in a group, it faced two others, with a glossy-topped table between. One of the facing seats was occupied by a man. He watched her with benign interest.

"I'm Sylvia Brand," she said, extending her hand. "Senior logistics manager at the Detroit Assembly Plant."

"Peter Williams." While his skin seemed unusually pale, his handshake was firm and businesslike. "Robotics engineer."

"This should be an exciting adventure," said Sylvia with a smile. "I've done a lot of traveling for the company, but always flying commercial. Never on a company jet."

"Likewise," replied Peter. "A person could get used to this." He leaned forward as if to share a confidence. "I'm going to be honest with you—I have no idea where we're going. I came to work this morning expecting to have a typical day. My boss, Saran, met me at the main entrance. He told me I was going on a special assignment and I'd be leaving right away. They put me into a company car and drove me here. That's all I know."

"And they took your phone, right?"

"Yes. Saran said they couldn't risk a leak. It was all very hush-hush. I really hope I get my phone back because it's got a bunch family videos that I haven't backed up yet."

"Oh—you have a family?"

"It was our daughter's sixteenth birthday yesterday. She didn't want a big party, so my wife and I took her out to her favorite restaurant. Then we brought her home and I gave her the keys to her new car—the new Sun self-driving electric. I have mixed feelings about that, because when I was sixteen I learned to drive in an old-fashioned manually operated car with a gas engine. It even had a stick shift, if you can imagine that!"

"A real antique," smiled Sylvia.

"I'm not sure if kids are getting the same kind of training these days, where they can just point the car in the direction they want to go and the safety features make getting into an accident practically impossible. Laconda has told me about kids who say, 'Hey, now you can get drunk and get into your car and drive home, because you can't crash!' That seems like very dangerous thinking."

"I agree," said Sylvia. She thought of her unborn child. Sixteen years from now, what sort of world would he or she inherit? How many of the old ways, like driving yourself in your own car, would have disappeared?

"Aside from the videos," continued Peter, "my phone is very useful because I can track the car with it. I'll always know where she is and if anyone's in the car with her."

Sylvia smiled. "Being able to keep an eye on your sixteen-year-old as she drives around town is a good thing." She paused and looked around the luxurious cabin. "This certainly is nice. I'd feel better if I knew where we're going."

Peter shrugged. "I don't care as long as I'm home tonight."

Sylvia felt the dull thud of the outside door being closed. A voice over the intercom said, "This is Lamar. I'll be your captain on this flight. Welcome to you all. As soon as we receive clearance from the tower, we'll be taking off. Our flying time will be approximately three hours and twenty minutes. Our stewards, Nancy and Miguel, will take very good care of you. Enjoy the flight."

Sylvia said to Peter, "Lamar has the voice of an autonomous humanoid operator."

"Yep. He's a Morta AHO 7-A. The next generation above the sixes they're using as managers. Unlike a human pilot, he never gets drunk, never oversleeps, and never asks for a raise. But to be honest, designing a robot to fly a plane is much easier than designing a self-driving automobile. As far back as before the Global Depression, commercial airliners were very nearly self-flying. The human pilots were only necessary to supervise takeoff and landing. In a plane, once you're in the air, there are none of the hazards you encounter on a street, and you're not operating within inches of other vehicles. Compared to a vehicle on the road, in the sky you have a huge margin for error."

The sound of the plane's jet engines increased in volume and the craft gently rolled forward along the taxiway before coming to a stop. After a moment, the engines suddenly roared to life. As the sound became deafening, Sylvia felt herself being pressed against the back of her seat. The plane gathered speed and she looked out the window. The grass bordering the runway seemed to fly past while the trees and low buildings in the distance didn't move. She felt the nose of the plane lift, and then a "thunk" as it left the ground. From underneath came the hum of the landing gear retracting. They ascended at a steep angle—much steeper than the commercial jets she was accustomed to taking.

From her window Sylvia looked down on the angular buildings of downtown Detroit, the curve of the Detroit River, the graceful boat shape of Belle Isle, and the shimmering grey-blue of Lake St. Claire. To get a sense of where they were going, she tried to track the plane's direction as it banked to the left, and through gaps in the clouds she saw they were making a broad arc around the lake. Then the plane was fully above the clouds, hiding the earth from sight. Below lay heaps of brilliant white, while above curved the blazing blue sky.

"Are you a native of Detroit?" Sylvia asked Peter.

"My hometown is a little city on Lake Huron called Cheboygan. Population about five thousand. We're best known as the home port of the U.S. Coast Guard cutter and icebreaker Mackinaw. I graduated from Michigan State with a degree in computer science, and then went to grad school for robotics. After I got my master's degree I got a job at Sun Motors. Then I got married and we had Laconda. During the Global Depression life was very tough, but we survived. I play golf and we keep a boat in the Marina District. A twenty-two foot runabout. We take it out on the lake. That's about it—just a normal all-American family."

"You must like your job. Robotics. That's a pretty cool area to be in today."

"Yeah. I must confess my particular line of work is not very glamorous. I help develop assembly line robots. The rock stars are the people who create autonomous vehicles. Right now they're building a car that's basically a Morta AHO on four wheels that can go one hundred and fifty miles an hour. You can sit in the back seat and have a conversation with the car the way you'd have a conversation with your driver."

"Except—let me guess—the computer driver never gets drunk, never oversleeps, and never asks for a raise."

"Exactly. Our president and CEO, Mr. Atkinson, has said he wants to be among the first to have one."

"Among the first, but not the first," laughed Sylvia.

"To be sure, it'll be tested extensively before we let him take a spin. But like I said, I'm not directly involved in that project. I work on the automated assembly line."

"Do you have a Morta robot manager?"

"Yes," nodded Peter. "Her name is Gamir."

"Her?"

Peter shrugged. "Around the office we wanted to choose one gender or the other. We flipped a coin and it came up heads, which meant female. So we pretend Gamir is a woman. It doesn't matter to anyone; it was a random choice. Some people have suggested a gender-free pronoun in the form of 'dee,' with the object form as 'deem.' We didn't go for that, but eventually it may have to happen.

"It's crazy how gender colors peoples' perceptions of performance. Here's an example. The other day one of my colleagues thought Gamir spoke to him sharply. The guy had screwed up and Gamir was correcting him—"

"Sorry to interrupt, but they can do that? Vary their vocal tone?"

"Yes, the new ones can. When they believe something they're saying is particularly important—that is, the risk of failure is high if the human on the other end doesn't affirmatively respond—they can sharpen their inflection. So Gamir told my colleague that he needed to fix a problem now, and then she walked away. Later, when we were in the men's room—no cameras there—he lit into her, calling her a bitch and all kinds of other names I can't repeat. He said women are terrible managers, they can't lead, blah, blah, blah. I listened to him for a few minutes and then I said, 'Dude, do you remember that we were the ones who made Gamir a female? Gamir has no gender. Gamir is a gender-neutral robot. We could have just as easily imagined it to be male.'

"He didn't like hearing that. I couldn't convince him, so I dropped the subject. And on the flip side of the coin, one of the women who work in our office is convinced that Gamir is her soul mate and that Gamir understands her in a special way because there's a feminine bond. We tell her, 'You can think whatever you want, but all Morta 6-C management robots are the same. They have no gender.'"

"But is it possible," said Sylvia, "that because Gamir is engaged in continuous machine learning, it—or she—could amass data that's skewed towards one point of view? That somehow she could place a higher priority on data that paints a more positive picture of women than of men? For example, a human male boss who's sexist—and believe me, I've had plenty of experience in that department—will see a mistake made by a male subordinate and think, 'He made a bad decision, but it doesn't mean he's a bad worker. Anybody can make a mistake. It's not a serious problem.' Meanwhile, a female worker can make exactly the same mistake and the male boss will say, 'See? That proves a woman can't do the job. She doesn't deserve a promotion, or to be paid as much as a man.' In an organization run by women, might the same problem arise? Might a female manager have a bias in favor of the women working under her?"

"By extension," said Peter, "you could apply that to any demographic subset. Religious managers would have a bias against workers who are secular. Thin managers would have a bias against workers who are heavy. Managers who are married with kids would have a bias against employees who are single. The only way to avoid that is by establishing a strong culture of fairness in which data about employee performance is evaluated with clarity and not through the distorting lens of bias. Or you can hire gender-free robots. But as far as Gamir is concerned, it—which is the precisely correct pronoun—may have only a passing knowledge of the gender assignment we've given to it. Gamir just does its job. Gamir has no opinion regarding the differences in job performance between men and women. Gamir sees only productivity or the lack thereof. Gamir, and the other Morta

AHO 6-C robots, may be the best solution for workplace bias. They are incapable of irrational discrimination."

CHAPTER SEVENTEEN

Nancy approached their seats. "Are you comfortable?" she asked.

"Yes, thank you," replied Sylvia. "Do you know where we're going? The pilot said we'd be airborne for three hours and twenty minutes. That's enough time to get us as far as Seattle or Los Angeles. Or, if we were going south, to Miami or Houston."

"I can't comment on that," replied Nancy. "We ask that you relax and enjoy the flight. The flight time may not be relevant to the distance to our destination. Can I get you a beverage?"

"It's early in the day," said Peter, "but I could use a beer."

"Certainly," said Nancy.

"I'll take one too," said Sylvia.

Nancy smiled at her and said, "Because of your condition, I'm able to offer you water or fruit juice."

"My condition?" replied Sylvia.

"Yes. I've been advised that you will not be consuming alcohol on this flight."

"And who advised you of that?" said Sylvia.

"The decision makers supervising this trip," replied Nancy. "I really don't want to discuss your personal health. I hope you understand."

"I've changed my mind," said Peter. "I'll have apple juice."

"I'll have the same," said Sylvia with displeasure.

Nancy smiled. "Coming right up. And something to eat? I can offer you a turkey, ham, or roast beef sandwich."

"And what if I happened to be a vegetarian?" said Sylvia. "Oh, but you already know that I'm not, isn't that true?"

"Why don't you bring us one ham and one turkey, and we'll figure it out," said Peter.

With a dry smile, Nancy turned and left.

"Well, there you go," said Sylvia. "Since the whole world seems to know, I might as well tell you I'm expecting a baby."

"Congratulations!" said Peter.

Sylvia leaned closer. "They may have cameras on this plane, but you know what? I don't care. I didn't ask to be on this trip. So I'm going to speak honestly. I love Sun Motors, but sometimes I feel like I'm living in a fishbowl. They made us join the Sun Motors Employee Wellness Plan and sign a pile of consent forms that give the company the right to know everything about us. They say it's for our own protection, but sometimes I wonder. I don't like the idea that a Barbie-doll flight attendant knows that I'm pregnant and has orders to refuse me a goddamn beer when I want one. It gives me the creeps."

"I understand how you feel," said Peter, "but look at it from their point of view. Healthcare can get incredibly expensive. If they agree to cover you, they have to do it even if you come down with an expensive illness. If you get a rare disease, your insurer—in this case Sun Motors—may find itself on the hook for millions of dollars in expenses. I can tell you that from my point of view, I'm glad to have the Sun Motors Employee Wellness Plan."

"If I may ask…. Why are you glad?"

"It's because I was recently diagnosed with a rare form of Diamond-Blackfan anemia, a genetic blood disorder that prevents your bone marrow from producing enough red blood cells. It can get progressively worse until it kills you. Of all the people with this disease, about half have inherited the mutation from a parent, while the other half have a new mutation, where it appears for the first time in the family. The treatment—typically bone marrow transplants—is very expensive, painful, and short-term. When I found out I had it, I thought for sure the company would find a way to cut me loose, but they say they'll stick by me."

"I'm sorry to hear about your diagnosis," said Sylvia. "Do you mind if I ask if your daughter has it?"

"She's being tested," he replied. "We're not sure yet."

Nancy appeared with their beverages and sandwiches. As they ate they talked about less personal things, including the state of Detroit's professional sports teams and the problems of pollution in Lake St. Clair.

The seat belt sign flashed on. Nancy came to their seats, told them they were preparing to land, and cleared away their cups and plates. The plane began its gradual descent. The clouds enveloped it and the view out the window became nothing but white. After a bit of turbulence the earth appeared below. Sylvia peered intently out the window, searching for a familiar landmark, but she saw only rugged mountains, the lower ones blanketed in fir trees with the higher peaks capped in white snow. Occasional small lakes glimmered in the afternoon light, and here and there the landscape showed the meandering brown scratch of a road. There were no towns and no signs of human industry.

Despite the lack of built structures suggesting a city or airport, the plane rapidly descended. The trees became individual green spikes and the hills seemed higher. Then with a rocking "thud" the plane touched down. From her window Sylvia saw only the edge of the concrete runway and a wide, flat field bordered by a wall of pines, beyond which loomed pale purple mountains. The plane slowed and turned to the left. Now Sylvia could see the end of the runway and a road beyond. Then a building came into view— a plain structure with a control tower attached to one side—and she concluded that they had landed at one of the thousands of regional airports dotted across the United Americas.

The plane came to a halt. Over the intercom Lamar said, "Please remain seated until Nancy and Miguel tell you it's time to deplane. You'll exit by the rear door. Have a pleasant day."

Peter and Sylvia sat in their seats while Nancy and Miguel busied themselves in the back of the plane. Presently the rear door was opened and by swiveling in her seat Sylvia could see the passengers behind them standing and moving towards the exit. Then Nancy came to Sylvia and Peter and said, "You may now disembark. It has been a pleasure to serve you."

They stood up and walked to the rear door of the plane. Idling a short distance from the aircraft was a white limousine bus of the kind high schoolers rent to go to the prom or groups of people use on a business trip. Before descending the stairs, Sylvia paused to take stock of the environment. It was indeed a small regional airport, with an administration building and attached tower, a cluster of hangers, and a handful of private planes and corporate jets. There were two runways, set at an angle to each other. Just beyond the perimeter of the airport, here and there houses or other small buildings peeked from the pine forest. To the east—judging by the angle of the sun—lay a line of whitecapped mountains. Sylvia assumed it was early afternoon, and the moderate outdoor temperature suggested the plane hadn't flown far from the same latitude as Detroit. To her that meant they had probably flown almost due west, and she could be looking at the Rocky Mountains, the Cascades, or the Sierra Nevadas.

She walked down the steps and then to the limousine bus. She took a seat near the front, and Peter sat next to her. Few people on the bus were talking. Nancy and Miguel took the two remaining empty seats. The doors closed and the driver—a man wearing not the blue pants and white shirt of Sun Motors but a dark green shirt and black pants—drew a curtain across the aisle, separating himself from his passengers and obscuring the view of the road ahead. It was then that Sylvia noticed the windows of the bus were deeply tinted, so much so that even in broad daylight she could see only vague forms and the difference between the lighter sky and the darker ground.

Sylvia leaned forward to address Nancy. "I'm getting the impression that whoever arranged this trip doesn't want us to know where we are. I don't even know if we're still in the United Americas, and we certainly can't see very much out of the windows."

Nancy smiled and said, "These are nothing more than basic security measures. In due time, you'll learn much more. The ride will not be long."

"Are you staying with us, or do you have to fly back?"

"Miguel and I are here to ensure you arrive at your destination safely. Then we'll be saying goodbye."

"Do you mean you're not flying home with us?"

"Don't worry, you'll be well taken care of."

The bus began to move. Sylvia sensed the usual starting and stopping. Neither she nor Peter wore a wristwatch, and she asked Nancy, "Do you know what time it is?"

"No, but we're right on schedule," she replied.

Sylvia turned and, half-standing in her seat, said in a loud voice, "Does anybody know what time it is?"

A few of the riders mumbled "no" or "sorry, don't know."

Nancy said, "Sylvia, please be assured everything is going as planned. We'll be getting off the bus soon."

There was a prolonged period of steady driving at a highway speed, then slowing down, stopping, and starting again. Intently Sylvia peered through the tinted window and tried to discern what she saw, but she could make out only broad shapes and areas of light and dark. She could not tell if they were driving through city or forest, mountain or desert.

The bus came to a stop. Nancy and Miguel stood up and pulled back the curtain. Through the windshield Sylvia saw they were in the parking lot of an office building. Where the parking lot ended the pine trees began.

"We've arrived!" said Nancy with a smile. "Please watch your step getting off the bus."

Because they were nearest to the front, Sylvia and Peter were the first to stand and move towards the door. Before she disembarked, Sylvia turned to the driver, who was still sitting behind the wheel, and said, "Thank you for a nice ride."

"My pleasure, ma'am," he replied, touching the visor of his driver's hat.

"Will we see you again?" asked Sylvia. "To take us back to the plane?"

"We'll see. You have a good day, ma'am."

Quickly Sylvia scanned the dashboard of the bus for any useful information—a clock, toll receipt, or folded newspaper. There was nothing. Becoming aware of the restive group lined up behind her, she turned and descended the steps.

On the pavement, she stood for a moment as an unfamiliar scent came into her nostrils. She inhaled deeply and slowly. Mixed with the scent of pines there was no mistaking the faint, tangy smell of an onshore breeze from the sea.

We're near an ocean, she thought.

The building in front of her rose three stories, was capped with a flat roof, and showed typically bland office construction. The dark frameless windows revealed nothing of the activities inside. The door was set exactly in the middle of the façade. Clearly this edifice had been designed for functionality, not to win any awards for architecture. Several cars were parked in front. They were not all Sun Motors vehicles. A number of golf carts were parked there too. Sylvia hoped this wasn't some sort of home for retirees.

Nancy said, "This way, please," as she gestured towards the front entrance.

As Sylvia approached the door a man came out. He looked to be about her age. Definitely not a senior citizen. Without making eye contact he went to one of the golf carts, started it, and drove away towards a path leading from the parking lot into the pines.

After watching as the man drove away in his golf cart, Sylvia led the group inside. She entered a nondescript office lobby devoid of any artwork or visual decoration. Under her feet a gray rubber mat covered the traffic area of the glossy pebble-finish floor. The ceiling was bone white and not high. To the left, a typical office sofa—upholstered in orange and looking hard—kept company with a ficus plant. Straight ahead were a door and a staircase going up. To the right was a desk, like in a hotel, and another door.

Two women were behind the desk. They were wearing the same colors as the bus driver—dark green blouses and black skirts. They also wore nametags—Janice and Ka'sah.

"Good afternoon," said Ka'sah. "You must be Sylvia Brand. Welcome to Juliette Island."

"Juliette Island?" replied Sylvia. "We're on an island?"

"Yes," said Ka'sah. "It's named in honor of Juliette Gant, the daughter of the president of the Industrial Council. It's a very special place for very special people."

"I'm a special person?"

"If you weren't, you wouldn't be here." She handed Sylvia what looked like a cheap burner. "Here's your phone. You can use it to call any company representative on the island, and as a personal timepiece."

"Is it connected to the internet?"

Ka'sah gave her a broad, cold smile. "I'm sorry, it is not. Please go to room twenty-three, just up the stairs. There's also an elevator, but it's rather slow. You'll find it through that door." She pointed to the door next to the desk.

Sylvia took the stairs to the second floor. Room twenty-three was to the right, a few doors down. She knocked and without waiting for a response turned the knob and entered. She found herself in what looked like a home office. A man was sitting behind a desk. He was bald and wore rimless eyeglasses. Unlike the sterile lobby, this room looked as though it was designed for human comfort. There was an easy chair, a Persian rug, and an overstuffed sofa with pillows. The beige walls were decorated with a mélange of paintings and photographs. Several photos showed the man behind the desk at the wheel of a sailboat.

"Ms. Brand, please make yourself comfortable," said the man with a wave in the direction of the armchair facing the desk.

Sylvia remained standing. "Who are you, and why am I here?"

He looked up from what he was reading. "Of course—how rude of me. I'm Doctor James Hyland. I'll be your primary care physician."

"Primary care physician? What the hell are you talking about? I have a doctor and her name is Rebecca Goldsmith at the Willowdale Center. Elizabeth Darcy at Detroit Hospital is my OB/GYN. I don't need any more doctors. What I need is to go home!"

"Please calm yourself, Ms. Brand. May I call you Sylvia? Please sit down and I will answer all your questions."

Feeling as though she had no choice but to play along, Sylvia took the chair. She gave Dr. Hyland a hard look. "Okay, I'm sitting."

"I know this has been a rather unsettling day for you," said Dr. Hyland as he removed his glasses. Taking a cloth from his desk drawer, he began to wipe the lenses. "We apologize for the secrecy, shall we say, surrounding your trip here to Juliette Island. Through painful experience, we've found that a swift extraction is always best. If we ask people to come here, they often say no, which is unacceptable. It's better to get them here and explain later."

"Why am I here?"

"You are a very special person."

"So I've been told. Why?"

"Two reasons. You are carrying a child. And as we have learned from your tests, you are also a carrier of extremely rare genetic disease called mitochondrial DNA-associated Leigh syndrome. If manifested in the child, it's a severe mitochondrial disorder characterized by encephalopathy, or brain disease; body lactic acidosis, or elevated levels of lactic acid in the body; seizures; heart disease; respiratory abnormalities; and developmental delays. The specific symptoms and severity of these disorders in each individual can vary greatly from one person to another and even among members of the same family."

"What are you saying? My child is going to die of a horrible genetic disease?"

"No one knows the answer. MILS often emerges during the first three months to one year of life. However, onset can occur at any time from birth through adulthood. Some victims die in the crib. Others live well into adulthood. Medical science has long sought a cure for this disease, but finding carriers has been a perennial challenge. That's why you're here."

CHAPTER EIGHTEEN

"How do you know I carry MILS but Dr. Darcy didn't tell me?" demanded Sylvia. "This business of everyone else knowing my medical history while I'm in the dark is wearing thin. I'm not someone's lab rat. I'm a citizen of the United Americas and I have rights."

"I understand your frustration," said Dr. Hyland. "Here are the facts. Because Dr. Darcy participates in the Sun Motors Employee Wellness Plan, and Sun Motors is fully integrated with the Industrial Council, we received your test results at the same instant she did. We simply advised her to hold off on notifying you because we were going to intervene. The decision was made to bring you to the Juliette Island Center for Health Research, and now here you are. We're very glad to have you."

"This place is operated by the Industrial Council? I never signed any contract with the Industrial Council."

Dr. Hyland smiled. "Of course you did. The consent forms that you read and approved very clearly state that Sun Motors has the right to transfer its obligations as a health provider to any organization it sees fit, including the Industrial Council. This is a tremendous benefit to you! Here on Juliette Island we provide health care that's second to none. All the top pharmaceutical companies participate in our health research."

"Health research? What does that mean? Is this some sort of clinical trial?"

"In a way, yes. It's a long-term search for a cure, not only for MILS but for many other terrible diseases as well. Together with our pharmaceutical company partners, the Juliette Island Center is breaking new ground in identifying treatments for many of today's most destructive diseases. Perhaps you've heard of Quaxil, the miracle drug that alleviates some forms of trichotillomania? It was developed in a joint venture between the Juliette Island Center and Pardo Pharmaceuticals."

"I've heard it costs five hundred dollars per pill."

"Believe me, when a child compulsively pulls out their own eyebrows and hair to the point of baldness, her parents are happy to pay any price for hope."

"So I'm here because I have MILS, and my unborn child may have it too?"

"Yes."

"What about the man who is my husband and the father of my child? What about Jason Quin?"

"MILS is a disease that is passed from mother to child. The father is not relevant."

"He's relevant to me and to our child!"

"He is being well taken care of. Our concern, and your concern, must be for the health of you and your child. I don't think you fully appreciate the opportunity you have. Your form of MILS affects one in five hundred thousand children. That's more than a million in the United Americas."

"Why don't you get one of those other one million mothers to volunteer?"

"We do have a few others, but for many reasons, such as other health or mental issues, or legal constraints, volunteers are very difficult to find. Sylvia, you and your child will play a key role in the search for a cure. You will help change many lives. And in return, you'll be well rewarded."

"Well rewarded? How?"

"You get to live here on Juliette Island! This is the kind of place that people dream about coming to, whether for vacation or retirement. The weather is pleasant year-round and the island boasts beautiful topography, with lovely pine-covered hills descending to kiss white sand beaches. You'll enjoy the all amenities of civilization including a cinema, eighteen-hole golf course, shopping, and a four-star restaurant. And of course the finest medical care in the world for you and your child."

"You're assuming that I want to keep this baby, despite its having a terrible genetic disease."

Dr. Hyland's placid expression changed to a frown. He leaned forward and folded his hands on the desktop. Peering hard at Sylvia through his glasses, he said, "Of course you must have your child. There's no question about it. Are you saying you want an abortion? We don't provide that service here."

"I'm not saying I want an abortion," she replied. "I'm saying I'm entitled to make that choice."

"So you want to keep your baby," smiled Dr. Hyland. "That's good! I'm happy we agree."

"That's not what I'm saying," replied Sylvia. "I'm saying the choice should be mine. My child has a serious disease and I'm the one who should decide if I am to carry it through to full term. You haven't even asked me how I feel. I'm willing to listen to reason, but I think I deserve to be a part of the conversation."

"With all due respect, your argument is academic," replied Dr. Hyland with a dismissive wave of his hand. "Except in very unusual cases, abortions are not provided here on Juliette Island."

"Very unusual cases? Please elaborate. Who decides if a case is extremely unusual?"

"The Juliette Island Center Medical Board."

"And who is on the medical board?"

"A group of highly qualified doctors and Industrial Council members."

"Are you a member?"

"As a matter of fact, I am."

"Any women serving on this medical board?"

"Not at the present time."

Sylvia thought for a moment. Then she said, "Dr. Hyland, if in fact you are to be my primary care physician for the duration of my stay here—however long that might be—I need to know that you will be working in my best interest and will be advocating for me and my child. You have a fiduciary responsibility, do you not? Is not your patient your paramount concern, to be placed above the interests of insurance companies, hospital administrators, employers, the government, or any other entity?"

"Yes, of course," said Dr. Hyland. "Within reason, of course. We have to live in the real world."

"Let's change the subject," said Sylvia. It seemed that her new doctor—hopefully her temporary doctor, until she returned to home to Detroit—had a slippery answer for every question. After a long day, she didn't have the energy to debate him. There was much she wanted to know about her present situation, and she began by asking, "Where exactly are we? Where is Juliette Island?"

"In the upper Puget Sound, roughly halfway between Seattle and Vancouver. It's the largest of what used to be called the San Juan Islands. The islands and the surrounding territory are under the direct jurisdiction of the Industrial Council."

"Not the state of Washington?"

"That's correct. During the recovery from the Global Depression and with the rising military threat from Rodinia, among many other parcels throughout the nation, the government granted to the Industrial Council the northwest corner of Washington State. Here we conduct non-partisan research and formulate policy for the good of all the citizens of the United Americas. No politics are allowed here. We are neither Democrats nor Republicans, liberal nor conservative. It's really a very beautiful and efficient system."

"It sounds like one-party rule by a group of oligarchs."

"I think once you learn to appreciate the benefits of life here in the Olympic Zone, as the area is called, you'll take a more charitable view." He glanced at the clock on the wall. "You must be tired after your flight. I'll see you tomorrow for your first round of tests. Meanwhile, I'm sure you'd like to get settled. In a few minutes your manager will be here to take you to your home."

"My manager?"

"For lack of a better word," shrugged Dr. Hyland. "Mentor, personal guide, teacher, ombudsman—all are close, but not precisely accurate. So we just call them 'managers.'" He stood and extended his hand. "Until eleven o'clock tomorrow morning."

In the lobby, Sylvia was greeted by a Morta AHO 6-C wearing the black and blue of the Industrial Council. "Hello, Sylvia. I'm Limar, your personal manager. Please allow me to show you to your house."

"What is your assigned gender?" asked Sylvia.

"I believe our human guests use female pronouns when referring to me."

The robot turned and walked toward the front door. Janice and Ka'sah were behind the front desk, engrossed in a conversation. Sylvia and Limar went outside to one of the golf carts. Limar took a key from her pocket. "Have you driven a golf cart before?"

"Yes, thanks," she said as she took the key. "No cars for us guests?"

"No. I think you'll find the golf cart to be quite satisfactory. In inclement weather you can call for the taxi."

Sylvia took the wheel while Limar sat beside her. "Follow Pine Path until you get to Apple Way, and turn left," said Limar.

"How many people live here on Juliette Island?" asked Sylvia as she guided the golf cart along the asphalt path.

"One thousand four hundred and thirty-five guests, two hundred human staff, and a confidential number of autonomous humanoid operators of various types."

"Why do you call them 'guests'? Are they free to leave whenever they want?"

"They're contractually bound to stay for the duration of their treatment or study participation."

"Am I contractually bound?"

"Yes."

"I don't recall signing any such contract."

"You should refer to your copies of the consent forms you signed."

"I don't have them. Carin said the company would keep them for me." She stopped the golf cart on the Pine Path and turned to face Limar. "This so-called business trip is starting to look more and more like old-fashioned kidnapping and indentured servitude. When can I go home?"

After a pause, Limar said, "Each of us makes his or her contribution to our country. Everyone should serve where they are most valuable, wouldn't you agree? If in one situation a person creates a certain amount of value for society, and in another situation creates more value, then by what rational reason should that person not serve in the second situation, where he or she creates more value? Isn't there more fulfillment and satisfaction in creating more value rather than less?"

"But who makes that decision?" asked Sylvia. "Shouldn't each person decide for themselves how they want to contribute to the greater good?"

"With people of ordinary value, that may be an acceptable solution," replied Limar. "In any given system with many individuals, the people will naturally distribute themselves so that each can succeed. For example, if you have a system consisting of one hundred people, those one hundred people will not all decide to become doctors. Individually, one by one, they'll recognize that would be absurd. Some will become doctors, while others will become engineers or lawyers or artists. So that each can succeed, they will distribute themselves evenly across various occupations."

"Yes, and I chose to become a senior logistics manager at Sun Motors," said Sylvia. "I happen to like my job and I think I'm good at it."

"But you could not see the big picture," said Limar. "You could not see that because of your rare disease, you and your child have immense value to society. You and your child are special people."

"Value to society or to a pharmaceutical company's profits?" demanded Sylvia.

"What's the difference?" replied Limar. "When the pharmaceutical company benefits, so does society. What's good for industry is good for the United Americas."

"L'etat, c'est moi," said Sylvia.

"I am the state?" replied Limar. "I'm not familiar with that expression."

"You know it now," said Sylvia. "King Louis the Fourteenth of France. Ruled from 1638 to 1715. He saw himself as an absolute monarch. People in power commonly hold the delusion that what's good for them is therefore good for everyone. They believe a system that increases wealth and power for people who already have wealth and power is somehow good for all citizens. In some sort of socialist utopia that might be true, but we both know that in real world when power is concentrated in the hands of the few, the majority suffers."

Limar looked at Sylvia. "Please keep driving. We are behind schedule."

Why am I wasting my time debating with a damn robot? Sylvia asked herself as she started the golf cart. Arriving at Apple Way, she turned left. They entered a cluster of houses, not unlike a suburban cul-de-sac, but woodsier and more rustic. The homes were simple wood frame boxes with shingle roofs. They were all painted the same soft gray color. There were no cars in the driveways, only golf carts.

"We're going to number fifteen," said Limar. "A few houses down on the left."

Identical in construction to the other houses on the road, 15 Apple Way was differentiated only by an unusually tall sycamore tree in the small front yard. To Sylvia, it looked like a nicer version of the cabin she had been assigned to at summer camp when she was twelve years old. She noticed two other golf carts parked in the short gravel driveway.

"Who else is staying here?" she asked as she pulled up next to them.

"Mandy and Reese," replied Limar. "I think you'll like them because they're both from the Midwest."

"That's totally irrelevant to our potential compatibility," replied Sylvia. "But you're a robot, so I wouldn't expect you to understand."

The front door was unlocked. "On Juliette Island, nobody locks their doors," said Limar. "Most people don't even have keys. Sylvia entered the small foyer. The floor was wood and the plaster walls painted a plain off-white color. In front of her, a narrow staircase ascended to the second floor. To the right was a living room and to the left a small dining room.

"We're in the kitchen," called a woman's voice. To Sylvia's ears, the accent sounded more like Texas than Michigan, but no matter. They walked through the dining room to the rear of the house, where they found two women seated at the kitchen table.

"Hi, I'm Mandy," said the one with red hair as she stood up and extended her hand. Reese had dark brown hair. She remained seated. After introductions were made, Limar said to Sylvia, "I'll show you to your quarters, and then I'll leave you to get settled." Followed by Mandy and Reese, they trooped up the back stairway, which was even more narrow than the front stairs. On the second floor there was a hallway punctuated by several doors, and Limar led the way to the end, where he opened the last door. Sylvia entered a sitting room with a small sofa and desk. To the left, at the rear of the house, was the bedroom, and attached to it a small private bathroom.

"We were wondering who was going to get the big suite," said Mandy.

"Do you mean all the rooms aren't like this?" asked Sylvia as she peered out the bedroom window at the pine woods beyond the small back yard.

"No," said Reese. "Ours don't have the sitting room, and we share a bathroom." She exchanged glances with Mandy. They both smiled. "Ah-ha— you're going to have a baby!" exclaimed Reese.

"Is that why I have a bigger space?" asked Sylvia.

Smiling, Limar nodded.

"Congratulations!" said Mandy. "How far along are you? You're not even showing yet."

"Almost seven weeks," replied Sylvia. She turned to Limar. "This is very nice, but what am I supposed to wear? I have absolutely nothing! Not even a toothbrush."

Limar went to the window facing the front of the house. "Your problem has been solved. Your things have arrived."

Sylvia looked out the window and saw two drones, each loaded with a large box, which they deposited on the front walkway before flitting away. The foursome went downstairs, brought the boxes up, and placed them on the floor of the sitting room. Sylvia opened one of the boxes and pulled out items of clothing—skirts, blouses, shoes, sweatshirts, underwear. "None of these things are mine," she said. "They're all brand new."

"They're yours now," smiled Limar. "I think you'll find they will fit you very well. We have your measurements on file. All the clothing is custom cut and assembled."

It was then that Sylvia noticed Reese and Mandy were both wearing skirts and blouses of the same design, which matched the clothing in the box. The effect was oddly theatrical, as if they were all appearing in a production of Our Town.

"Ladies, I will leave you to get acquainted," said Limar. "Have a pleasant evening." With those words she went downstairs and drove away in the golf cart.

SYLVIA BRAND

CHAPTER NINETEEN

Coffee cups in hand, the three women sat at the kitchen table. The setting sun cast a warm glow across the white walls.

"Welcome to Industrial Council Prison," said Reese. "The only difference between ICP and regular prison is that here there's no end to your sentence. No parole. No way out except across the river or release at the whim of the Juliette Island Center Medical Board."

"Reese, don't you think you're being overly dramatic?" said Mandy as she scooped a spoon of sugar into her coffee and stirred it. "I love it here. It's a beautiful island full of friendly people. You can do whatever you want—tennis, golf, games at the rec center, movie nights, fishing off the pier, swimming, shopping. No responsibilities other than taking care of yourself and showing up for your medical tests. No one likes to be poked and prodded and have needles stuck into them every day, but it sure beats working for a paycheck at a lousy insurance company."

"Is that what you did before they brought you here?" asked Sylvia. "Work at an insurance company? And why did they choose you?"

Mandy told her story.

She had been born and raised in Golden, Colorado, a town a few miles west of Denver. When Mandy was eight years old her abusive father abandoned her, her mother, and her older brother. Mother had to go to work to support the family, and Mandy was often left in the care of an aunt and uncle. Her Uncle Will molested her until his wife discovered what was going on. To Mandy's amazement, Aunt Rebecca kicked Mandy out of the house, as if she were the sexual predator! She bounced around the foster care circuit, managed to graduate from high school, and then earned her associate's degree in business management at Colorado Mesa University. She got a job selling final expense plans for Mountain Life Insurance, a Two Hundred K company, but because of her erratic performance she barely eked out a living.

She got pregnant by a guy who promised to marry her but instead took her credit cards and went to Las Vegas, where he racked up fifty thousand dollars in debt before she realized what he had done and cancelled the accounts.

Mandy had the baby, a boy whom she named Winslow, after his maternal grandfather.

Throughout all of this, she suffered unexplained health problems, regularly going to the doctor with a laundry list of complaints including fever, fatigue, muscle weakness, loss of appetite, weight loss, muscle and joint aches, rashes, numbness, and abdominal pain. Her doctors attributed her symptoms to the effects of adverse childhood experiences and advised her to seek mental health counseling. She did, but progress was slow. The only thing that kept her from being cast out among the aberrants was that her boss at Mountain Life felt sorry for her and made it her mission to salvage Mandy's shattered life. When the expanded Mountain Life Employee Health Plan was put into place, it included genetic testing. Mandy's tests revealed she suffered from polyarteritis nodosa, or PAN, a blood vessel disease characterized by inflammation of small and medium-sized arteries, preventing them from bringing oxygen and food to organs. PAN most commonly affected vessels related to the skin, joints, peripheral nerves, gastrointestinal tract, heart, eyes, and kidneys. The outward symptoms were caused by damage to affected organs.

"The underlying cause of PAN is unknown," said Mandy. "Some doctors believe it's an autoimmune disease. Others speculate it's triggered by the hepatitis B virus. No one's certain. That's why I'm here. Six months ago, my boss came to me and told me I'd been chosen for a special assignment. They put me on a company plane and sent me here. When I figured out what was going on, I was like, are you kidding? You want me to live out in the middle of nowhere so you can use me as a medical research subject? But I got used to it. Life is good here. Three meals a day, a beautiful place to live, good medical care—why should I complain?"

"What about your child?" asked Sylvia. "Where's Winslow?"

"They brought him here, too," she said. Her eyes lowered to look at the table. "But they said he was very sick. They couldn't save him."

"Save him? From what?" asked Sylvia.

"No one has said anything," interjected Reese. "It's all a big mystery. One day he was alive and the next day he was dead. That's the way it is around here. It's like Frankenstein's laboratory, with horrible things happening behind locked doors."

"Oh, I'm sure it's not like that," said Mandy. Still looking down, she fiddled nervously with her coffee cup. "The doctors here are very nice. They try hard. I'm sure they did their very best for Winslow. He's in a better place."

"A better place?" said Reese incredulously.

Seeking to diffuse the growing tension, Sylvia turned to Reese. "How about you? How did you end up here?"

Reese said she was raised in Houston, Texas. She wasn't sure where she had been born; at age two, she had been adopted by a couple who had raised her, and to that day they remained her parents. After high school she earned her degree in social work, and then got a job at a neighborhood rape crisis center in a small town near Amarillo, counseling women who had been sexually abused and arranging medical treatment for them. But she never knew her biological mother or father, and so one day she signed up for a commercial genetics testing company. After signing all the consent forms without reading them, she sent in her swab sample.

A week went by with no response, and then two weeks. She called the company. The customer service representative told her there was a slight delay in processing her sample, but not to worry.

Then one day four people came to the center and asked for her by name. She went to speak with them, and they told her they were from the Industrial Council Security Service, and could they please speak with her at their office in Amarillo. Willingly, Reese got into the van, but instead of going downtown the van got on the expressway towards the airport. She demanded to know where they were going, and the agents told her to be patient. She responded by kicking one of them and trying to open the door of the moving vehicle. They held her down and she saw a syringe. That's all she remembered until she woke up on an airplane. Groggy, she became belligerent, and was again subdued and drugged.

"I woke up in this house," she said. "That was exactly ninety-four days ago. Believe me, I count every minute that passes. During my first medical interview with Dr. Hyland—the creep!—I learned I was a carrier of an inherited gene mutation for Walker-Warburg syndrome, a severe form of congenital muscular dystrophy. Most children who have it don't live longer than three years. Hyland told me they had been looking for a carrier of Walker-Warburg and that I was a very special person. Ever since I arrived, they've been treating me like human lab rat, with endless blood tests and brain scans and tissue samples." She leaned forward for emphasis. "Last week, Dr. Hyland told me that while I was providing much valuable data in the fight against this deadly disease, it would be a huge breakthrough if I agreed to have a baby!"

"Are you serious?" asked Sylvia.

"Totally. Hyland said that if I became pregnant and carried the baby full term, I'd be given my own house with a view of Puget Sound and double the usual household budget. I told him to go to hell and that I wasn't going to be a farm animal producing babies for him and his cronies to use as test subjects. And besides, why would I deliberately have a child that I knew would be born with a terrible disease? It's ghastly."

"I don't mean to pry," said Sylvia, "but was the rape crisis center part of a larger Two Hundred K company?"

"Oh, no," laughed Reese. "We were part of the vast canaille. I'm a dyed-in-the-wool aberrant."

"I don't mean to be rude, but I've never before known an aberrant. Of course I've met them—gas station attendants and store clerks and so on—but you're the first one I've ever sat down and talked to, much less lived under the same roof with."

"Well, here I am," laughed Reese. "I won't bite you, I promise. I'm the same species as you—Homo sapiens. The only difference is that I don't accept the rule of the Industrial Council. To them I say, 'Screw you!'"

Mandy raised her hand in caution. "Reese, please. We don't want any trouble. And I'm sure you don't want to be sent to the cooler again."

"What do you mean?" asked Sylvia. "Is this place bugged?"

"Do bears crap in the woods?" said Reese. "One morning I was complaining to poor Mandy that I couldn't sleep. Anxiety or something. So that afternoon I went to my regular appointment with Dr. Hyland, and no sooner did I walk into his office than he handed me a bottle of pills. 'These will help you sleep,' he said.

"I replied, 'You bastards, you've got the house wired!'

"He just shrugged and said they had a responsibility to ensure and safeguard our welfare. I told them they only wanted to 'ensure and safeguard' the viability of their human cash cows."

Sylvia looked around the kitchen. The microwave, the ceiling light, the electrical outlets, the cabinets, the refrigerator, the stove, the canisters of salt and sugar, the cute little kitten clock on the wall—all suddenly took on a sinister aspect. Cameras and microphones could be hidden anywhere.

"Girls, who's hungry?" said Mandy with abrupt cheerfulness. "What do you say we all go to the Dockside tonight for dinner? Celebrate our new roommate."

Reese looked at Sylvia. "Be prepared to blow your entire week's restaurant allowance at the Dockside. But it will be fun and the food isn't half bad. Before we go, we absolutely must get some fresh air outside."

Mystified as to why they needed to go out and get fresh air, Sylvia went along with Reese's suggestion. In the gathering twilight, they filed out the back door to a small patio facing the gloomy woods. Reese went to an old earthenware planter that had nothing planted in it. Reaching in, she pulled out a bottle and three plastic cups. To Sylvia and Mandy she each handed a cup. After putting her finger to her lips, indicating silence, she uncorked the bottle and poured a shot into each cup.

Sylvia brought the cup to her nose and inhaled. It was whiskey. She took a sip. "This is pretty good stuff," she whispered to Reese. "Where did you get it?"

"I have my source," Reese whispered in reply. "Sip it slowly. You can't have more than one or two shots every few hours."

"Let me guess," said Sylvia. "The Morta managers will detect the alcohol on my breath."

"You got it," said Reese.

"They say when you're pregnant you shouldn't have any alcohol,' said Sylvia. "But it sure tastes good!"

Reese offered them one more shot each. As she was pouring their portions, Sylvia said, "Are you sure you want to do this? The bottle looks as if it's nearly empty. We don't want to take the last of it."

"Don't worry," replied Reese as she drained the bottle. "I can get more on Sunday."

When they were finished, Reese carefully put the bottle and cups back into the planter.

"Okay, let's roll out!" said Reese. "To the Dockside!"

.

CHAPTER TWENTY

Sylvia rode in Reese's golf cart, while Mandy drove herself. After a few minutes' trundling along the twisting asphalt paths, now lit by streetlights, they came to the restaurant. In the parking lot there were dozens of golf carts, a few cars, and one truck. The place had all the attributes of a seaside eatery— the faded grey wood siding, the railings connected by rope twists, the front door window in the form of a porthole, and the vast expanse of dark water behind it. Sylvia told the others she wanted to see the view, and together they walked around the side of the building. What Sylvia really wanted to see was how much water separated Juliette Island from the opposite land mass, at least in this location. On the horizon she could make out distant twinkling lights. They seemed to be from another world.

Reese sidled up to her. "I know what you're thinking," she whispered. "You're looking at Victoria, British Columbia. It's a good ten miles away. Unless you're an Olympic swimmer, you wouldn't stand a chance. This island is at least five miles from any other point of land, except for the other side— the eastern side—which is connected to the mainland by a mile-long causeway. When the bus brought you here, it came across the causeway. There are checkpoints at each end with armed guards."

They went into the restaurant, where they were greeted by a Morta AHO. The machine showed them to a booth. The place was nearly full, with a variety of people all wearing clothing similar to what Sylvia had been given, as if the cast of Our Town had grown to nearly a hundred actors.

"I don't see any of the Juliette Island staff here," said Sylvia.

"And you never will," replied Reese. "Unless they have a particular job to do, like performing a medical procedure on a resident or working here in the restaurant, they go home every evening, across the causeway to the mainland. After sunset, the island is managed by robots. Since they're all made by Morta Laboratories, we just call them Mortas."

Sylvia wanted to ask why the humans left at night, but the server came for their order, and the conversation went in another direction. The restaurant had a pleasant vibe and the food was boring but edible. When they were finished and each had paid with their island debit cards, they made their way outside to the golf carts. The night air was warm, and in the dark woods the tiny lights of fireflies blinked like Morse code signals.

Standing next to their golf carts, Reese drew them close together. "It's too early to go home. We should have some fun. What do you say we go skinny-dipping? There's a little beach about a mile from here. Totally secluded. If you didn't know it was there, you'd never find it."

"I don't think we should," said Mandy. "You know it's against the rules. After dark you need to be at home or at an approved location."

"That's crazy," said Sylvia. "It sounds like a curfew. I haven't had a curfew since I was sixteen years old and my parents made me come home by eleven o'clock."

"They say," said Reese, "it's because we're such special people, and if we had a medical emergency in some remote area of the island, the first responders would be delayed. It's for our own safety."

"It's a good point," nodded Mandy.

"It's ridiculous," whispered Sylvia. "Okay, let's go. It sounds like fun. Mandy, how about you? I'm sure it will be all right if we're out a little bit late."

Mandy looked around nervously before she said, "Okay, I'll come. But we can't stay long. I don't want to spend the night in the cooler."

"Don't worry," said Reese. "Get in your cart and follow me."

Sylvia got into Reese's cart, and they rolled out of the restaurant parking area. Instead of heading towards 15 Apple Way, Reese turned in the opposite direction. Mandy followed close behind. The asphalt path climbed through a grove of tall dark pines where the only light was from the yellowish jiggling headlights on each golf cart. Then the trees yielded to an open rocky pasture, dimly illuminated by the half moon emerging from behind the high thin clouds. Reese slowed down and turned into a gravel road. A jackrabbit darted through the narrow headlight beam as the golf cart bumped along before descending a gradual incline. Somewhere in the distance an owl hooted. The hill became steeper as the road wound its way toward the glimmering water visible through the tall trees. At a small clearing Reese parked the golf cart, and when the three women were gathered together she said, "This way," and she led them along a narrow path bounded by prickly beach roses. The gravel underfoot changed to sand, and suddenly Sylvia found herself stepping onto a small crescent beach. Under her feet the white sand shone in the moonlight.

Kicking off their shoes, they walked to the water's edge, where gentle waves lapped. From far across the dark water, lights twinkled.

"Oooh, this water's cold," said Sylvia.

"Don't worry, you'll get used to it,' laughed Reese. "Come this way." She walked to a big flat rock and began to pull off her skirt and blouse. "You can put your clothes here so they don't get sandy." In a moment she was naked. For a moment Sylvia was startled—she was not accustomed to seeing unclothed people in public spaces—but then she went to the rock, took off her clothes, and put them in a neat pile.

Mandy did the same, and the three women walked toward the phosphorescent ripples. Under Sylvia's feet the dry sand retained the warmth of the day, but as they neared the water it grew damp and cool. Reese boldly strode forward into the dark surf, and when the water was up to her waist she dove in.

Sylvia felt the cold water grip her legs. She hesitated before forcing herself deeper, up to her chest. The sensation was like a thousand tiny knives sticking into her skin. But she kept moving and the pain subsided. When she felt she was ready, she dove in, and the shock of the cold water against her face nearly made her turn around and run back to shore. But with Reese setting the example, Sylvia stayed in, and Mandy was soon in the water too.

Overhead the half moon gleamed and a few of the brightest stars twinkled through the high clouds. As she swam, the tensions and conflicts that had filled Sylvia's mind and heart seemed to be assuaged, and she found herself enjoying the moment without guilt or anxiety about her future. If it was her fate to be here, at this hour of this day, then so be it. It was foolish to become angry over something beyond your control. She was one with the dark water and its unseen inhabitants—the sleek silent fishes that swam in whatever direction they wanted, over uncounted leagues of open water, even to other lands and distant currents. Freedom was such a simple thing, if you looked at it from moment to moment. At this very second, in this water, Sylvia felt as free as she had ever felt.

Sylvia looked up. High overhead, a jet plane slowly crossed the sky. It was coming from somewhere and going somewhere. With a feeling of regret, the sight reminded her that her freedom was limited to this water on this crescent beach. She squinted at the tiny light. Was it a military plane or a commercial airliner? Were there passengers on board going where they had chosen to go—on a business trip or even a vacation—or was the plane full of "special" people being shipped to some remote Industrial Council facility?

Suddenly Reese appeared next to her. "What do you think? Pretty amazing, isn't it?" she said as she tread water. Her wet hair shone in the moonlight and her teeth flashed white.

"Yes—it almost makes you forget you're living in a prison camp," laughed Sylvia. She dove in and swam under water in the welcoming cold darkness for as long as her lungs could stand it. With powerful strokes she felt the water flow around and over her hands and legs. Then, with her lungs bursting from lack of oxygen, she broke the surface.

Wiping the water from her eyes, Sylvia was startled to see Reese's head illuminated by a bright light from above. Surrounded by darkness, the spot of light shining on the ocean seemed unreal, like a scene from a movie.

Suddenly Sylvia herself was caught by a spotlight from the sky. Shielding her eyes as she tread water, she heard the faint whirring of propellers. The light was then joined by a third, trained on Mandy. High over Sylvia's head, a trio of drones hovered in a group. Each had a powerful spotlight trained on one of the women in the water below it.

"Exit the water immediately," called a metallic voice from one of the drones. "You are not authorized to be at this location. Return to the beach."

With a sickening feeling of deep dread and horror, Sylvia swam to the shore until she felt her feet brush the sandy bottom. Then she walked out of the water onto the beach. Reese and Mandy were already there, dripping and shivering, trying to cover their nakedness.

A Morta strode out of the path leading to the clearing where they had parked their golf carts. In the moonlight his eyes gleamed red.

"I didn't want to be here," wailed Mandy. "They made me come! Please just let me go home!"

"Be silent," said the Morta. "All of you, get dressed."

Under the harsh glare of the drones' spotlights, the three women went to the rock and hurriedly donned their clothing.

The Morta came to them and ordered them to turn around. Starting with Reese, he deftly bound their hands behind their backs with zip ties. Mandy began to sob uncontrollably. Reese said nothing, but stood with her head held high. Taken by surprise at the speed with which the Morta had accomplished its task, Sylvia felt deep shock at the sensation, for the first time in her life, of having her hands pinned behind her back against her will. She knew now that she had truly crossed the line between being a free person and a prisoner.

"Stay together," said the Morta. "Don't try to run."

They had no choice but to obey. Under the lights of the watchful drones, they waited on the beach. Then they heard the sound of a boat approaching. With its spotlight cutting the darkness, it swung into view from around the point sheltering the crescent beach. The boat, low and black, came parallel to the beach, turned, and then ran toward the beach until its flat bow scraped onto the sand. The front gate dropped, like on a pickup truck.

"Get in," said the Morta.

The three women, with their hands restrained behind their backs, made their way along the beach to the yawning maw of the boat and stepped up the ramp. They found themselves on a flat deck in front of an enclosed wheelhouse. A Morta guard on the boat gestured to a long bench attached to the gunwales. "Sit there," it said. They sat down, uncomfortably, with their hands tied. As Mandy whimpered, Reese said to the Morta guard, "We weren't doing anything wrong. We just went for a moonlight swim."

Its red eyes gleaming in the night, the Morta guard made no response.

"You thought maybe we were trying to escape?" she continued. "That's funny! Three naked women were going to swim ten miles to the mainland, where you guys would be waiting for us. That would have been quite a sight! Don't you have better things to do than chase innocent people who are just trying to have some fun?"

"Be silent," said the Morta guard.

After the bow door had been raised, the boat's engines shifted to full reverse, and with a lurch the craft slid off the sand and backed away into open water. Turning toward the north, it picked up speed. The hovering drones, the Morta on the beach, and Sylvia's memories of freely swimming in the dark, cold water were left behind.

"Where are you taking us?" demanded Reese. "To the cooler?"

The Morta made no reply.

"What's the cooler?" Sylvia whispered to Reese.

"I think you're going to find out," she replied. "Just remember, it won't last forever. We're valuable people. They need to protect their investment in us. As long as we contribute to their profits, they'll keep us healthy."

"What if we don't contribute to their profits?" asked Sylvia.

"If you seem harmless, they'll turn you loose among the aberrants. If you pose a threat, they make you disappear."

"Sylvia Brand and Reese Carter—stop talking," said the Morta. To steady himself in the choppy seas he was holding onto the railing. Sylvia was beginning to feel a little bit ill, and she deliberately took slow, deep breaths. On the bench next her, Mandy softly whimpered.

The boat had cruised around the island, and while the night made reckoning difficult, Sylvia estimated they went halfway around in about twenty minutes. They did not pass the causeway to the mainland. The boat slowed and pulled up to an aluminum dock mounted on floats so that it went up and down with the tide. The Morta guard ascended a short set of steps to the gunwales and then stepped onto the dock. After tying the boat to a cleat on the dock, the Morta turned and said, "You will now disembark."

Sylvia stood up. Her legs were stiff and her arms ached. With the assistance of the Morta that had piloted the boat, together the three women ascended the short steps and were soon standing on the dock.

"When are you going to free our hands?" said Reese to the Morta guard.

"Follow me," came the reply.

"No, I don't want to," said Sylvia. She didn't quite know why she said this. Perhaps she had been emboldened by Reese's independent attitude, or perhaps she had gotten tired of being told what to do. But having said it, she clenched her jaw and stood with her spine straight.

The Morta guard walked over to her. His red gaze fixed on her eyes, with viper quickness he reached out with his hand and grasped the back of her neck. Suddenly white-hot pain shot from her spine into her brain. Gasping for breath, her knees buckled and her vision became blurred. With the Morta's hand still on her neck, she crumpled to the dock. Only once she was down did he release his grip.

Crouched on her knees, with her hands tied behind her back, Sylvia felt the pain slowly ease. Slowly her breath returned and her vision became clear. She looked up at the Morta standing over her.

"Your occipital nerve is just one of many very sensitive areas of your body," the Morta said. "We know them all. We know which ones to activate without permanently damaging either you or your baby. Now get up and get back in line."

Feeling dizzy, Sylvia struggled to her feet. "Okay, okay," she said. "I get it."

"Good," said the Morta without a smile. "Let's go."

With a Morta in front and one behind, the women shuffled through a gate in a high fence to a nondescript building. Inside was a room with a desk. A long hallway led from the room. The Morta led Sylvia down the hallway, which was lined with numbered doors. He slid open number eighteen. Sylvia entered a plain cinderblock cell furnished with a bed, toilet, and sink. The Morta told her to turn around, and he released her hands.

"Go to sleep," said the Morta. He closed the door.

Sylvia was alone in her cell. The only light came from a dim bulb in the center of the ceiling. There was a small barred window at the end of the cell, opposite the door, but she couldn't see anything through it other than darkness. She sat on the bed. The metal springs under the thin mattress creaked. She thought about her life in Detroit, and about Jason and the house they were buying together. Her previous life and love seemed so far away and so long ago, and yet she could almost hear Jason's voice and feel his gentle touch. She thought about her parents, and the love they had given her as a child. Those were happy times, when life seemed brighter and simpler, even through the difficult days of the Global Recession.

Where had Sylvia gone wrong? Why had she been singled out for abuse? She had always played by the rules and had been a good and loyal employee of Sun Motors. She was an obedient follower of the Industrial Council and its systems. She had even welcomed the oversight of Carin, in no small part because his arrival had marked the end of the abusive reign of Randolph Meekin. But no matter how much she tried to go along with the program, the company and its ally the Industrial Council always wanted more. They were never satisfied. And thanks to an accident of fate—a genetic fluke over which Sylvia Brand had no control—she had been identified as a "special person" who couldn't be trusted to manage her own body. Her condition had value to medical science, they said, but Sylvia knew they really meant her condition made her valuable to the health care industry and their pharmaceutical company partners. By simply existing, she was a source of marketable data, the rights to which she had foolishly signed away. And to make her bondage even more complete, under the terms of her consent forms the Industrial Council had the right to ensure that access to her health data was full, robust, and unimpeded by her own actions. She did not have the legal right to deprive the Industrial Council of data for which it, by its own reasoning, had paid through its subsidy of her Sun Motors Employee Wellness Plan. They wanted, and were legally entitled, to what they had paid for.

Mentally and physically exhausted, Sylvia lay on the bed, covered herself with the skimpy blanket, and fell into a fitful sleep.

CHAPTER TWENTY-ONE

Sylvia awoke. She didn't know how long she had been asleep. The dim bulb on the ceiling glowed. But there was other light, coming from the window.

Stiffly, she sat up. Her back ached from the thin, hard mattress. Her eyes were bleary and paste coated the inside of her mouth. The salt water had dried in her hair, making it feel coarse. Slowly she stood up. She went to the window. In order to look out she had to stand on tiptoes. Through the bars and the dirty glass she saw morning light on the pine woods. That's all she could see—just a wall of scraggly trees with a glimpse of grey sky between the uppermost branches.

At the sink she rinsed off her hands and face. There was neither soap nor towel. Then she paced in her cell, walking the five paces from the steel door to the wall with the window. She did deep knee bends and then some pushups. She went to the door to listen, but heard nothing. Another look out the window yielded only a slight change in the angle of the shadows in the trees.

Hunger gnawed at her stomach. She went to the door and pounded on it. "Hey!" she called through the narrow slit that showed nothing but a section of cinderblock wall, "If you want me to have a healthy baby for your experiments, you'd better take care of me!" She looked around the cell for a camera. There had to be a camera. They had to be watching her. She peered at the sink, the toilet, the cracks in the walls. She craned her neck to look at the lighting fixture on the ceiling.

From the door came a metallic sound. The door slid open. Limar walked in. Behind her lurked the Morta guard.

"I apologize for the poor accommodations," she said with a tone indicating a measure of kindness had been added to her voice. "I hope your evening was not too terrible."

"Yes, it was terrible," she spat. "I don't appreciate being handcuffed like a common criminal and thrown into a prison cell. I see you've got your mechanical goon standing right behind you. What is this, some sort of good cop-bad cop routine? Am I supposed to be grateful you're showing an imitation of human decency?"

Limar turned to the Morta. "Walmad, you may go. Thank you." With a nod, the robot guard left. Limar looked at Sylvia. "I'm sure you'd rather eat breakfast at home than sample the fare here at the Re-Orientation Center. We have transportation arranged for you and your housemates. Please follow me."

Sylvia followed Limar into the hallway and then to the central receiving room, where Reese and Mandy were waiting. Then Limar escorted them to the same limousine bus that had transported them from the airport—the one with the opaque windows and curtain behind the driver. "Sorry, but it's important the other residents not see you being driven from the Re-Orientation Center," said Limar. "We want to protect your privacy."

"You also want to ensure we don't know the exact location of the cooler," said Reese. "The number one rule around here is the less the so-called residents know, the better."

"Reese," said Limar, "as someone who has been a guest here for over three months, you should know the nighttime guards have their instructions. We can't have the residents wandering around the island after dark. We're all here for a purpose. We all have a job to do. I'm sorry if the rules seem severe, but it's in everyone's best interest to comply. Let's keep focused on the good we're accomplishing for our fellow citizens."

"Am I free to leave whenever I want?" asked Reese. "Do I have my rights?"

"You have a contract with your healthcare provider," replied Limar. "It's your healthcare provider's obligation to do what's best for you and for our nation. I hope I need not remind you that we are on the brink of war with Rodinia. We cannot expect to enjoy the same personal freedoms as we would in peacetime. We all must make sacrifices."

"Excuse me," said Sylvia, "but you're a goddamn robot. Exactly what sacrifices are you making? Do you even know what that means?"

"And what about this alleged war with Rodinia?" demanded Reese. "As a Morta autonomous human operator, your database of national knowledge is shared with every other Morta unit. We've been hearing about impending war with Rodinia for years. Hell, when I was a kid I heard about the horrors of Rodinia. According to Facts News, the people there were practically cannibals! I'm beginning to think this talk of war is nothing more than an excuse for the Industrial Council to solidify its power and strengthen the oligarchy."

At that moment the limousine bus arrived at 15 Apple Way. Instead of responding to the challenges from Sylvia and Reese, Limar stood up and said, "We are at our destination. I hope you have a pleasant and productive day. I hope I need not remind you of your individual appointments with your doctors—Mandy at eleven o'clock this morning, and Reese and Sylvia each at noon."

The three women filed off the bus and went into the house. On the way in, Sylvia noticed Reese and Mandy's golf carts had been returned and were parked alongside the gravel driveway.

In her private shower, with the warm water soothing her body, Sylvia ran her hands across her stomach. Soon she would be showing. Her first pregnancy had lasted ten weeks before her spontaneous abortion, as the doctors called it. She was at seven weeks now. The next three weeks would be especially nerve wracking—there was something about making it past ten weeks that seemed like an important goal. What seemed to her to be most bizarre about her situation was that on the one hand, she was living as a prisoner, which was stressful and not conducive to a healthy pregnancy, but on the other hand, her overlords had a tremendous financial interest in keeping her and her baby healthy. She was a dove in a gilded cage.

And when the baby was born, what kind of world would he or she enter? Would her child have a serious and life-threatening disease, dooming both of them to lives as human guinea pigs for the conglomerates that held the keys to healthcare?

After her shower, Sylvia joined Reese and Mandy in the kitchen for breakfast.

"My friend," said Reese as she poured Sylvia a glass of orange juice, "you may have the dubious distinction of being the first inmate of Juliette Island Prison to spend her very first night on the island in the cooler. It takes most people a few weeks to work up to that distinction."

"It wasn't exactly her idea to go to the beach at night," said Mandy. "Anyway, let's try to keep a low profile and do the best we can. I don't want any deductions on my island debit card, and I don't want to be seen as a troublemaker."

"Deductions?" asked Sylvia.

"Yes," replied Reese as she sprinkled some hot sauce on her scrambled eggs. "As a punitive measure they might put a charge on your debit card. You need to track your balance carefully, because you don't want to try to use your card somewhere and have it declined because you've been fined for some infraction you've forgotten about."

"What happens if you have no money at the end of the week?" asked Sylvia.

"Then you have to beg from your friends," said Mandy. "Believe me, it's humiliating, and an effective tool to keep people in line. It pays to follow the rules—literally."

At noon Sylvia reported to the office of Dr. James Hyland.

"I understand you had a run-in with the overnight Mortas," he said in his kindly voice.

"Yes. My roommates and I went to a beach to go swimming. They arrested us and took us to the so-called Re-Orientation Center. It was nothing more than a common jail. It was my first time behind bars in my entire life."

"I hope you learned your lesson," he said as he removed his rimless spectacles and cleaned them with a soft cloth. "Now then—we have important work to do. Mitochondrial DNA-associated Leigh syndrome, or MILS, is no laughing matter. While fate has placed a heavy burden on your shoulders, this means you have been given an opportunity to contribute to medical science in a way that few other people have. I hope you were able to get some rest last night, because we have a full schedule of tests today. Did you eat breakfast this morning?"

"Of course I did. Why?"

He looked at a paper on his desk. "That's too bad—we should have told you not to eat. We'll have to work around it. Okay, please follow me." He stood up.

"Where are we going?"

"To the medical research wing of this building."

After walking through a maze of corridors, they arrived at a reception area. "Sylvia Brand is here," Dr. Hyland said to the woman behind the desk.

The woman smiled at Sylvia. "Your first day here? Welcome. The nurse will escort you to your first appointment."

"How long will this take?" asked Sylvia.

"All day," replied the woman. "Don't worry, you'll get used to it. Think of it as being just like your old job. Nine to five."

Sylvia was shown to a room where a nurse gave her a standard physical examination including a complete blood count, cardiac stress test, liver function test, prothrombin time test, strep test, skin allergy test. For the lumbar puncture test, the nurse inserted a needle between her two lumbar vertebrae and removed a sample of cerebrospinal fluid. "This is the fluid that surrounds your brain and spinal cord to protect them from injury," she explained. "This can help us diagnose serious infections such as meningitis, other disorders such as Guillain-Barre syndrome and multiple sclerosis, or cancers of the brain or spinal cord."

Next came a flexible sigmoidoscopy, in which the nurse inserted a thin, flexible tube, or sigmoidoscope, into Sylvia's rectum. "It's a quick way to screen for colon cancer or other disorders," said the nurse.

Then it was into the stirrups for a colposcopy exam, in which the instrument produces an illuminated, magnified view of the cervix as well as the vagina and vulva. "Many pre-malignant lesions and malignant lesions in these areas have discernible characteristics that can be detected through the examination," said the nurse.

Next came an esophagogastroduodenoscopy. After giving Sylvia an intravenous muscle relaxer and an anxiety medication, plus a local anesthetic sprayed into her mouth to prevent her from coughing or gagging when the scope was inserted, the nurse inserted the scope through the esophagus and down to the stomach and duodenum, the first part of the small intestine. She examined the lining of the esophagus, stomach, and upper duodenum.

There were more—electromyography for evaluating and recording the electrical activity produced by skeletal muscles, an electrocardiograph to detect cardiac abnormalities, and a chest radiograph. Then came an ultrasound exam of the fetus and two maternal blood tests designed to measure two substances found in the blood of all pregnant women: pregnancy-associated plasma protein screening, a protein produced by the placenta in early pregnancy; and human chorionic gonadotropin, a hormone produced by the placenta in early pregnancy. "Abnormal levels," explained the nurse, "are associated with an increased risk for chromosome abnormality."

At five o'clock, the nurse announced the end of that day's testing. Sylvia felt as if her body had been invaded through every orifice and the fingers of strangers had probed her most private parts. Her body was a public resource, an open book to read by anyone, a living version of the cadavers sent to medical schools for dissection.

At home, as they were making dinner, Sylvia said to Reese and Mandy, "I can't live like this. I feel like a lab rat. They stuck needles into me as if I were a pincushion. They jammed instruments up my ass and down my throat. Dr. Hyland told me that during my next appointment on Monday they're going to put a camera into my vagina and film the fetus. They're going to do brain scans and full body x-rays. He tells me these things as if I were a willing and grateful partner to their twisted program."

"Just go with the flow," said Mandy, as she tossed the salad. "It's not an easy life, but think of the benefits. Everything is paid for. Your home, your food, your clothing—all taken care of by the Industrial Council. You have not a worry in the world. Look at us, right here, right now. We're safe in our house. We're making dinner in our kitchen. In our lives we have friends and people who care about us. Our island is peaceful and offers us everything we need. We have these things, while all over the world there are billions of people who live in wretched conditions and would gladly switch places with any one of us."

SYLVIA BRAND

CHAPTER TWENTY-TWO

The next day was Saturday. It was like any other day of the week, and Sylvia's tests began at ten o'clock in the morning, went until lunchtime at one o'clock, and then resumed at two o'clock for another five hours. Dr. Hyland was off that day, and Limar escorted her to the medical wing.

The first test was chorionic villus sampling, a prenatal test in which a sample of chorionic villi is removed from the placenta for testing. The nurse explained that the chorionic villi are wispy projections of placental tissue that share the baby's genetic makeup, and that chorionic villus sampling can provide information about the health of the fetus.

Another nurse—there seemed to be an endless supply of them—came to the examination room with a long, thin optical instrument with an eyepiece at one end, a rigid or flexible tube in the middle, and a tiny lens and light at the other end of the tube.

"What is that?" asked Sylvia, still groggy from the anesthetic administered for the chorionic villus sampling.

"It's a cystoscope," replied the nurse. "I'm going to use it to look at the lining of your urethra and bladder."

"But I don't have any urinary tract problems. Down there, everything is normal."

"That may be," said the nurse as she opened the flow of sedative into Sylvia's intravenous line. "But we need to establish a baseline condition. Please count backwards from one hundred for me."

Sylvia wanted to protest that this procedure was unnecessary and invasive, but as she became more relaxed the problem didn't seem to be worth mentioning. She started counting, and got as far as ninety-four before the world disappeared.

She woke up. She was in a hospital room, with beeping machines on each side of the bed. Her view was blocked by portable translucent curtains. Her pelvis and throat were sore. She looked at both her arms. Mercifully, the intravenous lines had been removed. The punctures were covered by bits of gauze secured with tape.

"Hello?" she called. Her voice sounded distant, weak. Summoning her strength, she called out, "Hey, I'm awake!"

The curtain was pulled aside. A nurse, dressed in white, stood at the foot of the bed. She was smiling and seemed friendly.

"Are you the same nurse who was here earlier?" asked Sylvia.

"No, I just came on duty. My name is Andrea. Now that you're up, it won't be long before we can send you home."

When the nurse said this, the first image that came into Sylvia's fuzzy mind was her home in Detroit. "Will Jason be picking me up?" she asked.

"Jason?"

"Yes, my husband. Jason. Should I call him, or is he waiting?"

"I'm sorry, Sylvia, but Jason's not here. In a few minutes you'll be driven home by one of the guards. You'll be free to enjoy the rest of your evening."

Then Sylvia remembered. She was on a distant island, living in a house that wasn't hers with roommates assigned to her by the company. She was a medical test subject. She was not going home to Jason. From deep inside her she felt a tidal surge of grief, and suddenly tears erupted from her eyes.

"I'm sorry," she stammered as she looked for something to dab her eyes. "It's been a very long week."

The nurse smiled and handed her a tissue. "I understand. I hope you don't mind if I tell you that you've been a model patient. You are very brave. The work we're doing here is very important, and you're a part of it."

"Thank you." She didn't know what else to say.

By the time the Morta guard dropped her off at home it was late afternoon. Mandy and Reese were still at their medical appointments. Feeling sore and groggy, Sylvia went up to her room, lay down on the bed, and feel asleep.

At breakfast the next morning, Reese told Sylvia that ordinarily there were no medical exams on Sunday. The island's staff was reduced to minimal levels, leaving the bulk of the work, including security, in the hands of the Mortas. Unlike their human creators, the Mortas never needed days off. They didn't sleep, exactly; to recharge and receive their software updates, they went dormant for an hour a day. Every few weeks they had to report to the local Morta maintenance facility, which Reese believed was somewhere near the island, but she wasn't sure because since arriving on the island she hadn't been off it, and she knew very little about the surrounding environment.

"Sun Motors has a plant in Tacoma," said Sylvia as she spooned strawberry jam onto her English muffin. "I was there a few years ago. They assemble internal guidance systems for the Comanche truck, which they ship to us in Detroit. A few days before I was sent here I had a video conference with the production manager, and he told me they had just gotten a Morta supervisor. He wanted to know what he should expect."

"What did you tell him?" asked Mandy.

"That our manager, Carin, was about as ideal a boss as you could hope for. No ego, ready to help with a problem, and always respectful. Of course, I told him these things via the company video conferencing service while I was sitting in my cubicle, which I knew was under surveillance. What I told the guy in Tacoma was half the truth. From a purely operational standpoint, Carin was a very good supervisor. But I had to get past the fact that he was a creepy control freak who knew more about me than I did!'

"I hear you," said Reese.

"I heard the territory north of here," said Mandy, "in what used to be Canada, was part of the canaille, occupied exclusively by the aberrants."

"You mean totally out of the control of the federal government and the Industrial Council?" asked Sylvia.

"Yes," said Mandy. "It's what used to be the province of Alberta. The center is the old city of Calgary, which the aberrants have supposedly re-named Swanta, after their so-called leader. Of course it's all a load of rubbish. I cannot imagine anyone living in the filth and lawlessness of the canaille. They can call their city whatever they want, it's still a disgusting swamp. Or so I've heard."

As they were cleaning up the dishes, Reese said, "Ladies, what do you want to do today?"

"I'm going to the movies with my friend Jacqui," said Mandy. "Then we're just going to hang out at the rec center. Maybe meet some cute guys."

"And if you meet some cute guys, what exactly do you plan to do with them?" laughed Reese.

"I try not to think about that," she replied.

Reese turned to Sylvia. "In case you're wondering, when you go in for your medical exam on Monday morning, the doctor will know if you've had sex. They'll find your partner's DNA in your vagina, or traces of a condom, or evidence of a lubricant. And if you try to wash that stuff out, they'll detect that too. Even an unusual stretching of your girl parts will be detected."

"Is it against the law to have sex?" asked Sylvia.

"You've got to remember there are no unusual laws here," corrected Reese. "Technically, we're governed by the same laws as everyone else. But we're also controlled by the contracts and consent forms we signed with the companies that employ us. Your actions are controlled by the policies set by Sun Motors, and by extension the Industrial Council, to which Sun Motors has assigned its signatory rights. To answer your question, your doctor, as the lawful representative of the Council, may determine that having sex could be detrimental to your mental or physical health. This would put into jeopardy the investment they've made in you, in the form of your paycheck. He may therefore impose a penalty if you disregard his professional medical advice. The medical board could also penalize your partner."

"Are you saying to me," said Sylvia, "that I could report for my medical exam, and Dr. Hyland could say, 'Tests indicate you recently had sex with Joe Smith, which is against my medical advice, and therefore I'm going to throw you both in the cooler.' He could do that?"

"Yes," replied Mandy as she dried the silverware and put it into the drawer. "Under the contracts and consent forms that we signed, he has the medical authority to do that."

"So by extension," said Sylvia, "If Dr. Hyland thought it would be therapeutic for me to have sex with Joe Smith, then he could order that as part of my treatment?"

Reese and Mandy looked at each other. "In theory, I suppose he could," said Reese. "But it's much more difficult to make someone do something against their will than to penalize them for doing something wrong."

"Especially something like having sex," added Mandy.

"Do we really know what they do to," said Sylvia, "I spent most of the day unconscious, with my feet in the stirrups and my legs open wide for anyone to see. Hell, for all I know every intern at that hospital had sex with me while I was lying there in dreamland. I have no way of knowing. My pelvis is sore from all the tests. Maybe it's actually sore from getting pounded by my doctor."

"I think I'm going to be sick," said Mandy.

"Ladies, let's get our minds off this morbid topic," said Reese. "Now that the dishes are put away, I'm going to get dressed."

Later in the morning, after Mandy had left to meet her friend Jacqui, Reese came up to Sylvia's room.

"Let's go explore the island," she said.

"What do you mean?" replied Sylvia, putting down her book, which she had found on the shelf in the living room downstairs. It was an old romance novel. All the books on the shelf were romance novels published decades earlier.

"I want to show you Tucker's Point." Then she added conspiratorially, "I also want to hook up with my friend Aldeen. He works weekends in the food and beverage office. He may have something for me."

"Is he the guy who gets the booze for you?"

"He might be."

"Okay, let's go. I'm sick of sitting around this boring house."

They went downstairs. "First we need to go to the kitchen," said Reese. She led the way to the kitchen closet, where she retrieved an old picnic basket. "Someone from a long time ago left this here. It's become very useful." She put the basket on the counter and opened it. Then, carrying a white towel, she disappeared out the back door. Sylvia went to the door and watched as

Reese took the empty bottle from the old planter and wrapped it in the towel. Then she came back inside and placed the bottle, wrapped in its towel, in the bottom of the picnic basket. "Get me some bread and cheese from the refrigerator," she told Sylvia. "I'll get some cups and napkins."

When they had loaded the basket with the basics for a picnic, they went to Reese's golf cart. The weather was cool for summer, and the sky was overcast. "Think it's going to rain?" asked Sylvia.

"Your guess is as good as mine," replied Reese as she turned the key. "But if it does rain, that would be very good for us."

"Good? Why? I don't want to get soaked."

Reese guided the cart along the short driveway to Apple Way. "Because the Mortas don't operate well in the rain. They have problems with moisture getting into their circuits, and their guidance systems—their cameras for visual information and their microwave sensors for basic orientation—don't function as well in the rain. The greater the amount of precipitation, the more unhappy they become. In their own peculiar robot way, of course. Unlike we humans, who are already sixty percent water and don't mind getting more dumped on our heads, most robots, including the Mortas, are zero percent water."

"The drones too?"

"Especially the drones. In the rain, they can barely fly. The fleet is grounded."

They made their way down Apple Way to Pine Path. The houses they passed seemed quiet. In the small front yards of a few, a man or a woman trimmed the hedge or swept the path. Reese waved to one—a man in his sixties. "That's Reginald Astor," she said when they were out of earshot. "He's a bit of a legend. They say he's the person who's lived here the longest. He arrived over twenty years ago, when the place first opened. He has Huntington's disease. It's getting progressively worse, and no one expects him to live more than a year or two."

"Does he have family?" asked Sylvia.

"Not on the island. I've hung out with him a few times, usually at the mess hall or the Dockside, and he never talks about his past life. But people who know him say that back in Denver, Colorado, he has a wife and two children. The kids are both adults now, of course. It's possible Reggie is a grandfather. No one's certain."

"Does he want to stay here, or are they making him stay here?"

Reese shrugged. "After so many years, they say you get used to it, and the question becomes moot. You stay because it's what you know."

They drove past the Juliette Island Center, and the road became wider and more well-paved.

"This is where Pine Path becomes Seaside Drive," said Reese. The landscape was mostly tall pines with a few dilapidated buildings nestled between. They passed an abandoned warehouse with a corrugated metal roof, an old gas station with weeds growing through the cement apron, and a cinderblock structure with a broken, faded sign reading "Wild Horse Bar."

"Years ago there were several thousand people living on what was then called Osprey Island," said Reese. "Then the Global Depression came, and many of them left. In the aftermath the Industrial Council convinced the government to turn it into a big medical research laboratory. The Council forcibly relocated all the remaining residents to the mainland, or turned them loose in the canaille to fend for themselves."

They came around a bend and suddenly Sylvia saw the gray waters of Puget Sound. The opposite shore was forested with pine trees. It seemed closer than when they were at the Dockside and looking across the water at the city of Victoria.

"You're looking east, towards Manafort Island," said Reese. "It's about five miles away. Even if you were an expert swimmer, the tidal currents are extremely treacherous. As far as I know, no one's ever swum it and lived to tell the tale."

They continued to follow Seaside Drive as Sylvia jealously watched the opposite shore. She thought she could make out the occasional building, and once she thought she saw a large truck, like a semi-trailer, ambling along a hidden road.

Suddenly the cart came to a halt. Startled from her reverie, Sylvia looked towards the front. Not ten feet ahead hovered a drone.

"Just sit quietly and do what it says," whispered Reese.

The drone fixed its cameras on them. The only sound was the whirring of its four propellers. Then it spoke: "Sylvia Brand and Reese Carter, please state your business."

"We're going on a picnic," replied Reese. She gestured to the basket.

"Where?" asked the drone.

"On Tucker's Point. As I'm sure you know, it's near the food and beverage office. We'll be within sight at all times."

"Show me the inside of the basket."

Sylvia took the basket, tilted it towards the drone, and opened the lid.

After a moment the drone said, "You may proceed."

"May I have your number please?" asked Reese.

"My number is three-seven-five." With those words the drone whirred into the sky and was lost among the trees.

"Why did you ask for its number?" asked Sylvia as Reese.

"If we get stopped again, we can tell the drone that we've been cleared by number three-seven-five. It will check its database and see that we're telling the truth. It will make our day less stressful."

They as they were making their way along Seashore Drive, they rounded a low hill that blocked the view of the water. When they emerged from behind the hill, Sylvia saw a long, low bridge that spanned the water, anchoring itself to the opposite shore.

Reese stopped the cart. "There it is," she said. "The causeway is the only road for travel on and off the island. It's the route the bus took when it brought you here. The causeway goes to Manafort Island, traverses the island, and then crosses another branch of Puget Sound to reach the mainland."

"How long do you think it takes to drive the length of the causeway and arrive on the mainland?" asked Sylvia.

"Once you get past the guards, no more than ten minutes."

Reese resumed the drive, and soon they came to a weather-beaten sign reading "Tucker's Point." About half a mile further beyond was a low office building. Reese headed for the office building.

"Aren't we going to Tucker's Point?" asked Sylvia.

"If we have time. First I need to see if Aldeen is here."

Reese steered the golf cart to an unmarked side door. There was a buzzer, which she rang. After a few moments the door opened. Sylvia saw Reese talking to a man. Then Reese walked back to the golf cart. The man watched from the door.

"You take the golf cart for a little drive around Tucker's Point," said Reese as she took the picnic basket. "Get out and enjoy the view. Come back for me in about fifteen minutes."

With the picnic basket in hand, Reese turned and hurried toward the door where the man was standing.

Mystified, Sylvia turned the golf cart around and steered in the direction of Tucker's Point. She parked on a high point of land overlooking the water. Below her the waves muscled against the rocks, surging and retreating, over and over again in a relentless cycle. Seagulls wheeled and cried, because that's just what seagulls do, even if their display seems pointless. To her left, about a mile away, the causeway, concrete pale against the dark water, reached in a gentle arc to the opposite shore—another island to be sure, but one step closer to the world she had left behind. The causeway was quiet now, with no traffic. Perhaps it was because it was late Sunday afternoon, and no one was coming or going. Squinting, she imagined the bus that had brought her to this island just three days earlier. Had it only been three days? It felt like a lifetime. In her mind she saw the bus, the windows opaque, the screen across the front, with its passengers who were unknowing of their destination and expecting a simple one-day business trip. How fantastical it was! She had a rare genetic disease, passed on to her baby, and for that reason she was a "special person" whom the Industrial Council and its doctors and pharmaceutical companies needed to keep under lock and key.

A boat came into view. It was not large—perhaps thirty feet—but with its aggressive, angular lines and gray color scheme it looked like a military vessel. It cruised slowly, perhaps a quarter of a mile offshore. Powered by its electric motor, the boat approached noiselessly, like a cat prowling the perimeter of a barn. Sylvia stood and watched it. Then she saw a figure emerge from the cabin and stand on the flat foredeck. As the boat passed the point opposite from where she was standing, she realized the figure was a Morta guard.

He was looking directly at her. She instinctively shrank back, but on the exposed point of land there was no place to hide. Then she remembered drone three-seven-five. It had cleared them to be in the area. Gathering her courage, Sylvia stood up straight, with her hands on her hips, and returned the guard's gaze. The boat did not change course, but slowly continued around the point. The Morta guard kept watching her until the trees obscured his view. After a moment all that was left of the passage of the patrol boat was the faint ripple of its wake.

Sylvia stood for a while, taking in the view. She was facing east, toward the mainland. In her imagination she flew across the miles all the way to Detroit. It would be almost dinnertime there. What was Jason doing at that moment? Sylvia had vanished Thursday morning. That was three days ago. Surely he would have contacted the police. But what if Carin told the cops that she had never shown up for work on Thursday morning? She tried to remember if she had seen any of her co-workers in the parking lot that morning. She didn't think she had. There was no proof that Sylvia Brand had ever arrived for work that day.

Perhaps Carin told Jason she was out of town on business. How long could that story hold up? And would the company then be forced to concoct a new story to explain her disappearance?

The third possibility was that the company had told Jason the truth—that his new wife had been spirited away to serve as a medical guinea pig on a secret island in the Pacific Northwest. No, that was not a possible choice, because if the company told every aggrieved spouse about the whereabouts of their loved ones, then Juliette Island would be quickly overrun by family members intent upon their rescue.

As the days and weeks passed and Sylvia never came home, what would Jason do? Yes, he might hold fast and keep the torch lit for her. Then she began to get a sick feeling in her stomach. The opposite might happen. Jason might get tired of waiting, or he might believe that she had run out on him. How long could she expect him to wait? A month? A year? Five years? And what were his feelings toward his unborn child? Would he ever see him or her?

Sylvia took a deep breath. Agonizing over her fate wasn't going to change it. Bitterness about working for Sun Motors—such a good job!—and signing the contracts and consent forms wasn't going to get her back to the life she had known. She had agreed to be a part of the system, and the system was now exacting its price.

She looked at her phone. Fifteen minutes had elapsed. She turned away from the dark water and went to the golf cart. She started the motor and drove back to the side door of the food and beverage office.

A moment later the door opened and Reese walked out, holding the picnic basket. With a smile on her face she put the basket in the back of the cart and climbed into the seat.

"Mission accomplished!" she announced.

"What does that mean?"

"I'll show you when we get home. Too risky out here. You never know when a drone is lurking."

Sylvia drove them home. Instead of going into the kitchen, Reese led Sylvia around the house to the back patio. She opened the basket and, after taking out the bread and cheese and utensils they had packed, she reached to the bottom and pulled out an object wrapped in a white cloth. Removing the cloth, she held up a bottle of Bourbon whiskey.

"Twenty years old," she said. "This is the stuff they serve to the doctors and big-shot administrators here on the island. Top shelf. Shall we have celebratory sample?" She went to the old planter and took out two cups. Sylvia uncorked the bottle and poured a shot into each cup.

"Wow, this is amazing," said Sylvia. "I feel like I'm a member of an exclusive club. I don't want to pry, but did your friend Aldeen simply give this to you?"

"Yes," said Reese. "I give him the empty bottle so there's no inventory problem, and he gives me a fresh one. No one's the wiser."

"He must really like you."

Reese shrugged. "I suppose so. He's not really my type."

"What do you mean he's not your type? You're not leading him on, are you? That wouldn't be very nice."

Reese laughed and took another sip of her whiskey. "Believe me, no one is leading him on! He knows exactly what he's getting."

"Reese, what do you mean?"

"I make him feel good, and in return he makes me feel good." She raised her cup. "Cheers."

"Oh my God, Reese, you have sex with this guy in exchange for booze!" Sylvia looked at the cup in her hand and grimaced.

Reese put her hand on Sylvia's arm. "First of all, it's not really sex. I mean, it's oral sex. That's all. He's not getting into my pants and he knows it. But on this lonely island, something is better than nothing, isn't it? He gets his rocks off and then he lets me take home a bottle of the good stuff. I'd say it's a fair trade."

"I'm sorry, it just seems so unsavory. Like you're… I don't know exactly what to call it…"

"Prostituting myself? It's all right, you can say it. But think about it—

aren't all of us prostituting ourselves? We allow the doctors to shove all kinds of gizmos into every orifice and peer with their cameras into every private part of our bodies. They take our blood and saliva and urine and hair follicles. They put us into MRI machines and take ultrasounds and x-rays. In return we get three square meals a day, a roof over our heads, and a nice island to live on. From my point of view, giving Aldeen a happy ending in return for a fifty-dollar bottle of Kentucky Bourbon is a pretty good deal. It makes me think the next time my doctor shoves a stainless steel scope up my ass, I should demand a bottle of Cognac."

Sylvia heard the sound of a golf cart in the driveway. "I think Mandy's home," she said.

Reese collected the cups and put them with the bottle in the planter. Then they went inside.

CHAPTER TWENTY-THREE

It seemed like Sylvia had no sooner fallen asleep in her bed when she was awakened by the sound of heavy footsteps on the stairs. Groggily she opened her eyes. Her door flew open, the lights came on, and two Morta guards entered her room, followed by a company security officer.

"Sylvia Brand," said the security officer. "Get up. We're taking you into custody."

"Why? What's going on?"

"You and Reese Carter made an unauthorized visit to a restricted area, where she engaged in a sex act. This is a violation of your contract. Now get up and get dressed."

Bewildered, Sylvia got out of bed and hastily put on her clothes while the security officer watched. After the guard had zip-tied her hands behind her back, the four of them marched down the stairs. Mandy stood in the living room, wearing her bathrobe, with its terrycloth belt tied tightly around her waist. With a stricken expression on her face, she said nothing.

Sylvia walked outside. In the driveway a van was idling. The night air was cool and damp. Overhead the stars shone bright and clear, while from the safety of the shadowy bushes crickets chirped to each other. From the open door of the van, the interior light threw a harsh blaze across the walkway. Reese, her hands behind her back, was already sitting inside the van, with a Morta guard next to her. After Sylvia had awkwardly climbed inside, the door was slammed shut and the van began to roll.

"What happened?" Sylvia asked Reese.

"We were caught on camera," she replied.

"You and Aldeen?"

"Yes. The security people had installed an additional camera that Aldeen didn't know about."

"You two, be quiet," interjected the Morta. "No talking."

The van trundled along the road. It was no surprise to Sylvia that the van had no windows, and also no surprise when they stopped, the doors were pulled open, and she saw they were parked by the gated entrance to the Re-Orientation Center.

"Back to the cooler," said Sylvia as she stepped onto the gravel driveway.

"Be strong," said Reese.

"No talking," said the Morta guard.

They were led through the gate, inside the building, and into separate cells. After her hands had been freed and the door clanged shut, Sylvia stood in the center of the cell. Overhead the naked bulb glowed. There was no sound—no crickets, no cars outside, no voices. She went to the steel door with its narrow slit. Sylvia listened. She heard footsteps. They came closer. She glimpsed the waist of a Morta guard as it passed her cell. Then the footsteps receded.

She sat on the metal-framed bed. It is me? she wondered. Am I out of step with reality? Do I have expectations that are unrealistic? I just got here—why do I keep getting into trouble? All I ever wanted to do was follow the rules and be a good person. Where did I go wrong?

Then she felt a wave of anger. It's not me—it's them! This horrible sick system has tricked me and made me into a zoo animal. I must never surrender! Never! For the sake of my child, I must resist the forces that want to turn me into a commodity and my disease—if you have to call it that—into a cash machine.

Then her practical mind stepped in. They aren't going to hurt me. They want me to be healthy for their experiments. This isn't ethnic cleansing or genocide, where people are targeted for elimination. It's not even like ordinary incarceration, where they don't particularly care if you happen to die while in custody. I'm a special person. They need me for both their research and their profits. They may want to make me uncomfortable and even scare me, but they won't do anything really bad to me.

Feeling physically and mentally exhausted, she lay down on the bed and drifted into a restless sleep.

The next morning she was driven to the Juliette Island Center for Medical Research, where Dr. Hyland met her and escorted her to the surgical wing.

"I'm tired and hungry," she told him. "I haven't had the opportunity to go home and get cleaned up. Whatever we're doing this morning, I hope it won't take long."

"No, it won't take long," he replied with a smile as they walked through the corridors.

"Am I going to be punished for what happened last night?"

"No. We can talk about that later. Ah—here we are." They had arrived at the surgical prep room. A nurse stood by. "Please lie down on the bed. No need for a hospital gown—you can leave your clothing on. Good. Now the nurse will roll up your sleeve and insert an IV line. I assume you're right-handed, is that correct?"

"Yes. What are you giving me?" she asked as the nurse swabbed her left arm.

"A small dose of midazolam, a short-acting sedative drug that blocks pain and makes you feel sleepy but doesn't render you unconscious. You should not require help with your breathing, but if necessary we'll give you extra oxygen through a mask as well as fluids through a catheter into a vein."

"What are you going to do to me today?" She asked the question not because she really wanted to know (they had already done so many things to her body that in her mind it hardly mattered) but because she didn't want Dr. Hyland or the nurse to think she had relinquished all of her rights as a patient. It was a childlike attempt to preserve the fiction that this was a true partnership between doctor and patient, which in her heart she knew was far from the case.

"Just a short procedure," he said. "We can talk more about it later. I'll come back in a few minutes to see how you're doing."

He walked away, and Sylvia was left staring at the ceiling tiles.

She began to feel drowsy. At first it aroused in her feelings of anxiety, and so she fought the sensation, but after a few minutes she realized that instead of slipping into unconsciousness she was hovering in a pleasant twilight between wakefulness and sleep. This isn't so bad, she thought. Very relaxing, in fact.

Dr. Hyland appeared at her bedside and peered down at her with a benign smile. "How do you feel?" he asked.

"Fine," she murmured. Her voice sounded far away.

"Can you feel this?" he said as he took her left hand and manipulated it. She glanced down and saw a syringe. He was giving her an injection into the muscle between the thumb and forefinger.

"No. What are you doing?" She asked more out of curiosity than concern.

"Giving you a local anesthetic. We're almost ready to proceed."

Let them do what they want, thought Sylvia. It doesn't matter to me.

With his right hand, Dr. Hyland picked up a white plastic syringe with a wide stainless steel needle that looked more like a straw with a sharp point. With his left hand, using pair of blunt forceps, he grasped a section of flesh between the thumb and forefinger, parallel to the index metacarpal bone, making a hump. With the white plastic injector in his right hand, he stuck the sharp end of the needle into the hump of flesh, parallel to the bone. When it had gone in about half an inch, he depressed the plunger on the injector, while at the same time slowly withdrawing the injector. After about ten seconds, the plunger was fully depressed. With his left hand, he then took a piece of gauze and pressed down on the entry wound while removing the stainless steel needle. When the injector was free, he set it aside.

After applying a bandage to the entrance wound he smiled and said, "There—all done! That was easy, wasn't it?"

"Yes, I suppose it was." Lifting her left hand, she looked at the bandage with vague interest. "Did I hurt my hand?"

"No—don't worry. Everything is fine. When you've come out of sedation, we'll talk. Then you can go home. Get some rest."

Sylvia lay in her bed, thinking about Jason, and how painting their new house yellow with white trim would make it look much nicer than its current hideous green, and her friends at Sun Motors, and how the contract for the Comanche truck battery system—a major component—needed to be renegotiated....

After a while she felt clear-headed, and there was a dull pain in her left hand.

The nurse came to her bed. "Do you feel like getting up?" she asked.

"Yes, I do." Sylvia sat up. The IV in her arm had been removed, and in its place was a little white bandage. She took a few deep breaths before standing on her feet. "Okay, now what? It's Monday morning, right? Can I go home and get something to eat before my tests today?"

"Yes," replied the nurse. "One of the guards will drive you home. Your hand will feel stiff and swollen—that's to be expected. Do not remove the bandage."

The Morta guard drove her in a golf cart. They did not speak to each other. When she got home, neither Reese nor Mandy were there. After making herself some eggs and toast, Sylvia took a shower, keeping her hand in a plastic bag, as the nurse had instructed. By the time she was dressed again it was time to go back to the Center for her regular appointment.

She found Dr. Hyland in his office.

"Ah, Sylvia, I see you've weathered the procedure very nicely," he said as she sat down. He took her left hand and gently removed the bandage. He examined the wound. "Some swelling, which is normal. No sign of infection. Good." With a satisfied expression he released his grip.

She looked at her hand, from which the bandage had been removed. She flexed her fingers and formed a fist. There was a small hole in her skin, from which blood oozed.

She looked closely at her hand. "Oh my God—there's something under my skin!" Gently she ran her fingertip over the bruised and tender flesh between her thumb and index finger. "I can feel something in there! It's hard, like a little cylinder. What did you do?"

Leaning forward and clasping his hands on the desktop, Dr. Hyland assumed a thoughtful demeanor. "Sylvia, last night both you and Reese got yourselves into serious trouble. Reese more so, of course, because she was consorting with that man, Aldeen. Sexual liaisons between residents and employees of the island are prohibited."

"Sorry, I guess she didn't see that in the guest handbook."

"Don't be a smart aleck. You're very lucky you aren't serving a week in the Re-Orientation Center, like Reese is."

"But the drone cleared us. Number three-seven-five."

"Drones have the authority to stop and question residents who are observed in unusual or off-limits places. They do not have the authority to approve a sexual encounter in an empty office in the food and beverage department building. Now then—about your hand. Because of your repeated infractions of the island travel policy, the Juliette Island Center Medical Board has decided that you are to carry an RFID tag. As I'm sure you know, the acronym stands for 'radio frequency identification.'"

"I know exactly what RFID means," she replied curtly. "At Sun Motors we've been using RFID tags for years."

"This morning I implanted one in your hand. It's actually a GPS device that transmits your location, twenty-four hours a day. I'll show you." He tapped a few keys on his computer and, after a moment, turned the screen to show Sylvia. "I've logged onto our patient management system. As you can see, it shows your location here, in my office. It's accurate to within two meters."

"You bastards!" she shouted. "You implanted a tracking device in my hand!"

"Yes, we did. Because you're carrying a child, we felt it was important to give you every opportunity to stay out of the Re-Orientation Center. Life there is not very pleasant, and we want to ensure the health of your baby."

"But you have no right to implant a foreign object in my body!"

Dr. Hyland nodded thoughtfully, as if pondering her question and showing empathy. He removed his rimless glasses and, taking a cloth from the pocket of his white coat, carefully cleaned the lenses. "To the contrary," he said as he replaced his glasses on his nose, "Our contract with you gives us the right to protect our very considerable investment in you and your child. We agree to provide a full range of medical services, and in return you agree to act responsibly and in the best interests of your own good health. If you are prone to wander around the island—to go swimming after dark at a deserted beach, or accompany your friend to a remote area so that she can have a sexual encounter—then the Medical Center Board sees the risk to your safety increasing. It's all about risk, Sylvia. Our goal is to enhance and maximize life, not jeopardize it. While we're in the business of medicine and healing, it would not be a stretch to say we're also in the business of insurance." He smiled. "I think with a little bit of perspective, you'll agree it's not such a big deal. Why, there are many people in business who eagerly have RFID tags implanted in their hands, just as you have. Having a tag in your hand allows you to access restricted areas without worrying about carrying a key or identification card. You simply approach the locked door, and instead of swiping your old-fashioned card or sticking your face into a camera lens, you hold up your hand, and the door opens. You can even pay for your dinner at a restaurant by waving your hand over the receptor carried by the server."

"I don't need to do any of those things on this island," replied Sylvia. "This thing in my hand does nothing but give you more control over me. Let me tell you something: I don't care if you don't trust me. I'm going to do whatever the hell I want, and if you want to send a drone or a Morta guard after me, be my guest. I'm not a cow or a sheep, content to graze in my little pasture. I'm going to live my life with something approaching human dignity."

"I understand," said Dr. Hyland. "You're still very new here. It takes a while to get acclimated. My advice is to relax and go with the flow. Juliette Island can be a very lovely place, if you're open to it."

Sylvia looked at his kindly face for a moment before turning her gaze to the window. Through the glass she saw the sun shining brightly against the greens and blues of the pine trees. Then she said, "I don't know why I'm here. How did this happen? Is this what my life is going to be?"

"Sylvia," he said, "I've been here a long time. I've seen many people come through these doors. They arrive with many different attitudes. Some are angry and resentful. Some are bewildered. Some are happy to be here— possibly because they have some issue in their previous life they're relieved to have put behind them. While people land on this island with different feelings, the ones who make the best adjustment and learn to enjoy themselves are the ones who trust in a higher power. They trust there's a deeper reason why the path of their life has led them here. Here on Juliette Island, everything hinges on trust. I need you to trust that we have your best interests at heart, and you have ours as well."

To Sylvia, the answer was this: There was no answer. The world was the way it was. Or rather, the United Americas was the way the Industrial Council had fashioned it. It was a place where the rules had been designed by faraway people who were much more powerful than she. She knew these people didn't trust her. They had brought her here under false pretenses, and it was clear she would not be allowed to leave. All this stuff about working for each others' best interests was a twisted diversion from reality.

But it was useless to debate Dr. Hyland. He held too much power over her—and her unborn child.

Sylvia raised her eyes to meet his. "Let's get down to business. What's my schedule for today?"

Sitting back in his chair, Dr. Hyland made a few clicks with his mouse. "In half an hour you will undergo a computerized tomography scan. Your CT scan will combine a series of X-ray images taken from different angles around your body and then use computer processing to create cross-sectional images, or slices, of the bones, blood vessels, and soft tissues inside your body. CT scan images provide more detailed information than plain X-rays. With a CT scan, we will not only detect any tumors, lung nodules, and liver masses, but muscle and bone disorders, heart disease, internal injuries, or internal bleeding. A CT scan can also help guide procedures such as surgery, biopsy, and radiation therapy. But perhaps most of all, it will give us a clear picture of your entire body at this moment in time—a baseline, if you will, against which we can make comparisons in the years to come."

"The years to come?"

"Sylvia, this is a long-term program. We're looking for data that spans not days or weeks, but years. Don't you understand? Nothing of value is created overnight. Deep knowledge takes time."

CHAPTER TWENTY-FOUR

Sylvia completed her CT scan and some other tests. At the end of the day, tired and feeling like a human pincushion, she went back to 15 Apple Way. Mandy was there, and the first thing Sylvia did was go to the back patio and look for the bottle of whiskey. It was still in the planter.

"Didn't they know?" Sylvia mused aloud.

"I guess they saw Aldeen and Reese getting it on, but didn't catch the payoff," replied Mandy. "When Reese comes back we'll drink a toast to freedom."

Together they made dinner.

"Getting a GPS implant is a serious thing," said Mandy as she tossed the salad. "They're not playing games with you. Do you know Charlie Ohan, who lives at 23 Plum Court? He's the skinny guy with the curly blond hair. He was once a feisty one! Always causing trouble and demanding to see his manager over every little thing. I heard that somehow he got hold of a real cellphone and tried to call his wife in Des Moines. They intercepted the call and scrambled it, and then found the phone. That earned him a week in the cooler. Then he tried to escape by hiding in a truck going across the causeway. That was a stupid thing to do because they search every vehicle very carefully. They tossed him in the cooler for a week, and they also planted a GPS device in his hand, just like yours. He didn't believe it was real, and one day he decided to go to the southern tip of the island and flag down a passing ship. You know, as if he were a castaway on a desert island. He hadn't gotten halfway there before they were all over him—drones and Morta guards both. Again he went to the cooler, only this time it was for two weeks. When he came out he was a changed person. Almost like a zombie. Whatever they did to him in there, it sucked the life right out of him. He became the mellowest person on the island, but it was fake, you know what I mean? You can go and talk to him, and it's like talking to a human Ken doll. They did something to him. I don't know what it was, but it changed him."

"When he came back from the cooler, did he have swollen eyes?" asked

Sylvia. In a saucepan she heated some oil and butter for the chicken cutlets.

"Yes, he did! Both his eyes were bruised. He looked like he had been in a boxing match. I asked him what had happened, and if they had beaten him. He said he didn't remember anything happening. He woke up in the Medical Center, in a hospital bed. Then they let him go home."

"It sounds as if they gave him a lobotomy," said Sylvia. She shivered at the thought.

"Why were his eyes bruised?"

"It's called a transorbital lobotomy. Also an icepick lobotomy. Very popular among medical professionals in the first half of the twentieth century. The surgeon inserts an icepick into the soft tissue just above the eyeball and below the eyebrow, and pushes it through the thin frontal bone of the eye socket. The tip penetrates into the frontal lobe of the brain, which controls personality, behavior, and emotions. The surgeon swishes the icepick around in there, severing neural connections. After doing one side of the brain through one eye socket, he'll do the other side through the other eye socket."

"That's so gruesome," said Mandy. She put the salad on the table and went to the drawer for silverware.

"Yes—and unpredictable. Because the doctor is cutting blindly, he has no idea what the result will be. But icepick lobotomies are cheap and fast, and unlike drugs like Thorazine, the effect is permanent. Do you know why Charlie is here on Juliette Island?"

"He told me he had UV-sensitive syndrome, a condition characterized by sensitivity to the ultraviolet rays in sunlight. That's why he never goes out in the sun—even a small amount of exposure can give him a sunburn. Pardo Pharmaceuticals is using him to develop new sunscreens, as well as testing a new drug for those afflicted with the disease."

"The fact that Charlie Ohan is a walking zombie with half a brain has no impact on his usefulness as a medical test subject," said Sylvia. "As long as he's capable of showing up for his appointments and enduring whatever they do to him, he's worth the investment."

After Sylvia had sautéed the chicken, they sat down at the table.

"I hope you don't mind my asking," said Sylvia, "but you seem to be very content here. Doesn't it bother you that you can't leave? And that your child is dead?"

Mandy took a serving of salad from the bowl. "I suppose I feel at home here because I have nowhere else to go. I have no family. My job at Mountain Life Insurance was just a paycheck. And I was sick all the time. When I first came here I was just like you—I was angry and resentful. But then I started to realize this was a good place for me. I've made some friends, and the medical care is amazing. I don't care if they use me as a guinea pig. It's a small price to pay for security. I don't have to worry about anything. I just show up when they tell me to, and the rest of the time I do what I want. Of course I miss Winslow, but what could I do? He had a serious illness."

"What did they do with his body after he died?"

"They cremated him. They have a place on the north end of the island where they do that."

"There's a crematorium here on Juliette Island?"

"Yes. Of course it's totally off limits. If you go north from here, along the coast, you eventually arrive at the causeway. The crematorium is about a mile beyond that. They took Winslow there, and they gave me his ashes in a little urn. They allowed me to go out in the boat and scatter them in the Sound."

"They let you go out in a boat?" Sylvia asked incredulously.

"Yes. They keep it in a boathouse next to the crematorium. It's not very big—it has a little outboard motor. I had to go with a couple of human security officers, of course. I don't think the Morta guards are allowed to go in small boats. Can you imagine what would happen if one of those things fell into the water? It would sink like a stone!"

"So when you die on the island, they cremate you?"

Mandy shrugged. "I suppose. I've never been to a funeral here. I don't even think there's a cemetery."

After dinner, Sylvia decided she needed to become more familiar with the approved places that residents could go. After all, she reasoned, if she were wearing an implant that alerted the guards the moment she strayed into forbidden territory, she might as well get to know the places she could go. I'm not a doormat, she told herself, but neither am I a masochist.

She got into her golf cart—a small and pathetic symbol of freedom, she thought, but nonetheless one that was very real. She drove around for a while in the gathering twilight, exploring the various roads and neighborhoods. All the houses looked like hers; the only differences were that some of them had little gardens in the front, while others had nothing but grass. She saw people here and there, puttering around their yards or walking along the roads. All were wearing the same cut and color of clothing that Sylvia had been issued. She saw no pets—no cats, no dogs. She heard no barking, which was odd, because at home at twilight you always heard dogs barking. Roosters crow at sunrise and dogs bark at sunset.

She came around a bend and before her she saw a playground, with a slide and swings and a jungle gym for climbing. A handful of children were playing there, supervised by their mothers and fathers. Feeling the pull on her heartstrings, Sylvia drove into the little gravel parking area. Leaving her golf cart among the others, she walked to the edge of the playground and watched for a few minutes. She imagined her own child, two or three years from that moment, taking her first steps into this exciting, big-kid world, learning how to climb and run, and meeting other children.

A little boy came running by, and he tripped and fell down. He began to cry. Instinctively Sylvia went to him and helped him up. As she was brushing the wood chips off his knees, a couple hurried over. They were both in their thirties, and the woman appeared to be pregnant.

The woman took the little boy in her arms and began to comfort him. As Sylvia stood there watching, she began to feel self-conscious, so she turned to the man and said, "Your son is a very energetic little boy!"

The man smiled and said, "Thank you—although I must confess, I'm not Timmy's father. My name is Jim Ryan. Pleased to meet you." He extended his hand.

"Sylvia Brand," she said as they shook. "I'm sorry—I just assumed—"

"Oh, no worries," said the mother. "I'm Natalie Downey. Jim and I are engaged to be married. Our child is due next April. My son is from my previous relationship."

Sylvia explained that she was new to the island and was exploring the permissible areas. Natalie glanced at the bandage on Sylvia's left hand. "I see you've got the implant," she said. She held up her own left hand. "Feel under the skin. There—next to the metacarpal bone."

Sylvia felt the outline of a small cylinder just like the one Dr. Hyland had implanted that morning in her flesh. "How long have you had it?" she asked Natalie.

"Three years. One day I decided to blow off my medical appointment and go for a drive. They found me on the western shore, brought me back, and put me in the cooler overnight. The next day they stuck this thing in me. For a while I hated it. I wanted to get a knife and cut it out. But I got used to it. I decided to go along—and I'm glad I did."

Intrigued, Sylvia hung around while Natalie soothed her son and sent him back to the playground. Then the three of them walked over to a bench and sat down. They chatted about inconsequential things until Jim excused himself, saying he had to get up early the next morning for a special medical test.

"Jim seems very nice," said Sylvia as he walked away.

"Oh, he's just wonderful!" replied Natalie. "I'm so glad they found him for me. Of course at first I was, like, 'Are you kidding? Is this an arranged marriage?' But much to my amazement, it's working out beautifully."

"I'm sorry—what did you say? They found him for you?"

"Yes, I know—crazy, isn't it? Scientific matchmaking! But it works!"

At Sylvia's urging, Natalie told her story.

Like Sylvia, Natalie had a good job with a Two Hundred K company—a plastics fabricator in Atlanta. And like Sun Motors, the company had brought in a Morta supervisor and had enrolled the employees in a comprehensive health plan doubling as an employment contract and non-disclosure agreement. Her supervisor—his name was Basor—had explained that instead of signing a dozen different forms, it was much more expedient to bundle all of them into one agreement. In retrospect, said Natalie, the resulting document was something close to an indentured servitude contract, but at the time she was grateful to have a good job with a top company, so she signed it. She met a man, Edwin, and they got married. After a few months, she got pregnant. Lab tests, provided free of charge by the company, revealed that her unborn child had a rare form of anemia, which he had contracted from Natalie and Edwin, who were both carriers. The doctors told them that the disease was unpredictable, and their child might die by the age of five or live a fairly normal life well into adulthood. After much soul searching, she and Edwin had decided to have the child and hope for the best—perhaps by the time he was a toddler, medical science would have found a cure.

One day as Natalie was going to work—this was when she was twelve weeks pregnant—Basor met her in the parking lot and told her she was going on a special assignment. She was whisked to the airport and put on a company plane. A few hours later, the plane landed, she was put in a van, and the next stop was the Juliette Island Center for Health Research.

At first she was angry and defiant, and made a few attempts to test the boundaries of her confinement. Eventually they got tired of putting her in the cooler, and gave her the RFID tag implant.

"When Timothy was born, that changed everything for me," said Natalie as she kept one eye on her child, who was climbing up the stairs to the slide. "I had to start thinking about him and his future. I became resigned to the fact Juliette Island was our home. I had a new career as a medical test subject. I had a good life with everything I wanted. I was sad about leaving Edwin behind, but I'm sure he found someone new. People do that, right? They don't sit around moaning. They get on with their lives, just as I was getting on with mine."

With a pang, Sylvia thought of her dear Jason. Would the same thing happen to them? Of course it would. Jason wasn't going to wait around for months or years with no word from Sylvia. He was going to find someone new—presumably a girl who didn't carry any genetic diseases and therefore was of no interest to Pardo Pharmaceuticals and the Industrial Council.

"How did you meet Jim?" she asked.

"Back in March—it was the fifteenth, I'll never forget the date—my doctor called me in and said he had some amazing news. Around that time I was feeling depressed, so I was like, 'Yeah?' He told me that they had identified a man of my age and background who was the carrier of a different genetic disease than mine, which meant that he and I could have children that were free of genetic diseases, although they could be carriers. At first I thought he was joking—was I no better than a farm animal used for breeding? But he kept talking, and then he showed me a video of Jim, and I thought he was very handsome. I said okay, I'll meet him for dinner. My doctor then gave me a form to sign. It was several pages long, and I asked him what it was, and he said it was just a formality—something about liability. He also said it was an agreement that if Jim and I had children, they'd be bound by the same agreements Jim and I had with our employers. The possibility of actually having more kids seemed far-fetched, and I wanted to meet this guy, so I signed.

"That night I met Jim at the Dockside, and at first I wasn't sure about him, but as the evening went on I started to like him. We dated some more, and then I got pregnant. I was deeply conflicted and thought about finding a way to terminate my pregnancy, but my doctor was delighted. He then arranged for Jim and I and Timothy to move into a private house and receive a bigger allowance. No more living with roommates! I later found out this was standard procedure—if you get pregnant through a sanctioned relationship, you and your partner go to the top of the list for a private home, and you get more money. Believe me, those are nice perks."

"Congratulations," said Sylvia—not because she thought Natalie's experience was in any way acceptable, but because Natalie herself seemed so happy that to say anything else would be cruel. "It sounds as if you're committed to staying here on Juliette Island."

"I think so," said Natalie. "Jim wants to, and we have nothing to complain about. Life is good here. A little bit boring, I'll admit, but there's safety and security."

"But what about your children?" asked Sylvia. "Timothy and your new one? Do you expect them to live here for the next eighty or ninety years?"

"I don't know," said Natalie. "But think about it—there are millions of people who live on islands in the South Pacific that are no bigger than Juliette Island. For generation after generation, they live in places like Tuvalu, a group of tiny islands midway between Hawaii and Australia. Eleven thousand people live out in the middle of nowhere! They have their own government, bank, and police force. Are they to be pitied because they live in isolation?"

"No, but the people who live on Tuvalu can leave if they want to," replied Sylvia. "The government doesn't implant tracking devices in their bodies."

"Every place is different," replied Natalie with irritation. Then, perhaps not wanting to start an argument, she smiled and said, "All I know is that we're happy here."

CHAPTER TWENTY-FIVE

The next day was Tuesday, and at ten o'clock in the morning Sylvia dutifully reported to the office of Dr. Hyland.

"Before we get started," she said, "I'd like to ask you about something."

"Sure—what is it?"

Sylvia told him about meeting Natalie and hearing about how Natalie had met and become engaged to Jim, and how they were having a child together. "How often does that happen?" she asked.

"It's interesting that you should bring that up," smiled Dr. Hyland. "Yes, it's true we proactively identify mates for our residents. We call it our partner match program. The criteria are not unlike those used by dating services— age, education, family background, and so forth. In addition, we have the advantage of knowing the complete genetic profile of each of our residents, enabling us to precisely align people on the basis of their inherited genetic variances."

"Don't you mean genetic diseases?" asked Sylvia.

"We prefer not to use that word, particularly when discussing making a match between two people. We feel that 'variances' is equally descriptive without being pejorative. After all, here on Juliette Island we regard genetic variances as opportunities, not defects."

"Opportunities for profit, wouldn't you say?"

"Yes, I would," nodded Dr. Hyland. "Profit is a powerful motivator. Don't you think most of the advances made by the human race have been spurred by the desire for profit? When Thomas Edison invented the light bulb, he didn't release his patent and make his invention free to all, did he? Of course not; he manufactured and sold light bulbs. When Steve Jobs revolutionized the personal computer, did he give away his designs? No, he retained his rights to them and made a profit from them."

"I don't want to get into a debate with you," replied Sylvia, "other than to say a stable, healthy society is based on three interest groups: labor, capital, and government. The first two, by nature, exist in opposition to each other. To maintain balance, the government must be an impartial arbiter between them. If either labor or capital becomes too powerful, the government must step in and balance the relationship. Unfortunately, in the United Americas we have a situation where the government and capital work together hand in glove. With the Industrial Council at the forefront, they act as one. Against such a combined force, labor is helpless. The unhealthy impulse to generate corporate profits at all costs cannot be held in check. This creates a situation like what we have today, with the rampant exploitation of the value created by labor and its transfer to the ruling oligarchs."

"Very impressive analysis," said Dr. Hyland as he peered at Sylvia through his rimless glasses. "Unfortunately, you've omitted a critical factor. This is efficiency. With its competing interests, the world you describe is woefully inefficient. Many would even call it wasteful. Why should there be tension between capital, labor, and the government? Think of all the pointless and wasteful labor strikes of the nineteenth and twentieth centuries. An entire industry could be shut down because some labor leader wanted to make a name for himself, thereby creating hardship, lost wages, and loss of production. If you thought about it, I'm sure you'd conclude that the Industrial Council, working shoulder to shoulder with the government, has produced impressive benefits."

"Impressive benefits for a few people," replied Sylvia, "but not for the majority. And at what cost? Whatever happened to personal freedom? To not only do what you want, but freedom from exploitation?"

Dr. Hyland leaned forward and said, "My dear Sylvia, it must be nice to hold such high ideals. I prefer to live in the real world. Now then, before we find ourselves spending all day pursuing this fascinating topic, let's return to the business at hand. You asked about your friends, Natalie and Jim. You have implied that there was a profit motive behind our selection of Jim for Natalie, or vice-versa, depending on whose point of view you take. All I can say is that we take every factor into consideration, including personal, emotional, and medical issues. We want success, not failure. Now then...." He paused to click through some files on his computer. "Yes, there he is! After much careful research and meticulous mapping of thousands of touch points, as we call them, as well as consideration of your respective genetic structures, the Medical Board has determined that you qualify for the partner match program, and we've found the ideal man for you."

"You've done what?"

Dr. Hyland turned the computer so that Sylvia could see the screen. She saw a photo of a man wearing a plaid sports jacket and a broad smile with astonishingly perfect teeth. "Meet Don Gardner. Age twenty-nine. Unmarried, no children. Born and raised in Topeka, Kansas. Worked as a sports reporter for Fact News in Kansas City. He's been a resident here for about a year. Well adjusted. Enjoys playing tennis. Have you seen the tennis courts yet? If not, I suggest you visit them. People who play tell me they're very fine. Don lives on Peachtree Way, a short drive from you." Dr. Hyland smiled and lowered his voice, as if what he was saying were confidential. "I took the liberty of showing him your photo. I must tell you, I think he's quite smitten. He's looking forward to meeting you."

Sylvia felt the old familiar pain clutch the back of her neck and jab its bony fingers into the base of her skull. A drop of sweat tickled her forehead and her lungs couldn't get enough air. Struggling to present an image of composure, she stammered, "That's very nice, but I'm not looking for someone. I have a husband."

"Oh, you mean Jason Quin. That's been taken care of. He's been granted his freedom."

"What do you mean, granted his freedom?" Now her stomach was churning and she hoped it wasn't obvious that she was gripping the arms of the chair as if she were riding a roller coaster.

"When married employees are re-assigned to the Juliette Island program," said Dr. Hyland, "their marital bonds are annulled. We've found that a clean break is much better for both partners. Jason has been sent an official letter from the Industrial Council informing him that he is free to seek another partner. I'm sure he appreciates the opportunity to start over."

"Start over? What are you talking about? I'm carrying his child!"

"But Jason is a thousand miles away," said Dr. Hyland. "He's a part of your past. And frankly, despite your feelings for him, which I'm sure are very real, from the standpoint of data he was a rather poor match for you. There were many areas of incompatibility. You are very different personality types. For example, our data shows that your personality falls under the category of extroverted-intuitive-thinking-acting, or EITA. In contrast, Jason's personality fits the profile of introverted-logical-feeling-dreaming, or ILFD. This, along with several hundred other personality touchpoints, led the Medical Board to conclude that you and Jason have a compatibility rating of two out of five, which is a poor prognosticator of marital success."

"But we love each other!"

"I understand you have those feelings," said Dr. Hyland, "but they aren't enough to sustain you through life's trials and tribulations. It may interest you to know that Don Gardner is an ELTA personality—a much closer match to you. The prognosis for a long-term relationship with Don Gardner is much better than with Jason Quin. We believe—we know—that careful analysis, coupled with a cool, detached examination of the data and the facts, results in matches that are far more long-lasting than when subjects are left to their own devices and vagaries of chance."

"I've heard enough," said Sylvia. "Not only do you poke and probe into every corner of my body, but now you assert the same authority over my heart? I'm sorry, but I reject the premise. Love cannot be quantified or put onto a spreadsheet. It cannot be summed up in a set of data points or personality types. It defies logic, which is its beauty. People who fall in love often do so despite their outward differences because they feel completed by each other. Each feels the other fills in the gaps in their own personality. If I'm an EITA personality, or whatever you call it, then why would I be attracted to someone of the same type? In your own words, wouldn't such a union be terribly inefficient, because it would perpetuate a redundancy?"

"The algorithms include the variances to which you allude," replied Dr. Hyland wearily. He glanced at the clock. Noting they were falling behind schedule, he frowned. "I must tell you," he continued, "that while you are free to say 'no,' there are penalties for declining to support the path laid out for you and Don. If you refuse, there will be subsequent reductions in your living arrangements and privileges. In contrast, if you embrace the decision of the Medical Board, which is based on sound research, you and your children will enjoy a higher level of benefits."

"Did you say 'children,' in the plural form?"

"Of course," replied Dr. Hyland. Behind his rimless glasses his eyes twinkled. "Just between you and me, Don is very anxious to start a family. He told me that he wants at least three children. Isn't that marvelous? And because of our genetic screening, it's likely these children will not suffer from the genetic conditions carried by you and Don—although you can never be certain."

"I'm sorry, but do I have any say in this? Does my opinion count?"

"As I said before, you have a choice. You can choose to live in the women's dormitory, or you can choose to live in a spacious private home with Don and your family."

"If I choose to live in the dormitory, where will my child live?"

"In foster care. We have several families on the island who would be delighted to take in a fatherless child."

Inwardly seething, Sylvia said nothing. Dr. Hyland pretended to look at some papers. The seconds ticked by. Sylvia's anger subsided enough so that she could logically consider her choices. Neither were acceptable. It wasn't that she disliked Don Gardner; she didn't even know him. The problem was that ever since she had set foot on Juliette Island—rather, ever since Carin had entered her life—her fundamental rights as a human being had been chipped away. Oh, but there was always a good reason! Giving up her rights was good for the company, or led to greater efficiency, or helped the effort in the nation's perpetually looming war against Rodinia, or was even good for Sylvia herself in some roundabout way. All of these so-called good things, and all the contracts and consent forms, added up like grains of sand until they had formed a bottomless pool of quicksand into which she felt herself sinking.

"You need not decide today," said Dr. Hyland. "Let's think about what we need to accomplish this morning."

The subject was dropped, and Sylvia worked her way through the day's portfolio of tests. The nurse reported that her baby, now at seven weeks, was developing normally. In her womb it was about the size of a blueberry, and growing rapidly, with most of the growth concentrated in the head as new brain cells were generated at the rate of one hundred per minute. At seven weeks, Sylvia might start feeling morning sickness (not yet, she replied) and food aversions (again, Sylvia reported no problems there). Then Sylvia asked the nurse why the mountains of data didn't predict how she would feel at seven weeks. The nurse smiled and said that every woman was different, and currently there were no tests to assess a woman's likelihood of having various sensations. How a person was likely to feel was still a mystery.

At home that night, with Reese still in the cooler, Sylvia made dinner with Mandy, and she revealed to Mandy Dr. Hyland's offer of a match with Don Gardner. "Dr. Hyland told me my marriage to Jason had been annulled," said Sylvia as she sautéed some onions. "Can they really do that?"

"They can erase the digital record," replied Mandy, molding some ground beef into two patties. "You could go online and search for your marriage license and record of your ceremony, and you would find nothing. If you had a paper copy, I'm sure it's been removed from your house or office. Therefore you can think or believe whatever you want, but as far as the state is concerned, you're a single woman. And you're pregnant. This will create additional problems for you. It will make life here on Juliette Island more difficult."

"Dr. Hyland told me that if I didn't hook up with Don Gardner, I'd be moved into the women's dormitory and my baby would be put up for adoption."

"He's playing hardball with you, that's for sure." She put the burgers on the skillet and went to the refrigerator for cheese. "They say that possession is nine-tenths of the law. Well, they possess both of us. They tricked us into coming to this island from which there's no escape. In my case, I've learned to accept it. Better to switch than fight. I'm at peace with myself."

"Until they do something really awful to you," said Sylvia. "Then we'll see how much inner peace you have."

At that moment, Sylvia heard the front door open. "In the kitchen," she called.

Limar entered. "How was your day today?"

"Fine, thank you," replied Mandy.

"Very pleasant," said Sylvia.

"Are either of you planning on leaving the house tonight?" asked Limar.

"No" was the answer from both.

"I see you're making dinner," said Limar. "I won't keep you. Enjoy your evening."

"Say, Limar," said Sylvia, "before you go, is there any word on when Reese's going to be released from the cooler?"

"If you mean the Re-Orientation Center," said Limar, "I do not have that information." She turned and left.

Mandy went to the window, and from behind the curtain she watched as Limar walked down the path and over to the next house. Then she turned to Sylvia. "You shouldn't ask questions like that! You'll get into trouble. You might even be sent to the cooler yourself."

"Please tell me again how happy you are to be living on Juliette Island," replied Sylvia. Mandy gave her a sour look. "Okay, we've both made our points," said Sylvia. "Let's forget about our mechanical prison guard and enjoy our dinners."

As the last rays of twilight painted the tops of the trees red, they sat down to eat. "We need to grow some tomatoes," said Sylvia, poking at the slice on her plate. "These things we buy at the market taste like cardboard. Please pass the pickles."

"We could make our own pickles, too," said Mandy. "We'd need to get some decent cucumbers and some dill. So—have you thought any more about Don Gardner? I wish they'd find a man for me. Maybe if you don't want Don Gardner, they'd let me try him."

"Mandy, really," replied Sylvia. "Is that any way to talk? Besides, it's not up to us. The matches are based on algorithms. If you match, you get the green light. No match means no green light."

"If I were you, I'd accept reality and at least give the guy a shot," said Mandy. "If the Industrial Council has really deleted your marriage, and if you're going to be living here indefinitely, why not make the best of it? It's possible that Don Gardner is a perfectly nice guy. I'm sure you could do much worse."

"But I'd feel terrible about Jason," said Sylvia. "In my heart I still love him. Nobody could ever take his place."

"Okay, I agree: no other man could take his place. But does that mean you have to become an old spinster? You've got one life to live, sister—there are no second chances."

"All right, I'll think about it."

CHAPTER TWENTY-SIX

On Wednesday morning at ten o'clock, Sylvia reported to Dr. Hyland's office.

"I hope you've brought good news regarding Don Gardner," he said when she sat down at his desk.

"Yes," she replied. "I would like to meet him for dinner."

"Splendid!" he replied. "You may call Limar on your phone. She will contact Don and make the arrangements."

"I can't call him myself?"

"We believe that in these initial stages, it's better for everyone to stick with the island protocol."

At seven o'clock that night, Sylvia met Don for dinner at the Dockside. She found him already seated at the table, and he did not stand up when she approached, offering only a bland puppy smile. He was dressed in the male equivalent of the female island uniform—a boxy blue sports jacket and white shirt that looked like they came out of an old twentieth-century Sears catalogue. His hair was longish and carefully parted on the side and plastered down with some sort of gel.

They exchanged pleasantries—how the weather was nice and the restaurant not too crowded. Then they sat in silence as they perused their menus, which took Sylvia about thirty seconds because she quickly decided she wanted the spinach ravioli; and then, for lack of anything better to do, she pretended to keep looking at the selections. With brows furrowed, Don studied his menu for a few minutes. Then, without lifting his eyes, he said, "Should I have the sirloin steak or the Statler chicken?"

"Excuse me—what?" Sylvia had been daydreaming.

He looked at her with condescending annoyance. "I said, should I have the sirloin steak or the Statler chicken?"

"Oh, I don't know. They both sound good. I haven't had either one yet—as I'm sure you know, I only arrived on the island six days ago."

"Yes—you're a newbie," he replied. "From Detroit, is that right?"

"That's right. I work in the logistics office of Sun Motors."

"Did you guys ever fix that problem with the radar system of the Comet SUV? That was a major product defect."

Sylvia cringed. The Comet radar system software had been poorly designed, had led to a recall of fifty thousand vehicles, and had cost the company tens of millions of dollars. The episode was the biggest product recall since the Global Depression and had been a major embarrassment for the company. No one who worked at Sun liked to talk about it, and especially not with a casual acquaintance.

"It was fixed," replied Sylvia. "It's in the past. I thought you would have known that, since you worked at Facts News."

"I was a sportscaster," he said without looking up from his menu.

The server came to the table and asked if they were ready to order. Without waiting for Sylvia to reply, Gardner said, "The sirloin steak—it comes with a mushroom sauce?"

The server replied, "Yes, just as it says on the menu. It hasn't changed. Always with a mushroom sauce."

He thought some more. "The salmon looks good—is that farm raised or wild?"

"Farm raised. The season for wild salmon won't start for another few weeks."

"That's no good," mused Gardner as he stroked his chin with his hand. He looked up. "Sylvia, why don't you go ahead and order."

"I'll have the tossed salad with vinaigrette dressing and the spinach ravioli," she said.

"Something to drink?" asked the server.

"Water, please."

After writing this on her pad, the server turned her attention back to Gardner.

"Let's see…. I had the roast beef last week, so that's out. Not sure if I'm in the mood for chicken. The salmon is farm raised, so I'll pass on that. You're having the spinach ravioli, so there's no point in my getting the same thing. I've had the meat loaf recently too."

"Try the steak tips," said Sylvia, trying not to show her annoyance at Gardner's indecisiveness.

"Okay, but if they're no good, I'll blame you," he said. This time he was smiling. Sylvia was not.

"Very good," said the server. "And a salad?"

"I've had the garden salad and the Caesar salad. Sylvia, do you think the coleslaw will go well with the steak tips?"

"Yes, I'm sure it will."

"And a glass of wine… let's see…."

"Sir," said the server, "we offer a choice of red or white wine. It's the same choice we've had for several years."

"I'll have the red."

"Very good."

Sylvia decided that to keep the evening moving along, she needed to be proactive in the conversation. "How did you get into sportscasting?" she asked.

Gardner explained he had been in high school and had been cut from the varsity football team—which he thought was highly unfair, even though he admitted missing key practice sessions—and so he started reporting on the team for the school newspaper. He revealed to Sylvia that for snaring girls, being associated with the team as a reporter was nearly as good as being a player, and therefore he had no shortage of girlfriends. There were lots of beer parties and wild weekends, which Gardner described in great detail.

After the salads arrived, he continued his memoirs by detailing how in college he had expanded his sports reporting platforms to include the college radio station and then the local cable access TV station. There were more beer parties and more girls.

By the time the server brought their main courses, Gardner's life story had progressed to his first full-time job as a sportscaster for a television station in Wichita. He spent two years there covering mostly high school and college games (the hottest girls were at Kansas State in Manhattan, Kansas, he reported) before joining Facts News in Kansas City.

The server cleared their plates and brought coffee.

"You've had quite a career," said Sylvia as she stirred in her sugar and cream. "Very impressive. So—if I may ask—why are you here? I don't want to pry, but we're all here for a reason."

"It was time to make a move," he said without a trace of irony. "I got caught up in a very unfair accusation from a female colleague. The station's owners were lined up against me. At around the same time, my dentin dysplasia had progressed enough to become a problem."

"Oh, I'm sorry," said Sylvia. "Since I've been here I've become something of an expert on genetic diseases—I have mitochondrial DNA-associated Leigh syndrome—but I've never heard of dentin dysplasia."

"It's also called 'rootless teeth,'" replied Gardner. "It's an accurate description. Your teeth look normal, but they have stunted roots. Over time, they become loose and eventually fall out of your mouth. Just like that—pop, pop, pop. That's why I have these nice new choppers." He grinned, showing perfect white rows of teeth. "One day the station told me they were sending me on a special assignment. I got on the plane and got off here." He waved his hand, indicating the room around them. "That was one year ago. At first I was resentful, but then I figured, hey, why not make the best of it? If I could raise a family here on Juliette Island, why not?"

"Yes—why not?" replied Sylvia. In her mind's eye, she could see nothing but his toothless gums. She signaled for the server, to whom she gave her debit card. In a moment her bill was paid and the card returned. As soon as her companion had finished his coffee, Sylvia said, "Don, this has been a very pleasant evening. Thank you." She pushed back her chair and stood up.

Caught off guard, he scrambled to his feet. "Just let me get my bill—I'll go to the door with you." Sylvia waited while he paid. Outside in the parking area, Gardner turned to her. "Will you walk me to my golf cart?"

"All right," replied Sylvia, overruling the warning voice in her head. "Where is it?"

"Over there," he gestured vaguely towards the far edge of the gravel lot.

They walked together toward a stand of dark trees. Sure enough, in the shadows under the branches, outside the pool of light from the restaurant, a golf cart was parked.

"Your chariot awaits you," said Sylvia brightly.

"How about a kiss goodnight?" He moved close.

"Well, all right," she replied she offered him her cheek. "But I really must be going. I have an early day tomorrow."

Suddenly he put his arm around her waist and drew her against his body. He mashed his lips against hers and probed her mouth with his tongue.

Turning her face away and pushing against him, she struggled to twist free. His grip was strong. She felt his other hand on her breast, squeezing it. As she tried to grab his wrist and wrench it free, in a twisted tango move he kicked her feet out from under her and she toppled backward onto the grass bordering the gravel lot. He lay on top of her with his full weight pressing down. With one hand he tried to hold her head steady while he kissed her mouth. The other hand crawled down from her back to her buttocks, fingers groping, trying to hike up her dress.

Summoning all her strength, she slammed her fist into his throat. He cried out in pain and relaxed his hold on her, allowing her to break free, stand up, and run towards the light of the restaurant.

"Stupid bitch," she heard him gasp.

When she got home, she went straight for the planter on the patio. After swallowing a shot of whiskey, she went upstairs and took a shower, but the sensation of being violated wouldn't wash off. She went to bed and drifted into a troubled sleep.

The next morning, Sylvia reported to Dr. Hyland's office. Through his rimless glasses, he peered at her with an expression of disapproval.

"Don Gardner called me this morning," he said.

"Did he tell you that he sexually assaulted me in the parking lot of the Dockside?"

"He told me you punched him in the throat. He could have been seriously injured. I'd say if there was an assault, he bore the brunt of it."

"He's a predator."

"That's a strong word," said Dr. Hyland. His tone softened. "He's been here a year, without female companionship. Please try to understand how difficult it must be for him. Men have needs. Perhaps he was a little bit clumsy in his overtures. I hope you can forgive him."

"Actually," said Sylvia, "his assault on me—which back in the real world could earn him jail time—was the least of my issues with him. The bigger problem is that he's a raging bore. We spent over an hour at dinner, and during ninety percent of that time I sat and listened while he told me his life story, right down to the quantity and quality of his girlfriends. The man is both extremely dull and extremely determined that he should dominate the conversation. That's a fatal combination. His sense of entitlement is truly appalling. I urge you to re-examine your data points and find some other girl for him to victimize, both physically and emotionally."

Dr. Hyland slowly shook his head. "You may have gotten off to a rough start with Don, but I assure you he's a good man. All the data point to one conclusion: he'll be a good husband for you and a good father for your children. I'm sure that if you made an effort to see the situation from his point of view, you'd be much more empathetic. And remember that marriage to your chosen partner will bring many substantial rewards, while refusing to go along with the program will bring equal and opposite sanctions."

"Is that a threat?" asked Sylvia.

"Come now, let's not be dramatic. It's just reality. We each have a job to do here. I have mine and you have yours. Don has his. Let me ask you—did you make any effort to please him? To see the world from his point of view?"

"I made a huge effort to sit there and listen to him brag about his years as a young stud working as a sportscaster. It was one female conquest after another, interspersed with boasts about all the famous athletes he knew. He didn't let me get a word in edgewise. I'd be amazed if he even knows my name. Go ahead, call him on the phone. Ask him the name of the girl he had dinner with last night."

Dr. Hyland held up his hands in a double "stop" sign. "Sylvia, that's enough. The Medical Board has spoken. You will marry Don Gardner. You will live with him and have children with him. Perhaps you don't realize what a valuable service you will be performing for humanity. When combined, your individual genetic profiles will create in your children unique combinations we haven't seen before. And one more thing—you should also count yourself extremely lucky that Don, out of the goodness of his heart, is willing to raise your expected child as his own."

"I'm sure he's also eagerly looking forward to the fattening of his debit card balance once he's a so-called 'head of household' with a child on the way," said Sylvia.

Ignoring her comment, Dr. Hyland leaned forward and looked directly into her eyes. "Sylvia Brand, from this moment on, your happiness is in your hands. If you're determined to be miserable, then miserable you shall be. But I advise you to keep your winter of discontent to yourself. Don Gardner deserves a partner who's loving and supportive, not a shrew who cannot be tamed. Do you understand?"

Knowing she had lost this battle, Sylvia gritted her teeth and said, "Yes."

"Within the month, your marriage will be consummated. In the meantime, I encourage you to spend time with Don and get to know him." Dr. Hyland closed the file and set it aside before clicking on his computer. "Very well. Let's see what your medical examination schedule looks like today."

CHAPTER TWENTY-SEVEN

At the end of the day, Sylvia drove home, parked her golf cart in front of 15 Apple Way, and turned off the motor. She sat quietly, thinking about her life. What had she done wrong? Why did she deserve to be forcibly married to an odious clown just because the Medical Board thought his and her DNA would make an interesting and profitable combination? Was she only valuable to her fellow human beings because by some random stroke of fate she had an unusual flaw in her genetics? She felt like she had fallen into a deep, dark well from which there was no escape. What had become her reason for living? Was it to bear the baby she and Jason had conceived in love, only to have that innocent child raised by a creep allied with the Medical Board? This scenario loomed large in her heart, blocking out the light, like a vast black cloud overspreading the sky and blotting out the sun.

Sluggishly, she roused herself. Sitting like a lump in her golf cart wasn't going to help. She trudged to the front door and went inside. Entering the kitchen, she found Mandy slicing potatoes for dinner.

"I haven't seen you since before you met Don Gardner for dinner last night," Mandy said as she laid the slices on a greased pan. "How did it go?"

"Please do me a favor and don't mention that man's name," replied Sylvia. "He's a horrible boring person and he sexually assaulted me right there in the parking lot. And Dr. Hyland is just as bad. He told me I had no choice—I was to marry Don Gardner and carry his little rug rats."

"I'm so sorry," said Mandy. She put the pan in the oven. "But maybe it will all work out. After all, what else can you do? This is our life. Some higher power—call it God or fate—put us on this island. It's now our home. We need to make the best of it."

"Mandy, God did not put us here!" said Sylvia. "The Industrial Council put us here! Greedy men and women put us here! People who have power put us here and are keeping us here! We're on this island by the deliberate choice of those who are no better than us and who seek to profit from our bodies and our diseases."

"Okay, okay—I understand how you feel," said Mandy. "I didn't mean to say we have no free will. We do. Listen, I'm sure you're hungry. I'm going to make hamburgers. Do you want one?"

Sylvia took a deep breath. In a peculiar way, she wished she could be like Mandy—a carefree leaf in the wind, willing to accept whatever fate brought her. The Buddhists said that desire was the root of all unhappiness. This was true. Sylvia knew her misery was the product of her desire to control her own life in defiance of her present circumstances. She could choose to roll over and go with the flow. But that would be both morally unacceptable and physically dangerous. If her soon-to-be life partner, Don Gardner, beat her and abused her, she would find no sympathy from the Medical Board, from Dr. Hyland, or anyone else in authority. Don Gardner could even make her disappear, and as long as he wasn't stupid about it, the Medical Council would undertake nothing more than a token investigation. Her doctors could kill her. Then her body would be cremated and her name erased from the database. And her child? Knowing no other environment but Juliette Island, who could imagine what her life would be like? Would her child become an obedient sheep, making no trouble for the Medical Board and expressing gratitude for whatever tasty little scraps they tossed to her, the way a dog eagerly waits underneath the banquet table?

With a heavy heart, Sylvia ate her dinner and washed the dishes. It was hopeless. She was doomed. Without saying goodnight to Mandy she went upstairs to her room. Fully clothed, she lay down on the bed. Yes, she decided, the only solution was to end her miserable existence. To die was better than to live as a prisoner. Taking her own life meant taking that of her child, and she prayed that Jason, if he were still walking on the earth, would forgive her.

As if she were watching someone else do it, she got up from her bed and looked around her room. She had no weapon, no poison. But she had a belt, and she could hang herself. She saw herself go to her closet and take the leather belt hanging from the hook. The belt was slender but strong. She could fasten the two ends together, as if she were wearing it, and slip it around her neck. Then she could place it over the hook. How long would it take to die? Hopefully not very much time. The last thing she wanted was to be discovered not quite dead, and taken to the Medical Center and revived, and for Dr. Hyland to shake his head and tell her what a weak and pathetic woman she was.

The smooth, hard leather encircled her neck. Now was the time. She closed her eyes and relaxed her body, letting it slide down the side of the door. The belt gripped her neck. As it became tighter, she felt the blood pressure build in her face. Okay—this is it. Let your legs go. You don't need them any more.

A noise came from the hallway. A soft knock on her door.

"Sylvia—are you awake?" The voice belonged to Reese.

Damn you, Reese! Why did you have to interrupt? Sylvia struggled to her feet and the noose loosened its deadly hold. "Uh—yes, just a minute," she stammered. Feeling dizzy, she held onto the side of the door. She slipped off the belt, undid the buckle, and hung it on the hook. After talking a few breaths, Sylvia opened the door.

"My God, Reese!" she exclaimed. "What have they done to you? Please— come in."

As she entered, Reese said, "Oh, they just roughed me up. I lost a few pounds too—being fed nothing but bread and water will do that to you. But they knew they couldn't hurt me too badly because I'm too valuable. They need me for more tests." She stopped and looked at Sylvia. "Are you okay? You seem depressed." Her fingers went to Sylvia's neck. "And you've got a rash or something."

Sylvia turned and sat on her bed. Suddenly, despite her effort to hold them inside, the tears flooded from her eyes. Reese sat next to her and tenderly put her arm around her. Sobbing, Sylvia said, "I'm so sorry. I just couldn't take it anymore. I was going to—I don't know how to say this, I feel so stupid—I was trying to end it. I didn't want to live. I'm sorry."

"Sorry?" said Reese. "What on earth are you sorry for?"

"For not being strong. For complaining."

Reese took her by the shoulders. "Sylvia, you have nothing to be sorry for." She reached for a tissue from the box on the night table. "Dry your eyes. You're lucky I came upstairs when I did! A few minutes later and you might have succeeded. Now listen to me: I've had enough of this place. So have you. I'm ready to get the hell out of here."

"What are you talking about?" she said as she dabbed her tears. "Do you mean escape?"

"Sister, that's exactly what I mean. We can't continue to live like this. We live like animals in a zoo. What's the end game? I want you to think about something. Have you noticed there are very few old people living here? There's Reginald Astor. He's in his sixties. Hardly a geriatric. There are one or two elderly residents who have Alzheimer's disease, and that's why they're here. But there's no one else who's beyond middle aged. Do you know why?"

"No, I don't. Maybe they send them home when they're no longer useful medical subjects."

"Are you kidding? Send them home? So they can tell everyone about Juliette Island and all the people who are forced to live here? Get real. That's not going to happen."

"So what happens to them?"

"You mean, what will happen to us. To you and me. I'll tell you what's in store for us: I have a friend who works in the crematorium."

"Reese, you couldn't mean…"

"Yes, that's exactly what I mean. When you're no longer useful, they tell you to report for your normal medical tests. When you're on the table, they tell you they need to give you a general anesthetic. You say, go ahead, I don't care, I've gone to sleep too many times to count. They pump you full of Propofol. You drift off to slumber land and you never wake up. They slice you open, harvest your organs, take out your brain, suck out your bone marrow, and when there's nothing left but a hollow carcass they put it in a body bag, throw it into the back of a truck, take it to the crematorium, and fire it up. At two thousand degrees Fahrenheit, within two hours your pathetic cadaver has been reduced to five pounds of bone and ash. Then the remains are fed through a crusher to break up the bone fragments—although at the Juliette Island corpse roaster, they probably skip this step. They pour your ashes into a big bucket. When the bucket is full, they take it out in the boat and dump the cinders into Puget Sound. Within a few years, your fried molecules will have traveled on ocean currents all around the world."

"You're talking about the boat they keep in the boathouse next to the crematorium?" asked Sylvia. "The one they let Mandy ride in with her son's ashes?"

"That's the one. If your child dies, the Medical Board treats it like a normal death, with some vestige of dignity. They don't want the grieving parents to freak out. But when they kill you, they do it very quietly."

"I don't want to die here," said Sylvia. "And I don't want my child to grow up here. But what can we do? How can we get off this ghastly island?"

Reese leaned closer, as if the walls had ears. "I know a guy who has keys to the boathouse. He's one of the human guards at the cooler."

"Reese, how do you know this?"

"Let's just say I get around. Most of the guys who work on this godforsaken pimple of an island have two useful qualities: they aren't very loyal to the Industrial Council, and they're starved for sex."

"Reese—do you mean—just like Aldeen—?"

"It's the coin of the realm, my dear. To get what you need, you use the money God gave you. I have something guys want, and I'm ready to do business. Actually, I like Khaleed. He's cute. But the important thing for us is this: he's worried about his future. He's got an unusual genetic disorder— something called Factor X deficiency, which affects the blood's ability to clot. He told me the Medical Board has brought him in for testing, and he's scared that at any moment he'll be converted from a prison employee to an inmate. He's seen the way the inmates leave the island—in the bucket on the boat. So he's ready to jump. He'll take us with him."

"Why doesn't he just take the boat and go?"

"My dear, the Mortas weren't born yesterday. Or manufactured yesterday, as the case may be. They track every movement around the island, and if Khaleed took the boat on an unscheduled cruise, they'd be all over him. He'd never make it."

"So how can he do it?"

"By waiting until it rains. In a good hard rain, the Mortas are less efficient and the drones can't fly. We get in the boat and race away at top speed. If we're lucky, the Morta patrol boat won't catch us in time."

"And if we're unlucky?"

"They'll try to stop us, and if they can't, they'll blow us out of the water."

"Okay," said Sylvia. Looking at the flesh of her hand, she ran her fingertip over the bump in the skin above the tiny pill-shaped transponder. "What about these?"

Reese's eyes narrowed. "We've got to remove them."

"How?"

"By cutting them out."

A bolt of nausea flashed through Sylvia's body. "I don't know if I can do that."

Taking Sylvia by the hand, Reese looked into her eyes. "Trust me, the pain will be a very small price to pay for your freedom. We'll do it together. It will take only a few seconds. One quick cut and it's done. But we need to get a razor and some bandages."

Fighting back her fear, Sylvia nodded. "Okay."

Suddenly they heard Mandy's cheery voice from the bottom of the stairs. "Hey you guys," she called. "I'm making some popcorn. Want some?"

"Yeah," called Reese. "We'll be down in a second!" She turned to Sylvia. "I like Mandy, but there's no way we can tell her about this. She's a loyalist. Even if she didn't object to our escaping, she'd have a problem keeping her mouth shut. One question from Limar and she'd spill her guts, and we'd both be dead."

CHAPTER TWENTY-EIGHT

The next morning at her usual appointment, Dr. Hyland asked Sylvia if she had reconsidered her attitude toward Don Gardner. She told him that although he was a bit rough around the edges, after thinking about the proposed marriage she had seen him in a new light. She had stepped back and looked at the big picture, and realized that the Medical Board had shown good judgment. She promised to do her very best to create a happy home for her husband, herself, and their children.

"I'm so very pleased to hear that," said Dr. Hyland. "I'll convey to Don the good news."

"But you must tell him one thing," said Sylvia. "I'm a woman of high moral character. While I'm looking forward to consummating our marriage and raising our children, I insist that we save our intimate relations until after we're married. This is very important to me. I'm sure that he will enjoy great piece of mind knowing that his wife takes her vows very seriously, and that an intimate relationship outside of marriage is something that will never happen with me."

"Excellent!" Dr. Hyland beamed. "Of course I will impress upon him the importance of your virtue. I can personally guarantee that he will conduct himself like a perfect gentleman—or he will have to answer to me. I'll contact the island administrator and set a date for your marriage. I know you will be very happy."

Having for the time being cleared that particular hurdle, for the rest of the day Sylvia dutifully endured the familiar rounds of tests and probing and MRIs and tubes and needles.

During the last test, an ultrasound of her fetus, the nurse received a summons and excused herself from the examination room.

Sylvia had been alone in the room before, and had never thought much of it. But today was different. She slid off the table and looked around. Bandages were easy to find—they were in plain sight, and she stuffed a fistful in her pocket. Keeping her ears attentive to the sound of the door opening, she went to a cabinet and pulled open one drawer after another. She saw lots of medical devices and sundries, but no scalpels. She went to a small table that had a single drawer. Pulling it open, she saw surgical instruments in sterile plastic bags. She took a scalpel, put it in her pocket, and closed the drawer. Then she got back up on the table.

That night, the mood at the house was relaxed and congenial. Over a dinner of grilled chicken and rice, Sylvia told Mandy that she had decided to marry Don Gardner. Mandy seemed genuinely pleased, but expressed her personal sadness that once Sylvia and Don were united, her friend and roommate would be moving to a new home. "The three of us have such a good rapport," she said. "I'm going to miss you! I'm sure Reese feels the same way."

"Oh yes, absolutely," said Reese. "Sylvia, it won't be the same without you."

There was a knock on the front door. "In the kitchen," called Reese.

Limar came in and said, "How is everyone tonight?"

Everyone agreed that they were fine. Never better.

"I understand you, Sylvia, will soon be starting your own household with Don Gardner," said Limar. "I'm sure you're very excited."

"Oh yes—very excited," replied Sylvia. Then she added, "I see that word travels quickly."

"We're all plugged into the same database," said Limar with a pointless smile. "The minute Dr. Hyland entered it into your file, all the Morta autonomous humanoid operators knew."

"All of them?" asked Sylvia. "Do you mean to say, all of them everywhere in the nation?"

Limar nodded. "Of course that particular fifty-kilobyte morsel would have been filed away with the many terabytes of other data, like one grain of sand being added to a beach; but if the data were relevant to the operator or there's query, then the information would be instantly accessed."

"Oh, I get it," said Mandy.

Sylvia was silent. She was thinking about Carin and her circle of colleagues in Detroit—and especially of Jason.

"It's Friday night—anyone going out?" asked Limar.

No, no one was going out. They were all staying in.

"If that's all," said Limar, "then I wish you a good evening."

Limar left the house. Sylvia noted the time—it was exactly twenty minutes after seven. Every night, without fail, Limar came for her inspection between seven o'clock and seven-thirty. Sylvia and Reese needed to make their escape after Limar's visit.

The weather that night was clear. Khaleed, Reese reported, had access to weather reports. He was watching the forecasts. There was nothing on the horizon. Every day when Sylvia left the house, and again when she came home in the evening, she'd scan the heavens, looking for rain clouds. All she saw were friendly white clouds.

On Sunday night, Sylvia had her second date with Don Gardner. They met at the Dockside. Perhaps Dr. Hyland had given him a stern lecture, because in Sylvia's opinion he was slightly less obnoxious than during their first meeting. He even asked Sylvia about her life at 15 Apple Way, and he lasted about thirty seconds into her answer before he started to fidget and look bored. Sylvia saw this and, with a feeling of sadness, quickly ended her story, at which point Gardner, with the spotlight again turned in his direction, launched into a detailed description of a frat party he had attended while in college, and to which the campus police had been called because too many of the boys were lewdly grabbing the girls and/or drunkenly vomiting on the lawn in front of the frat house. Of course, because the cops were from the college and not the town, the offenders suffered no consequences other than a friendly admonition to "keep it cool, okay?"

Late on Monday afternoon, when Sylvia was released from her daily medical tests she stepped outside the Juliette Island Center for Health Research and looked up to the sky. The clouds directly overhead were high and thin, but to the west she saw a dark line, and the westerly breeze felt unusually cool. She hurried home, and neither Mandy nor Reese were there. A few minutes later, as Sylvia was puttering around in the kitchen, Reese arrived.

"Have you seen the clouds?" Sylvia asked. "Looks like rain."

"Yes I did, and on the way home I stopped to see Khaleed. We're getting a storm tonight. It's supposed to start at eight o'clock and last until midnight. We need to be at the boathouse at eight-thirty."

Sylvia felt as if she had been hit by a lightning bolt. This was it! The hour was upon her. By dawn tomorrow, she'd either be dead or free. There was no middle choice. She would not allow herself to be captured. They would have to kill her.

"Are you with us?" asked Reese. Her eyes were bright and shining.

"Yes," replied Sylvia. "Absolutely. One hundred percent."

At that moment they heard Mandy's golf cart crunch on the gravel driveway.

"What are we going to do with our roommate?" whispered Sylvia.

"You'll see. Shhh—she's coming."

Mandy came into the kitchen. "Hey guys," she said cheerily. "On the way home, I picked up two frozen pizzas. Pepperoni and sausage. I thought we could have an easy dinner tonight."

"Sounds good to me," replied Sylvia.

At seven thirty, when they were eating, Sylvia got up to look out the window.

"Is there something out there?" asked Mandy as she picked a pepperoni off the last piece of pizza. "You've been up and down like a jack-in-the-box."

"Oh, nothing—sorry," she said. "I saw an unusual bird in the yard today. It looked like some kind of big hawk. Just curious to see if it were still hanging around."

A few minutes later the sky suddenly darkened. A few splats of raindrops hit the window—at first just one or two at a time, but the pace slowly increased until it became a steady drumbeat.

"Wow—we haven't had a good storm in a while," said Mandy. She went to the window and looked out. "It's really coming down."

Limar did not come to the house for the regular inspection. This was a good sign—it confirmed the Morta robots didn't like operating in the rain.

At eight o'clock, Sylvia met Reese in her room. She was carrying a length of clothesline. "It's still raining," said Reese. "We're going to go for it. Give me your scalpel."

Sylvia handed it over.

"Okay, let's go see Mandy."

They found their roommate on her bed, reading a book. "Hey guys, what's up?" she asked.

Brandishing the scalpel, Reese approached her. "Mandy, I need you to lie on your stomach with your hands behind your back."

"Why—what?"

"Just do it. Sylvia and I are leaving. We need you to stay out of the way. Believe me, it's for your own good. They must not think you were a part of this. You need to be a victim. Make a sound and I'll cut your throat."

"But why are you leaving?" said Mandy. "If they catch you they'll kill you."

"You and I have very different levels of tolerance for tyrants," said Reese. "If you want to live your life as a slave in golden chains, that's your choice. No one can make that decision for you. Sylvia and I can't do it. We can't live here. We'd rather die. That's just the way it is. Now please—turn over and put your hands behind your back. Don't make me kill you."

Dutifully—perhaps because obedience was in her blood—Mandy rolled over, face down, on the bed, and offered her hands to the rope. While Reese held the scalpel on Mandy, Sylvia quickly tied her hands and feet. "I'm sorry to do this," she said, "but we have no choice." She then cut a strip of cloth from a towel and tied it around Mandy's mouth.

With Mandy immobilized, Sylvia and Reese went to the kitchen. They sat down at the table. Reese extended her hand, palm down, on the table. She handed Sylvia the scalpel. ""Do it. Now."

"I can't," said Sylvia. "I've never—"

"Do you want to die? That's what's going to happen if we don't get out of here. Do it for your unborn child. Come on, make the cut."

"All right," said Sylvia. With one hand she pinched the flesh around the cylinder, forming a small hump. With the other hand she took the scalpel and pressed the sharp tip against the soft flesh covering the cylindrical shape.

"Breathe slowly," commanded Reese. "Steady your hand."

Sylvia pressed down and drew the blade towards her. Reese stiffened but did not cry out. Sylvia felt the tip of the blade scrape along the top of the cylinder as the blood began to ooze out.

"Okay, that's enough," gasped Reese. With her thumb and forefinger, Sylvia pinched the skin tighter. She could feel the hard cylinder, and she tried to work it upwards. Suddenly it popped free.

Reese gasped. After flicking away the cylinder, Sylvia reached for a bandage and pressed it down hard on the wound.

Reese was breathing hard. "God, that hurts!" After a moment she composed herself. "We've got to hurry. You're next. Put your hand on the table."

With fear pouring through her heart, Sylvia extended her left hand.

"Close your eyes," said Reese. "Think of a faraway happy place."

Sylvia felt Reese pinch the flesh between her thumb and forefinger. Suddenly a savage pain shot from her hand up her arm to her brain. Involuntarily she cried out. She tried jerk back her hand but Reese held it in place with a tight grip.

"One more second," she heard Reese say.

The pain obliterated every other sensation. Tears welled up in Sylvia's eyes. She gasped for air. God, when was it going to end? She felt Reese squeezing harder.

"Come on, come on," muttered Reese. Just as the agony was becoming unbearable and Sylvia was ready to yank her hand free of the grasp of her tormentor, Reese said, "Okay—good!" The pinching sensation ended and was replaced by hard pressure on a dull throbbing ache.

Sylvia opened her bleary eyes. Reese smiled as she held the bandage tight against Sylvia's hand. "Are you all right?" she asked.

"Yes—I think so," replied Sylvia, wiping away tears with the back of her hand.

"It's all over. See, you survived!" Reese removed the bloody bandage and replaced it with a fresh one, which she taped tightly to Sylvia's hand.

Sylvia looked at the clock. Eight-fifteen. "We need to get out of here. Where are the transponders?"

"Right there on the table, doing their jobs," replied Reese, pointing to the two little cylinders covered in thick, coagulating blood. "We'll leave them as little gifts."

With her hand pulsing with pain, Sylvia went to the front vestibule and took her raincoat and hat from the rack. After putting them on, she opened the door and stepped out into the downpour. Reese followed. They went to Sylvia's golf cart, got in, and set off down Apple Way.

Helpless against the mass of water droplets, the golf cart's little headlight beam refracted into an ineffectual cloud, and Sylvia could see no more than ten feet in front of her.

Within moments they were both soaked. Her left hand throbbing, Sylvia guided the golf cart to Pine Path, and then past the Juliette Island Center, which was dark. No other vehicles were on the pathways. Pine Path became Seaside Drive, and they passed the abandoned warehouse with its corrugated metal roof drumming loud in the rain, the old gas station, and the gloomy Wild Horse Bar. Rounding the hill, they came to the spot where normally you could see the causeway, but in the heavy rain they saw only darkness. They passed the sign for Tucker's Point and the food and beverage office.

"Keep going straight," said Reese, the water running off her hat.

Squinting into the deluge, Sylvia guided the golf cart along the path. They came to a chain link fence with an open gate. Sylvia drove through and a moment later the headlight revealed a door to a big industrial building. Next to the door, a utility vehicle sat in the rain. Called a "Rhino," it was made by Sun Motors, and was typically used on farms and estates for hauling tools and lightweight cargo. Here on Juliette Island, the Rhinos were used by the Morta guards and human employees.

Reese alighted from the golf cart and ran through the muddy puddles to the door, where she huddled under the small canopy. She knocked. She looked around nervously. No sign of a drone or Morta guard. Reese knocked again. The door opened and a man came out. Hunched over against the rain, he ran to the Rhino. Reese followed him, and waved to Sylvia to join them. She ran to the Rhino and climbed into the small back seat. The water poured off the canvas roof in sheets.

"Sylvia, meet Khaleed," said Reese.

Khaleed turned and quickly shook Sylvia's hand. His eyes did not linger on her and his jaw was set at a determined angle. He turned the key to the Rhino and the little two-cylinder gas engine sprang to life with a staccato roar. He flicked on the headlights and steered the Rhino further north, past the perimeter of the building that bore no markings but that Sylvia knew must be the ghastly crematorium.

They bumped along a path under dripping trees until the headlights caught a wooden boathouse. As they approached, Sylvia saw the dock, beyond which loomed vast wild darkness. Khaleed halted the Rhino by the boathouse and motioned for them to get out. Together they went to a door. Khaleed produced a key, and as the rain beat down he fumbled for the lock and, finding it, turned the key. The metal door swung open. They entered, and before them in the deep gloom a white powerboat with an open wheel rocked gently in the wavelets coming through the open entrance. Aft of the driver's seat, a red faux-leather banquette formed a U-shape around the stern, with the engine compartment acting as a sort of table. Khaleed jumped down into the boat, took the wheel, turned the key, and pressed the starter button.

Sylvia and Reese untied the lines, climbed on board, and took seats on the banquette.

Suddenly from outside a sharp light raked across the entrance to the boathouse.

"Attention—you inside!" called an amplified voice. "Come out with your hands up!"

CHAPTER TWENTY-NINE

"Damn!" muttered Khaleed. "One of the human guards on patrol. Get down! We've got to get out of here!"

Khaleed shoved the throttle forward, and with a roar from its engine the boat leaped from the narrow slip into the blinding light. As Sylvia threw herself onto the floor of the cockpit the spotlight pinned the boat in its glare. A shot rang out, then two more. Sylvia felt a bullet slam into the side of the boat inches from her head.

With the boat at full throttle, within a few seconds it had outrun the spotlight. As it raced across the waves in the pouring rain, Sylvia lifted her head.

"Oh my God," she said. In the driver's seat, Khaleed sat slumped over the wheel, his arms hanging slack by his sides. Springing to her feet, she put her hands on his shoulders. Then she saw the hole in his back, running red mixed with rainwater.

Reese was at her side. She reached over Khaleed's body and pulled back on the throttle. The boat slowed. Sylvia looked behind them. On the distant shore, the brilliant finger of the spotlight probed the darkness.

"Help me get him out of the chair,' said Sylvia. Together they lifted him from the seat and laid him on the floor. Sylvia looked at his eyes and felt for a pulse.

"He's dead," she said.

The rain lashed them. Aside from the glimmering light on the shore, deathly darkness surrounded them.

"We'll use their light to ensure we're headed in the right direction," said Sylvia. "We want to go east. We'll keep it behind us."

Suddenly the spotlight was extinguished.

"Without it, we're lost," said Reese. It was true—as Sylvia swiveled in her seat and peered into the rain, she couldn't see more than a few yards. Unless they had a landmark, they could easily head off in the wrong direction—even back to Juliette Island.

"We need to find the causeway," said Sylvia. "It's the only way we'll know where we're going. We'll follow it to the other side."

"Remember," said Reese, "the land adjacent to the causeway, and most of it along the coast, is part of the United Americas and controlled by the Industrial Union. Once you get a few miles inland, you cross into the Western Canaille Zone."

Sylvia took the wheel and pointed the boat in the direction of what she thought was south, towards the causeway. "Look at the wave patterns," she said. "They're coming from behind us. Let's make sure we maintain the same orientation."

Gingerly they crept forward through the downpour. A moment later Sylvia saw the dark shape of the concrete causeway and the phosphorescent gleam of waves breaking on the rocks.

"Okay, let's keep the causeway to our starboard," said Sylvia. She advanced the throttle and the boat's nose rose out of the water.

Through the dense rain, from the direction of the island a set of headlights appeared on the causeway and a searchlight swept the dark water. "They're looking for us," said Reese. The lights gained on them, and Sylvia increased the boat's speed. Then from the mainland side another set of headlights appeared, also with a searchlight piercing the rain-swept night.

Sylvia throttled back. "We're trapped," she said. "We have no choice but to head out into the open water." She turned the wheel and accelerated, and, with a second to spare before the searchlights caught them, the darkness of the storm enveloped the boat.

The rain poured down. Water sloshed in the bottom of the cockpit. Sylvia had long since given up any hope of staying dry—she was soaked to the skin. She looked at the body of Khaleed. Except for one handshake and greeting, she didn't know him. He looked like a boy, too young to die. His expression was peaceful. The uncaring drops of water bounced off his skin and, merging together, ran in rivulets down his motionless face. He had saved her life at the cost of his own. She wanted to cover him up. It seemed like the right thing to do. But there was no blanket, no sheet. Only the pounding rain.

She looked over the side of the boat. The water was choppy and it was hard to tell where the waves were coming from. The vessel could be slowly rotating in a current. They had no way of knowing.

"It can't be later than nine o'clock," said Sylvia. "It'll be dark for another six or seven hours. If they send out a boat, we'll see its lights. The best thing for us to do is wait for the weather to clear. If we can see the moon or the stars, we'll know which direction is east. Meanwhile, I think it's best if we put Khaleed into the ocean."

"All right," said Reese. "If they find him, they may think we've all died."

Sloshing on the deck, Sylvia took Khaleed's right arm near the shoulder, while Reese took his left arm. With a mighty effort the two women lifted the body with its water-soaked clothing so that the head and torso rested on the gunwale. While Sylvia held Khaleed by his shoulders, Reese lifted one leg and then the other. For a moment the dripping body lay balanced on the gunwale, and then both women gave it a shove and it splashed into the sea. They watched it slowly drift away into the darkness.

Sylvia and Reese sat in the boat as the rain continued its steady drumbeat. The hours passed, or so it seemed. The rain eased, then dwindled to a light drizzle. The two women talked about their previous lives and what they were going to do when they reached freedom.

"I suppose I'll just start over from scratch," said Reese. "My adoptive parents still live in Houston, but I can never set foot in the United Americas again. Visiting them will be out of the question. It makes me sad to think they'll never know what really happened to me. I'm sure the Industrial Council security people denied kidnapping me and made up some story, like I ran away with my boyfriend. Perhaps there's some way I can contact them. Maybe on social media?"

"The government blocks internet traffic from outside the country," said Sylvia.

"I guess you're right," said Reese. Then she brightened up. "Do you think there's cell phone service between the canaille and the United Americas?"

Sylvia shrugged. She didn't know.

"I hope I can find work at a women's health center," said Reese. "They must have those things, right? I mean, it's not like we're escaping to some sort of Stone Age nation, are we?"

"No, I don't think so. From what I've heard—stories, really—life in the canaille is just like life at home, only a century behind. Maybe like the Wild West was in the old days, where you had places with no law enforcement interspersed with settlements that had a sheriff. I've read about the old Gold Rush towns, where you had thousands of people living in the middle of nowhere, practically self-governing, with no legal system. People figured right and wrong out for themselves. Neighbors helped their neighbors. There was no Industrial Council that told you what you had to do. Nobody knew your business. You were judged on what you actually did, not on what some doctor though you might do in the future."

The rain was little more than a mist now, and Sylvia scanned the dark sky for a break in the clouds signified by the faint glow of the moon or a twinkle of a single star. She saw only inky blackness. The water was calm, with only the occasional soft wave lapping at the side of the boat. The boat floated lazily, in which direction they knew not.

"How about you?" asked Reese. "You're going to have a child. What are you going to do when you first set foot on free soil?"

"I need to contact my child's father. I owe that much to both my child and to Jason. That's number one. After that, I don't know. Find a job, like anyone else would. Find a place to live. At home, I have money in the bank, though I suppose that doesn't matter now." She paused. "Above all, I just want to get my body back. I don't want to be a human lab rat. I don't want some guy in his corner office on the thirtieth floor of the Bigshot Building to know more about my own body than I do. And I definitely don't want him to make decisions on my behalf! That's just crazy."

Sylvia looked directly overhead. Was there a glimmer of star? Yes, there was! There was one, and then another, and a third.

The two women huddled in the drifting boat, watching the sky. Stars became visible, only to disappear again as the clouds broke up, re-formed, and passed overhead. In the bottom of the boat, the water sloshed gently.

"Look!" said Reese as she pointed into the gloom. "Do you see that? The sky is lighter over there."

Sylvia looked, and at first she wasn't sure, but after a few minutes she had to agree the horizon was lighter there than when she looked in the opposite direction. "At last!" she said. "Now we know which direction is east. Let's go!"

Sylvia started the engine and turned the wheel to the east.

"Look!" shouted Reese. She pointed behind them, towards the island. Sylvia saw a boat with a spotlight speeding in their direction.

"A Morta patrol boat," said Sylvia grimly. She slammed the throttle down and the boat roared forward. She glanced behind. The Morta boat was gaining ground.

The sky had lightened and Sylvia peered ahead, looking for land. She saw only gloomy gray mist. The boat bounced along the waves, throwing up white curls of water from its bow.

Shots rang out, and then more. Sylvia turned. A Morta stood on the front deck of the patrol boat, holding an automatic weapon. The patrol boat was pitching in the waves, but the closer they got the more likely it was the Morta could fire accurately.

There! Up ahead Sylvia saw a dark gray line of land. A volley of bullets splashed in the water to port. Violently Sylvia jerked the wheel to starboard and the boat careened across the waves. More shots, this time falling behind in the foaming wake.

"Stop your boat!" the amplified command came across the water. "If you surrender you will live!"

The motorboat was now speeding parallel to the rocky shore. There was no place to stop, and the patrol boat was close behind. Sylvia desperately scanned the shore—too many trees, too many rocks! To run the boat onto the rocks would be fatal, and to stop the boat and get off would be equally fatal.

A volley of shots slammed into the hull of the boat, sending shards of fiberglass flying. Reese huddled on the floor. Sylvia jerked the wheel back and forth as the boat zig-zagged through the choppy seas.

"Stop!" the voice called again. "You cannot escape!"

Suddenly—up ahead—the mouth of a narrow river! Sylvia roared towards it, and in a moment the boat plunged into the shallow waters of an intertidal estuary. On each side the tall reeds swayed as the wake from her boat hit them. Ahead the river curved, and Sylvia, still at full throttle, hurtled deeper into its mouth.

The patrol boat followed, with the Morta on deck squeezing off bursts of bullets. The windshield of the speedboat shattered, crumpling the safety glass into a twisted sheet. Sylvia felt the bottom of the boat strike something and bump upward, but the propeller kept turning and the boat kept moving. Tall reeds and half-submerged rocks flew past in a blur.

Entering a straight stretch of river, she dared to glance behind her. She saw the patrol boat close behind, and the Morta on deck taking careful aim with his weapon. She was looking down the deathly barrel of the gun when suddenly the patrol boat lurched into the air and seemed to abruptly slow down. With his gun in his hands, the Morta flew off the bow of the boat and landed with a massive splash in the water.

Sylvia watched as the patrol boat came to a dead stop on the sandbar that Sylvia, in her smaller boat, had just barely made it over.

But they were not safe yet. Reducing her speed, Sylvia navigated further upstream, among the reeds and rocks, as the river narrowed and the tree-covered banks closed in. She had gone perhaps a mile up the river when she came to a shallow, rocky section where the current moved quickly. This was as far as she could go. She ran the boat up onto the marshy bank among the reeds and shut off the motor.

She turned to Reese, who was still huddled on the floor.

"Hey—we made it!" she exclaimed. "We lost them!"

Reese didn't move.

Sylvia went to her and touched her shoulder. Reese moaned and moved her head.

"Oh my God—you've been hit!" said Sylvia.

"It's nothing—I'll be fine," she whispered. She opened her eyes and looked at Sylvia. "Just hold me for a moment, would you? I feel so cold."

Sylvia reached down, put her arms around Reese, and raised her out of the water sloshing in the floor of the boat. "You're going to be all right," said Sylvia. "We'll get you to a doctor. Hang in there."

"Did we make it?" asked Reese.

"Not yet," replied Sylvia. "We need to keep moving. Let me help you up."

Reese made no reply. Her eyes lost their focus and her body went slack.

"Reese! Reese!" said Sylvia. "Don't leave me! Stay with me!" She put her ear next to Reese's mouth. Her breathing had stopped. Sylvia felt her neck for a pulse. There was nothing.

For several minutes Sylvia sat in the boat, cradling Reese in her arms. There was no doubt—she was dead.

CHAPTER THIRTY

Sylvia laid her friend on the deck of the boat. Stiff from fatigue and the cold, she stood up. She hated leaving Reese in the bottom of a waterlogged boat, but she knew that the Mortas and their drones and guns would soon come, looking for revenge, and she had to leave.

"My friend, you're beyond whatever they would do to you," she said. "Thank you for saving my life. I won't forget."

With those words she climbed out of the boat and went to the bow. Pushing with all of her strength, she moved it a few inches closer to the open water. After pausing to catch her breath, she pushed again. This time the boat broke free of the suction of the muck and floated into the current of the river. She watched as it lazily drifted downstream and out of sight.

Sylvia stepped through the mire to dry land. She looked around. The landscape was wild and desolate, without a house or road in sight. As long as the river flows from the east, she thought, I'm going to follow it. She set off, picking her way through reeds and bushes, climbing over felled logs and massive buried boulders, crossing little tributary creeks. The sun had fully risen into the eastern sky and the day was growing warmer.

She glanced behind her. The stranded patrol boat was a mile downriver, far out of sight. Soon the hijacked powerboat, carrying Reese's body, would be upon it. What was the scene there? Was the Morta guard hopelessly disabled after being immersed in water? Had others been dispatched to kill or capture Sylvia?

Suddenly in the distance, above the river, she saw a dot in the sky. It didn't fly erratically, like a bird. At an altitude of a few hundred feet it kept a straight course, coming up the river.

A drone!

Quickly Sylvia hustled to the nearest big tree and slid around behind it. Flattening herself on the ground, she brushed rain-soaked leaves and loose branches over her body.

Then she waited.

She dared not raise her head and peek—the drone's sensitive cameras could detect the slightest anomaly in the patterns of the landscape. Her heart beat fast in her chest. Her fingers gripped the muddy earth. She heard only the rustle of the wind in the trees and the cheery calls of songbirds. Then she heard another sound—a sinister whirring and the hum of motors. It approached and lingered. She held her breath and dared not even blink. Then the evil vibrations faded away.

She raised her head and listened intently. The sound was gone. She crept out of her hiding place behind the tree. She looked up and down the river. The drone was not in sight. But to stay on the banks of the river was too dangerous—if the wind picked up, shielding the sound of a drone, or if she were inattentive for even a moment, that drone, or another one, could catch her in its sights.

Clamoring through the rugged woods, keeping the river in view, she followed its banks eastward. The sun was high, and under its warm rays the trees and vegetation were drying. After crossing another tributary creek, she came to the first sign of civilization: an old barbed-wire fence, half collapsed and rusty. Made from wooden posts, it ran from the river straight into the woods and up a low hill, where it vanished in the underbrush. She crossed the fence and continued on until the woods ended and she came to a cleared field. Pausing at the edge of the woods, she surveyed the landscape. The field was about two or three acres in size, and had been recently mowed. It was dotted with trees. On the other side, the woods resumed. Clearly the field served no agricultural purpose; it was maintained by its owner simply to look nice, or perhaps as a habitat for native insect and animal species. Sylvia inhaled deeply, savoring the freshness of the damp grass and earth warming in the sun.

She turned and walked north along the edge of the field. The land rose at a gentle incline. She came to a line of blueberry bushes that marked the northern end of the field, beyond which was a green lawn, and then a house.

The house was an old wood-frame structure, painted plain pale yellow with white trim. Two stories tall it stood, topped with a peaked roof of green shingles. A big brick chimney anchored one end, and a porch closed the other.

Sylvia saw no people in or around the house. She made her way through the muddy path between the blueberry bushes and walked toward the house. Coming around the porch, she saw a car parked in the gravel driveway. It was an old Sun Motors model, called the Bluebird. The sight was startling because she hadn't seen a Sun Motors car since being kidnapped. Sylvia was particularly fond of the Bluebird, a sweet little family car with a perky profile. She hoped its presence was a good omen. She kept walking until she came to the front door of the house. It was painted blue, with a bronze pineapple for a knocker. She raised the knocker and gently tapped it against its striker. The percussive noise seemed too loud for the serene and bucolic environment.

She heard footsteps, and the door opened. An elderly man peered at her. His expression was cautious but kindly. "Yes? How may I help you?"

Sylvia took a deep breath and stood up straight. Her left hand was throbbing and her damp clothes were sticking to her. Her matted hair clung to her dirty face. She knew this man could either save her or cause her to be killed.

"I'm sorry to bother you," she heard herself say, "but I've escaped from Juliette Island."

His eyebrows furrowed and his gaze became piercing.

"When?" he asked.

"Last night, during the storm. My friend and I took a boat. They killed her. I survived." Despite her effort to put on a brave face, Sylvia felt tears well up in her eyes. "I'm sorry. I didn't mean to bother you." The tears trickled down her cheeks and she wiped them with her muddy sleeve. "I'm so sorry. I don't know where to go."

The man reached out his hand. "Quickly—come inside!" His touch was warm and comforting. Sylvia walked through the door. Her knees buckled, the room began to spin, and everything went dark.

She woke up. She was lying on a couch in a room. The ceiling overhead was white plaster with lots of little cracks. Her mouth was pasty and her hand hurt.

"Ah—there you are," said a man's voice.

She turned her head.

"Oh," she said in a faraway voice. "You're the man who opened the door. You live here."

"Yes, I do," he said, smiling. He reminded Sylvia of her grandfather, who had died long ago. "Here, have some water."

He helped her sit up, and offered her a glass of water. It was cool and refreshing.

"Thank you," she said.

"What's your name?"

"Sylvia Brand."

"Where are you from? I mean, originally."

"Detroit. I work at Sun Motors. Umm... who are you?"

"My name is Theodore Flowers. Doctor Theodore Flowers."

Sylvia recoiled. A doctor? Her brain rebelled and her soul became sickened.

"Oh, don't worry," he smiled as he reached to pat her hand. "I'm a regular doctor. No longer with the Medical Center."

"What do you mean, 'no longer with' the Medical Center?"

"I retired. I have nothing to do with them any more. I'll tell you all about it after you get cleaned up and have some breakfast. And I want to look at that hand. We don't want it to get infected. Come into the bathroom."

Sylvia stood up on stiff legs and followed Dr. Flowers. The cheery yellow walls and white tiled floor of the bathroom lifted her spirits. After he gently removed the bandage, he cleaned the open cut. Sylvia grimaced. "Sorry for the pain," he said, "but we've got to irrigate it. To properly close this wound, you need stitches. I can do it now." He left the room for a moment and returned with a medical bag. After giving her a local anesthetic, he stitched up the cut. "How did this happen?" he asked. She told him the story of the implant. He shook his head. "Barbaric. Absolutely criminal. It took quite a bit of courage to cut it out."

When he was finished stitching and applying a new bandage, he left her alone to take a shower. "My daughter comes to visit once in a while," he said at the bathroom door, "and for convenience she leaves some clothing here. You look to be the same size. Her bedroom is down the hall. Help yourself."

After Sylvia had found a pair of jeans and a sweatshirt, she went down to the kitchen, where Dr. Flowers was making scrambled eggs and toast. She sat down to eat, and with a cup of coffee he sat with her at the table.

Dr. Flowers told Sylvia that when the Industrial Council first established Juliette Island shortly after the Global Recession, he had been hired as a staff physician. The Council wanted to leverage the enormous potential of digital human data, and the idea of operating a remote island facility where scientists and their subjects could work without interruption was enormously appealing.

"At first, it was ethical and we did some good work," he said as he cradled his coffee mug. "But it wasn't long before the profit motive took over. The Medical Center began luring patients to the island under false pretenses. Then they started getting people who clearly didn't want to be there. The Industrial Council wrote legislation that President Deacon signed into law that gave them the right to enforce the fine print of their standard consent forms, which most people never read. This gave the Industrial Council the legal right to "re-assign"—that is, forcibly abduct—corporate employees who had valuable medical data, and send them to Juliette Island. I saw what was going on. It became almost like a concentration camp. And when they were done with you, suddenly you died during a routine procedure. I didn't do that— one of the other doctors did. It wasn't long before we figured out that any time an elderly patient was referred to Dr. Gladstone, they never came back. When I turned sixty-five, I put in for retirement. I had to get out."

"But you saw what was happening and you said nothing."

Dr. Flowers hung his head. He folded his hands in his lap and kneaded his fingers. "It's true. I remained silent. I let them do their dirty work. I thought, how can one person oppose their vast machine? If I protested, they would kill me. So I put a smile on my face and pretended everything was fine. It broke my heart to see what we were doing to perfectly ordinary, nice people. Surprisingly, some of the 'guests'—that's what we called them— adapted very well to their new environment. They liked being subjugated. But most people didn't like it. Some tried to escape. When they got caught they were either tossed in the cooler or, if they were deemed particularly recalcitrant, they were provided with a permanent Propofol vacation."

Sylvia looked around the comfortable living room with its patterned carpet and gold-framed paintings on the walls and marble fireplace surround. "You played your cards well," she said. "Today you are living here, in this lovely house, without a worry in the world."

"I made my choices," he said. "I have to live with them. Right now, at this moment, all that matters is that you need my help, and I'm going to give it to you." He looked at Sylvia the way a doctor looks at a patient. "You're pregnant, aren't you?"

Sylvia nodded. "Yes, I am."

He smiled. "So you and your child escaped together. After all that you've been through, there is hope. How far along are you?"

"Eight weeks, I think. I'm nervous because I was pregnant once before, and I had a miscarriage at ten weeks."

"Statistically, you're no more at risk than any other woman," smiled Dr. Flowers. He stood up. "Let's talk about your future. You cannot stay here— they will be searching for you. It is too dangerous. We need to get you to New Hudson as quickly as possible."

"New Hudson?"

Dr. Flowers laughed. "I'm amazed at how effectively the federal government and Facts News control the information doled out to our citizens. You didn't know the disorganized regions of the canaille had banded together to form New Hudson? This was a few years ago. And while President Deacon makes noise about going in there and taking over, he's never followed through. He knows a quagmire when he sees one! Now then—let's get you out of here."

Sylvia had no personal belongings other than some things belonging to Dr. Flower's daughter, so there was nothing to do except walk out to the car. Dr. Flowers opened the trunk of the Bluebird. "I'm sorry to say that until we clear the city limits of Winslow—the town you're in right now—you need to ride back here. I'm certain the Morta guards will stop me and question me. I can handle them as long as you're out of sight."

Having worked to acquire the parts from which the Sun Bluebird had been assembled, Sylvia was very familiar with the trunk of the car; but this professional familiarity did not prevent a wave of anxiety from surging through her. Dr. Flowers, seeing her stricken expression, said, "Please don't be afraid. If you feel claustrophobic, knock on the front panel. I will hear you, pull over, and pop the trunk to give you some air. Okay? Now please— we have not a moment to lose."

With her heart pounding, Sylvia climbed into the trunk. Laying on her side, she drew up her knees. "Okay," she said. "Close it."

The lid came down and Sylvia was plunged into darkness.

She heard and felt Dr. Flowers get in the car and start the engine. The car began to move. In the darkness, Sylvia tried to stay calm and comfortable, but while the trunk was carpeted the ride was rough. The car went faster and then slower, and then faster again.

Sylvia heard music. The doctor was playing a symphony. It sounded familiar—yes, it was Tchaikovsky's Swan Lake. The sweeping tones brought back memories of her childhood, when every year her mother would take her to the ballet. This was before the Global Depression, which had put the ballet company out of business. The music was soothing and allowed Sylvia to close her eyes and, at least for a while, forget her dire predicament.

The car came to a stop. The music ended. Sylvia waited in the dark. She was about to knock on the panel and implore Dr. Flowers to open the trunk when she heard talking.

"Who are you and what's your business?" said a distinctively genderless voice.

"Being a Morta autonomous humanoid operator fully plugged into the central database," replied Dr. Flowers, "you should already know who I am. But in case you can't pull up the data, my name is Dr. Theodore Flowers and I'm on my way to see a patient."

"We need to search your vehicle," said the Morta. "A fugitive is on the loose. She's considered extremely dangerous."

"I can assure you I have not seen any fugitives," said Dr. Flowers.

"We need for you to open the trunk."

Sylvia's blood ran cold. She held her breath and prepared for a bad end to her few hours of freedom.

She felt Dr. Flowers get out of the car. "Now you listen to me," he said sternly. "You know I spent twelve years working at the highest levels of the Medical Center. You should also know that despite having retired from active service, I remain personal friends with Dr. Peyton, the chair of the Medical Board. I'm sure he would be extremely displeased to learn that you have taken it upon yourself to question my loyalty and patriotism."

There was moment of silence. Inside the trunk of the car, Sylvia waited in darkness and suspense. She resolved that if the trunk were opened, she would fight back and make them kill her. To die today was better than to live as a prisoner tomorrow.

"Very well," said the Morta. "You may proceed."

She heard Dr. Flowers get back into the car, the door close, and the engine start. Then there was motion. They drove for a while—Sylvia had no idea how long—as Dr. Flowers played his classical music.

The car stopped. Dr. Flowers opened his door and got out. Then the trunk lid swung open. Sunlight flooded the cramped space as Sylvia slowly unfolded herself and unsteadily swung her legs onto the pavement. Blinking, she looked around. She saw nothing but a vast expanse of fields stretching out to a line of mountains in the distance.

"Where are we?"

"Outside the town of Chilliwack," replied Dr. Flowers. "On what used to be the old Trans-Canada Highway. This is the first place it was safe to stop, because we can see if anybody is coming long before they can see us. Stretch your legs for a minute, and then we'll get back on the road."

Sylvia stood in the afternoon brilliance and breathed deeply. High overhead in the cloudless sky, a hawk turned lazy circles. The only sound was the gentle rustle of the wind caressing endless acres of golden wheat stalks. "Where are we going?" she asked.

"The first friendly city is Banton. It's a ten-hour drive northeast of here. Crossing the border will be tricky—you'll have to get back in the trunk. But Banton is securely in the canaille. You'll be safe there."

"Do aberrants live there?"

Dr. Flowers laughed. "Aberrants? Yes, they do. I always thought that was a stupid expression. The Industrial Council invented the concept as part of its propaganda campaign. They want to make folks believe that anyone not living in the United Americas is somehow subhuman. It's just another tool of the dictatorship. Authoritarian states have been doing it since the dawn of time. You control your population by knowing everything about them, making them believe you're protecting them from a terrible enemy, and by identifying a class of people who are both 'bad' and are easy targets. President Deacon and the Industrial Council have done all three very effectively." He looked at his watch. "We'll drive for a few more hours and then stop and get something to eat. I know a safe restaurant where the patrols are rarely seen."

Dr. Flowers allowed Sylvia to ride with him in the front seat of the car. They drove through miles of farmland, seeing few other vehicles. The plains yielded to the Cascade Mountains, tall and rugged. Next to a crystal blue lake they stopped at the Timber Café, and after stepping over the threshold to make certain there were no police, Dr. Flowers signaled for Sylvia to come inside. When the bill came, Sylvia realized with horror she had no money except for her Juliette Island debit card, which was worthless.

"I think you'll do well for yourself," smiled Dr. Flowers. "This one's on me. When you can, I know you'll pay back the favor—perhaps by helping someone else in their time of need."

They drove on, winding their way through the Rocky Mountains, alongside spectacular gorges and over high bridges. The sun set, casting long purple shadows from the cold, craggy peaks. It was after dark when Dr. Flowers pulled over to the side of the road. He turned to Sylvia. "We're a few miles from the border with Banton. The police presence will intensify until we cross the last checkpoint near the river. For this final leg of our journey, I need you to get back into the trunk."

"I understand," replied Sylvia. She stepped out of the car and climbed into her familiar little prison. Dr. Flowers closed the lid. The car started up, and in the darkness Sylvia prayed the last few miles of her long journey would not be her last.

They drove for a while, and then the car slowed and came to a stop. From her hideaway, Sylvia strained to hear the conversation between Dr. Flowers and whoever was outside. Dr. Flowers said he was visiting a patient. The guard asked for the name of the patient. Dr. Flowers replied that it was confidential and a matter of doctor-patient privilege. The guard persisted. Suddenly the car accelerated, slamming her against the rear panel. She heard shouts, and then gunfire. With the force of a sledgehammer, a bullet punched a hole into the lid of the trunk inches above her head. The car careened and she felt it plunge downward. It landed with a splash. Within seconds Sylvia felt cold water trickling into the closed compartment. She screamed and pounded on the lid of the trunk. The water rose higher, soaking her clothes. Now it was encircling her head. She screamed and pounded. Suddenly the lid flew open and Dr. Flowers, standing in running water up to his chest, reached in and helped her out. Just as her legs cleared the lip of the opening, the car lurched in the shallow rapids and flipped over. In a moment it had been swept downstream. Fighting to keep her head above water, Sylvia held onto Dr. Flowers's hand as they fought to reach the opposite shore. When she thought she had no more strength and would be hurled against the rocks, her feet felt traction on the gravelly stream bed, and together they hauled themselves out of the torrent and onto dry land.

"You made it," breathed Dr. Flowers. "No more Juliette Island. You're in New Hudson. You're free."

CHAPTER THIRTY-ONE

"I'm happy, and very grateful," said Sylvia. "But what about you? You left your home! Your car is gone. What are you going to do?"

"I'm going to start over," said Dr. Flowers. "To be honest, since my wife passed away, living in that house all by myself became boring. I didn't want to leave because it seemed like too much effort. You can get into a rut, you know? The days go by, you do what you do, and suddenly you realize your life is in a holding pattern. So here I am! I cannot go back. Just like you, I need to start over. But we're not without resources. I've got some money and know a few people in New Hudson. Let's get started."

They got up and, in their wet clothes, walked up the embankment. When they reached the top they found themselves standing on the shoulder of a paved road. Dr. Flowers looked around. "That way," he pointed, "is north. About three miles from here, in a town called East Fork, there's a diner with rooms for rent on the second floor. It's been there since I was a kid. The same family has owned it for two generations. Let's go."

They started walking. The cool night air caressed Sylvia's cheek. The dark woods and fields made her feel protected, as if she belonged there. The moonless sky was ablaze with more stars than she had seen in years. Looking up in wonderment at their profusion and beauty, she thought about how far she had come, and how in the grand scheme of things her personal journey had been both miniscule and monumental, and that both descriptions were perfectly okay.

Eventually the lights of the Tip Top Diner came into view. As they approached, Sylvia looked at it with curiosity. It was not unlike any other roadside diner in the rural countryside outside of Detroit. The roof was a little bit saggy, the neon sign too bright, and the parking lot too weedy, but the place looked sturdy and inviting. She noticed the cars parked in the lot— they were older models, showing years of use, but presumably they got people where they needed to be.

"Ah—they haven't changed a thing!" said Dr. Flowers as he pulled open the front screen door. Inside, the space was divided between a bar where you could sit and a dining room with tables and booths. The customers—a mixed bunch of couples and singletons—regarded the damp newcomers with curiosity.

Dr. Flowers went to the counter. "Is Madge here?" he asked.

The girl turned her head and shouted, "Hey Madge, ya got a visitor!"

From the swinging kitchen door a woman emerged. When she saw Dr. Flowers her eyes lit up. "Teddy! This is an unexpected surprise! How are you?" She paused and looked at Dr. Flowers and Sylvia. "Have you and your friend been rolling in the mud? Of course it's none of my business, but..."

Dr. Flowers laughed. "Madge, this is Sylvia. I drove my car into the river a few miles down the road. We both got a bit waterlogged. The car's gone—swept downstream."

"How did you manage to do that?" asked Madge. "You're not drunk, are you?"

Dr. Flowers leaned closer. "No, Madge, I'm not drunk. We were escaping from the robo-cops. Sylvia is from Detroit, by way of Juliette Island. This morning she showed up at my house. I decided to drive her here."

Madge's eyes widened and she looked at Sylvia. "My child, you're from that awful island where they kill people for medical tests?"

"Yes. I was there for ten days. I couldn't take it—I had to get out. Some friends helped me escape. So did Dr. Flowers. I'm very fortunate."

"I want you both to go upstairs and get cleaned up," said Madge. She opened a drawer behind the counter, rummaged through it, and found a key. "This will let you into room number eight. Last one on the right at the top of the stairs. Then come back down and I'll give you something to eat."

Twenty minutes later, Sylvia and Dr. Flowers came downstairs and took seats at the bar.

"Now that you feel more comfortable," said Sylvia, "what can I get you? On the house. My treat."

"Madge," said Sylvia, "you're being very generous, but I don't want charity. I want to pay for what I get. I saw you have a help wanted sign in the window. I want you to hire me. I worked in restaurants all through college. I'll wash dishes, wait tables—whatever you need."

"Madge, I wouldn't argue with her," laughed Dr. Flowers. "She's a tough customer."

Madge agreed to give Sylvia a job. "You can start right now," she said. "But you can't work hungry, so you'll have your dinner first, and then I'll put you to work."

After they had eaten, Sylvia turned to Dr. Flowers. "I cannot thank you enough. You saved my life. But what are you going to do? You can't go back home."

"I own some property north of here, up in the lake country," he said. "I'll rent a car and go up there. I'm sure they could use a country doctor, and maybe I'll build a house by the water." He stood up. "Sylvia, it's been my very good fortune to meet you. I wish you the very best of luck."

She watched him walk out the door. Suddenly she felt very alone. She was a stranger in a small town, pregnant, friendless, and broke.

Madge put her arm around her. "Don't worry. You're one of us now. We take care of each other. Now let's get you started making some money."

Life at the Tip Top Diner was like going back to a world that Sylvia had forgotten once existed. The work was hard and the customers came in all shapes and sizes. Some were nice, some were brusque, and a few were just plain jerks. Madge was the same. Some days she was like a sister to Sylvia, while other days she was more like the Wicked Witch of the West. But she was relentless in taking care of her customers, and Sylvia knew at the end of the day when she counted her tips that Madge knew how to run a business. She did it without hidden cameras, GPS wristbands, or computers with screens through which your manager could talk to you. She did it without contracts and consent forms. She did it without management robots. If Sylvia had a problem, she knew she could go to Madge and at the very least get a fair hearing.

Physically, she never felt better. Despite the hard work, she never got the headaches and neck spasms to which she had become accustomed at Sun Motors. But the problem she could not solve was the fact that in just a few months her child would be born without a father. The brutal separation from Jason was a worm that ate at her heart during every waking moment. Madge knew this; every once in a while, when business was slow, she would catch Sylvia with that faraway sadness in her eyes, and come over and put her arm around her and say, "I know. I know."

One day a customer walked through the door—a middle-aged man wearing jeans and a leather jacket. He took a seat at the counter. Sylvia was in the kitchen, and she saw him through the window. As she was turning to go through the swinging doors and serve him, Madge grabbed her by the shoulders. "You stay here," she urgently whispered. "I'll take care of him. Don't go out there until he's gone."

Bewildered, Sylvia said, "Okay, I'll stay here in the kitchen and help out."

Madge pushed open the door and left the kitchen. As Sylvia went about her chores, every few minutes she glanced through the window. The man seemed perfectly ordinary. He ordered a cheeseburger, salad, and a beer. He seemed to be minding his own business. After a while, he paid his bill and left.

Madge came to the kitchen door. "The coast is clear," she said to Sylvia. "What was that all about?"

"He's a spy," said Madge, "from the Industrial Council. His job is to look for fugitives like you. Someone may have phoned in a tip, or he may have simply come here randomly."

"But isn't New Hudson a sovereign nation?"

Madge smiled. "On paper, yes. But in reality, no. The United Americas makes sure our government is very friendly to Washington. The canaille, as they call us, is a client state they use as a human dumping ground, or at least that's how they see it. It's been done before. Back in the eighteenth and nineteenth centuries, England shipped hundreds of thousands of convicts to Australia, where, despite the hardships inflicted upon them, they settled and began new lives. Today about twenty percent of the population of Australia can claim lineage from an English convict. Among the Aussies, it's become a badge of honor! The English—such nice people!—also sent fifty thousand convicts to colonial America. Many of them wound up working on tobacco plantations in Virginia, right alongside African slaves. The colony of Georgia, in the southern United Americas, was first founded by James Edward Oglethorpe as a debtor's colony populated by prisoners from English debtors' prisons. In the eighteenth century, France shipped thousands of convicts to Louisiana. And of course Russia used Siberia as a penal colony." Madge smiled and spread her arms. "Welcome to New Hudson, the land of the aberrants! We're the human jetsam thrown overboard by Washington. As for me, I'm descended from a family exiled right after the Global Depression. My parents were followers of a preacher named Isiah Gold. I'll admit he was a flaky guy—he rode around on a white horse. But by all accounts he was harmless. I have no idea what the problem was with the government—I mean, isn't the United Americas supposed to be the land of religious freedom? But they settled here and eventually opened this diner. And I'm still here today. I would never go back, even if I could. The United Americas has become a police state."

Madge took Sylvia into the back office, where there was an old computer on the desk. "I want to show you something," she said as she clicked through a series of windows. "Ah—here it is!" She swiveled the computer so Sylvia could see it.

"Oh my God—that's a photo of me!" she exclaimed. "What is this website?"

"It's called 'Counterspy.' It's our underground news service. Some smart guy figured out how to hack into Facts News, which gets local feeds by satellite from all over the country. This is the press release from Juliette Island stating you've escaped and for the good citizens of the Northwest Province to be on the lookout for you. Luckily Dr. Flowers got you across the border quickly. But you need to be careful—the UA police have long tentacles."

With her pregnancy advancing, Sylvia needed to find a prenatal healthcare provider. Madge asked her if she needed help in locating one, but Sylvia, beset by anxiety about doctors, kept putting it off. The last thing she wanted was to be re-immersed in the oppressive world of the Sun Motors Employee

Wellness Plan, not to mention the horrors of Juliette Island.

Madge came to her one day and said, "Sylvia, you're off duty the rest of the afternoon. Come with me. I'm going to take you to a doctor."

Despite Sylvia's protests, Madge got Sylvia into her car and drove her to the next town, where there was a clinic. Madge walked with Sylvia into the simple one-story building, where they were met by the receptionist, who gave Sylvia one of those ubiquitous clipboards with a sheaf of medical forms attached, and a pen on a string.

"No! I'm not doing this," said Sylvia as she turned to leave.

"These papers are different from what you're used to," said Marge, firmly taking her by the arm. "Here, let's review them together." They sat down in the waiting area and examined the forms one by one. The first page was an insurance from.

Sylvia went to the receptionist. "Does the Sun Motors Employee Wellness Plan work here?"

"No," she smiled, "but there's no need to worry. We'll get you signed up for New Hudson universal health care. It's free for everyone."

"What do you mean, free? Nothing's free."

"Corporate and personal taxes pay for it."

"Isn't that called socialism?"

The receptionist smiled at her. "Down in the UA they use that outdated term. That's because each person has been taught to believe the other guy is getting a better deal or is cheating the system. Therefore you need to screw him before he screws you. Up here in New Hudson, we call it 'neighbors taking care of neighbors.' Our system is built on trust, not suspicion."

Sylvia returned to her seat. There was a liability form. Lastly was a form that Sylvia didn't recognize. Attached to her medical history form was something called a Personal Health Data Release.

"This says," explained Madge, "that in regard to your health data, you have a choice. You may elect to keep all of your health data as your own personal property, not to be shared or sold at any price to any third party. In this case, your relationship to your doctor is the same as your relationship with your lawyer, who must take an oath to keep the details of your client-lawyer conversations absolutely confidential. This is a right only you can forfeit. No one can take it from you.

"Or, you may choose to lease your data for a price. If you choose this, you're placing your data on the market the same way you'd put your car or house on the market. From a reputable broker, you'll receive a fair price for your data. The system is tightly controlled and supported by blockchain technology."

"Blockchain?" said Sylvia. "I thought New Hudson was some sort of technological backwater."

Madge shook her head. "That's another myth spewed out by the United

Americas propaganda machine. Blockchain technology is the foundation of all of our contracts, both personal (like marriage) and business." She pointed to an apple in a bowl on the receptionist's desk. "We use blockchain to track and verify the journey of that apple from the orchard to the store. The beauty of blockchain contracts is that they require a low level of trust. Since every transaction is verified by the blockchain's public record, it's both safe and reliable. At this moment, you have a fair choice: you can keep your medical data private, or you can be paid what it's worth while a reputable company uses it for a clearly defined purpose."

"After what I've been through, I'd rather keep it private," said Sylvia as she signed the form.

"No problem," replied Madge. "If you ever change your mind, you can file a new form. The records of your choices will all be right there on the blockchain."

Sylvia met her new doctor, who examined her and said that she and her baby were both healthy. She left the clinic feeling as though a new day had dawned. No longer would she be a victim of an oppressive medical establishment that used her as a human research subject. She was in control now, and her self-image as a strong, independent woman began to blossom again.

Later that day, as Sylvia was cleaning tables at the diner, a man entered and sat down at the counter. She fetched a menu and was walking towards him when she stopped in her tracks.

The man was Randolph Meekin. He looked the same as the last time she had seen him on his final Friday afternoon at Sun Motors—well-fed and smug.

Taking a deep breath, Sylvia approached him. "Mr. Meekin, this is an unexpected pleasure," she said as she handed him the menu.

He looked at her and said, "Sylvia? Sylvia Brand? What the hell are you doing here?"

"It's a long story," she replied. "But here I am. What can I get for you?"

His eyes gave her the painfully familiar crude once-over. "Let me think about that for a minute. I gotta say, Sylvia, you are looking good! Better than ever. I'm amazed our paths have crossed out here in the middle of nowhere. I think it means something. Damn! We definitely need to get together. And you know what? It's going to be a lot easier for us now that we don't work together. Those rules about fraternization at Sun Motors were a nuisance." He broke out into a grin from ear to ear. "I swear, this is my lucky day! So tell me, where are you staying? You got a place around here? I live over in Red Hook. I work as a driver for a bread company. Make good money, too. Of course my wife lives there too, but we can figure out that little problem, right?" He winked at her and then stared at her with his greedy eyes.

At these words, Sylvia felt a volcano of anger rise up inside her. When she had worked under Meekin at Sun Motors she had suppressed her rage by sheer force of will, but now it was forcing its way into her consciousness, implacable and unstoppable.

She leaned close to Meekin and, parting her lips seductively, said, "Randy, this is your lucky day. I've got something special for you. Meet me behind the diner. I'll be waiting."

With those words and a warm smile she disappeared behind the door to the kitchen.

Sure enough, within a minute Meekin came around the corner of the building. With a lascivious grin he said, "I always thought you were playing hard to get! Maybe we were just in the wrong place at the wrong time." He put his arms around her and drew her close. She went along with the game.

"Say," she said, putting her hand on his chest, "I heard you were getting it on with Judy Loring. I don't know if I like that."

"Judy Loring? Are you kidding? I wouldn't go near her. She's crazy."

"Have you seen her?"

"Just once. She and that loser husband of hers live down in Rocky Falls. She works at an insurance company. But who cares? Right now I have you. C'mon, give me a kiss."

"I'm going to give you something I've wanted to give you for a long time," she whispered.

Randolph Meekin was bigger and stronger than Sylvia. She knew she had just one shot at him. It had to be right on target, or else she'd have a serious problem.

One shot.

With as much force and speed as she could muster, she slammed her right knee up into his crotch.

Meekin howled in pain. Eyes went glassy. Doubled over and fell to the grass. Legs twitching. Gasping for air.

Sylvia took a knife she had concealed in her pocket and held it in front of his nose. "If you show your face here again, I'm going to turn you from a bull into a steer. Then you can explain to your wife why you have a headache every night. Now get out of here."

Pocketing the knife, she went inside the restaurant.

Meekin did not return to his stool at the counter. She never saw him again.

The next day, Sylvia went into town and rented a car. She drove to Rocky Falls. It was a small town with a couple of gas stations, churches, and convenience stores. It didn't take her long to find an insurance office—John Quimbly Associates. She parked and went inside.

She found herself in one large room. Behind the service counter were a dozen desks. Seated at one of the desks, peering at a computer, was Judy Loring.

"Hey old friend," called Sylvia.

Judy looked up and gave a cry of joy. She ran to Sylvia and they embraced. "I can't believe it's you!" exclaimed Judy. "Did they exile you too? How long have you been here?"

Sylvia briefly told her story.

"Oh my God," said Judy, "we've all heard about Juliette Island. Horrible things! They say people who go there never come back. They use you and then they kill you. And you escaped! I cannot tell you how overjoyed I am to see you! Listen—you absolutely must come to our house for dinner. Tim and the kids would be thrilled to see you." Sylvia tried to demur, but Judy insisted, and Sylvia relented.

The Lorings lived in a small cabin next to a big apple orchard. At the dinner table, Judy said, "When they exile you, they literally drop you off on the sidewalk, give you a hundred dollars, and tell you to fend for yourself. So there we were, the four of us, wondering what we were going to do. We were hundreds of miles from home, we had next to nothing, and we didn't know a soul. But you know what? Throughout New Hudson there are networks of volunteers. They keep their eyes open for new arrivals. You can spot the exiles—they're the bewildered people standing by the side of the road, looking as if they've just dropped out of the sky. We were standing there when a woman approached us. Her name was Yvette. She befriended us, and put us in touch with Mr. Madrid, who owns this farm. This cabin was empty, and he let us have it."

"I'm so happy that you've managed to rebuild your lives," said Sylvia. "But you must dream of going back, right?"

Tim shrugged. "We're getting used to being here. The people are friendly, and while our life is not as glitzy as it used to be, in many ways it's better. We've seen just how much the UA government lies to its citizens. President Deacon acts like he's the savior of the nation, and the supposedly impending war with Rodinia is used to justify any number of abuses. The Industrial Council is driven by nothing but the profit motive, and they teach the people to be suspicious of each other. Technology is used to disenfranchise people, not uplift them. Here in New Hudson, we all have a shared set of values— simple things like honesty and fair play. And there are some very smart people here! When you create an environment where smart, educated people are viewed as the enemy, guess what? Eventually they leave. The woman who lives down the road from us is a computer scientist. She was so sickened by what the Industrial Council wanted her to do that she emigrated here."

"People come to New Hudson willingly?" asked Sylvia.

"The UA government will never admit it, but yes, they do," replied Judy. "They decide the United Americas isn't what it used to be, and all hope is lost, so they pack up and slip over the border."

Sylvia left their house that night resolved to contact Jason and urge him to emigrate to New Hudson. But how?

When she returned to the Tip Top Diner she asked Madge, "Who's the smart guy who runs Counterspy News and who hacked the Facts News satellite feed?"

The next day, Sylvia drove two hundred miles to the city of Hopewell. She went to an address Madge had found, and rang the bell on the door marked Lakelands LLC. A bearded man wearing glasses opened the door.

"Are you Neil Gormley?" she asked.

The man looked at her suspiciously, and then his expression changed to surprise and he said, "Wait a minute—I recognize you! You're the woman who escaped from Juliette Island." He glanced up and down the street. "Please—come in."

The office was small and crammed with computers. Sylvia sat on a metal folding chair.

After telling Gormley her story, she said, "I have a great favor to ask of you."

"I'll do my best to oblige," he replied as he pushed his glasses higher on his nose.

"Can you send an email to an address in Detroit?"

Gormley thought for a moment. "The firewalls set up by the UA government are extremely effective," he said. "But because many Two Hundred K companies are engaged in trade with firms in New Hudson, a limited amount of business-to-business communication is allowed. Is your email address at a company?"

"Yes. It's called Hilltop Financial. The person I need to contact is an employee named Jason Quin."

Gormley nodded and began to work at his computer keyboard. As he peered and pecked, the minutes ticked by. Sylvia began to lose hope. It was a stupid idea! Suddenly Gormley swiveled the computer on its base and showed Sylvia the screen. To her astonishment, she saw Jason, sitting at his desk!

Tears flooded her eyes. "I can't believe it," she said. "There he is! How did you do that?"

"Many companies have computer networks with old operating systems," shrugged Gormley. "They spend millions on perks for the firm's partners and brag about their cutting edge technology, and yet the computers sitting on their desks have operating systems that date back to before the Global Depression. I hacked into your husband's computer and took over the built-in camera. A fifth-grader could have done it."

"Can I talk to him?"

"No, but you can send him an email. Do not reference yourself directly, because his work account is being monitored by his Morta boss. Among the Two Hundred K companies, nearly all have blanket monitoring of employee communications. Nothing escapes their scrutiny. In addition, they may be watching him very closely because they know he's your husband. You must be extremely careful."

"Okay," she said. She typed an email:

"Dear Mr. Quin,

"I have heard about your company, and I would like to inquire about your financial services. Let me tell you a little bit about myself. Until recently I lived in Mexicantown, but two weeks ago I was relocated to the West Coast. I didn't like it there and have since taken up residence in the Northwest. I'm eight weeks pregnant, but unfortunately my husband, who is the child's father, has been separated from us. I confess I have very few assets: I suppose the most valuable is the diamond ring my husband gave me when he proposed. It was evening, and we were in a park, seated on a bench under a willow tree. He got down on one knee, just like in the movies. At that moment I knew I'd love him forever.

"Unfortunately I cannot travel to meet with you in person. I hope you make client visits. I live in a lovely apartment above a restaurant. If you ask around, you'll find me.

"Sincerely,

"Winifred Pearson."

"My mother's maiden name," said Sylvia as she clicked the "send" button. With the email on its way, they both watched Jason's face as he continued to work at his computer.

Minutes passed. Five, then ten. After fifteen minutes, Gormley said, "He's checking his email."

For a few seconds Jason showed no response. Then he suddenly peered intently at the screen. He seemed to be reading something intently. He looked around at the office before returning his gaze to the screen. A disbelieving smile flickered across his face. He typed.

His email response arrived:

"Dear Client,

"Thank you for contacting me. I'd be delighted to arrange a meeting so that we can discuss your future. While it's unfortunate that your husband was separated from you and your unborn child, I'm sure this terrible situation can, and will, be rectified as soon as possible.

"Sincerely, Jason Quin."

Then he put his palm flat against the screen of his computer. He held it there.

Sylvia did the same, and for a moment they stayed like that, electronically united over the miles.

@richieetwaru

ABOUT THE AUTHOR

Richie Etwaru is the eldest of two brothers born in a rural farming village in Guyana, South America in the late 1970s to parents who were both schoolteachers. He was raised to believe that the most important ingredient of life is courage. Courage not mistaken with risk but consistent with the bravery required to embark upon something never attempted.

He has been quoted in NPR, The Wall Street Journal, The New York Times, The Financial Times, The Washington Post, Computer World, Forbes, VentureBeat, WIRED, and has appeared on dozens of television stations and media outlets globally. Richie is most known for founding the 31st Human Right: "everyone has the right to legal ownership of their inherent human data as property." He is driven to reshape the world by creating a new data economy, where inherent human data is legally human property.

Richie currently lives with his wife and two sons in the Northern mountains of New Jersey USA, where this novel was written during the summer of 2019.